MW01252886

War and Peace in Jewish Tradition

The transition between the reality of war and a hope for peace has accompanied the Jewish people since biblical times. However, the ways in which both concepts are understood have changed many times over the ages, and both have different implications for an independent nation in its own land than they do for a community of exiles living as a minority in foreign countries.

This book explores the concepts of war and peace throughout the history of Judaism. Combining three branches of learning – classical Jewish sources, from the Bible to modern times; related academic disciplines of Jewish studies, humanities, social and political sciences; and public discussion of these issues on political, military, ideological and moral levels – contributors from Israel and the US open new vistas of investigation for the future as well as an awareness of the past. Chapters touch on personal and collective morality in warfare, survival though a long and often violent history, and creation of some of the world's great cultural assets, in literature, philosophy and religion, as well as in the fields of community life and social autonomy.

An important addition to the current literature on Jewish thought and philosophy, this book will be of considerable interest to scholars working in the areas of Jewish studies, theology, modern politics, the Middle East and biblical studies.

Yigal Levin is a senior lecturer at the Israel and Golda Koschitzky Department of Jewish History at Bar-Ilan University, Israel, and at the Department of Israel's Heritage at the Ariel University Center of Samaria, Israel.

Amnon Shapira is a senior lecturer at the Department of Israel's Heritage at the Ariel University Center of Samaria, Israel, and a past member of the Department of Bible at Bar-Ilan University, Israel.

Routledge Jewish studies series
Edited by Oliver Leaman
University of Kentucky

Studies, which are interpreted to cover the disciplines of history, sociology, anthropology, culture, politics, philosophy, theology, religion, as they relate to Jewish affairs. The remit includes texts that have as their primary focus issues, ideas, personalities and events of relevance to Jews, Jewish life and the concepts that have characterised Jewish culture both in the past and today. The series is interested in receiving appropriate scripts or proposals.

War and Peace in Jewish Tradition

From the biblical world
to the present

The Third Annual Conference of the Israel Heritage Department
The Ariel University Center of Samaria
Ariel, Israel

Edited by Yigal Levin
and Amnon Shapira

Routledge
Taylor & Francis Group

LONDON AND NEW YORK

First published 2012
by Routledge
2 Park Square, Milton Park, Abingdon, Oxon OX14 4RN

Simultaneously published in the USA and Canada
by Routledge
711 Third Avenue, New York, NY 10017

Routledge is an imprint of the Taylor & Francis Group, an informa business

British Library Cataloguing in Publication Data
A catalogue record for this book is available from the British Library

Library of Congress Cataloging in Publication Data
War and peace in Jewish tradition: from the biblical world to the
present/edited by Yigal Levin and Amnon Shapira.
   p. cm.
   Includes bibliographical references and index.
   1. War – Religious aspects – Judaism. 2. War – Biblical teaching.
3. War in rabbinical literature. 4. War (Jewish law). 5. Just war
doctrine. 6. Peace – Religious aspects – Judaism. 7. Jewish ethics.
8. War – Press coverage – Israel. 9. War – Press coverage – United
States. I. Levin, Yigal. II. Shapira, Amnon.
   BM538.P3W37 2011
   296.3′827 – dc23   2011025000

ISBN: 978-0-415-58715-0 (hbk)
ISBN: 978-0-203-80219-9 (ebk)

Typeset in Baskerville
by Florence Production Ltd, Stoodleigh, Devon

Contents

Contributors

Meir Bar-Ilan, Israel and Golda Koschitzky Department of Jewish History and the Department of Talmud, Bar-Ilan University

David Calabro, Department of Near Eastern Languages and Civilizations, University of Chicago

Yuval Cherlow, Yeshivat Hesder Petach Tikva and the Jerusalem Center for Ethics

Carol Lea Clark, Department of English, University of Texas at El Paso

Yoel Cohen, The School of Communication, Ariel University Center of Samaria

David Elgavish, Department of Bible, Bar-Ilan University

Ziva Feldman, Israel Heritage Department, Ariel University Center of Samaria

Yossi Goldstein, Israel Heritage Department, Ariel University Center of Samaria

Isaac Hershkowitz, Department of Philosophy, Bar-Ilan University and the Israel Democracy Institute

Alick Isaacs, Melton Centre for Jewish Education, Hebrew University of Jerusalem, the Shalom Hartman Institute and the Talking Peace Project

Yishai Kiel, Department of Talmud, Hebrew University of Jerusalem

Yigal Levin, Israel Heritage Department, Ariel University Center of Samaria and the Israel and Golda Koschitzky Department of Jewish History, Bar-Ilan University

Joseph Isaac Lifshitz, Shalem Center, Jerusalem

Amichai Nachshon, Ashkelon Academic College, Bar-Ilan University, Orot and Sha'anan Colleges of Education

Kalman Neuman, Department of History, Herzog College and the Israel Democracy Institute

Gil Ribak, Schusterman Postdoctoral Fellow, Arizona Center for Judaic Studies, University of Arizona

Avinoam Rosenak, Department of Jewish Thought, Hebrew University of Jerusalem and the Van Leer Institute in Jerusalem

Amnon Shapira, Israel Heritage Department, Ariel University Center of Samaria

Jacob L. Wright, Candler School of Theology, Emory University

Foreword

On July 23, 2009, the Israel Heritage Department at the Ariel University Center of Samaria held its third annual conference, in conjunction with the Schwarcz Institute for Ethics, Judaism and the State at Beit Morasha in Jerusalem. The conference was titled "War and Peace in Jewish Tradition – An Interdisciplinary Conference," and included 25 papers by academic scholars and religious leaders from Israel and from abroad. The topics discussed in these papers ranged from warfare in the Bible and in rabbinic sources, through the ethical and political issues raised by modern Israel's military operations, obviously a much discussed topic in modern Israel and in Jewish society as a whole. The various issues discussed were approached through a range of methodologies: historical, sociological, hermeneutic, literary and ethical. The conference itself was well attended (around 200 participants throughout the day) and some of the papers elicited lively discussions.

While full publication of the proceedings was not seen as a primary goal of the conference, the success of the gathering and the wide interest that became evident after the conference encouraged us to go ahead with publication. Since not all of the presenters were willing or able to submit papers for review within a reasonable time, and a few colleagues that did not participate in the original conference expressed their wish to contribute, the present volume is not strictly speaking the conference proceedings, but rather an edited collection of papers based on the original conference. The final outcome, we think, is far more than the sum of the individual papers; rather, it affords the reader an opportunity to sample the way in which various sources within the Jewish tradition treat the subject of war and peace in many of its varied aspects: theology, morals, literature, statehood and more. Chronologically, this volume offers the reader a journey through Jewish history from Abraham all the way to the first decade of the twenty-first century. And while certain historical periods, such as that of the Second Temple and parts of the Middle Ages, are underrepresented, we feel that the reader does get a good understanding of the way in which the Jewish attitudes towards war, and towards peace, developed through time.

A great many people helped bring this volume to completion. First and foremost we wish to acknowledge the help we received from our home institution, the Israel Heritage Department at the Ariel University Center of Samaria and the former department chair, Dr. Uri Zur. We also received support for the project from the office of the president of the Ariel University Center of Samaria and from its research authority. We wish to thank our partners in organizing the conference, Rabbi Dr. Yehuda Brandes and Dr. Moshe Hellinger of the Schwarcz Institute for Ethics, Judaism and the State at Beit Morasha in Jerusalem as well as the rest of the staff at Beit Morasha. We wish to thank Professor Oliver Leaman, Director of the Judaic Studies Program at the University of Kentucky, who as editor of the Routledge Jewish studies series, first suggested that we publish this volume through Routledge and then walked us through the process of putting together and submitting a proposal. Joe Whiting, Acquisitions Editor for Middle Eastern & Islamic Studies at Routledge/Taylor & Francis and Suzanne Richardson, Senior Editorial Assistant for Middle East and Islamic Studies at Routledge/Taylor & Francis advised and aided us through the entire process of putting together this volume and bringing it to press. The rest of the Routledge/Taylor & Francis staff and the Florence Production team led by Rosie Stewart, who worked with us on the actual production process. Special thanks to C. Michael Copeland who translated several of the articles and prepared the index for this volume. And of course, the nineteen authors of the individual articles that have been included in this book, without whom none of this would have happened – it has been a pleasure to work with you all!

Yigal Levin and Amnon Shapira

Introduction

The transition between the reality of war and a hope for peace has accompanied the Jewish people since the dawn of their history. A study of Jewish sources from the Bible through modern thought and literature will immediately discern both an aspiration for peace and an acknowledgment of the reality of never-ending war. However, the ways in which both concepts are understood have changed many times over the ages. Both the meaning of war and the hope for peace have different implications for an independent nation in its own land than they do for a community of exiles living as a minority in a foreign country. As the environment changed, so did the people's needs and perceptions. The paradigm remains, but is expressed in different ways.

In this volume, we have endeavored to combine three branches of learning: the classical Jewish sources from the Bible to modern times; related academic disciplines of Jewish studies, humanities, social and political sciences; and finally, a look at the public discussion of these issues on all levels – political, military, media, ideological and moral.

The purpose of the volume, then, is to allow scholars and other interested readers to follow and to appreciate the development of the concepts of war and peace throughout the history of Judaism, from biblical to modern times. It is not a systematic survey, but rather a collection of individual essays that allow the reader to sample different approaches – historical, literary, philosophical and sociological. It is our belief that presenting the reader with these different methodologies will open new vistas of investigation for the future as well as an awareness of the past.

The eighteen papers included in this book are divided into four sections. The first section deals with concepts of war and peace in the Hebrew Bible. The questions asked here are not historical per se; not whether this war or that actually happened. The purpose of all of the chapters in this section is to understand the basic attitude of the biblical writers towards the moral, ethical, theological and political issues related to war and peace. Does the Bible show specific attitudes? In what ways are these attitudes different from those prevalent in the ancient world of which biblical Israel was a part? Can we trace an ethical stance through the various strands of biblical literature?

The first two essays in the book deal with the question of freeing prisoners, as represented in the Bible. David Elgavish shows that in the world of the Ancient

Near East, the freeing of prisoners, both military and civilian, was not considered a priority even by their own people, and certainly not by their captors. We know of no case in which a state went to war in order to free prisoners. This is also true within the Bible – never does the Bible describe the state as responsible for freeing prisoners. On the other hand, we do find that both Abraham and David, as leaders of families and of bands of men, did give chase after their dependants' captors, and two prophetic stories in which the prophets instruct the Israelites to treat their captives humanely, in both cases setting what later Judaism, to this very day, considers to be a moral standard. In the following article, Amichai Nachshon studies one of those prophetic tales in depth, showing how Elisha's command to free Israel's Aramean captives both provided Israel with a strategic advantage at that moment, and furthermore sent a message of humanity and of non-violence to the readers of the biblical text.

Yigal Levin's paper focuses on another aspect of warfare in the Bible, that of divine intervention. In his view, the wars of Joshua to conquer the land are seen as a pivotal point in God's military support of Israel; whereas during the Exodus and Wanderings the Israelites were totally under God's protection; as soon as they settled the land, God's "hand" was withdrawn to a safe distance away, and his support became much less direct. In the view of the Deuteronomistic authors of Joshua, God had fulfilled his primary role in the realization of the Covenant – its continued implementation was now up to Israel.

God's "hand" and human hands are the subject of David Calabro's essay, showing how ritual gestures were an essential part of the psychology of warfare in the ancient world and how the deity was pictured as making similar gestures. The contribution of Jacob L. Wright focuses on "making a name," especially by kings' going to war. In Wright's view, whereas in the literature of the Ancient Near East such actions are considered to border on the divine, within the Bible Israel's kings are "demystified and demythologized" and thus brought to the status of "constitutional monarchs," which is what they are assumed to have been in later Jewish law and tradition. Wright's essay is also the first in this volume that introduces the ideas of "obligatory" or "commanded" war versus "authorized" or "permitted" war, which, while based on ideas set out in biblical law and narrative, become especially relevant in later halakhic discourse.

The final two papers in this section deal with the moral and ideological issues raised by the reality of internal or "civil" war within the society of biblical Israel. To the two categories of war mentioned above Amnon Shapira adds a third – "prohibited war," wars that the Israelites are forbidden to wage. He then asks himself, and the reader as well, why the Bible does not seem to protest the many internecine wars that it describes, especially the many wars waged between the two "brethren" kingdoms of Israel and Judah? As the title of his article indicates, he does not really offer an answer. He does, however, suggest that violence is part of the nature of any ancient monarchy, and that Israel's monarchy was no different.

Meir Bar-Ilan's answer to almost the same question is different than Shapira's. He considers violence and greed to be a part of human nature in general, and shows that biblical Israel was no different in this regard than other ancient societies. In his opinion, internal warfare was not limited to the monarchical period, and remains a largely under-treated topic in Jewish history.

Joseph Isaac Lifshitz's article introduces us to the second section of our volume, which surveys the way in which rabbinic attitudes towards war and peace developed from the Talmud, through the Middle Ages and up to the modern era. As in many other matters, the rabbis' point of view is based on their interpretation of the biblical text by means of *midrash*, exegesis, and expressed through the medium of *halakhah*, Jewish law. In his essay, Lifshitz cites the majority opinion of the rabbis in the Mishnah, according to which a man may not carry a sword on the Sabbath, because, unlike jewelry, which has aesthetic value, carrying a sword is "a disgrace." From this Lifshitz goes on to discuss the rabbis' view of war in general as a necessary evil, but devoid of aesthetic value. The rabbis even reinterpreted biblical passages that seem to glorify war and warriors, including God himself, as actually extolling other, more palatable virtues such as Torah study. In contemporary *halakhah*, the question of carrying arms is no longer one of aesthetics but only of utility.

Yishai Kiel's article compares rabbinic views of war to the modern standards of "Just War Theory" as formulated by Michael Walzer and others. Once again, the rabbis' positions are expressed through *midrash halakhah*, interpreting biblical passages as legal formulations. In this case, Kiel asks whether the rabbis' understanding of Deuteronomy 20's stipulation that "far away cities" (those outside the land of Canaan) be offered the choice of peace or conquest, as well as what they considered to be limitations placed on the besiegement of a city, are in any way comparable to modern ethics of warfare. His answer is basically that the two ideologies, the rabbinic and the modern, have little in common, although he does show that as *halakhah* developed from the Talmud to such medieval authorities as Maimonides, it did begin to take ethical considerations into account.

Avinoam Rosenak and Alick Isaacs take the conflict between traditional Jewish views and those of Western thought into the twentieth century with their juxtaposition of Kant's ideas of humanistic rationalism and the mystical and theological views of two leaders of pre-state religious Zionism, Rabbi Abraham Isaac Hakohen Kook and Rabbi Moses Amiel. Quoting extensively from the writings of each in turn, Rosenak and Isaacs show how their views of a Torah-based society, which would live in peace with the surrounding world by its very nature, differed from both the ideas prevalent in Western thought and from those of the secular Zionism that was then the leading force in the effort to create a modern Jewish state.

The "Just War Theory" reappears in Isaac Hershkowitz's discussion of rabbinic criticism of the Warsaw Ghetto Uprising and its subsequent inclusion in the Zionist ethos of "destruction and redemption." All of the four rabbis surveyed in his paper disapproved of the Uprising, but for different reasons. In Hershkowitz's analysis, the more "moderate" rabbis disapproved for reasons that are close to those cited by "Just War Theory," while the more extreme (and anti-Zionist) rabbis operated under a totally different set of moral assumptions.

Kalman Neuman takes the discussion one step further, to the halakhic reaction to the actual creation of a Jewish state, for the first time in two millennia. As Neuman shows, the leading rabbis of the early decades of the state turned to the Talmudic concepts of "obligatory war" and "permitted war" in their attempts to apply the *halakhah*, which was formulated by Jews who were stateless and army-less to the modern state and its military, in such questions as military activity on the Sabbath, putting civilians at risk and retention of conquered territory.

However, in the modern world, rabbis are not the only movers of Jewish thought and practice. The reality of the modern Jewish world is often far removed from that of halakhic discourse. Since their emancipation from the ghettos of the Middle Ages and their achievement of citizenship in the nation-states of modern Europe and America, Jews as individuals and as communities have been involved in many of the wars of the modern world. The Holocaust and the establishment of the State of Israel once more forced Jews to deal with warfare as a nation, rather than as a religious community. The third section of our book presents us with three examples taken from three different parts of the modern Jewish experience. Gil Ribak takes us to the immigrant society of early twentieth-century New York and the way that the approach of global conflict was seen through the Yiddish press of the time. He shows that the Jews' perceptions of the conflict were a direct result of their recent experiences in "the old country" – boorish anti-Semitic Russians against cultured and civilized Germans.

The second essay of this section takes us to a totally different reality: that of the Land of Israel in the mid-1940s, with decades of strife with the local Arab population and the newly-revealed horrors of the Holocaust fresh in the minds of the leaders of the Jewish *Yeshuv*. In this paper, Yossi Goldstein traces David Ben Gurion's developing realization that war with the Arabs would be inevitable and that the *Yeshuv* would have to be ready when it came. He does this by citing Ben Gurion's writings and speeches and analyzing the ideology behind them.

The war that broke out on November 30, 1947, known to Israelis as "The War of Independence" and to most of the world as the first Arab-Israeli war, was unfortunately not the last. Since the foundation of the State of Israel, war has become an essential part of the Israeli experience and by extension a part of the world Jewish experience as well, albeit in a very different way. Not surprisingly, a very high percentage of modern Israeli literature deals with various aspects of the experience of war. In Ziva Feldman's literary analysis, Israeli author Yitzhak Orpaz-Auerbach's *The Voyage of Daniel* is about a shell-shocked "secular pilgrim" trying to deal with the horrors that he experienced during war.

The final section of the book is about the relationship between modern Israel, war and the media. In the opening paper, Yoel Cohen analyzes the reasons behind the foreign media's constant and continuous coverage of Israel. In his analysis, Israel's status as the Jewish and Christian "Holy Land" is a "trigger," which draws the interest of foreign audiences to such issues as the Arab-Israel conflict; there is almost no coverage of religious affairs items per se. One disadvantage of this focus on the conflict is that it is all that many audiences actually see, leaving them with the impression that it is the conflict that actually defines Israel and even Judaism itself.

In the second paper of this section, Carol Lea Clark studies one particular example of the media's treatment of the Arab-Israeli conflict: the *New York Times'* Coverage of the Gaza war of December 2008–January 2009, or "Operation Cast Lead" as it was called in Israel. As Clark argues, the *New York Times* could easily be considered the most important outlet for foreign news in the US, and is certainly instrumental in forming public opinion about foreign affairs. During the Gaza war, the *Times* was accused of bias by supporters of both the Israeli and Palestinian sides. Clark then proceeds to analyze a column called "Standing Between Enemies," published during the conflict by Clark Hoyt, public editor of the *Times*, which she classifies as "an apologia," to be compared with other examples of this genre.

In the final essay of the section and of the book, Rabbi Yuval Cherlow attempts to bridge the gap between modern media and contemporary *halakhah*. And the gap, to be sure, is quite wide. While modern media ethics are based on reporters' supposed "neutrality" and on the principle of the public's "right to know" pretty much anything, Rabbi Cherlow's assumption is that the reporter, as a citizen and a member of the society in which he lives (in this case Israeli society), has a primary responsibility to that society. Additionally, *halakhah* does not consider the individual as having a "right to know," but rather as having a responsibility to be informed on issues that are important to the well-being of society. Other information, especially information of a personal nature, is considered gossip or "evil tongue" and should not be publicized. And what is true in peacetime is even more valid in times of war. While Rabbi Cherlow extols the values of a free press, he feels that the individual journalist's fundamental responsibility is to his own society and that he must understand the power that the press holds as a part of the war effort and use that power responsibly. He is opposed to official censorship of the press but feels that responsible journalists should exercise a good measure of self-censorship.

So is there a particularly "Jewish" attitude towards the issues of war and peace? It is probably safer to state that there are multiple Jewish attitudes, arising from the multiplicity of the Jewish experience. Historically, Iron Age Israel and Judah were probably similar to other small states in the ancient Levant, but their prophets envisioned a future age of peace, in which "nation shall not lift up sword against nation, neither shall they learn war any more" (Isaiah 2:4). The authors of the Bible, however, also realized that war was a part of reality, and sought to civilize warfare in the present by formulating codes of behavior during war. These codes were further developed by the rabbis, mostly as theoretical constructs, since in their day Jews, as an often persecuted minority spread over many different lands, had very little opportunity to practice war as a community. Throughout most of the past two millennia, Jewish communities eschewed warfare, and war usually meant bad news. The prayer for peace became a paramount force in

Judaism, but only since the re-establishment of Jewish life in the Land of Israel and especially since the declaration of the State of Israel, have the hope for peace and the necessity of war been once again put to the test. The way in which the Jewish state and world Jewry have handled this test is the accumulated outcome of those two millennia of tradition and experience.

Yigal Levin and Amnon Shapira

Part I

War and peace in the Bible

1   The freeing of captives in the Ancient Near East and in the Bible

David Elgavish

The Bible's attitude toward military or civilian action undertaken to free captives can be deduced primarily from two campaigns: Abram's fight against the four kings to free his nephew Lot (Genesis 14); and David's attack on the Amalekites to free the wives and children of himself and his men who had been taken from Ziklag (1 Samuel 30). In neither case were the Israelite king or the sovereign Israelite state involved; rather these are stories about individuals or militias interested in freeing members of their own families. This is even more apparent in the legal sections of the Bible. No biblical law explicitly determines that someone must act to free a captive. Such an attitude contrasts with the extensive coverage in later Jewish tradition of the obligation to ransom captives.[1] In order to assess the extent, and even the very existence, of the conception of the freeing of captives in the Bible more accurately and whether it concerned military action or other means, we will first consider some of the Ancient Near Eastern sources that deal with this issue.

1. Freeing captives in the Ancient Near East

Clear and significant evidence regarding the freeing of captives has been found in Hittite sources. Some of the factors that contributed to the development of the problem around the area surrounding Ḫatti can be found in "The Deeds of Šuppiluliuma" king of Ḫatti and in the annals of his son Muršili II. Following a victory, the Hittites usually burned their enemies' cities, combatants were killed and survivors and any of the population who did not escape were taken into captivity along with the booty.[2]

Even when attacking an enemy who had previously taken captives, the freeing of those captives did not seem to be of primary importance. The emphasis is rather that of victory over an enemy who had offended the victor. King Tukultī-Ninurta I of Assyria (1243–1207 BCE) wrote as follows:

> Five fortified cities of the land Katmuḫu, rebellious capitals, which, during a deceitful peace, had dragged off my people (and) plundered my land, I conquered in the fullness of time. Like an earthquake I shook their shrines. I carried off captives (and) property (and) brought (them) to my city, Aššur.[3]

Despite the claim that Assyrian citizens were captured and the king of Assyria went to war, there is no evidence that the captives were freed. Apparently an individual was not considered important unless he was a defector who knew sensitive information and whose defection harmed his former ruler. The Hittites considered refusal to hand over defectors according to the obligation set in a treaty, as sufficient reason to declare war.[4] An example of this is the Hittite King Muršili's self-justification for his campaign against Arzawa since her king had refused to return the Hittite captives and exiles who had found refuge in his country. As he explained: "Because I asked you to return my subjects who came to you and you did not give them . . . Now, come, we will fight. Let the storm-god, my lord, decide our lawsuit."[5]

Under what circumstances were captives freed? Primarily when the captor could profit from it politically. The freeing could serve as an incentive to make a treaty, as did King Muršili II of Ḫatti and King Manapa-Tarhunta of the land of the Sehah River: "Gather up the civilian captives and turn them [over] to me. If you carry out all these matters, [then] I will take [you] as a vassal."[6] Such a passage could also appear in the treaty form as in the treaty between Ir-Addu King of Tunip and Niqmepa King of Mukiš: "If there are captives from my country whom they sell in your country you must seize them along with the one who sold them, and give them to me."[7] Sections of this contract are formulated in the second person command form, despite the fact that the contract is egalitarian. The text does not specify who is dictating the terms and who is accepting them. In principle, it could suit either of the parties.

Another motive for freeing captives might have been to win over a captured people. For this reason the clever diplomat Šamši-Addu directed his son King Yasmaḫ-Addu of Mari to clothe his captives from Zalmaqum and free them so that Assyria could rule over Zalmaqum peacefully. So he said to his son: "You have already taken the captives as slaves. From now on release every one whom your hand reached, so that when I start to go to that land, all that land will change sides to me like one person!"[8] Samsu-iluna, son of Hammurabi, King of Babylon (1749–1712 BCE), acted likewise. He captured Ida-maraṣ, but two months later freed its captives as well as many other prisoners he had taken.[9]

The ruler wished to win over his own citizens, especially when he began to rule. This is what happened in Sam'al where the local king Bar-ṣur was murdered, and his son Panamuwa escaped to Assyria where he received the protection of Assyria's King Tiglath-Pileser III. The Assyrian king killed the rebel and placed Panamuwa on his father's throne. Upon becoming the ruler, Panamawa carried out reforms that were generally accepted, among which were the opening of the prisons in Sam'al and freeing of the captives incarcerated there.[10]

Ninurta-Kudurrī-Uṣur, a clerk during the Neo-Assyrian period, expressed a different political attitude in his account of his care for Aramean captives: "I removed the hands and lower lips of 80 of their troops; and I let them go free to (spread the news of my) glory."[11]

To summarize, in the Ancient Near East prisoners were released, for the most part, when the releasing ruler had something to gain from their release, either in his relationship with the ruler of the country from which the prisoners were taken or in the upgrading of his status in the eyes of his own countrymen and their neighbors.

2. Wars to free captives in the Bible

a. Abram's campaign to free Lot (Genesis 14)

The campaign of the four kings

Genesis 14 tells a story of how five kings of the Dead Sea area rebelled against their overlords, four kings that seem to have been from Mesopotamia. Consequently, the four great kings traveled to the eastern side of the Jordan River (Genesis 14:1–4), attacking a number of nations besides the five rebellious kings. Then they turned back and confronted the five kings. One may guess that there was widespread rebellion in the area, and the northern kings came to repress them.[12] Our story, however, focuses on the kings of the Dead Sea area since Lot, Abram's nephew, lived in Sodom. Because of Lot, Abram confronted the four great kings.[13] Since the rebellion of the five kings against the four was doomed to failure, it attests to the irresponsibility of the rebel kings. The battle itself is not described. All it states is that ". . . the kings of Sodom and Gomorrah, in their flight, threw themselves into them [bitumen pits], while the rest escaped to the hill country" (v. 10). The account opens and ends with the flight of the inhabitants of Sodom and Gomorrah, which attests to a shameful defeat; since no fighting is described, the rebels apparently fled without even fighting.

The victors took booty, as it is written: "They took all the wealth of Sodom and Gomorrah and all their provisions, and went away. They also took Lot, the son of Abram's brother, and his possessions and went away" (vv. 11–12). The description is divided into two accounts that begin with the words "they took" (an anaphora) and end with the verb "and went away" (an epistrophe). At first the capture of the possessions of Sodom and Gomorrah is described, and afterwards, the text adds another account, the principal one concerning its focal point – the capture of Lot and his possessions. The words "and his possessions" interrupt the particulars regarding Lot and his family relationship. Ordinarily, we would expect the formulation: "and they took Lot, son of Abram's brother, and his possessions, and they went away." This modification calls to mind that the possessions brought about the separation between Abram and Lot; Lot decided to go to Sodom for economic reasons, and now he had to bear the consequences.

Abram's campaign to rescue Lot from captivity

Abram learned from a refugee that Lot had been taken into captivity and had to determine a course of action. Abram had good reasons not to become involved. Militarily he was not capable of fighting four important kings whose might he knew well, as one who had arrived at Canaan from Mesopotamia, and as he could have learned from the fate of the five kings who had confronted the Mesopotamian kings. Similarly, from a religious point of view, the Sodomites, the ideological and religious rivals of Abram, deserved their punishment. It was good for the world that they had been uprooted from their homes, and this applied to Lot as well, for he had abandoned Abram and gone to the wealthy provinces of Sodom to dwell there with wicked people.

Nevertheless, it states "When Abram heard that his kinsman (אחיו) had been taken captive" (v. 14), feelings of brotherliness enveloped Abram, compelling him to draw his sword in order to rescue his nephew from captivity. The text states: "a fugitive brought the news to Abram the Hebrew, who was dwelling in the terebinths of Mamre the Amorite, kinsman of Eshkol and Aner, these being Abram's allies" (v. 13). Mention of Abram's allies in the current context hints at their participation in the campaign at his side. So one can learn also from the closing verse of the story: "as for the share of the men who went with me – Aner, Eshkol, and Mamre – let them take their share" (v. 24). Abram had made a treaty with the leaders of the local clans; therefore, it is reasonable to assume, they joined him in this campaign. In addition to the participation of allies, it is said of Abram, "he mustered his retainers" (v. 14). Since Abram was the inferior party on the battlefield, he opted for tactics characteristic of the weaker side, as the text states, "at night, he and his servants deployed against them and defeated them and pursued them" (v. 15). Abram divided his men into a few units, surprised the enemy by fighting at night, and pursued them over a long distance. Abram's enemy was comprised of soldiers from different peoples, and therefore they did not present a united front, especially not during the night when they were coerced into fighting. Abram's tactics were similar to that of Gideon against the Midianites (Judges 7–8): each of them fought with a small force against an enemy who had greater forces, divided his force into separate units and pursued the enemy over a long distance; Abram fought to save his nephew; Gideon fought against an enemy who had killed his brothers (Judges 8:19).

Freeing the captives

Abram went out to battle and freed his nephew, Lot, and additional captives. Those captives were not mentioned when the taking of the Sodomites' possessions and of Lot was mentioned (vv. 11–12). This can be seen as a stinging criticism of Sodomite culture that considered the taking of the possessions as the great loss. Sodom, which prided itself on its possessions (Genesis 13:10), did not welcome visitors and did not proffer them food, was punished measure for measure: its possessions, especially its food that had been withheld from visitors, became booty. Only when Abram entered the scene were the men and women who had been taken into captivity brought to the knowledge of the reader. The list of returned captives was composed from Abram's point of view, and Abram valued people above possessions.

Abram, the king of Sodom and the king of Salem

The king of Sodom said to Abram: "Give me the people, but take the goods for yourself" (Genesis 14:21), because there is no king without citizens. The king of Sodom thought he could award the possessions to Abram, perhaps indulgently and not according to the strict letter of the law, although Abram had the right to the possessions. One may imagine that if the results had been the reverse, the king of Sodom would have taken the people and sold them as slaves, in contrast to Abram who refused the booty. Yet Abram did not relinquish the share that his allies and the priest Melchizedek merited. He gave them what they deserved of the booty.

In the account of the meeting between Abram and the king of Sodom, we are informed that Melchizedek king of Salem went out to meet Abram who was returning from his successful campaign, and said to him, "And blessed be God Most high, Who has delivered your foes into your hand" (v. 20). And so Melchizedek gave his moral support to Abram, the stranger who had fought in Canaan, and to his campaign. This was justified because the Mesopotamian kings had taken Lot, Abram's nephew, into captivity and they were therefore Abram's enemies. Melchizedek argued that God had determined the battle in favor of Abram. Perhaps the term "your foes" was used by the king of Salem to refer not only to the kings of Mesopotamia, but also to the inhabitants of the Dead Sea area whom Abram had taken. The people of Sodom were notorious for their villainy, and their ways were diametrically opposed to Abram's; now they were in his hands.

Why was the account of the meeting between Abram and the king of Salem set within the account of the meeting between Abram and the king of Sodom?[14] According to the fifteenth-century commentator Isaac Abrabanel,[15] the king of Sodom presented himself to Abram without asking for a thing, but Abram's generosity to Melchizedek influenced him to make a request. The commentary *Or Hachayim* suggests the opposite.[16] The king of Sodom asked for nothing of Abram, but when he saw the nature of the meeting between Abram and Melchizedek, he said to Abram, ". . . take the goods for yourself." It is also possible that the king of Sodom did not dare request anything of Abram, but when King Melchizedek of Salem appeared, and he saw the mutual warmth between them, he decided to take advantage of the circumstances, and made his request.

The integration of the two cases makes the reader compare them. The identical number of times the names Abram and Sodom appear also leads one to make a comparison. Each of them is mentioned eight times. The comparisons reveal profound differences between them. The king of Sodom is named Bera (=evil), which, compared to Melchizedek (=justice) attests to the moral contrast between them, as do the words they speak.[17] Melchizedek blessed Abram, whereas the king of Sodom proffered no words of greeting before presenting his demands. Even though Melchizedek did not owe Abram anything, he greeted him with bread and wine and blessings. Abram in return gave him tithes – ten percent of all. In contrast, the king of Sodom, who owed Abram for the freeing of his men, presented himself before Abram empty-handed. He did not bring food for the fighters who had returned from the battlefield. He also had no good words to say. The behavior of the king of Sodom corresponded to what was acceptable in his city, but contrasted with the way of life in Abram's household where the importance of serving food and drink to guests and travelers was accentuated.[18]

Abram apparently made a treaty with Melchizedek.[19] In contrast, his meeting with the king of Sodom contains elements that are antithetical to a treaty, that denote political distancing from the king of Sodom: The oath, which is an important element of a covenant, is used here by Abram to buttress his commitment not to form a tie with the king of Sodom: "I swear to the Lord, God Most High, . . . I will not take so much as . . . of what is yours" (vv. 22–3). When drawing up a treaty, it is customary to exchange gifts. Here, Abram swears that he will not take anything from the king of Sodom or from his possessions, in order not to create any obligation. Abram acted one-sidedly with regard to the possessions of Sodom that were released in the battle. He gave tithes to Melchizedek, and expressed his wish that the men who had joined him in the campaign should take their shares of the spoils. They merited the shares not because of any agreement with of the king of Sodom, but rather due to their military activities and their covenant with Abram. The meal that usually accompanies the drawing up of a treaty is deliberately missing here; there are no mutual statements regarding cooperation and rapprochement. On the contrary, Abram's statements express a severance from the king of Sodom. Smith reasons well when he argues that that whereas Abram accepted Melchizedek under his protection, he refused to take any of Sodom's possessions in order not to take that city under his protection. Abram swore to the king of Sodom, using language similar to what Melchizedek used: "I raise my hand [i.e. take an oath] to the Lord, God Most High . . ." (v. 22), thus clearly demonstrating to which of the two men he was linked. Indeed, the behavior toward the king of Sodom can serve as a model for **not** making a treaty.

The message and significance of the story

It is fascinating that biblical tradition attributes the importance of freeing captives to none other than Abram. To achieve this goal he was willing to sacrifice his life, attacking armies more powerful than his own in order to free his nephew. He acted immediately, confronting the enemy while they were still in Transjordan. However, the story does not tell of a meeting between Abram and Lot after the latter's release, perhaps because Lot was unfitting for such consideration. This makes Abram's act even more exemplary.

The sinful inhabitants of Sodom were taken into captivity, but released later on thanks to the goodness of Abram's heart. This event should have served as a warning to the inhabitants, but their worldview did not change. Lot, too, continued to live among them after his release. Therefore, the sinners had to be destroyed, and that event is depicted in Genesis 19.

While still en route, the four kings from Mesopotamia struck and defeated some nations whose territories stretched eastward and southward of the Jordan rift valley.

Later on, Abram defeated these kings and thus acquired the right to the territories they had conquered. This was in addition to the right derived from God's promise of the land to him. The four kings traveled on the highway from Ashteroth-karnaim to Kadesh; the Israelites would pass this way in the opposite direction. Ashteroth would be the end of Moses' conquests in the northern part that was east of the Jordan River (Joshua 12:4). Abram pursued the kings until Dan, which marks the northern part of the settlement borders of the Israelites in the Land.

b. David's war against Amalek to free his captured men (1 Samuel 30)

Amalek's attack against Ziklag

The Philistines and the Israelites went northward to fight the battle of Gilboa. Thus the Amalekites had the opportunity to attack broad areas of the southern land of Judah and the land of the Philistines. Nevertheless, the Amalekites burned only Ziklag, for the raids on them had started from there. They took the women and children that David and his men had left behind into captivity, presumably in order to sell them as slaves (1 Samuel 30:1–2).

David and his men, having been sent back by Achish, saw their city burned and their women and children missing and began crying in deep despair, for they realized it would be difficult to find the Amalekites in the desert. David himself had to deal not only with the capture of his family, but also with his men who wished to stone him for leaving the city without any guards, when he should have expected some reprisals on the part of the Amalekites (vv. 3–6).

David's pursuit of Amalek and rescuing the captives

From this low point, David gradually rose to the highest levels of leadership. He placed his trust in God and requested that he be able to continue moving forward and succeed in his endeavors. God answered David beyond what he had asked: not only would he overtake his enemies, but he would rescue the captives. This meant that they were still alive. Within the larger narrative of the book of Samuel, at the same time that David was inquiring of God, Saul was visiting the woman who consulted ghosts (1 Samuel 28); Saul went out to war depressed, whereas David who had inquired of God, was answered and went out to battle confidently. David was invigorated by his God, and swept his men along. The embittered 600 soldiers – the size of a battalion in the Bible – who had recently wanted to stone David, now united around their leader who had become stronger and strengthened the others, and together they went out in pursuit of the Amalekite battalion (1 Samuel 30:7–9).

During the pursuit, David reached the stream of Besor. Hertzberg considers the single mention in the Bible of this name as heralding good news for David.[20] At this point 200 of David's men did not have the strength to continue the pursuit for they had already participated in the long march from Ziklag to Aphek and back, and from there to the Besor. Perhaps the 400 men who followed David were the 400 fighters from the original nucleus of David's men (1 Samuel 22:2); and the 200 men who guarded the vessels were those who joined later on, and became an addition that did not consolidate with the original group (ibid., 23:13). Therefore he left them behind to guard the equipment (ibid., 30:24). Thus it became feasible to free the other fighters from the extra burden and from the need to supply the remainder with water and food in the desert south of the Besor. This custom of dividing the force into 400 men who go out to fight and 200 who remain to guard the equipment and provisions was familiar to David from the conflict between himself and Nabal (ibid., 25:13).

While in pursuit, they found an unconscious man whom they identified as Egyptian because of his clothing. They gave him food and drink, and he revived. His origin is pointed out to inform us that they took care of him not to help them locate the battalion, for he was not an Amalekite, but as a moral obligation. Nevertheless, the Egyptian was able to tell them that he had served an Amalekite and that his master had abandoned him when he became ill, though his illness must have been mild as he lasted three days without food, and though the Amalekites had camels to carry him and plenty of food, for as it states later on, they were celebrating with food and drink. Nevertheless they left him without food. This informs us of their cruelty. Perhaps they figured that since they were on the way to Egypt to sell captives, they would not be able to sell the Egyptian there; moreover he was ill and might slow them down. The Amalekites' cruelty brought about their downfall. Their treatment of the Egyptian explains his readiness to cooperate with David who had revived him. The immoral act the Amalekites committed determined their fate, whereas the generosity of David and his men earned them victory over the Amalekites.

The servant informed David of what had happened in Ziklag, and where the Amalekites planned to celebrate. So the servant saved David much time and effort that would be exerted in searching the wide-open spaces of the Negev and enabled him to surprise his enemy. The Amalekites, who had not learned from the mistakes of their opponents, did not place guards suitably; instead they focused on celebrating. So David managed to strike them while they were spread out over a large area, partying with all the spoils and not set up for battle. In this, he reminds us of Gideon (Judges 8:11).

David's success was complete. Four hundred men set out on the campaign, and four hundred men returned; all the captives were found alive; all the possessions were restored. The three verses that discuss David's success (1 Samuel 30:18–20) mention the word "all" four times and repeat the inclusive "from . . . to" to indicate that everything was returned: "from small to great," "from sons to daughters," "from booty to all that was taken from them." These merisms reinforce the sense of David's complete success. The Amalekites did not harm the captives, for they wished to sell them in good condition. Even though the Amalekites celebrated and ate of the spoils taken at Ziklag, David took spoils from the Amalekites and thus compensated for his losses. All of the success was attributed to David whose name is mentioned five times in the three verses. The fighters announced "this is David's spoil" (v. 20) in contrast to the attitude they had expressed at the beginning of the story. David's status was solidified; he emerged stronger after the crisis in leadership.

David sets the rule for division of spoils

Upon their return to the Besor stream the fighters met the 200 men who had been left in the rear. Some of the more negative characters of those who had gone with David said, "we will not give them any of the spoil that we seized – except that each may take his wife and children and go" (v. 22). This fits the conception that the loser loses his right to his property, and that ownership passes over to the victor. Such a philosophy is reflected also in the words of the king of Sodom (Genesis 14:21). Here again we witness David's skill in leadership. At first he addressed the speakers in a spirit of appeasement: "You must not do that, my brothers, in view of what the Lord has granted us" (1 Samuel 30:23). That is, he states that they had received their spoils from God, and because of God they had remained alive and been victorious. Therefore they could not treat those who had remained in the rear in such a manner. Since these words did not change the opinions of the evil men, David formulated his next statement more harshly: "how could anyone agree with you in this matter?" (v. 24). So David overruled the men in his group. He determined: "the share of those who remain with the baggage shall be the same as the share of those who go down to battle; they shall share alike" (v. 24). Apparently this refers to the division of the spoils taken from the enemy; the possessions of David's men who had been in captivity, on the other hand, were to be returned completely to their former owners.[21]

The message and significance of the story

In this story we see how the wives, children and property of David's militiamen were captured by his enemies. In such a situation, taking action to free captives was absolutely necessary. Additionally, this event harmed David's status as leader of his own men and the effectiveness of his militia towards others. We can learn something of the extent of the damage done by comparing this episode with David's earlier decision to destroy the entire household of Nabal simply because the latter had cursed David and his men (1 Samuel 25:10–22). David asked for and received God's permission for his actions, something which Abram had not done.[22] The story of David's action is also more generous with details on the factors leading to his victory: his finding the Egyptian who told him where to find the Amalekites, who were busy with their victory feast, which made them easy to defeat. This may illuminate Abram's victory as well: he too struck at night, and his enemy might have also been feasting or sleeping.

We have here a succession of episodes that cannot be treated as occurring by chance. David and his men returned from Aphek before the war, so they managed to pursue the Amalekites and seize the captives; and it so happened that a sick Egyptian slave remained alive for three days and led David's battalion to its destination. The narrator thus points to God's intervention in the course of episodes in order to help David. The story is built in a concentric structure suited to the arena of events: Ziklag, the Besor stream, the place where the Amalekites encamped, the Besor stream, Ziklag. The structure informs us of the revolution in David's status in the wake of the campaign against the Amalekites.

David's campaign stands in contrast to Saul's war against Amalek with regard to taking the spoils of Amalek. In contrast to the prohibition on Saul to take spoils from Amalek (1 Samuel 15:3), David nails down for generations the procedure for division of the spoils, when he divides Amalek's spoils among the soldiers. Apparently, taking spoils was forbidden in a war intended to wipe out the memory of Amalek, whereas David went out on the campaign to rescue the captives of his camp. Moreover, Saul did not succeed in controlling the people's lust for booty, maintaining that "I yielded to the voice of the people" (v. 24), whereas David succeeded in restraining his soldiers and is presented as an effective legislator. Besides forcing his opinion on the dissenters in his camp, David took care of those among his men who lagged behind, in contrast to Amalek who left behind a sick person who found it difficult to maintain their pace. David remained humane despite the difficulties of life that are especially severe among nomads. So David is revealed as a discerning person; he is that much closer to becoming a king.

c. *Freeing of captives by other acts of violence*

The freeing of Dinah

Dinah was kept by Shechem son of Hamor in his house even after her rape. Only after the act of Simeon and Levi against the inhabitants of Shechem could her brothers take her away from there (Genesis 34:26). Thus the brothers' act to free their sister from the rapist's house could be justified. But the brothers were not satisfied with punishing Shechem and freeing Dinah; they also killed the men of the city of Shechem and took captives (ibid., 29). Apparently the brothers' act exceeded the bounds of punishing sinners and degenerated into wild pillaging that tarnished their argument for justification. For this reason, Jacob feared retribution by the local cities and hastily left the area.

Johanan son of Kareah against Ishmael son of Nethaniah

The act of Johanan son of Kareah against Ishmael son of Nethaniah is included within this framework. Jeremiah 41:10–12 says of Ishmael:

> Then Ishmael took captive all the rest of the people who were in Mizpah, the king's daughters and all the people who were left at Mizpah . . . and set out to cross over to the Ammonites. But when Johanan the son of Kareah and all the leaders of the forces with him heard of all the evil which Ishmael the son of Nethaniah had done, they took all their men and went to fight against Ishmael.

But finally Johanan did not have to fight because as soon as he appeared, Ishmael escaped and all the captives were freed and joined Johanan (Jeremiah 41:14).

d. Freeing of captives at the request of a prophet

Freeing captives of Judah held by Israel (2 Chronicles 28: 9–15)

During the war of Pekah and Rezin against Ahaz, Israelite soldiers took captives from Judah. As the text states, "The Israelites captured 200,000 of their kinsmen, women, boys, and girls; they also took a large amount of booty from them and brought the booty to Samaria" (2 Chronicles 28:8). The victors thought that they would be honored for this, but the prophet Oded reproved them: "Because of the fury of the Lord, God of your fathers, against Judah, He delivered them over to you, and you killed them in a rage that reached heaven!" (ibid., 9). That is, the soldiers should not have attributed their victory to themselves, but to God who punished Judah by means of Israel that had become God's rod of anger. God expected his agents to behave with self-restraint.[23] Instead, they gave vent to their destructive impulses.[24] The prophet added: "Do you now intend to subjugate the men and women of Judah and Jerusalem to be your slaves? As it is, you have nothing but offenses against the Lord your God" (v. 10). Israel must not add fuel to the flames by taking captives. He therefore demanded "Send back the captives you have taken from your kinsmen, for the wrath of the Lord is upon you!" (v. 11). At first the prophet refers to the captives as "men and women of Judah and Jerusalem." When he advocates a course of action to the Israelites, however, he calls the captives "your kinsmen."

The response was immediate and affirmative. The initiative did not come from the government, but from the "chief men of the Ephraimites" who internalized the words of the prophet and repeated them. The soldiers cooperated willingly. The realization that they had become "a rod of wrath" lacking a spark of humanity, created in them an existential need to return to sanity, to the spiritual image of humanity and to brotherhood. The prophet demanded "send back the captives"; they responded above and beyond this demand. They did not even wait for royal endorsement. Their acts of kindness are mentioned in succession: "they clothed them and shod them and gave them to eat and drink and anointed them and provided donkeys for all who were failing and brought them to Jericho" (v. 15). The northern Israelites relinquished their rights to the spoils as victors; and they freed the captives after clothing and feeding them; they even anointed them with oil as was customary with honored guests.

This exemplary behavior of the people of Samaria was cited generations later in the Mishnaic formulation of the proclamation to be recited to the soldiers of Israel by "the priest anointed for war":

> "And shall say unto them, Hear, O Israel, etc.," against your enemies and not against your brethren, not Judah against Simeon, and not Simeon against

Benjamin, for if you fall into their hand they will have mercy upon you, as it is said: ". . . and took the captives, and with the spoil clothed all that were naked among them, and arrayed them, and shod hem, and gave them to eat and to drink, and anointed them, and carried all the feeble of them upon asses, and brought them to Jericho." (Mishnah *Sotah* 8:1)[25]

The place of this story in Chronicles and its contents are problematic for several reasons. First of all, the story interrupts the review of the blows struck at Ahaz and his appeal to the king of Assyria for help (v. 16). Unlike the usual situation in Chronicles, the northern kingdom is presented in this story positively in contrast with the kingdom of Judah.[26] Judah has left God and Israel is the victor; the prophet is a northerner, and Israel prides itself on the fact that its people acknowledge their sins. There is no parallel to this story in Kings or in Isaiah. Moreover, nowhere in the Bible is there an event in which a community acts on behalf of war captives solely for humanitarian and religious reasons. The writer-editor seems to have integrated a story that originated from prophetic circles into his survey. It teaches us that in the eyes of that writer, the members of the northern kingdom were an organic part of the People of Israel, though they were immersed in sins due to their severance from Jerusalem and the House of David. According to this approach, the blame for these sins falls primarily on the shoulders of the kings of Israel and less on the people. At the same time, the writer integrated this particular story not out of love for Samaria, which is mentioned three times in the story, but out of hatred for Ahaz, because the event teaches us that the king of Judah had sunk even lower that the people of the northern kingdom.

The freeing of Aramean soldiers by the king of Israel (2 Kings 6:8–23)

When the king of Aram became agitated upon realizing that the king of Israel knew of his military plans, his servants informed him that the prophet Elisha provided the king of Israel with updated military knowledge. Therefore the king of Aram decided to capture Elisha and sent a military unit that included chariots and horsemen. They encircled the town of Dothan where Elisha was staying (2 Kings 6:12–14). Then God struck the Aramean force with blindness and they were brought to the king of Israel in Samaria. Thus the potential conquerors became captives. The king of Israel was surprised to see the Aramean captives and asked Elisha, "Father, shall I strike them down?" (v. 21). The king understood that he must not act without the permission of the revered prophet, whom he calls, "Father"; on the other hand, he was eager to take advantage of the opportunity that had come his way, and strike his enemies. But the prophet replied, "No, do not . . . did you take them captive with your sword and bow that you would strike them down?" (v. 22).

How should we interpret the prophet's rhetorical question? Does it refer to the Aramean captives and mean that the king of Israel was not permitted to strike them because he had not captured them, or does it define a general rule according to which the king of Israel should not put to death those he captured during a war? The second possibility is based on the verb מַכֶּה "strike" in the present tense in contrast to its two appearances in the king's question, and the prophet begins his answer in the future tense as well.[27] However, within its context, the first explanation is preferable. For if the king of Israel requests permission to strike captives whom he had not captured, one may assume that he generally struck captives that he did capture. Moreover, the combination "sword and bow" is usually used in the Bible in connection with the hand of God rather than with a human force.[28] Therefore the prophet asserts that the king had not captured these people, and he is not referring to behavioral patterns. It seems that the medieval commentators who preferred the second interpretation did so because of their own conception of the proper way to treat captives (centuries before the Geneva Convention!), in contrast to the view of the biblical narrator.

The prophet was not satisfied with this; he demanded more: "set food and drink before them, and let them eat and drink and return to their master" (ibid.). This statement creates a contrast between the beginning of the story and its end by means of plays on words: the king of Aram נלחם "was waging war" (v. 8), whereas the king of Israel was to put לחם (literally: bread) in front of the soldiers of the king of Aram. The prophet thus adopted the advice of the wise man: "If your enemy is hungry, give him bread to eat; if he is thirsty, give him water to drink. You will be heaping live coals on his head, and the Lord will reward you" (Proverbs 25:21–2). The king of Israel indeed carried out the words of the prophet: "So he prepared a lavish feast for them" (2 Kings 6:23). Assuming that the king is the subject of the sentence, he did even more than he was asked to do. He was told to give bread and water; he prepared a festive meal. Then, following the prophet's speech, the Aramean soldiers who had come to paralyze Israel were freed.

Some scholars attribute Elisha's generosity to the Aramean enemy to the prophet's humane personality. In the opinion of Ehrlich, stories in the Bible can be dated according to the moral level they reflect. Whereas the story, "Go away, baldhead!" (2 Kings 2:23–5) was written in "pre-culture days," this story was written about two hundred years later.[29] This evolutionary idea seems naive today. Some think that Elisha demanded that the Arameans be freed in order to publicize the miracle and to glorify himself and publicize the glory of God outside the boundaries of Israel. In this spirit, Yael Shemesh argues that the story is intended to teach that true power is not in the hands of the two kings but in the hand of God and his emissary, the prophet. With the extraordinary restraint the king was asked to demonstrate toward the enemy, he validates the words of the prophet – these are not his own captives, and therefore he cannot treat them as he pleases.[30] A similar conception derives from Ahab's war against Aram in which the prophet reproves the king of Israel for freeing Ben-hadad (1 Kings 20:42). In both stories the prophets argue that the king of Israel cannot do as he pleases with the captives, because they are not his captives but God's.[31]

It seems more likely that Elisha acted for political reasons, in order to establish peace between Israel and Aram. Indeed the text that closes the story, "and the Aramean bands stopped invading the land of Israel" (2 Kings 6:23), supports this view. The story begins with the wars of the king of Aram against Israel and the invasions into its territory, whereas it ends with Aram's cessation of acts against Israel. If at the beginning of the story Elisha helped the Israelite army against Aramean invasions, at the end he appears as the one who put a stop to war in Israel.[32]

3. Conclusions

In our initial survey of Ancient Near Eastern sources, we did not uncover any evidence from those sources of a war being fought for the specific purpose of freeing captives. Apparently, the individual was not considered important enough to warrant a country going to war in order to free him.[33] Even the demand to free a captive is quite rare in Ancient Near Eastern sources; captives were freed primarily when this suited the interests of the captor.

Conversely, in the Bible we do find evidence of fighting to free captives. These were not wars conducted by the state, but rather actions taken by militias set up by the captives' families for this purpose. Such was Abram's campaign against the four kings to rescue Lot; such was the war waged by David and his men to free their families from the Amalekites. The purpose of the action in both cases was to free the captives, but the fighters also took back the possessions that had been taken, and the campaigns earned Abram and David the praise awarded victors and leaders. Abram is no longer considered an immigrant dependent upon the kindness of the local inhabitants; rather he is a hero who acted to guard their security and possessions. David, too, recovered his status in the eyes of his followers, and was thus able to continue on the road to becoming a king. Following these actions, there were discussions regarding the booty. The action taken by Dinah's brothers against Shechem was also carried out by her brothers, in other words by relatives of the captive. Here, too, the possessions of Shechem were taken, even though the capture of Dinah did not include taking possessions. The brothers did not earn praise; on the contrary, their father rebuked them (Genesis 34:30).

How can we explain the biblical documentation of campaigns to free captives, when such documentation does not exist regarding the ancient Near East? Perhaps one may explain this against the background of the nomadic origins of the ancient Israelite community, where obligations derived from closer blood links. The biblical reports therefore relate to the earliest days of the people, and even then it is not the state that initiated the fight to free the captives but the captives' relatives. Besides actions to free captives, the Bible contains statements against taking brethren-Israelites as captives, such as, "Thus said the Lord of Hosts: The people of Israel are oppressed, and so too the people of Judah; all their captors held them, they refused to let them go" (Jeremiah 50:33). Therefore one expects a third party not to stand aside when he sees Israelites being taken into captivity. Accordingly, the prophet Obadiah rebukes Edom, Jacob's brother, "In the day that thou stood on the other side; in the day that the strangers carried away captive his forces,[34] and foreigners entered into his gates and cast lots upon Jerusalem even thou wast as one of them" (Obadiah 11).

Besides the campaigns to free captives, we have also surveyed two cases of freeing captives at the demand of a prophet. In both cases, the prophet asserted that victory over the enemy was accomplished with the help of God, and therefore it was not reasonable to keep the captives or to harm them. The listeners then acted even more generously than had been demanded of them.

Jewish tradition has developed a special sensitivity to the issue of freeing captives. While there is no specific biblical injunction that commands such sensitivity, throughout the ages of exile, persecution and pogroms Jews have looked back at these and other biblical passages for guidance and have assigned extreme importance to the freeing of captives by almost any means. This sensitivity has carried over to the modern State of Israel, which has acted to free captives both by force (such as in the famous raid on Entebbe in 1976) and by negotiation (as in the various deals struck with Lebanese and Palestinian terror organizations), sometimes even to the extent of weakening Israel's military or political position.

Notes

1. See J. Hager-Lau, *The Redemption and the Magnificence: Guarantor's Expressions in Redemption of Captives from Ancient Times until our Days*, Jerusalem: The Religious Institute in Or-Ezion, 2009 (Hebrew); N. Efrati, "Captives, Ransoming of," in F. Skolnic (Ed.), *Encyclopedia Judaica*, 2nd ed. vol. 4, New York: Keter Publishing House, 2007, pp. 456–7.
2. H.A. Hoffner, Jr., "Deeds of Šuppiluliuma," fragments 11, 13, in W.W. Hallo (Ed.), *The Context of Scripture: Canonical Compositions from the Biblical World* II, Leiden: Brill, 2000, p. 186; R.H. Beal, "The Ten Year Annals of Great King Muršili II of Hatti," year 1, ibid. p. 84; A. Altman, "Tracing the Earliest Recorded Concepts of International Law (4): The Near East in the Late Bronze Age (1600–1200 BCE)," *Journal of the History of International Law* 11, 2009, p. 145.
3. A.K. Grayson, *Assyrian Rulers of the Third and Second Millennia BC (to 1115 BC)* (RIMA I), Toronto: University of Toronto Press, 1987, p. 235: A.0.78.1, iii, 21–9.
4. A. Altman, "Hittite Imperialism in Perspective: The Hittite and the Roman Treatment of Subordinate States Compared," in G. Wilhelm (Ed.), *Hattuša – Bogazköy: Das Hethiterreich im Spannungsfeld des Alten Orients*, 6 (Internationales Colloquium der Deutschen Orient-Gesellschaft, Würzburg 22.–24. März 2006), Wiesbaden: Harrassowitz Verlag, 2008, p. 391.
5. Beal, "The Ten Years Annals of Muršili II," p. 86.
6. *CTH* 69 in G. Beckman, *Hittite Diplomatic Texts* (2nd ed.), Atlanta: Scholars Press, 1999, p. 12: §4, A, i, 58–9.
7. Hallo, *The Context of Scripture*, p. 330: 2.128, 20–1.
8. G. Dossin, *Correspondance de Šamsi-Addu* (Archives royals de Mari I), Paris: Imprimerie nationale, 1950, 29: 5–24; Wu Yuhong, *A Political History of Eshnunna, Mari and Assyria during the Early Old Babylonian Period: From the End of Ur III to the Death of Samsi-Adad*, Changchun: Institute of History of Ancient Civilizations, Northeast Normal University, 1994, p. 243.
9. *The Context of Scripture*, p. 258: 2.108, 42–9.
10. Hallo, ibid., p. 159: 2.37.
11. Hallo, ibid., p. 280: 2.115B, ii, 19.
12. There is no extra-biblical source attest to any of the kings or events mentioned in this chapter. The opinions regarding the historical credibility of this story are divided: E.A. Speiser, *Genesis* (Anchor Bible), Garden City: Doubleday, 1964, p. 108, claimed that this chapter was derived from "a foreign source"; other scholars date this story to the

exilic period and later; see J. Van Seters, *Abraham in History and Tradition*, New Haven: Yale University Press, 1975, p. 305; F.I. Andersen, "Genesis 14: An Enigma," in D.P. Wright, D.N. Freedman and A. Hurvitz (Eds.), *Pomegranates and Golden Bells: Studies in Biblical, Jewish, and Near Eastern Ritual, Law and Literature in honor of Jacob Milgrom*, Winona Lake: Eisenbrauns, 1995, p. 506.

13. H. Brodsky, "Did Abram wage a just war?," *Jewish Bible Quarterly* 31, 2003, p. 170, asserts that the strike against the areas outside the five cities was a tactical move intended to frighten the inhabitants of the cities. But it seems unlikely that such a preliminary strike was necessary to frighten them, for the cities were so feeble that they were crushed as soon as they were attacked.

14. The commonly held assumption is that the Melchizedek narrative is a late insertion into the narrative of Abram's campaign. See J. Emerton, "The Riddle of Genesis XIV," *Vetus Testamentum* 21, 1971, p. 407. Such an argument, however, does not exempt us from understanding why the later redactor saw fit to incorporate one episode within another.

15. Don Itzhak Abrabanel, *Torah Commentary, Genesis*, Jerusalem: Bene Arbeel Publishing, 1964, pp. 198–9 (Hebrew).

16. Chayim ben Attar, *Or Hachayim: Commentary on the Torah*; translated and annotated by Eliyahu Munk, Jerusalem: Lambda Publishers, 1999, I, p. 133.

17. See M. Garsiel, *Biblical Names: A Literary Study of Midrashic Derivations and Puns* (trans. P. Hackett), Ramat-Gan: Bar-Ilan University Press, 1991, p. 34; V.P. Hamilton, *The Book of Genesis* (NICOT), Grand Rapids: Eerdmans, 1990, p. 401.

18. See Genesis 18:2–8; 24:14.

19. See D. Elgavish, "The Encounter of Abram and Melchizedek: Covenant Establishment," in A. Wénin (Ed.), *Studies in the Book of Genesis: Literature, Redaction and History (Bibliotheca Ephemeridum Theologicarum Lovaniensium CLV)*, Leuven: University Press, 2001, pp. 495–508.

20. H.W. Hertzberg, *I and II Samuel* (Old Testament Library), London: SCM Press, 1964, p. 227.

21. For the division of the spoils see D. Elgavish, "The Divisions of the Spoils of War in the Bible and in the Ancient Near East," *Zeitschrift für Altorientalische und Biblische Rechtsgeschichte* 8, 2002, pp. 242–73.

22. Nowhere in the Abraham cycle does Abraham actually appeal to God for permission.

23. See D. Elgavish, "Restraint in the Wars between Israel and Judah," in Z.H. Erlich and Y. Eshel (Eds.), *Judea and Samaria Research Studies – Proceedings of the 4th Annual Meeting – 1994*, Kedumim – Ariel: The College of Judea and Samaria, 1995, pp. 59–68 (Hebrew with English abstract).

24. Similarly, Isaiah (10:5–7) accused the Assyrians of not comprehending their role as a rod of God's anger and consequently behaving with excessive cruelty.

25. P. Blackman, *Mishnayoth* III (pointed Hebrew text, English trans., introductions, notes, suppl., appendix; 2nd ed.), New York: Judaica Press, 1963, p. 367.

26. S. Japhet, *The Ideology of the Book of Chronicles and its Place in Biblical Thought* (trans. Anna Barber), Frankfurt am Main: Lang, 1997, pp. 267–324.

27. This was noted by Rashi in the eleventh century, by his contemporary Joseph Kara and by Levi ben Gershon (Gersonides or Ralbag) in the fifteenth century. See M. Cohen (Ed.), *Kings I & II, Mikra'ot Gedolot 'Haketer': A Revised and Augmented Scientific edition of 'Mikra'ot Gedolot' Based on the Aleppo Codex and Early Medieval Mss*, Jerusalem: Keter, 1995, p. 186 (Hebrew).

28. See Josh. 24:12; Ps. 44:7. For the verb מַכֶּה *makkeh* as an indicator of a one-time act in the present, see S.R. Driver, *A Treatise on the Use of the Tenses in Hebrew and Some Other Syntactical Questions* (2nd ed.), Grand Rapids: Eerdmans, 1998, p. 167.

29. A.B. Ehrlich, *Mikrâ Ki-pheschutô*, Berlin: M. Poppelauer's Buchhandlung, 1890, (print-offset New York: Ktav Publishing House 1969), II, p. 347 (Hebrew).

30. Y. Shemesh, "The Stories of Elisha: A Literary Analysis," Ph.D. Dissertation, Ramat-Gan: Bar-Ilan University, 1997, p. 221 (Hebrew).

31. The two stories differ. Israel's king wished to kill the Aramean military unit, but Elisha prevented this. Ahab, in contrast, was rebuked for pardoning the king of Aram. The reactions of the prophets reflected different circumstances. Elisha ordered the release of the Aramean force that had come to capture him, because striking the minor force would not bring about a significant military advantage to Israel. On the contrary, the gesture would constitute a moral victory and was preferable. Ahab, on the other hand, released the Aramean king who had initiated and conducted two major wars against Israel. The consequences of the moves prove the wisdom of the prophets. Ahab's generosity toward Ben-Hadad led to another war between Aram and Israel only three years later and Ahab was killed in that war. In contrast, the release of the Aramean soldiers led to a cessation of Aramean invasions of Israel (v. 23).

32. Because of constrains of place we did not discuss the following sources: Exodus 3–12 (in which God acts to free his captive people), Numbers 21:1–3 and Judges 8:18–19.

33. The story of the Trojan war has its roots in a similar situation. Paris, a Trojan prince, abducted Helen the wife of Menelaus King of Sparta and also carried off much of Menelaus' wealth. Following this, the Greeks waged war against Troy. They burned the city and plundered it, and returned Helen to her husband. However, this exceptional story does not deal with prisoners of war but with the kidnapping of a queen. In circumstances such as these the king will fight to regain his wife.

34. The term חילו, *ḥêlô*, here translated, in the tradition of the Vulgate, as "his forces" (referring to people), can also mean property and even fortresses. The Septuagint uses a more ambiguous term, δύναμιν. See D. Stuart, *Hosea-Jonah* (WBC 31), Waco: Word Books, 1987, p. 413.

2 "Set bread and water before them"

Elisha's order to treat the enemy with mercy and its implications*

Amichai Nachshon

1. Introduction

One episode in the Elisha cycle (2 Kings 6:8–23) recounts a miraculous deliverance after the prophet acts with uncommon morality. The story, which the scholarly literature refers to as a "political legend" (a subcategory of the saints' legend),[1] makes readers aware of the prophet's righteousness and wisdom. It describes how Elisha put an end to the repeated incursions by Aramean brigades (vv. 8–23). Like the stories of Naaman (2 Kings 5) and of the siege of Samaria (2 Kings 6:4–7, 20), which bracket it,[2] the narrator never names the two kings who are characters in this story (those of Israel and Aram).[3] This is apparently his way of emphasizing the superiority of the prophetic institution over the royal and highlighting how the kings of Israel needed to rely on the spiritual and moral powers of the prophets of the Lord.[4]

According to the account in 2 Kings 6:8–14, the Aramean king dispatched his soldiers to capture Elisha after his ministers blamed the frustration of all his military plans on the prophet's supernatural powers. In the wake of Elisha's prayer,[5] the soldiers are struck blind (v. 18).[6] Exploiting their blindness, Elisha leads them to the Israelite capital of Samaria. After he entreats the Lord to restore their sight, they find themselves prisoners in Samaria (v. 20). The king of Israel asks the prophet's permission to strike them down, but Elisha adamantly refuses: "You shall not slay them. Would you slay those whom you have taken captive with your sword and with your bow?" (v. 22).[7] Instead, the prophet orders that the Aramean captives be feasted and then sent back to their master (vv. 22–23). The narrator concludes this pericope with the observation that in the wake of this incident the Arameans stopped raiding the kingdom of Israel: "And the Aramean bands stopped invading the land of Israel" (2 Kings 6:23).

The present article analyzes Elisha's prophetic attitude toward the captured Arameans on two levels:

1. The moral level: what is the moral worldview that can be extracted from the story?
2. The cognitive level: what is the political craft behind the prophet's actions? Are they merely a tactical maneuver?

2. The moral implications of the story

The moral superiority of Elisha's action—forbidding the king of Israel to kill enemies other than on the field of battle[8]—is clear. As Rashi puts it: "Are you in the habit of killing your prisoners after capturing them?"[9] Elisha's message may be that there is no need for force when the Lord is fighting on behalf of Israel, as He told Moses before the splitting of the sea: "The Lord will fight for you, and you have only to be still" (Exodus 14:14).[10]

Elisha's behavior here resembles that of the Israelite commanders toward their Judahite prisoners in Pekah son of Remaliah's war against Ahaz: "[They] took the captives, and with the spoil they clothed all that were naked among them; they clothed them, gave them sandals, provided them with food and drink, and anointed them; and carrying all the feeble among them on asses" (2 Chronicles 28:15). The prophet's compassionate treatment of the Aramean enemy fits in with the idea, expounded several times in the prophetic literature, that the ways of the Lord, which include mercy, apply even to enemies in time of war.[11]

The prophet's extraordinary mercy toward the Aramean band, which includes ordering that "a great feast" be made for them, stands in striking contrast to the story of Adoni-bezek in Judges 1:7. As that king noted, after his Judahite and Simeonite captors cut off his thumbs and big toes, "seventy kings with their thumbs and their great toes cut off used to pick up scraps under my table; as I have done, so God has requited me." Amit maintains that Adoni-bezek permitted the captive kings to eat his table scraps, like dogs.[12] His self-condemnation of this behavior as justification for his punishment—"as I have done, so God has requited me"—reflects the underlying ethical perspective of the story: one must not humiliate captive enemies.

According to Koole,[13] Elisha's perspective in our story is similar to that of the prophet Isaiah, who expects rulers to be "merciful kings" and to treat captives with compassion.[14] He indicts the Babylonians for their unnecessary brutality during their conquest of Jerusalem. Jerusalem, he holds, had been "given" to the Babylonians by the Lord: "I gave them into your hand, [but] you showed them no mercy" (Isaiah 47:6). That is, the Babylonians are considered to be instruments of the Lord, and as such are required to obey Him and to show mercy to vanquished Jerusalem and its people. Their cruelty during the occupation of the city is accounted a sin for which they will be punished.[15]

In addition to Elisha's explicit instruction to the king of Israel to treat his prisoners mercifully, Elisha's miraculous victory, achieved with the assistance of angels, can be seen as censure of the Aramean pillagers. This reading is backed by many biblical passages that apply pejorative terms to armed bands that engage in political mischief. In the account of Jehoiakim's reign, they are referred to as "destroyers" (2 Kings 24:2). During Solomon's reign, the Edomite and Aramean rebels are referred to disapprovingly as *śatan* "adversary" (1 Kings 11:14–25).[16] The language of the text, that Rezon the Aramean "was an *adversary* of Israel all the days of Solomon, doing mischief as Hadad did; and he abhorred Israel" (1 Kings 11:25),[17] indicates that the hostile actions (שטנה) by Solomon's adversaries are evil; as he informs Hiram: "there is neither adversary (שטן) nor misfortune (פגע רע)" (1 Kings 5:18). Klein and Goerg argue for an affinity of the roots *ś.t.n* and *ś.t.m*, which means hatred: e.g., "Esau hated (וישטם) Jacob" (Genesis 27:41).[18] The same term is applied to David by the Philistine lords, who are dubious of his loyalty—"lest in the battle he become an adversary to us" (1 Samuel 29:4)[19]— and to the psalmist's foes who seek evil for him: "may my accusers (שטני נפשי) be put to shame and consumed; with scorn and disgrace may they be covered who seek my hurt" (Psalm 71:13).[20] Fitting in perfectly with this meaning is the notice that "in the reign of Ahasuerus, at the start of his reign, they wrote an accusation *(śitnah)* against the inhabitants of Judah and Jerusalem" (Ezra 4:6); here the political damage—suspension of the construction of the Temple (vv. 23–24)—is undoubted. In all of these cases the *śitnah* or antagonistic action involves political damage.[21]

In this context, Elisha's treatment of the Aramean marauders, who have injured Israel in the past (2 Kings 5:1–2) and in the present (6:8–14), is a lofty and sophisticated reaction. The prophet shows them his ability to control the course of events, forcing them to recognize his military superiority. At the same time, the mercy shown them at his instigation is the utter antithesis of their habit of pillage and plunder. Serving them a feast constitutes a sort of protest against the injustices they wreak.

It seems, then, that this story illustrates how the prophet, working miracles, can induce both the king of Israel and enemies from afar to demonstrate some form of morality even in war. The people of Israel learn to treat their prisoners decently, while the Arameans learn to refrain from murder and plunder. The prophet's moral teachings motivate those around him to recognize and honor God.[22]

3. Political craft in Elisha's actions

Elisha chalks up a significant military victory, putting an end to the depredations by the Aramean raiders, without the use of military force. We may identify his action as a sophisticated psychological ploy to influence the Aramean enemies and make them see that their raids gain no political advantage and ought to be halted for everyone's sake. This major political achievement is mentioned at the end of the story, where we read that after the captives returned to their master, the Aramean bands no longer invaded the country. Readers are supposed to learn from this that kings are obligated to rely on the power of the prophets of God, who, in addition to their moral superiority, are also blessed with political insight.[23]

Five episodes in the story can be seen as elements of the prophet's stratagem:

1. Elisha prays to God, asking that he strike the Arameans with both physical and mental blindness (v. 18).
2. Elisha exploits the Arameans' blindness when they ask him for directions and leads them to Samaria (v. 19).
3. After the Arameans are safely within Samaria Elisha prays for their sight to be restored. The Arameans look around and realize their military

vulnerability, inasmuch as they are inside the walls of the city (v. 20). No doubt they discover that they are surrounded by the soldiers of the king of Israel.

4. At this stage there is an unexpected colloquy between king and prophet. The king asks for permission to kill the captives (v. 21), but the prophet sternly forbids him to do so and instead enjoins him prepare a feast for the Arameans and then to release them (v. 22).
5. The king complies, prepares a lavish feast for the Aramean captives, and sets them free (v. 23).

The prophet's series of actions can be seen as constituting a moral and psychological trap. Elisha plays with the Arameans' emotions; we may easily conjecture what they were feeling at each stage of the plot. At first, struck blind, they were hurting and humiliated, painfully aware of their sudden vulnerability and of the terrible price they would pay for their aggression. Next, Elisha renders the Arameans tense and anxious, as they blindly follow a stranger (the prophet incognito) to what turns out to be the enemy's capital. Arrived there, they are still not aware of their perilous situation. Only after the prophet prays again—"open the eyes of these men, that they may see" (2 Kings 6:20)—do the Arameans become aware of their mortal danger. By opening their eyes, Elisha intensifies the dread that struck them when they lost their sight. The notice that "they saw; *and lo*, they were inside Samaria" (ibid.) indicates the unexpected scene they now had to deal with. When they realize the dramatic reversal in their situation, from attackers to vanquished, trapped in the heart of the enemy city, they expect that they are about to die. According to Robinson, the Arameans would have feared that they were about to be the victims of a ritual execution, with their end similar to that of Agag: "Samuel hewed Agag in pieces before the Lord in Gilgal" (1 Samuel 15:33).[24]

But now there is a radical reversal. Quite unexpectedly, Elisha enjoins the king of Israel to treat the Aramean captives mercifully and to prepare a feast for the two armies. This produces an emotional and cognitive reversal among the Arameans: from existential panic to utter relief. The prophet's answer to the king must have astonished all who heard it—both the Aramean prisoners and their Israelite captors. The preparations for the feast were undoubtedly a source of wonder for the captives, who, having expected the worst, were instead regaled with a royal banquet.

Axskjöld suggests that the feast was part of the ceremonial signing of a peace treaty, such as that between Isaac and Abimelech: "let us make a covenant with you. . . . So he made them a feast, and they ate and drank. In the morning they rose early and took oath with one another; and Isaac set them on their way, and they departed from him in peace" (Genesis 26:28, 30–31).[25] It is important to note that, as prisoners, the Arameans had no choice in the matter of the banquet. Set in front of them before the threat of death had been removed, it would have inspired them with deep humiliation, as a public demonstration of their moral inferiority to the prophet and his people.

The book of Proverbs recommends this very tactic of humiliating one's enemies by feeding them: "If your enemy is hungry, give him bread to eat; and if he is thirsty, give him water to drink" (Prov. 25:21). The underlying idea is explained in *Seder Eliyahu Rabbah*:

> "Wisdom is better than weapons of war" (Ecclesiastes 9:18): The *poston*[26] made by Elisha with the king of Israel was greater than all the wars conducted by Jehoram son of Ahab king of Israel, as it says: "When the king of Israel saw them he said to Elisha, 'My father, shall I slay them? Shall I slay them?' He answered, "You shall not slay them" (2 Kings 6:21–22). And it says further, "So he prepared for them a great feast" (2 Kings 6:23)—and the "feast" mentioned here is a term for "peace."[27]

That is, according to the homilist, a meal eaten together with a defeated enemy leads to maximum diplomatic success: peace with no fear of future aggression by the foe.

It is plausible that the banquet overseen by the prophet, after which he gave instructions that they be paroled to their own country, produced a strong emotional upheaval for the Arameans and reversed their conception of the Israelite enemy,[28] motivated by their gratitude and esteem for the noble prophet to whom they owed their lives and self-respect.[29]

4. Evaluation of Elisha's action

Elisha's stratagem achieved its objective—an end to Aramean raids—and provided the kingdom of Israel with a military deterrent: "the Aramean bands stopped invading the land of Israel" (2 Kings 6:23). Abravanel clearly understood the diplomacy involved: "The meaning is that the banquet that the prophet gave to the Arameans who came to capture him was of more benefit when it came to getting the Aramean bands to stop invading the land of Israel and deterred them more than all the wars of Jehoram deterred them."[30] The Aramean rulers realized the uselessness of fighting against an adversary protected by a miracle-working prophet and reached an important political conclusion: there was no point in continuing the incursions and raids into the kingdom of Israel.[31]

Our story burnishes the prophet's prestige for readers of the Elisha cycle, as noted by Rofé in his treatment of the king's visit to the dying Elisha, who promises Israel victory over its enemies: "The narrative reveals the belief that Elisha in his person constitutes 'Israel's charity and cavalry'; i.e., he is the equal of the northern kingdom's entire chariot corps, decimated in the Aramaean wars."[32] The ironic implication is that the might of the prophet who prays frequently and receives heavenly assistance exceeds the strength of the fainéant ruler of Samaria.[33]

Furthermore, the statement that "the Aramean bands *no longer invaded* the land of *Israel*" (2 Kings 6:23) echoes a similar line in the summary of the career of the prophet Samuel: "The Philistines were subdued and *no longer invaded* the territory of *Israel*" (1 Samuel 7:13). This reference to Samuel's overwhelming victory, which deterred the Philistines for many years, comes right before the people's request for a king (8:5), whose main function will be to defend them against the Philistines (9:16). The juxtaposition emphasizes the people's folly in demanding a king like all the nations, when it is the prophet Samuel who has delivered them from the Philistines. This echo serves to highlight the great power of Elisha, who achieves a political victory similar to the triumph that won Samuel such historical prominence and esteem.[34]

Despite the important achievement reported at the end of our story—the suspension of the Aramean raids into Israel—the relentless conflict between the two kingdoms continued for the rest of Elisha's life.[35] Hence we must limit the significance of Elisha's coup. Although the sudden incursions in search of booty ended, open warfare between the two states, for which military preparations could be taken, continued for many years.[36] Thus Elisha's effort did not produce full peace, but did bring about a fundamental improvement in the personal security of the residents of the Northern Kingdom.

We may conclude that, in addition to the moral advantages of the prophet's action, he also gained four tactical advantages:

1. Elisha took the initiative and caught the enemy unaware. This allowed him to control events and direct them toward the desired outcome.
2. Elisha placed the civilian population of Israel outside the battle zone.
3. Elisha caused the enemy to recognize that the prophet's power exceeds theirs and that he is impervious to their attacks.
4. His magnanimous conduct, which caused no causalities, produced diplomatic respect for his country.

5. Summary and conclusions

According to the reading proposed above, in addition to the universal prophetic lesson contained in Elisha's refusal to allow the king to harm the captive Arameans, the prophet employed a clever psychological ploy that achieved his goal. His prayer that the Aramean invaders lose their sight produced the anticipated miracle that led to their finding themselves trapped inside Samaria. This set them on an emotional rollercoaster that at first produced panic and helplessness. Then, when they were feasted rather than killed, they were inspired to respect the prophet and to acknowledge his superior physical and moral power. It is clear from the story that the prophetic stratagem surpassed what could have been achieved by open warfare, since it put an end to the frequent incursions by the Aramean bands and improved the security situation.

To summarize, the story presents three key ideas that relate to Elisha's role in teaching the people of the kingdom of Israel to treat their enemies morally and respectfully:

1. The story buttresses the status of the prophet, the legitimate emissary of the Lord, and shows the hollowness of the power of the idolatrous king of the

House of Omri, who in his weakness had been allowing the Aramean bands free run of his kingdom. Only the magnanimous prophet could put end to this appalling and dangerous situation.[37]

2.   The story teaches the obligation to deal mercifully with one's enemies and to respect their dignity. The king may not employ the violence of the battlefield against foes that fell into his power through a miracle. He must take advantage of this victory by showing mercy and compassion, as the prophet enjoins.

3.   The story has a universal message. We learn from the sequence of events that the enemy marauders can be defeated by the Lord's intervention through his prophet. It derides the military power of the Aramean enemy, defeated by a lone prophet by means of prayer and cleverness. We may also see here a principled condemnation of the use of freebooters to ravage and plunder an enemy country.

In addition to the moral lessons on the importance of compassion, even in war, an analysis of the stratagem and its advantages heightens the irony: the folly of the weak political leader of Israel is contrasted with the resourcefulness of the devious but moral man of spirit. This contrast intensifies the appreciation of diverse aspects of the ethical code of war in the Bible and leads readers to search for means to avoid killing whenever possible.

Notes

*   I wish to thank the research fund of the Ashkelon Academic College for its generous help.

1.   A. Rofé, *The Prophetical Stories: The Narratives About the Prophets in the Hebrew Bible, Their Literary Types and History*, Jerusalem: Magnes Press, 1988, deals with this topic at length. For a specific treatment associated with this story, see pp. 58–63. For a recent detailed study, see Yael Shemesh, "The Elisha Stories as Saints' Legends," *Journal of Hebrew Scriptures* 8, 2008, pp. 2–14, which deals with the full Elisha cycle in its cultural and political context. See her discussion there on pp. 2–10.

2.   The present study focuses on a single short episode, 2 Kings 6:8–23. The stories that bracket it create a thematic problem. According to our story, Elisha's coup produced an important achievement: "the Aramean bands stopped invading the land of Israel" (2 Kings 6:23). But the very next verse describes a lengthy siege of the city of Samaria: "Sometime later, King Ben-hadad of Aram mustered his entire army and marched upon Samaria and besieged it" (2 Kings 6:24). The narrator is aware of the difference between the threat posed by the raiders who pillaged the hinterland of the kingdom and the serious danger represented by the siege of its capital. According to Jones, the end of the hostile incursions is a historical fact that corresponds to a specific event unrelated to the adjacent stories: "Thus the climax provided for vv. 8–23 not only forms a link between this section and other narratives in Kings but reflects more correctly historical circumstances" (G.H. Jones, *1 and 2 Kings. Volume II, 1 Kings 17:1–2 Kings 25:30*, London: Marshall Morgan & Scott, 1984, p. 429). This issue requires separate treatment. Here we shall deal only with Elisha's prophetic stratagem for eliminating the threat posed by the raiders.

3.   G. Galil, *The Chronology of the Kings of Israel and Judah*, Leiden: Brill, 1996, pp. 51–52, esp. n. 25, deals with the problem of identification of the historical events alluded to in 2 Kings 6–7. The reference to Elisha links the episode to events in the kingdom of Israel during his career; that is, from the time of Jehoram son of Ahab, who ruled in the middle of the ninth century BCE through that of Jehoash at the start of the eighth

century. This covers the reigns of Jehoram son of Ahab, of Jehu, and of his two sons, Jehoahaz and Jehoash (see the chronology in Galil, ibid. p. 147). The present study is not the appropriate place to investigate the associated historical questions.

4. According to Rofé, *The Prophetical Stories*, p. 57, "the authenticity of this account, which portrays the prophet as the king's associate involved in national political life, should not be doubted."

5. According to Rofé, *The Prophetical Stories*, p. 61, the presentation of Elisha as acting through prayer, rather than by means of magic and miracles, reflects the refined and exalted character of the prophet, who is shown to be generous and merciful. Elisha prays three times: that his servant's eyes be opened (6:17), that the Aramean band be struck blind (v. 18), and that they recover from their blindness (v. 20). According to T.E. Fretheim, *First and Second Kings*, Louisville: Westminster John Knox Press, 1994, p. 158, the main message of the story is that a prophet's prayer is more powerful than the military might of kings.

6. According to Rofé, *The Prophetical Stories*, pp. 62–63, this physical blindness is a sequel to the absurd political blindness reflected in the foolish attempt to abduct a true prophet who enjoys miraculous protection. This observation fits in with the reading by S. Laniado, *Keli Yaqar on the Former Prophets. 2 Kings*, Jerusalem: Makhon Ha-ketav, 1994, p. 139 (Hebrew), who explains the purpose of the sudden blindness: "Inasmuch as their eyes saw Elisha's wondrous act and their mouths said that he 'tells the king of Israel the words that you speak in your bedchamber,' how could they be so witless as to try to capture him, since he knew they were pursuing him and would go else-where at once. Could there be any greater blindness? This is why he prayed, saying, 'Strike this people, I pray thee, with blindness,' for such a blow befitted them more than any other." Physical blindness can be interpreted as a metaphor for intellectual blindness, as in the case of Adam and Eve: "Then the eyes of both were opened, and they knew that they were naked" (Genesis 3:7). See the commentary of Meir Leibish Weiser (the Malbim) on Kings, "It is clear that the blindness here is not blindness of the eyes but rather mental confusion" (in *Miqra'ot Gedolot. Kings*, Tel Aviv: Brody-Katz, 1975, p. 283 [Hebrew]). See also C.-J. Axskjöld, *Aram as the Enemy Friend: the Ideological Role of Aram in the Composition of Genesis – 2 Kings*, Stockholm: Almqvist & Wiksell International, 1998, p. 131. In my view, in this story vision is to be understood as both physical and intellectual. For the methodology of dual interpretation of biblical narrative, see at length Y. Grossman, "Dual Meaning in the Biblical Narrative and its Contribution to Molding the Story," Ph.D. dissertation, Ramat-Gan: Bar-Ilan University, 2006 (Hebrew).

7. Thus translated in RSV. The NJPS understands the prophet's rhetorical question differently: not that it is wrong to kill prisoners in general, but that the king has no right to kill those whom he did not capture on the field of battle: "Did you take them captive with your sword and bow that you would strike them down?"

8. On reading the story as a pacifist tract that rejects military violence in every situation, see J.A. Wood, *Perspectives on War in the Bible*, Macon: Mercer University Press, 1998, p. 109. This idea is possible if one takes the story to be the account of an unusual incident. Since, however, the Elisha cycle is replete with numerous acts of retribution and sudden death, affecting both Israel and its enemies (the she-bears who mangle the lads from Jericho [2 Kings 2:23–25], the prophecy of the destruction of Moab [3:18–19], the prophecy of the punishment of the house of Ahab [9:1–10], and the prophecy of Israel's victory over Aram [13:14–19]), it is simply impossible to hold that Elisha was a pacifist. See A. Shapira, *The First Democracy in the Bible: Ancient Foundations of Democratic Values*, Tel Aviv: Hillel Ben-Hayyim, 2009 (Hebrew) which addresses this issue at length (pp. 9–186).

9. Rashi, in *Miqra'ot Gedolot ha-Keter. 2 Kings*, Ramat Gan: Bar-Ilan University Press, 1995, p. 187 (Hebrew). The same interpretation is offered by Joseph Kara and Gersonides

(ibid.), by H.M.Y. Gevaryahu, "From the Bible Study Group at David Ben-Gurion's House: On the Prophet Elisha," *Beit Mikra* 33, 1988, p. 207 (Hebrew), and by others.

10. See also 2 Chronicles 20:17. This was the reading of Isaac Abravanel, *Commentary on the Prophets and Hagiographa*, Hamburg, 1687; Reprinted Jerusalem: Elisha Press, 1956 (Hebrew), and of S. Niditch, *War in the Hebrew Bible: A Study in the Ethics of Violence* Oxford: Oxford University Press, 1993, p. 148.

11. See Niditch, ibid., pp. 137–149, esp. p. 148.

12. Yaira Amit, *Judges with Introduction and Commentary*, Jerusalem: Magnes Press, 1999, p. 33 (Hebrew).

13. J.L. Koole, *Isaiah III. Vol. 1: Isaiah 40–48* (Historical Commentary on the Old Testament), trans. A.P. Runia, Kampen: Kok Pharos, 1997, p. 534.

14. These are righteous monarchs who show mercy to foreign captives (1 Kings 20:31–32). In that story, the "merciful king" *(melekh hesed)* has a positive connotation as a paragon of political conduct. This is not the place to consider the complexity of the account in 1 Kings, which sees Ahab's action as political folly performed without prior consultation of a prophet. The term *rahamim* "mercy" employed in this prophecy (Isaiah 47:6) echoes the prophets' calls to the Israelites to treat their fellows mercifully. Zechariah, for example, mandates such conduct: "Thus says the Lord of Hosts, 'Render true judgments, show kindness and mercy each to his brother'" (Zechariah 7:9).

15. See now D. Rom-Shiloni, *God in an Age of Destruction and Exile: Biblical Theology*, Jerusalem: Magnes Press, 2009, pp. 185–192 (Hebrew). On other implications of Isaiah 47:6 see A. Nachshon, "The Lord's Demands of Gentiles in the Historical and Prophetic Books of the Bible," Ph.D. dissertation, Ramat-Gan: Bar-Ilan University, 2003, pp. 41–43 (Hebrew). On this prophecy see further S. Paul, *Isaiah 40–66 with Introduction and Commentary*, Jerusalem: Magnes Press, 2008, pp. 257–258 (Hebrew).

16. On this see at length D. Edelman, "Solomon's Adversaries Hadad, Rezon and Jeroboam: A Trio of Bad Guy Characters Illustrating the Theology of Immediate Retribution," in S.W. Holloway and L.K. Handy (Eds.), *The Pitcher is Broken: Memorial Essays for Gosta W. Ahlström*, Sheffield: Sheffield Academic Press, 1995, pp. 166–191.

17. Hebrew ויקץ. The root *q.w.ṣ* has the sense of repulsion or loathing; e.g.: "I am disgusted *(qaṣti)* with my life because of the Hittite women" (Gen. 27:46); "we loathe *(qaṣah)* this worthless food" (Num. 21:5). But the present verse could also be understood along with the Peshitta, which reflects the metathetical ויצק "he did harm." See S. Abramski "The Revival of the Damascene Kingdom in the time of Solomon and its Mark on Historiography," in J. Blau and Y. Avishur (Eds.), *Studies in Bible and the Ancient Near East Presented to Samuel E. Loewenstamm*, Jerusalem: Rubinstein, 1978, pp. 15–24 (Hebrew); M.Z. Kaddari, קוץ, *Dictionary of Biblical Hebrew*, Ramat Gan: Bar-Ilan University Press, 2006, pp. 940–941 (Hebrew).

18. J. Klein, *Job* (Olam Hatanakh), Tel Aviv: Davidson Azati, 1996, pp. 29–30 (Hebrew); M. Goerg, "Der 'Satan': der 'Vollstrecker' Gottes?," *Biblische Notizen* 82, 1996, pp. 9–12. See also Genesis 49:23; 50:15; Job 16:9; *et passim*.

19. Achish bows to the other Philistine rulers' demand and sends David away from the battle. To justify this action he tells the latter, "go peaceably, that you may not displease [*lit.* do anything that is evil in the eyes of] the lords of the Philistines" (1 Sam. 29:7). Similar is David's censure of the sons of Zeruiah: "What have I to do with you, you sons of Zeruiah, that you should this day be as an adversary *(śatan)* to me?" (2 Samuel 19:23 [RSV 22]). S. Bar-Efrat, *First Samuel With Introduction and Commentary*, Jerusalem: Magnes Press, 1996, p. 209 (Hebrew) explains that in the incident with Abishai the word *śatan* has the sense of "hindrance, annoyance"; that is, the adversary interferes with the king's ability to run his kingdom. P.L. Day, "Abishai the Sāṭān in 2 Samuel 19:17–24," *Catholic Biblical Quarterly* 49, 1987, pp. 546–547, argues that Abishai's advice that David kill Shimei, if followed, would harm the prospects of

reconciling the Benjaminite families to David as king; that is, Abishai the adversary is undermining the legitimacy of David's rule.

20. See also Psalms 38:21; 109:4; 20.
21. See A. Frisch, "The Solomon Stories in the Book of Kings," Ph.D. dissertation, Ramat-Gan: Bar-Ilan University, 1986, p. 313 n. 1 (Hebrew).
22. This is the subject of Nachshon's dissertation, "The Lord's Demands of Gentiles." See also Shemesh, "The Elisha Stories as Saints Legends," p. 8, and her interpretation of Elisha's miracles in a universal context.
23. N. Avraham, "On the Social Status of Elisha and the Disciples of the Prophets," in M. Heltzer and M. Malul (Eds.), *Teshurot leAvishur: Studies in the Bible and the Ancient Near East, in Hebrew and Semitic Languages*, Tel Aviv: Archeological Center Publications, 2004, pp. 41–54 (Hebrew). See there at length about the social status of Elisha and his disciples as a unified group with a spiritual platform, rather different from that of the surrounding population.
24. J. Robinson, *The Second Book of Kings*, Cambridge: Cambridge University Press, 1976, p. 61. On the ritual significance of Samuel's action, see M.D. Fowler, "The Meaning of 'Lipne YHWH' in the Old Testament," *Zeitschrift für die Alttestamentliche Wissenschaft* 99, 1987, p. 390.
25. Axskjöld, *Aram as the Enemy Friend*, p. 133.
26. Y. Shemesh, "The Elisha Stories: A Literary Analysis," Ph.D. dissertation, Ramat-Gan: Bar-Ilan University, 1997, p. 221 (Hebrew) proposes reading *pistin*, from the Greek, meaning "faith" or "trust." Nahan ben Jehiel, *Arukh*, s.v. פסט (Pardes: New York, 1955, p. 378), suggests "ambush" or "security." According to Y. Ariel, *Mikdash Melekh: Studies in the Book of Kings*, Hispin: Midreshet Hagolan, 1994, p. 272, n. 21 (Hebrew), the variant in *Yalqut Shimoni, pasqin*, could mean "armistice."
27. M. Ish-Shalom (Ed.), *Seder Eliyahu Rabbah ve-Seder Eliyahu Zuta*, Vienna: Bamberger, 1902; Jerusalem: Wohrman, 1969, p. 39 (Hebrew). This idea has been accepted by most scholars of this story.
28. In an interdisciplinary article that I co-authored with my father, A. and I. Nachshon, "Moral-Psychological Manipulation in a Prophetic Story: An Interdisciplinary Analysis," *Moreshet-Israel* 7, 2010, pp. 31–45 (Hebrew with English abstract), we conjecture that here we have an intelligent use of cognitive dissonance. That is, Elisha cleverly and intentionally generated severe cognitive dissonance among the Arameans by creating an acute conflict between their expectations of cruel treatment and the compassion they actually experienced. Because the intensity of the dissonance produces a reaction of equal intensity to dissipate it, the conflict was resolved quickly. As in many cases, this meant a drastic change in the Arameans' conduct and attitudes. It is plausible that this change among the junior ranks percolated upward to the higher echelons of the Aramean leaders and ultimately led to a long-term strategic change by the Aramean king and his counselors (note the plural *adoneihem*—"their masters"— in the Hebrew of vv. 22–23), to whom they related the story. Thus Elisha's actions led the Arameans to suspend their hostile raids into the territory of Israel.
29. E. Samet, *The Elisha Chapters*, Ma'ale Adumim: Ma'aliyot, 2003, pp. 462–463 (Hebrew), conjectures that the Arameans were quite animated when they reported back to their king. This is plausible, because the text links the prophet's act with the end of the Aramean depredations. According to Samet, Elisha displayed both military and moral superiority vis-à-vis the Arameans.
30. Abravanel, *Commentary on the Prophets and Hagiographa*, pp. 622–623 (Hebrew).
31. According to Axskjöld, *Aram as the Enemy Friend*, p. 265, the members of the Aramean band served as witnesses of the prophet's power and enhanced his reputation in their first-hand report.
32. A. Rofé, *Introduction to the Literature of the Hebrew Bible* Jerusalem: Simor, 2009, p. 37.

33. According to R. LaBarbera, "The Man of War and the Man of God: Social Satire in 2 Kings 6:8–7:20," *Catholic Biblical Quarterly* 46, 1984, p. 651, the story "draws on traditional folkloric material rich in irony, puns, and humor to create a biting social commentary." T.R. Hobbs, *2 Kings*, Waco: Word Books, 1985, p. 74, refers to it as a "comedy of manners."

34. Samuel's lofty status is reflected in Psalms: "Moses and Aaron among His priests, Samuel, among those who call on His name; when they called to the Lord, He answered them" (Ps. 99:6); and in Jeremiah: "Though Moses and Samuel stood before me . . ." (Jeremiah 15:1). As Garsiel recently put it: "The author [of 1 Samuel] has given a local triumph, of limited scope in time and place, extraordinary proportions: the broadest territorial expanse and a maximum duration for the Philistines' subjugation ('all the days of Samuel'). In this way Samuel is presented as a national leader who delivered his people from the hand of the Philistines so that peace prevailed in the country during his tenure, like the judge-deliverers who preceded him." See M. Garsiel, *The Beginning of the Kingdom in Israel: Studies in the Book of Samuel*, vol. 1, Tel Aviv: The Open University, 2008, p. 154 (Hebrew). There are similar descriptions of the successes of other judges who brought peace to the land: Othniel son of Kenaz, 40 years (Judges 3:10); Ehud son of Gera, 80 years (ibid, v. 30); Deborah, 40 years (5:31); and Gideon, 40 years (8:28).

35. This is clear from the stories of the siege of Samaria (2 Kings 6:24–7:2), the anointing of Hazael (8:7–15), and Elisha's death (13:14–19). Even Elisha's deathbed prophecy deals with a future military victory over Aram: "Elisha said, 'An arrow of victory for the Lord! An arrow of victory over Aram! You shall rout Aram completely at Aphek'" (2 Kings 13:17).

36. The possibilities for defense against open attack are many and diverse: espionage, lookouts, building and training a military force, concluding military pacts with other states, attacking the enemies' fighters and supply lines and so on. Moreover, in the prophetic worldview military victory could be won through prayer, sacrifice, and obedience to the prophets—behavior that makes one eligible to be the beneficiary of great miracles. As for the possibility of changing God's will through prayer, see Y. Zimran, "And He Heard their Voice: On God's Changing His Mind in Response to Human Prayer," M.A. thesis, Ramat-Gan: Bar-Ilan University, 2009 (Hebrew).

37. According to Shemesh, "The Elisha Stories as Saints' Legends," p. 5, the three stories in 2 Kings 5, 6:8–23, and 6:24–7:20 are religious and social satires directed against the socioeconomic elite of the kingdom of Israel in the ninth century BCE.

3   The wars of Joshua

Weaning away from the divine

Yigal Levin

The first eleven chapters of the book of Joshua recount a succession of military campaigns, at the end of which Joshua, as leader of the Israelite nation, is in possession of the entire land of Canaan: "So Joshua took all that land: the hill country and all the Negeb and all the land of Goshen and the lowland and the Arabah and the hill country of Israel and its lowland, from Mount Halak, which rises toward Seir, as far as Baal-gad in the valley of Lebanon below Mount Hermon. He took all their kings, struck them down, and put them to death" (Joshua 11:16–17).[1] The story is a dramatic one, filled with such famous scenes as the crossing of the Jordan, the toppling of the walls of Jericho, the stoning of Achan, the convocation on Mounts Gerizim and Ebal, the ruse of the Gibeonites, the sun and the moon standing still and finally the great battle against Jabin of Hazor and his allies. Many of these tales have become biblical icons, working their way into art, literature, theology and indeed into the very way in which countless generations have imagined the Bible. In modern scholarship, different issues have come to the fore: on one hand the moral question of Joshua's being commanded by God to totally annihilate the inhabitants of Canaan;[2] on the other hand the historical and archaeological questions of whether any of the above ever actually happened.[3]

To the author of the book of Joshua, however, these questions were irrelevant. While the precise date and provenance of the book's composition and the editorial process that it went through has been debated since the beginning of modern biblical scholarship,[4] one thing is clear: the author of Joshua was neither a moralist nor a historian, in the modern sense of the word. The purpose of the conquest narrative in Joshua, broadly speaking, is to show how the God of Israel fulfilled his part in the covenant he had made with his people by giving them the land of Canaan. Now that the land had been conquered, it was Israel's turn to fulfill their part, by living in the land according to the laws and statutes that they had been given, and specifically to refrain from worshipping other gods.[5]

The wars of Joshua, then, are a part of the fulfillment of the divine promise. This is clear from the very start, when God commands Joshua:

> "Now proceed to cross the Jordan, you and all this people, into the land that
> I am giving to them, to the Israelites. Every place that the sole of your foot

will tread upon I have given to you, as I promised to Moses . . . Only be
strong and very courageous, being careful to act in accordance with all the
law that my servant Moses commanded you; do not turn from it to the right
hand or to the left, so that you may be successful wherever you go. This book
of the law shall not depart out of your mouth; you shall meditate on it day
and night, so that you may be careful to act in accordance with all that is
written in it. For then you shall make your way prosperous, and then you
shall be successful."

(Joshua 1:2–3, 78)[6]

Indeed, reading through the narrative, God's presence and involvement is seen
everywhere. In chapter 1 God charges and encourages Joshua, "No one shall be
able to stand against you all the days of your life. As I was with Moses, so I will
be with you; I will not fail you or forsake you" (verse 5).[7] In chapter 2 Rahab
confesses her fear of the Israelites' God (verse 9) and the two spies end their report
by saying "Truly the Lord has given all the land into our hands; moreover all the
inhabitants of the land melt in fear before us" (verse 24). In chapters 3 and 4,
God miraculously stops the waters of the Jordan, guides the Israelites across into
the land and instructs them to set up the memorial stones. He then commands
the people to circumcise themselves and to offer sacrifices, while the Canaanites'
are paralyzed with fear (chapter 5).

The actual fighting begins with the conquest of Jericho in chapter 6. This, of
course, is the most obvious and well-known example of divine intervention:
actually, the Israelites barely have to fight at all – they circle the city once a day
for six days and seven times on the seventh, the priests blow their horns, the people
shout, the walls come tumbling down and the Israelites storm the city, killing
everyone except the prostitute Rahab and burning and looting everything in sight,
dedicating the spoils to God. God is also involved in the battle of Ai (see especially
8:1, 18) although less manifestly. In chapter 10, the battle of Gibeon and the
Beth-horon pass, God's hand is again clearly visible in the hailstones that he rains
down on the enemy and of course in the stopping of the sun and moon in
mid-course (verses 11–13). And while in the southern campaign that follows this
battle there are no such miraculous events, God's hand is still evident to the
writer: "The Lord gave it [Libnah] also and its king into the hand of Israel" (verse
30); "The Lord gave Lachish into the hand of Israel" (verse 32); and finally, "Joshua
took all these kings and their land at one time, because the Lord God of Israel
fought for Israel" (verse 42). The same is true for the battle against the northern
kings at the waters of Merom; while no miraculous events are described, the author
is unambiguous: "And the Lord handed them over to Israel" (11:8). To him, it
was God who fought for Israel, and it was God who gave the land to Israel, not
just in promise, but in deeds as well.

However, upon close examination of God's involvement in the conquest of the
land, as it is portrayed by the author of Joshua, a pattern emerges – one of a
gradual diminishing of God's direct involvement. In my view, this is a purposeful
literary formation, with a specific objective in mind. In order to demonstrate this,

we must briefly survey the wars of conquest, again with an eye on just how involved God was in each individual battle.

As stated above, the first actual war fought by the Israelites in Canaan was the siege of Jericho. This military campaign was preceded by the mission of the two spies (chapter 2), the miraculous events of the Jordan crossing and the Israelites' first few days on Canaanite soil (chapters 3–5).[8]

Then comes the battle of Jericho (chapter 6). In verse 1 we read that "Jericho was shut up inside and out because of the Israelites; no one came out and no one went in." The people of Jericho, despite their advance knowledge of God's "giving the land to Israel" (2:9–11; 5:1), apparently thought that simply shutting themselves behind their fortifications would save them. God, however, wished to make an example of them. He instructed Joshua to order the armed men and seven priests carrying horns to circle the city once a day for six days.[9] On the seventh day they circled seven times, and after the seventh time, when the horns were blown, the people shouted, the walls fell flat, and the city was theirs for the taking.

At first reading it would seem that Jericho was conquered by God Himself, without human help. As put by Fleming, "Yahweh himself seizes the first Canaanite stronghold in the path of his people."[10] The writer of Joshua, however, does not quite see it that way. According to verse 20, after hearing Joshua's instructions, shouting and seeing the walls fall, the people still had to "go up into the city" and capture it. Once God had removed the obstacle of the walls, the Israelites still had work to do. The actual conquest, killing the inhabitants (except for Rahab and her family) and gathering the spoils to be consecrated still had to be done by the Israelites themselves. Why was this necessary? God could have dealt with Jericho as he had with Sodom and Gomorrah, destroying the city and all of its inhabitants after allowing Rahab and her family escape. But, according to the author, he chose not to. What message did the author wish to convey?

Joshua's next battle was that of Ai, told over most of chapters 7 and 8.[11] This campaign is actually divided into two stages. In the first, Joshua again sent spies, who advised that Ai was an easy target,[12] Joshua sent up a relatively small force, and, for the first time in almost 40 years (since Numbers 14:44–45), the Israelites were defeated in battle, losing "about thirty-six men" (Joshua 7:5). At experiencing defeat for the first time, "the hearts of the people melted and turned to water" (ibid.) and the shell-shocked Joshua turned to God with very serious complaints, basically stating that this one defeat symbolized the end of Israel! However, we, the readers, already know what God's answer will be, since the author has already told us how Achan, unbeknown to Joshua, had helped himself to some of the consecrated spoils.[13] Now, after the humiliating defeat, God instructs Joshua to purify his own camp, and once this is done, encourages Joshua to attack Ai once more (8:1).[14]

Superficially, the second battle of Ai seems to have been accomplished without divine intervention. Indeed, the city does not fall at the sound of a trumpet-blast and no obvious miracles occur. The Israelites, led by Joshua himself, ambushed the city's king and army and then attacked the undefended city, killing all its inhabitants, destroying the city itself and taking its spoils for themselves.[15] However,

God is far from absent from the story. After encouraging Joshua, God then acts as the grand strategist, instructing Joshua on how to take the city. This is emphasized in verse 7.[16] Moreover, this is not the end of God's involvement in the matter. In verse 18, God commands Joshua, "'Stretch out the spear that is in your hand toward Ai; for I will give it into your hand.' And Joshua stretched out the spear that was in his hand toward the city." Seemingly, a sign for the warriors to attack the city. But in verse 26 we find an interesting comment: "For Joshua did not draw back his hand, with which he stretched out the spear, until he had utterly destroyed all the inhabitants of Ai." Joshua stood on a hilltop overlooking the battlefield all day with his spear outstretched, until the enemy was defeated. The similarity to Exodus 17:10–13 is obvious, only then it was Moses who stood with his hands outstretched (holding a staff instead of a spear) and Joshua who was fighting. Furthermore, in both episodes, the upheld staff/spear is more than just a sign of encouragement; it is a miraculous device, through which God's involvement in the fighting is made manifest.[17] God is as involved in the conquest of Ai as he was in the conquest of Jericho, but in a different way.

The final six verses of chapter 8 and all of chapter 9 recount two episodes that are not about fighting: first the building of the altar on Mount Ebal and the ceremony on Mounts Gerizim and Ebal, and then the ruse of the Gibeonites and their accepting servitude to the Israelites. In both episodes, the Israelites are shown fulfilling Deuteronomic law: the Gerizim-Ebal ceremony appears in Deuteronomy 11:29–31 and in chapter 27,[18] and the commandment to "make peace" with cities that are "far away" from the nations of Canaan is spelled out in Deuteronomy 20:10–15.[19] But beyond that, God's presence is evident in both episodes. In the case of the Gibeonites, when they finally confess their subterfuge, they also admit that it was their fear of the Israelites' God that compelled them do what they did (9:24).[20] In the Israelites' journey to mounts Gerizim and Ebal it is less obvious, but the very fact that they could travel through enemy territory and perform their ceremonies on the peaks surrounding the major Canaanite city of Shechem, must mean that they were somehow under God's protection.[21] Seen in context, the Israelites sinned (Achan), were punished (the initial defeat at Ai), repaired their sin (by stoning Achan), and then regained God's aid and protection. The cycle was restarted: the Gerizim-Ebal ceremony can be compared to the ceremonies at Gilgal, the surrender of the Gibeonites to the surrender of Rahab, and the destruction of Ai to the destruction of Jericho (all with subtle differences – see 9:2).

Chapter 10 includes two war stories, connected by a brief etiology and followed by an editorial summary. In verses 1–15, "the five kings of the Amorites – the king of Jerusalem, the king of Hebron, the king of Jarmuth, the king of Lachish, and the king of Eglon," led by Adonizedek of Jerusalem, attack Gibeon in retaliation for its "defection" to the Israelite side. The Gibeonites call upon Joshua, and the Israelites, after marching uphill all night, attack at dawn and inflict heavy losses, as "the Lord threw them into a panic before Israel, who inflicted a great slaughter on them at Gibeon, chased them by the way of the ascent of Beth-horon, and struck them down as far as Azekah and Makkedah" (verse 10). This, however, was not enough: as they were fleeing, "the Lord threw down huge stones from heaven on them as far as Azekah, and they died; there were more who died because of the hailstones than the Israelites killed with the sword" (verse 11), and then "Joshua spoke to the Lord; and he said in the sight of Israel, 'Sun, stand still at Gibeon, and Moon, in the valley of Aijalon'. And the sun stood still, and the moon stopped, until the nation took vengeance on their enemies" (verses 12–13). And then the people returned to their camp at Gilgal.

In this part of this chapter, the divine is clear and present, beginning with God's words of encouragement in verse 8, his throwing the enemy into a panic in verse 10, his raining huge hailstones on them in verse 11, and finally the grand gesture of making the sun and the moon stand still verses 12–13, summarized with "and the Lord fought for Israel" in verse 16.[22] Then again, the Israelites were not released from doing some of the fighting themselves. They marched uphill all night, attacked at dawn, inflicted great casualties and chased the enemy kings all the way to Azekah and Makkedah, where they were executed by Joshua. So while God was definitely involved in the fighting the actual victory was Israel's.

It should also be emphasized that despite the various theories that have been suggested over the years, neither the heavenly hailstones nor the stopping of the sun and the moon had any direct military purpose whatsoever. According to verses 11–14, the hailstones rained down on the enemy forces after they were already in flight, and Joshua's call to the sun and the moon came even after that![23] The sole purpose of these "signs and wonders" was, to borrow a phrase from a much more recent war, "to shock and awe."[24] Even the Israelites' chase after the five kings was not to defeat them, but rather "until the nation took vengeance on their enemies." An ancillary purpose may have been to prove to all that once the Gibeonites had surrendered to Israel, they too were under God's protection.

In verses 28–39, Joshua and the Israelites capture six towns in the southern part of Canaan: Makkedah, Libnah, Lachish, Eglon, Hebron, and Debir. Additionally, they defeat the king of Gezer who arrived to aid Lachish. The fact that only three of the six cities now captured had participated in the attack on Gibeon shows that the southern campaign had no direct relation to the previous confrontation, and this section may well have originally been based on a totally separate tradition.[25] In fact, even the connection to Makkedah is tenuous. In verse 28, the destruction of Makkedah is compared to that of Jericho. The same is said of the destruction of Libnah in verse 30. But from that point on, a connection is made between each of the sequentially conquered cities: Lachish was destroyed like Libnah, Eglon like Lachish, Hebron like Eglon, Debir like Hebron. We would have expected Libnah to be compared to Makkedah and Makkedah to Jericho (or to Ai); the fact that Libnah is compared directly to Jericho shows that it was originally the first town in the list. The conquest of Makkedah is a secondary addition, meant to "bring us back" to the five kings' hiding place, from which it was convenient for Joshua to begin his southern campaign.

Compared to the battle of Gibeon, the southern campaign seems to have been as non-miraculous as could be. While the text does not give us any tactical details about the capture of the six cities, the military activity seems fairly straightforward:

Joshua approached each town in turn, laid siege, captured it within a day or two, and killed all of its inhabitants. When the king of Gezer came to help Lachish, "Joshua struck him and his people, leaving him no survivors" (verse 33). However the divine is not absent from this section either. This should have been obvious from the comparison to Jericho, and if not that, then from the extreme speed at which the cities were taken and the total lack of opposition. Furthermore, twice the text emphasizes that "the Lord gave" a particular city to Israel (verses 30 and 32), and the editorial summary of the southern campaign (verse 42) again repeats "Joshua took all these kings and their land at one time, *because the Lord God of Israel fought for Israel.*"

Chapter 11 tells of Joshua's northern campaign. The list of adversaries here begins similarly to that of the southern coalition: Jabin king of Hazor called upon Jobab king of Madon, the king of Shimron and the king of Achshaph. Unlike the southern list in 10:3, some of the northern kings remain unnamed. Furthermore, over the next two verses, the described coalition goes from the specific to the very broad and unspecific: "and to the kings who were in the northern hill country, and in the Arabah south of Chinneroth, and in the lowland, and in Naphoth-dor on the west, to the Canaanites in the east and the west, the Amorites, the Hittites, the Perizzites, and the Jebusites in the hill country, and the Hivites under Hermon in the land of Mizpah" (11:2–3). In other words, Jabin, Jobab, and their allies were just the tip of the iceberg: the battle by the Waters of Merom was fought against all of the remaining inhabitants of Canaan, "a great army, in number like the sand on the seashore, with very many horses and chariots" (verse 5). And as may be expected, in verse 6 God promises Joshua that he will "hand them over dead to Israel," which he does in verse 8. However, despite the rather literal NRSV translation quoted here (JPS, NIV, and others have "deliver them up all slain" and the like, which is basically the same), the enemy do not miraculously drop dead before Israel. Joshua and his troops defeat them, chase them, and slaughter them. God actually takes no further action. In fact, even in the final summary of all of Joshua's conquest, God's hand is conspicuously absent. In stark contrast to 10:42, "Joshua took all these kings and their land at one time, *because the Lord God of Israel fought for Israel,*" all 11:20 allows is that "it was the Lord's doing to harden their hearts so that they would come against Israel in battle, in order that they might be utterly destroyed, and might receive no mercy, but be exterminated, just as the Lord had commanded Moses." God commanded, God "set up" the Canaanites; the fighting itself was done by Israel.

As is clear from the above survey, to the writer of Joshua, God seems to have always been present, however his presence is manifested in different ways and on different levels. In some cases, God is seen as actually fighting for Israel, leaving the Israelites with little to do but to collect the spoils. In other cases, God "opens the way" for Israel to defeat its enemies. In yet others, all God does is "set the stage" by hardening the enemies' hearts and in yet others, God is conspicuously absent from the scene (although he continues to exercise overall responsibility for Israel's fate, as he does everywhere in the Bible).

In the second half of his work on the Joshua conquest narrative, Assis lays out his view, according to which the four conquest stories (Jericho, Ai, south, north) are arranged in two pairs, in which the first of each (Jericho and the war against the southern kings) features conquest by divine intervention, while the second (Ai and the northern campaign) are achieved by natural means. Assis' thesis, which he goes on to substantiate over the next few chapters, is that by switching back and forth from the miraculous to the natural, the writer defuses some of the tension that exists between the two states of being, as part of his description of Israel's transition from the miraculous period in its history under Moses to the more natural time under the judges.[26]

Although we agree in principle with Assis, our analysis of the various units and the role of the divine in each one shows a more consistent pattern of progression from the miraculous to the natural. The Jordan crossing, of course, is one big wonder, "the Exodus reenacted." Israel does nothing but march and worship. The conquest of Jericho is similar, although as we pointed out, Israel was expected to take part in killing the inhabitants and collecting the spoils. The double battle of Ai seems less so, until we note that the first attempt failed not because of Israel's military inferiority but because of their moral failing (Achan), and once this was rectified they were able to win. In the second attempt, God was present not only as prime tactician but through Joshua's upheld spear as well. God stays in a protective background role during the journey to Mounts Gerizim and Ebal. In the battle of Gibeon God once again awes with his power, but that's exactly what God's role is – wonder and awe. The actual fighting, the chase and capture of the five kings and their execution are all done by Israel – God doesn't even tell Joshua where the kings are hiding. In the subsequent southern campaign, despite the allusion to Jericho and the assurance that it was indeed God who gave the land to Israel, God himself plays no part in the fighting. And in the final northern campaign this trend is even more pronounced as, despite the mythic descriptions of the enemy multitude, God's roll is reduced to that of encouragement and overall control of events. All of the actual fighting is done by Joshua and his forces, with no divine intervention whatsoever.

What, then, is the significance of this pattern? It is obviously an integral part of the narrative sections of the book as a whole, and thus should be understood within the framework of our understanding of the date and purpose of the book of Joshua as a whole, and of the conquest narratives in particular. This issue has been debated among scholars since the very beginnings of modern biblical research and cannot be solved in this short paper. Very generally, the dates given for the composition of at least the "kernel" of what we call the book of Joshua range from the early Iron Age (twelfth to eleventh centuries BCE), not long after the described events occurred, all the way to the Hasmonean period in the late second century. But since Martin Noth's monumental work in the 1940s, the general consensus, such as there is, sees the book of Joshua, more-or-less as we know it, in the context of a larger "Deuteronomistic History," written in the late pre-exilic, exilic or early post-exilic periods (that is, the sixth through the fourth centuries BCE). This "history" tells the story of the people of Israel from their entrance to the Land until their exile from it, as evaluated by the standards set in the Deuteronomic Covenant. One of the basic tenets of this covenant is that the Land was given to Israel by God, on condition that they observe the rules set down in the Law – and above all else, totally refrain from worshipping other gods. It is for this reason that they were commanded to annihilate the previous, idol-worshipping inhabitants of the land:

> When the Lord your God brings you into the land that you are about to enter and occupy, and he clears away many nations before you—the Hittites, the Girgashites, the Amorites, the Canaanites, the Perizzites, the Hivites, and the Jebusites, seven nations mightier and more numerous than you—and when the Lord your God gives them over to you and you defeat them, then you must utterly destroy them. Make no covenant with them and show them no mercy. Do not intermarry with them, giving your daughters to their sons or taking their daughters for your sons, for that would turn away your children from following me, to serve other gods. Then the anger of the Lord would be kindled against you, and he would destroy you quickly. But this is how you must deal with them: break down their altars, smash their pillars, hew down their sacred poles, and burn their idols with fire. For you are a people holy to the Lord your God; the Lord your God has chosen you out of all the peoples on earth to be his people, his treasured possession.
>
> (Deuteronomy 7:1–6)

Once the land was conquered and its inhabitants wiped out, Israel would continue to live in the Land, only as long as they kept the stipulations of the covenant:

> When you have had children and children's children, and become complacent in the land, if you act corruptly by making an idol in the form of anything, thus doing what is evil in the sight of the Lord your God, and provoking him to anger, I call heaven and earth to witness against you today that you will soon utterly perish from the land that you are crossing the Jordan to occupy; you will not live long on it, but will be utterly destroyed. The Lord will scatter you among the peoples; only a few of you will be left among the nations where the Lord will lead you. There you will serve other gods made by human hands, objects of wood and stone that neither see, nor hear, nor eat, nor smell. From there you will seek the Lord your God, and you will find him if you search after him with all your heart and soul. In your distress, when all these things have happened to you in time to come, you will return to the Lord your God and heed him. Because the Lord your God is a merciful God, he will neither abandon you nor destroy you; he will not forget the covenant with your ancestors that he swore to them
>
> (Deuteronomy 4:25–31)

The following Deuteronomistic History then traces the fulfillment of this covenant, beginning with the conquest under Joshua, an initial period of trial and error under the judges, the establishment of the monarchy, an institution which was supposed to preserve and keep the covenant (Deuteronomy 17:18–20), and its subsequent failure to do so. The division of the kingdom, the fall and exile of the northern tribes, and eventually the destruction of Jerusalem, are all seen as God's justified reaction to Israel's constant breaking of the covenant.

However, within this continuum there is a major break, which occurs during the conquest of the land. During the time of Moses, while the Israelites were in the wilderness, their very existence under such conditions was dependant on God's constant presence: "and in the wilderness, where you saw how the Lord your God carried you, just as one carries a child, all the way that you traveled until you reached this place" (Deuteronomy 1:31). In warfare as well, "The Lord your God, who goes before you, is the one who will fight for you, just as he did for you in Egypt before your very eyes" (Deuteronomy 1:30). Which he did, in the war against Sihon (Deuteronomy 2:32–36) and Og (Deuteronomy 3:3).

As we have already shown, the Jordan crossing follows the same pattern of divine action, but as soon as the Israelites enter the land, God's hand begins to gradually withdraw. This is symbolized by the cessation of the Manna that had sustained them in the wilderness and their beginning to eat the produce of the land (Joshua 5:11–12): from this time forward, they were to procure their food in the normal fashion. The age of "signs and wonders," a recognized Deuteronomic concept, was coming to a close.[27]

The same is true for God's involvement in Israel's wars. While the conquest of the land is part of God's side of the covenant and thus his responsibility to provide, it is not his alone. As proven by the spy incident (the Deuteronomic version of which is in Deuteronomy 1:22–45), Israel must be willing to make the effort. And so even at Jericho, the Israelites were required to do their part, a part that became bigger with each ensuing battle. By the time Israel was ready to take on Jabin of Hazor and his allied multitude, they no longer needed miracles. They were weaned off their dependence on the divine. God's encouragement was enough. Having conquered the land, all they had to do now was to keep it – not through miracles, but by observance of God's law.

Notes

1. All biblical quotations are from the NRSV unless otherwise specified.
2. Much has been written about this issue, especially within Jewish and Israeli scholarship and educational circles. Generally speaking, there are four basic approaches: a. the "classic" approach of the rabbis, going back to Talmudic literature, according to which the commandments to exterminate the Canaanites and Amalek were one-time events, no longer applicable in later times; b. the "academic" approach by which the texts should be seen in the context of the time and society that produced them, without attempting to apply their values to our own time; c. the "educational" approach which attempts to interpret the text in a way which would fit modern values; d. the "apologetic" approach which maintains that since the historicity of the story is in doubt, it can pretty much be ignored by modern educators. For a sampling of recent literature see A. Sagi, "The Punishment of Amalek in Jewish Tradition: Coping with the Moral Problem," *Harvard Theological Review* 87, 1994, pp. 323–346; Y. Medan, "The Question

of the Conquest of the Land Following Moral Values – A Look at the Book of Joshua,"
in *Morality, War and Conquest*, Alon Shevut: Tenuvot, 1994, pp. 19–30 (Hebrew);
Y. Binnun, "The Book of Joshua – *Peshat* and the Sages' Interpretation," ibid. pp. 31–40
(Hebrew); S. Rosenberg, "War and Peace – Joshua and Isaiah," ibid. pp. 41–52
(Hebrew); C.S. Ehrlich, "Joshua, Judaism, and Genocide," in J. Targarona Borrás and
A. Sáenz-Badillos (Eds.), *Jewish Studies at the Turn of the Twentieth Century I: Proceedings of
the 6th EAJS Congress, Toledo, July 1998*, vol. I–II, Leiden: Brill, 1999, pp. 117–124;
Y. Zakovitch, "Teaching the Book of Joshua in Our Times," in M.L. Frankel and
H. Deitcher (Eds.), *Understanding the Bible in Our Times: Implications for Education* (Studies
in Jewish Education IX), Jerusalem: The Hebrew University Magnes Press, 2003,
pp. 11–20 (Hebrew with English abstract); L. Mazor, "The Rise and Fall of the Book
of Joshua in the *Mamlakhti* School System in View of Ideological Shifts in Israeli Society,"
ibid. pp. 21–46 (Hebrew with English abstract); G.L. Cohen, "The Book of Joshua
as Reflected in Midrashic Exegesis," ibid. pp. 47–59 (Hebrew with English abstract);
E.L. Greenstein, "Interpreting the Bible by Way of Its Ancient Cultural Milieu," ibid.
pp. 61–73 (Hebrew with English abstract); S. Trigano, "Les guerres de Josué: origine
et violence," in S. Trigano (Ed.), *Guerre et paix dans le jidaïsme*, Paris: In Press, 2004,
pp. 13–22; J. Cazeaux, "Le livre de Josué: De la conquête au dernier des Justes," ibid.
pp. 43–62; S. Carmy, "The Origin of Nations and the Shadow of Violence: Theological
Perspectives on Canaan and Amalek," in L. Schiffman and T.B. Wulowelsky (Eds.),
War and Peace in Jewish Tradition, New York: Yeshiva University Press, 2007,
pp. 163–199; N. Lamm, "Amalek and the Seven Nations: A Case of Law vs. Morality,"
ibid. pp. 201–238. For a useful summary of modern Christian approaches see T.R.
Hobbs, *A Time for War: A Study of Warfare in the Old Testament*, Wilmington: Michael
Galzier, pp. 199–233. For more general treatments see S. Niditch, *War in the Hebrew
Bible: A Study of the Ethics of Violence*, New York – Oxford: Oxford University Press, 1993;
N.K. Gottwald, "Theological Education as a Theory-Praxis Loop: Situating the Book
of Joshua in a Cultural, Social, Ethical and Theological Matrix," in J.M. Rogerson,
M. Davies and M. Daniel Carrol R. (Eds.), *The Bible in Ethics* (JSOT Sup. 207),
Sheffield: Sheffield Academic Press, 1995, pp. 107–118; L.L. Rowlett, *Joshua and the
Rhetoric of Violence: A New Historical Analysis* (JSOT Sup. 226), Sheffield: Sheffield
Academic Press, 1996; P. Pitkänen, "Memory, Witnesses and Genocide in the Book
of Joshua," in J.G. McConville and K. Möller (Eds.), *Reading the Law: Studies in Honour
of Gordon J. Wenham*, New York – London: T&T Clark, 2007, pp. 267–282. For a
specifically post-9/11 treatment see R. Albertz, "Monotheism and Violence: How to
Handle a Dangerous Biblical Tradition," in J. van Ruiten and J. Cornelius de Vos
(Eds.), *The Land of Israel in Bible, History and Theology – Studies in Honour of Ed Noort*
(VT Sup. 124), Leiden – Boston: Brill, 2009, pp. 373–387.
3. For which see A. Mazar, *Archaeology of the Land of the Bible, 10,000–586 B.C.E.* (ABRL),
New York: Doubleday, 1990, pp. 328–355; N. Na'aman, "The 'Conquest of Canaan'
in the Book of Joshua and in History," in I. Finkelstein and N. Na'aman (Eds.), *From
Nomadism to Monarchy: Archaeological Aspects of Early Israel*, Jerusalem: Yad Yitzhak Ben-
Zvi and the Israel Exploration Society, 1994, pp. 218–281; F.S. Frick, *A Journey through
the Hebrew Scriptures* (2nd ed.), Belmont: Wadsworth/Thomson, 2003, pp. 240–263 and
most any other modern treatment of the history, archaeology or biblical traditions of
the early Iron Age.
4. For discussion on the date and process of composition of the book of Joshua, its possible
sources and the genres it employs see any modern commentary on Joshua, and
additionally: J. Van Seters, "Joshua's Campaign of Canaan and Near Eastern
Historiography," *Scandinavian Journal of the Old Testament* 2, 1990, pp. 1–12; J. Strange,
"The Book of Joshua – Origin and Dating," *Scandinavian Journal of the Old Testament* 16,
2002, pp. 44–51; A. Rofé, "Joshua son of Nun in the History of Biblical Tradition,"
Tarbiz 73, 2003–2004, pp. 333–364 (Hebrew with English abstract); D.N. Pienaar,

"Some Observations on Conquest Reports in the Book of Joshua," *Journal of Northwest Semitic Languages* 30, 2004, pp. 151–164; E. Assis, "Divine Versus Human Leadership: An Examination of Joshua's Succession," in M. Poorthuis and J. Schwartz (Eds.), *Saints and Role Models in Judaism and Christianity*, Leiden: Brill, 2004, pp. 25–42; idem, *From Moses to Joshua and from the Miraculous to the Ordinary: A Literary Analysis of the Conquest Narrative in the Book of Joshua*, Jerusalem: The Hebrew University Magnes Press, 2005, pp. 1–7 (Hebrew). For the basic editorial and literary unity of Josh. 1–12 see I. Rozenson, "The Story of the Failure at Ai and the Literary Structure of Joshua 1–11," *Beit Mikra* 42, 1997, pp. 137–143 (Hebrew); Assis, *From Moses to Joshua*, pp. 8–32 and references there.

5. For more on this theme and the way in which it is played out in Joshua see P.D. Miller, "The Story of the First Commandment: The Book of Joshua," in A.D.H. Mayes and R.B. Salters (Eds.), *Covenant as Context; Essays in Honour of E.W. Nicholson*, Oxford: Oxford University Press, 2003, pp. 310–324.

6. C.H. Gordon, "War and Peace: The Theoretical Structure of Israelite Society," in V.D. Sanua (Ed.), *Fields of Offerings; Studies in Honor of Raphael Patai*, Rutherford: Fairleigh Dickinson University Press, 1983, pp. 299–303, goes as far as to claim that in theory, all later "true Israelites" were supposedly descended from those who had participated in the conquest and had received an inheritance.

7. Assis, *From Moses to Joshua*, pp. 31–52, sees the continuity of leadership implied in the title of his book as one of the main themes of the conquest narrative.

8. J. Van Seters, "Joshua's Campaign of Canaan," emphasizes the thematic and literary similarities between these episodes and some of the Neo-Assyrian conquest reports. Following this, he considers most of them to be late additions to the DtrH. We, on the other hand, agree with Noth in seeing them mostly as integral parts of the story. See also Assis, *From Moses to Joshua*, pp. 53–119. However, in this paper we wish to focus on the battle narratives themselves.

9. It is worth noting that Joshua actually expanded upon the instructions that he had received: he added the Ark to the procession, dividing the men into front and rear guards, and had the priests blow the horns while the people remained silent. See Assis, *From Moses to Joshua*, pp. 127–131, who sees Joshua as trying to make the attack more "military" and less "miraculous."

10. D.E. Fleming, "The Seven-Day Siege of Jericho in Holy War," in, R. Chazan, W.W. Hallo and L.H. Schiffman (Eds.), *Ki Baruch Hu: Ancient Near Eastern, Biblical, and Judaic Studies in Honor of Baruch A. Levine*, Winona Lake: Eisenbrauns, 1999, pp. 211–228. In this paper Fleming shows that the seven-day period of rituals is a common topos, using examples from Ugarit, Mari and the Bible. For more on the literary aspects of this pericope see R.B. Robinson, "The Coherence of the Jericho Narrative: A Literary Reading of Joshua 6," in B. von Rüdiger, T. Krüger and H. Utzschneider (Ed.), *Konsequente Traditionsgeschichte: Festschrift für Klaus Baltzer*, Freiburg – Göttingen: Universitätsverlag – Vandenhoeck & Ruprecht, 1993, pp. 311–335.

11. More than any other site mentioned in the Joshua conquest narrative, the geographical identification of Ai has been debated over the years. While the geographical references point to the site of Khirbet et-Tell, the archaeological data there do not match the biblical narrative. See: Z. Zevit, "The Problem of Ai: New Theory Rejects the Battle as Described in the Bible but Explains How the Story Evolved," *Biblical Archaeology Review* 11, 2, 1985, pp. 58–69; J.A. Callaway, "Ai (et-Tell): Problem Site for Biblical Archaeologists," in Leo G. Perdue (Ed.), *Archaeology and Biblical Interpretation; Essays in Memory of D. Glenn Rose*, Atlanta: John Knox Press, 1987 pp. 87–99. This has led some scholars to look for alternative sites, while others have chosen to interpret the biblical text "creatively." See, among others, Y. Binnun, "'Comes to Ayyat . . .' – A New Solution for the Identification of Ai," in Z.H. Erlich and Y. Eshel (Eds.), *Judea and*

Samaria Research Studies – Proceedings of the 2nd Annual Meeting – 1992, Kedumim – Ariel: The College of Judea and Samaria, 1993, pp. 43–64 (Hebrew); Sh. Riklin, "A New Proposal for the Identification of the City Hai near Ma'aleh Michmash," in Y. Eshel (Ed.), *Judea and Samaria Research Studies – Proceedings of the 5th Annual Meeting – 1995*, Kedumim – Ariel: The College of Judea and Samaria, 1996, pp. 27–32 (Hebrew). However, as shown by M. Gichon, "The Veracity of Biblical Battles," in Y. Eshel (Ed.), *Judea and Samaria Research Studies – Proceedings of the 6th Annual Meeting – 1996*, Kedumim – Ariel: The College of Judea and Samaria, 1997, pp. 17–33 (Hebrew with English abstract), the biblical description of the battle does best fit Khirbet et-Tell; unlike Gichon, we do not take this as "proof" of the historicity of the story – only as evidence that the author (or his source) was familiar with the territory.

12. Rozenson, "The Story of the Failure at Ai," pp. 144–145 emphasizes that the spies first gave their opinions and advice and only then reported the facts – not what would be expected of professional spies.

13. Rozenson, "The Story of the Failure at Ai," p. 143, calls verse 1 an "exposition," which empowers the reader with knowledge that the protagonists do not yet have.

14. As mentioned above, some scholars consider the Achan episode to be a "late" addition to the Ai narrative, and M. Noth, *Das Buch Josua* (2nd ed.), Tübingen: Mohr, 1953, pp. 43–46, suggested that the story in DtrH was based on two separate, pre-existing etiologies. However, Assis, *From Moses to Joshua*, pp. 141–142, correctly emphasizes that the stories are intertwined; neither could exist as is without the other.

15. As pointed out by Rozenson, "The Story of the Failure at Ai," pp. 147–149, the first, failed attack was characterized by three major lapses, which do appear in other battles: in this case there is no preceding divine order, no mention of "the people" or "the fighting men," and Joshua himself does not command the troops. All these lapses are rectified in chapter 8.

16. As noted by Assis, *From Moses to Joshua*, p. 143, this is the only case in the Bible of God acting as a strategist.

17. For further comparison between the two narratives see E. Noort, "Josua und Amalek: Exodus 17:8–16," in R. Roukema (Ed.), *The Interpretation of Exodus: Studies in Honour of Cornelis Houtman*, Leuven: Peeters, 2006, pp. 155–170. Assis, *From Moses to Joshua*, pp. 153–156, while admitting that the spear is "a sign of Joshua's dependence on God," does not recognize it as a miraculous device, but rather "a symbolic act, expressing the presence of God behind the scenes." To me, the parallelism to Exodus 17:10–13 is too close for that.

18. For the origin of this periscope see M. Anbar, *Joshua and the Covenant at Shechem (Jos. 24:1–28)*, Jerusalem: Bialik Institute, 1999, pp. 135–143 (Hebrew), who concludes that it is a late addition to Joshua, from a time in which it was important to show that Joshua had fulfilled Torah law to the letter on one hand, and when a convocation at or near Shechem was no longer seen as a threat to the centrality of Jerusalem on the other. This of course assumes that other parts of Joshua are "early." Seeing all of Joshua within a Deuteronomistic History seems to answer both demands. See also N. Na'aman, "The Law of the Altar in Deuteronomy and the Cultic Site Near Shechem," in S.L. McKenzie and T. Römer (Eds.), *Rethinking the Foundations: Historiography in the Ancient World and in the Bible, Essays in Honour of John Van Seters*, Berlin: Walter de Gruyter, 2000, pp. 141–161.

19. Though it should be noted that "to make peace" basically means to accept the city's surrender. The term שלום is used in the same way in the description of Solomon's dominion in 1 Kings 5:4 [Eng. 4:24]. See also: P.D. Hanson, "War, Peace and Justice in Early Israel," *Bible Review*, 3, 3, 1987, pp. 32–45; J.A. Fischer, "War and Peace: A Methodological Consideration," in A.J. Tambasco (Ed.), *Blessed Are the Peacemakers; Biblical Perspectives on Peace and Its Social Foundations*, New York: Paulist Press, 1989,

pp. 17–39; C. Westermann, "Peace (Shalom) in the Old Testament," in P.B. Yoder and W.M. Swartley (Eds.), *The Meaning of Peace: Biblical Studies*, Louisville: Westminster – John Knox Press, 1992, pp. 16–48.

20. Although there is also a question of whether this story was a part of the "original" Deuteronomistic Joshua. For example K. Latvus, "From Army Campsite to Partners in Peace: The Changing Role of the Gibeonites in the Redaction Process of Josh. x 1–8; xi 19," in K.-D. Schunck and M. Augustin (Eds.), *"Lasset uns Brücken bauen . . .";* *Collected Communications to the XVth Congress of the International Organization for the Study of the Old Testament, Cambridge, 1995*, Frankfurt: P. Lang, 1998, pp. 111–115, has concluded that in the original version Gibeon was simply the site of the battle against the southern coalition, with the story of the Gibeonites' surrender being a post-DtrH addition. In his opinion, Joshua 8:30–35 is "obviously even a later addition." Another view is that of A.D.H. Mayes, "Deuteronomy 29, Joshua 9, and the place of the Gibeonites in Israel," in N. Lohfink (Ed.), *Das Deuteronomium; Entstehung, Gestalt und Botschaft*, Leuven: Peeters, 1985, pp. 321–325, who connects the story to Deuteronomy 29 and sees it as paving the way for the Gibeonites' inclusion in the community of Israel as *gērîm*. See also J. Day, "Gibeon and the Gibeonites in the Old Testament," in R. Rezetko, T.H. Lim and W.B. Aucker (Eds.), *Reflection and Refraction: Studies in Biblical Historiography in Honour of A. Graeme Auld*, Leiden – Boston: Brill, 2007, pp. 117–120.

21. For some of the geographical, textual and historical issues surrounding these texts see E. Noort, "The Traditions of Ebal and Gerizim: Theological Positions in the Book of Joshua," in M. Vervenne and J. Lust, *Deuteronomy and Deuteronomic Literature, Festschrift C.H.W. Brekelmans*, Leuven: Peeters, 1997, pp. 161–180.

22. The divine act of making the sun and the moon stand still, seemingly changing the natural order of creation, has been the focus of speculation since antiquity. See J.S. Holladay, Jr., "The Day(s) the Moon Stood Still [Jos. 10:12–13]," *Journal of Biblical Literature* 87, 1968, pp. 166–178; M. Görg, "Mythos und Geschichte in Jos 10, 12–14," *Aegyptiaca – Biblica; Notizen und Beiträge zu den Beziehungen zwischen Ägypten und Israel*, Wiesbaden: Otto Harrassowitz, 1991, pp. 347–360; B. Margalit, "The Day the Sun did not Stand Still: A New Look at Joshua X 8–15," *Vetus Testamentum* 42, 1992, pp. 466–491; J.H. Walton, "Joshua 10:12–15 and Mesopotamian Celestial Omen Texts," in A.R. Millard, J.K. Hoffmeier and D.W. Baker (Eds.), *Faith, Tradition and History: Old Testament Historiography in Its Near Eastern Context*, Winona Lake: Eisenbrauns, 1994, pp. 181–190; R.S. Hess, "Joshua 10 and the Sun that Stood Still," *Buried History* 35, 1999, pp. 26–33; H.A.J. Kruger, "Sun and Moon Marking Time: A Cursory Survey of Exegetical Possibilities in Joshua 10:9–14," *Journal of Northwest Semitic Languages* 26, 2000, pp. 137–152; Day, "Gibeon and the Gibeonites in the Old Testament," pp. 120–122.

23. Although the geography should also be noted: with the sun over Gibeon in the east and the moon over Aijalon in the west, this miracle must have occurred in early morning!

24. Assis, *From Moses to Joshua*, p. 193, put it slightly differently: "The story of the southern conquest brings the reader to the conclusion that there is no need for miracles."

25. Noth, *Das Buch Josua*, 60–67; J.K. Hoffmeier, "The Structure of Joshua 1–11 and the Annals of Thutmose III," in A.R. Millard, J.K. Hoffmeier and D.W. Baker (Eds.), *Faith, Tradition and History: Old Testament Historiography in its Near Eastern Context*, Winona Lake: Eisenbrauns, 1994, pp. 165–179, compares this section to New Kingdom Egyptian conquest accounts, and especially adopts the idea that a "daybook" is behind some of these accounts. For further literary analysis see K.L. Younger, Jr., "The 'Conquest' of the South (Jos 10, 28–39)," *Biblische Zeitschrift* 9, 1995, pp. 255–264; Assis, *From Moses to Joshua*, pp. 160–163. For the relationship of this section to the story of the conquest of Hebron and Debir by Caleb and Othniel in Judges 1 see M. Weinfeld,

"Judges 1.1–2.5: The Conquest Under the Leadership of the House of Judah," in A.G. Auld (Ed.), *Understanding Poets and Prophets: Essays in Honour of George Wishart Anderson* (SJOT Sup. 152), Sheffield: Sheffield Academic Press, 1993, pp. 388–400.

26. Assis, *From Moses to Joshua*, p. 121.

27. For "signs and wonders" (אתות ומפתים) in Deuteronomy see 4:34, 6:22, 7:19, 26:8, 29:2, 34:11, and in the singular (אות ומופת), 13:2–3, 28:46. See also W. Johnstone, "The Deuteronomistic Cycles of 'signs' and 'wonders' in Exodus 1–13," in A.G. Auld (Ed.), *Understanding Poets and Prophets: Essays in Honour of George Wishart Anderson* (SJOT Sup. 152), Sheffield: Sheffield Academic Press, 1993, pp. 166–185.

4 "He teaches my hands to war"

The semiotics of ritual hand gestures in ancient Israelite warfare

David Calabro

For the ancient Israelites, as for the people of neighboring cultures in Mesopotamia and Egypt, warfare was not just a conflict between humans, but one that also involved divine action. However, despite the fact that the Hebrew Bible contains many allusions to anthropomorphic aspects of Israel's God, it does not describe him as a visible warrior on the battlefield, smiting down foes with a weapon.[1] Instead, God's bellicose actions in warfare are represented as a sort of mystery, a sign that is either divined or revealed. My purpose in what follows is to explore one aspect of divinely aided warfare as represented in ancient Hebrew literature, namely gestures of raising or extending the hand to destroy, which are described as being performed by both God and prophets. I shall point out what the relevant passages reveal about how signs were interpreted, transmitted, and thought to be efficacious in ancient Israelite culture.

Especially prominent among biblical references to God's body parts are the hands, and in particular, what God does with his hands. We find a great deal of focus in the Hebrew Bible on how God uses his hands in battle to deliver his people. An example of this is in the Song at the Sea in Exodus 15:

...ה' איש מלחמה ה' שמו

...ימינך ה' נאדרי בכח / ימינך ה' תרעץ אויב

מי כמכה באלם ה' / מי כמכה נאדר בקדש

נורא תהלת עשה פלא / נטית ימינך תבלעמו ארץ

The LORD is a warrior; the LORD is his name . . .
With your right hand, O LORD glorious in strength—[2]
  With your right hand, O LORD, you shattered the enemy . . .
Who is like you among the gods, O LORD?
  Who is like you, O Glorious One, in the sanctuary?
Revered with praises, Doer of wonders,
  You extended your right hand, and the earth swallowed them up.
(Exodus 15:3, 6, 11, 12)

We notice here the repetition of the word ימין "right hand" in relation to God's role as a warrior. In particular, the focus is on the actions God performs with his right hand. By performing a gesture of extending his right hand against the enemy, God shattered the enemy and caused the earth to swallow them up. This gesture is quite frequently attested in the Hebrew Bible, with 46 occurrences.[3] In every case where the gesture is used against humans, the effect is to destroy. The gesture can also be performed against the elements of nature, and in these cases, the effect is to move or change the elements.[4]

Z. Bahrani, in her book *Rituals of War: The Body and Violence in Mesopotamia*, has discussed an ancient Babylonian semiotic of the body that emphasizes the characteristics of the body, the manner in which it is shaped and marked by the gods. This semiotic system is exemplified in the enormous corpus of divination texts found in Mesopotamia. In the Babylonian semiotic system, the characteristics of the body (be it the body of a human being or an animal) act as signs of past, present, and future events, and as such can be read using a logic that is based on the cuneiform script.[5] In ancient Hebrew literature, we lack a semiotic corpus comparable in size to that of Mesopotamia. However, we find traces of a semiotic system, one that is distinct from that in Mesopotamia, in textual references to gestures. The focus in this semiotic is not the characteristics of the body, that is, how the body is shaped by deity or shaped like deity, but rather the actions performed by the body, that is, how the body has been instructed by deity or instructed to act like deity. The logic of this system is based on wordplay in the spoken language. We find this kind of semiotic logic in divine utterances embedded in narrative texts like the following:

ושלחתי את־ידי והכיתי את־מצרים בכל נפלאתי אשר אעשה בקרבו ואחרי־כן ישלח אתכם

I will stretch out my hand and smite Egypt with all the wonders that I will do in his (Pharaoh's) midst. After that, **he will let you go**.

(Exodus 3:20)

Here the verb שלח is used for the same gesture as that described above, where the idiom was נטה ימין "extend the right hand." The most common idiom used to describe this gesture is נטה יד "extend the hand," but the verbs הרים "raise," הניף "elevate," נשא "lift up," and נתן "put forth" are also used. In Exodus 3:20, the use of the verb שלח is unusual. The idiom שלח יד is usually used for gestures with other purposes, including utilitarian ones.[6] The unusual use of this idiom here is understandable, however, in light of the wordplay with ישלח "he will let go." Notice how the wordplay is specifically between the action of the gesture and its result. When the LORD "shalakhs," it will force Pharaoh to "shillakh."[7] As the narrator here reports it to us, the LORD is performing a kind of semiosis of the gesture of extending the hand, assigning it an outcome via a cognate in the spoken language.

The same kind of semiotic reasoning that we find in Exodus 3:20 proliferates in the book of Ezekiel.[8]

בן־אדם ארץ כי תחטא־לי למעל־מעל ונטיתי ידי עליה ושברתי לה מטה־לחם

Son of man, if a nation sins against me my being unfaithful, **I will extend my hand** against it and break its **staff** of bread.

(Ezekiel 14:13)

לכן כה אמר אדני ה' אני נשאתי את־ידי אם־לא הגוים אשר לכם מסביב המה כלמתם ישאו

Therefore thus says the Lord GOD: "**I lift up my hand**. If the nations which are around you do not **bear** their reproach, . . .!"

(Ezekiel 36:7)

על־כן נשאתי ידי עליהם נאם אדני ה' ונשאו עונם

Therefore, **I lift up my hand** concerning them, says the Lord GOD, and **they will bear** their iniquity.

(Ezekiel 44:12)

The gesture in the last two passages is not the extended hand of destruction but the uplifted hand of making an oath.

In all the passages from Exodus and Ezekiel quoted above, the wordplay is based on the verb in the gesture idiom, not the body part itself. It is the actions that the hand performs, not its strength or other characteristics, that provide the key to reading the gestures as signs in the Hebrew system. It is also important to note that in each one of these instances, the semiosis of the gesture act is placed in the mouth of the LORD; the mode by which it is obtained by the prophet is revelatory, and the channel by which it is obtained is verbal. These observations give us a fair idea of some features of the Israelite semiotic system, which can be compared with the features of the Mesopotamian system (see Table 4.1).

While prophets are the ones through whom God's gestural acts are revealed, they are also God's specially commissioned servants who are directed, again through verbal revelation, to perform these gestures themselves. In biblical passages that describe these gestures being performed by prophets, we find ambiguity as to whose gesture it is considered to be: the prophet's or God's. It is likely that the gestures were considered efficacious precisely because of their contiguity with and similarity to God's gestures. This contiguity often receives special emphasis in the

Table 4.1 Israelite and Mesopotamian Semiotic Systems

	Israelite System	*Mesopotamian System*
Logic of analysis:	Verbal, spoken language	Writing system (cuneiform)
Method of obtaining:	Prophets obtain verbal revelation from deity	Divination specialists read signs in entrails, stars, events
Analysis focuses on:	Actions	Static characteristics

biblical passages, being described in the form of theophany scenes or implied in the use of objects that are evidence of a prior divine encounter.

In several passages in the book of Exodus, Moses uses the gesture of the outstretched hand to alter elements and destroy enemies. In every case, Moses' use of the gesture is linked to a divine command and/or an object representing divine authority, namely his staff (see Exodus 4:17). For example, the description of each of the ten plagues in Egypt follows a specific pattern in which God commands Moses or Aaron to stretch forth the hand against parts of Egypt, with or without the staff, and Moses or Aaron does so (Exodus 7:19–20; 8:1–2, 12–13; 9:22–3; 10:12–13, 21–2). As we have seen in Exodus 3:20 (see also Exodus 7:4–5), though the action is actually performed by Moses, the gesture of extending the hand to enact the plagues is attributed to the LORD.

Moses uses the same gesture in the crossing of the sea. Again, the pattern of divine command and obedience to the command is apparent.

ויאמר ה' אל־משה...דבר אל־בני־ישראל ויסעו : ואתה הרם את־מטך ונטה את־ידך על־הים ובקעהו
ויבאו בני־ישראל בתוך הים ביבשה...ויט משה את־ידו על־הים ויולך ה' את־הים ברוח קדים
עזה...ויאמר ה' אל־משה נטה את־ידך על־הים וישבו המים על־מצרים על־רכבו ועל־פרשיו : ויט
משה את־ידו על־הים וישב הים...וינער ה' את־מצרים בתוך הים :

The LORD said to Moses, "Tell the children of Israel to take up their journey. As for you, raise your staff, **extend your hand** against the sea, and divide it, so the children of Israel can enter the midst of the sea on dry land." . . . Then **Moses extended his hand** against the sea, and the LORD made the sea move by means of a strong east wind. . .The LORD said to Moses, "**Extend your hand** against the sea, so that the water comes down on Egypt—on its cavalry and chariotry." Then **Moses extended his hand** against the sea, and the sea came down. The LORD shook off Egypt in the midst of the sea.

(Exodus 14:15, 16, 21, 26, 27)

Again, in other passages also, the gesture of stretching forth the hand is attributed not to Moses, but to the LORD (see Exodus 15:12; Isaiah 10:26).[9]

Moses uses a similar gesture in the war against the Amalekites in Exodus 17:9–13. This passage describes a ritual that is rescued from being infelicitous. Moses is supposed to stand with his hand or hands raised, a posture similar to that of God in Psalm 10:12, and thereby exert divine power against the Amalekites until they are defeated.[10] However, due to Moses' advanced age and the consequent difficulty of maintaining this posture, Aaron and Hur have him sit on a rock while they help hold up his hands. Again, it is God, not Moses, who is at last said to have "war with Amalek from generation to generation" (Exodus 17:16).

A similar ideology applies to the gesture of baring the arm as a display of power. The gesture is performed both by God and by mortals, but more frequently the former, and the latter only when God commands the person to perform it. God performs the gesture in Isaiah 30:30; 52:10; and 53:1, but he commands Ezekiel to perform it in Ezekiel 4:7.

This ideology also continues beyond the biblical period, as it is found in the War Scroll of the Dead Sea Scrolls. Here, the role of the prophet who carries out God's gestures in earlier biblical literature is performed by the Sons of Light.

ובעומדם שלושה סדרים ותקעו להם הכוהנים תרועה שנית קול נוח וסמוך ידי מפשע עד קורבם
למערכת האויב ונטו ידם בכלי המלחמה והכוהנים יריעו בשש חצוצרות החללים קול חד טרוד לנצח
מלחמה והלויים וכול עם השופרות יריעו קול אחד תרועת מלחמה גדולה להמס לב אויב ועם קול
התרועה יצאו זרקות המלחמה להפיל חללים

As they stand in three formations, the priests shall blow for them a second blast, a low legato (?) note: signal for advancing up to the battle line of the enemy. **They shall extend their hands** with (their) weapons. Then the priests shall sound the six trumpets of the slain, one staccato note, to direct the battle. Then the Levites, all those with shofars, shall sound one note, a great battle blast to melt the heart of the enemy. With the sound of the blast, the javelins shall fly out to fell the wounded.

(1QM 8:6–11)

וכול יקום הוותם מהר ימלו [...]ץ בק[...] התחזקו למלחמת אל כיא יום ^{מועד} מלחמה היום הזה
[...]אל על כול הג[וים ...]ט על כול בשר אל ישראל מרים ידו ב[...]ת פלאו [...] כול רוחי
רש[...]עה [...]

As for every living thing, their desires will wither quickly [. . .] strengthen yourselves for the battle of God, for this day is the ~~day~~ ^{appointed time} of battle, [. . .] God against all na[tions . . .] against all flesh. The God of Israel **is raising his hand** in his wondrous [. . .] all the spirits of wick[edness . . .]
(1QM 15:11–14)

ובעומדם ליד מארכת כתיים כדי הטל ירימו איש ידו בכלי מלחמתו ושש[ת ... ח]צוצרות החללים
קול חד טרוד לנצח מלחמה

When they are standing near the battle line of the Kittim, within throwing range, each man **shall raise his hand** with his weapon. The six [. . . t]rumpets of the slain one staccato note to direct the battle.

(1QM 16:6–7)

ובה[נ]שא יד אל הגדולה על בליעל ועל כול [...]ל ממשלתו במגפת עולמים [...] ותרועת [...]
קדושים ברדף אשור ונפלו בני יפת לאין קום וכתיים יכתו לאין [...] משאת יד אל ישראל על כול
המון בליעל בעת ההיאה יריעו הכוהנים [... חצוצ]רות הזכרון ונאספו אליהם כול מערכות המלחמה
ונחלקו על כול מ[... כ]תיים להחרימם

[. . .] when the great **hand** of God shall be **li[f]ted up** against Belial and against all the [. . .] of his dominion with an eternal slaughter [. . .] and the shout of the sanctified ones when they pursue Assyria. The sons of Japheth will fall never to rise again, and the Kittim will be crushed [. . .] **the lifting**

up of the God of Israel's **hand** against the whole multitude of Belial. At that time the priests shall sound [. . . trum]pets of remembrance. Then all the battle lines shall be gathered to them and shall be divided against all the [. . .] of the Kittim to annihilate them.

(1QM 18:1–5)

Some translators render the phrase ונטו ידם בכלי המלחמה in 1QM 8:8 as, "and they shall take hold of their weapons" or similarly.[11] However, this phrase is a clear continuation of the biblical gesture of destruction. In biblical idiom, as here, נטה יד בכלי means "stretch out one's hand with or by means of (object)." In 1QM 16:6–7, it is interesting that this gesture (here with the verb הרים instead of נטה) is performed when the gesturers are within throwing range of the enemy. Thus it is clearly not a utilitarian hitting gesture, but a magical one that is effective at a distance. In Columns 15, 16, and 18, one sees a striking alternation between God's gestures and the same gestures performed by humans, both described as means of destroying the enemy. It is not only the gestures that do this. For example, the blasting of the shofar in 1QM 8:9–10 recalls the sound made by God on Mount Sinai:

ויהי ביום השלישי בהיות הבקר ויהי קלת וברקים וענן כבד על־ההר וקל שופר חזק מאד ויחרד
כל־העם אשר במחנה

On the third day, when it was morning, there were sounds, flashes, and heavy smoke on the mountain, and a very loud sound of a shofar. All the people in the camp trembled.

(Exodus 19:16)

Thus the War Scroll describes situations in which the Sons of Light assault the Sons of Darkness with images and sounds that invoke the power of God.

The attribution of human gesture acts to God and the ubiquity of divine commands in the performance of these gestures imply that the human gesturer acts as a representative of God. The gesture, then, stands as a sign of God's gesture. To be more specific, the gesture is both an icon of God's gesture (that is, it resembles the gesture God is performing or would perform) and an index of God's gesture (that is, it presupposes that there has been contact between the gesturing God and the gesturing mortal). In using the gesture, the human performing it asserts that he has been involved in at least one sacred encounter previously, in which he learned the form of God's gesture and was divinely authorized to perform it. This is another way in which the Israelite semiotic of the body differs from that of Mesopotamia. In the Mesopotamian system, the shape and features of the body serve as indices of the work of the deity, both past and future. In the Israelite system, the actions of the body serve as indices of divinely imparted instruction, authority, and exercise of power.

The use of ritual gestures in Israelite warfare, therefore, calls attention to the manner in which these gestures are learned. Few scholars have delved into this area of inquiry. H. P. L'Orange, in his discussion of the destructive gesture of extending one hand, which he called "Cosmocrator's Sign," suggested that there was a ritual context for the learning of this gesture, namely initiation ceremonies for priests and kings.[12] S. D. Ricks and J. Sroka placed the learning of the gesture in the context of a temple coronation ceremony. According to Ricks and Sroka, the new king, having been instructed in the use of this gesture, then used it to defeat the forces of chaos in the ritual combat that was part of the coronation ceremony.[13] Both of these reconstructions are true to the general milieu of the ancient Near East. However, the extent to which they might apply specifically to the Israelite culture has not yet been established, nor is it likely that it will be, since we lack direct evidence. What we can be certain of is how the learning of gestures for warfare is portrayed in the Hebrew Bible, and I will now explore this in more detail.

In Psalms 18:35 and 144:1, the Psalmist asserts that "[God] teaches my hands to war," presumably meaning that he had learned his gestures from God himself. This could include both the utilitarian gestures of using weapons and the supernaturally effective gestures discussed here. How does God himself instruct people to use gestures? The account of Moses in Exodus 3–14 provides an interesting case study to answer this question. Exodus 3–4 describes a personal encounter between Moses and God, a theophany. Exodus 3:20, quoted above, in which God promises to free the Israelites from Egyptian bondage by stretching out his hand, occurs in this theophany context, and that passage is the first instance where Moses is given specific knowledge of the gesture that will bring about the supernatural effects in the following chapters (though he has not yet been directed to use the gesture himself). Elsewhere in chapter 3, the dialogue between Moses and God is quite heavily occupied with the topic of signs, especially gestural signs. In 3:11–12, Moses expresses concern about his ability to confront Pharaoh and free the children of Israel. In response, God tells him:

כי־אהיה עמך וזה־לך האות כי אנכי שלחתיך בהוציאך את־העם ממצרים תעבדון את־האלהים על ההר הזה

For I will be with you, and this is the sign for you, for I have sent you. When you bring the people out of Egypt, you shall worship God on this mountain. (Exodus 3:12)

This is a somewhat perplexing passage.[14] The problem is identifying the antecedent of זה "this" in the clause "and this is for you the sign." The antecedent could be the promise that God will be with Moses in the previous clause or the commandment to worship God on the mountain in the second part of the verse, but both of these interpretations are problematic. Elsewhere in this portion of Exodus, a "sign" (אות) is usually something that can be visually perceived and serves as convincing evidence; it would not do much good to give a sign that cannot be seen or that will not take place until after the crisis is over. It is likely that זה refers to a gesture or other visual sign that is given to Moses but not explicitly described in the text.[15] Moses fails to see this gesture because he has hidden his face, being "too afraid to look at God," as related earlier in verse 6; thus the narrator leaves the gesture undescribed. However, it is possible that the implied gesture is a handclasp, in which case the sign would be perceptible through touch.[16] Moses then asks God to reveal his name to Moses as an additional sign. The LORD gives a somewhat evasive response to this request, but he does disclose to Moses the gesture by which he will smite Egypt (verse 20).[17] In 4:1–9, the LORD instructs Moses through demonstration and verbal command to perform a series of gestures which, through their supernatural effects, are designed to convince the Israelites and the Egyptians that Moses has indeed been commissioned by the LORD: casting down a staff to turn it into a snake, putting his hand into his tunic to make it turn leprous, and putting water on dry land to turn the water into blood. The LORD closes the theophany by providing Moses with a tool that is both significant of the past encounter and portentous:

ואת־המטה הזה תקח בידך אשר תעשה־בו את־האתת

Take this staff, by which you will perform the signs, in your hand.

(Exodus 4:17)

Throughout the account of the plagues and the crossing of the sea, God gives verbal commands that Moses then carries out, usually with explicit use of the staff. The verbal commands include specific instructions about the gesture to be performed, which is the same in all cases, extending the hand with the staff against various inanimate addressees. The use of the staff apparently helps to reinforce Moses' assertion of divine authority in the "sign" of the outstretched hand, since it serves as concrete evidence of having had an encounter with God.[18]

The elements of Moses' instruction, therefore, include a theophany, visual demonstration, and instruction through the spoken, revealed word. A similar sequence appears in the account of Joshua. In Joshua 5:13–6:5, the "captain of the LORD's host" appears with a drawn sword in his hand and proceeds to give Joshua specific instructions about how to conquer Jericho, including circumambulating the city and blowing shofars. Later, in Joshua 8:18, the LORD gives Joshua a verbal command to extend his hand with his sword against the city of Ai to enable his armies to conquer that city.[19] Therefore, whereas L'Orange, Ricks, and Sroka situated the learning of the Israelite gesture of destruction in the context of the coronation ceremony, it is perhaps better situated in the context of theophany.[20] In the case of the king (as in Psalms 18:35; 144:1 and instances referred to by L'Orange), the learning of the gesture could have been connected with a theophany or visionary experience following the installation of the king, similar to Solomon's dream in 1 Kings 3:5–14.

To summarize, ancient Israelite literature describes both God and humans performing ritual gestures in warfare. God's gestures could be carried out through his servants, and their gestures were indicative of God's. These gestures, along with semiotic analyses of the acts based on wordplay, were thought to be revealed through verbal oracles to prophets and other leaders, who then carried out the acts. The use of these gestures by humans thus called attention to previous situations in which instruction and authorization to perform the gesture were imparted. It is likely that these situations of contact with the divine were thought to be theophanies such as those found in the biblical accounts of Moses and Joshua.

Notes

1. A possible exception to this is Judges 4:14–15. Though some delete the phrase "by the edge of the sword" (לפי חרב) in verse 15, this emendation is unnecessary and lacks textual support; see R. G. Boling, *Judges* (Anchor Bible), Garden City, NY: Doubleday, 1975, p. 97; cf. NRSV, NJB. In such passages as Isaiah 42:13; 66:16; Jeremiah 12:12; and Psalm 17:13, it is questionable whether the reference is to a literal, anthropomorphic appearance of the LORD in battle. For a general treatment of the Israelite concept of the roles of the LORD and his people in warfare, see P. D. Miller, *The Divine Warrior in Early Israel*, Cambridge, MA: Harvard University Press, 1973, pp. 155–65.

2. Although Gesenius and Brown both consider the form נאדרי to be a Niphal masculine singular participle in construct with בכח (W. Gesenius, E. Kautzch, and A. E. Cowley, *Hebrew Grammar*, Oxford: Clarendon Press, 1910, §90 l; F. Brown, S. R. Driver, and C. A. Briggs, *The Brown-Driver-Briggs Hebrew and English Lexicon*, Peabody, Massachusetts: Hendrickson, 1999, p. 12; for the participle in construct with a prepositional phrase, cf. B. K. Waltke and M. O'Connor, *An Introduction to Biblical Hebrew Syntax*, Winona Lake: Eisenbrauns, 1990, §9.6 b), the participle is most likely in the absolute state such as the forms with the definite article in Psalms 113:5–6; 114:8; 123:1 (cf. Gesenius-Kautsch-Cowley, op. cit., §90 m; I wish to thank Prof. Dennis Pardee for pointing out this interpretation). In either case, this is an epithet of the LORD rather than a description of his right hand, which is grammatically feminine. The parallelism would then support interpreting ימינך as an adverbial rather than as the subject in both cola. Alternatively, the form נאדרי could be emended to נאדרה, a predicate adjective modifying ימינך (Gesenius-Kautsch-Cowley, loc. cit.). The LXX has *dedoxastai* "has been glorified," a third-person verb, which would support the emendation. However, in the absence of textual variation in the Masoretic tradition, it is preferable to translate the Hebrew text according to the form as it is given here.

3. Exodus 7:5, 19; 8:1, 2, 12, 13; 9:22, 23; 10:12, 13, 21, 22; 14:16, 21, 26, 27; Joshua 8:18 (2x), 19, 26; Isaiah 5:25 (2x); 9:11, 16, 20; 10:4; 14:26, 27; 23:11; 31:3; Jeremiah 6:12; 15:6; 21:5; 51:25; Ezekiel 6:14; 14:9, 13; 16:27; 25:7, 13, 16; 30:25; 35:3; Zephaniah 1:4; 2:13; 1 Chronicles 21:16. This list includes instances where the hand itself is not mentioned explicitly.

4. The most thorough discussion of this gesture to date is that of P. Humbert, "Etendre la main," *Vetus Testamentum* 12, 1962, pp. 383–95. See also P. D. Miller, *Divine Warrior*, p. 135.

5. Z. Bahrani, *Rituals of War: The Body and Violence in Mesopotamia*, New York: Zone Books, 2008, pp. 57–65, 77, 80–1, 110.

6. Other examples of this usage may be found in Exodus 9:15; 24:11; 2 Samuel 24:16; Psalm 138:7; Job 1:11–12; 2:5. Even so, these passages together represent only a small proportion of the total occurrences of שלח יד (55 occurrences in the Hebrew Bible, plus a few attestations in early Northwest Semitic inscriptions).

7. Similar wordplays may be found for this idiom in Exodus 9:15 (cf. verses 14, 17) and perhaps 2 Samuel 24:16 (cf. verse 13). Also compare Genesis 3:22–3, where God says, "Now, lest he stretch out his hand (ישלח ידו) and partake (ולקח) also of the Tree of

Life," and the narrator continues, "the LORD God drove him out (וַיְגָרֶשׁ) from the garden of Eden to work the ground from which he was taken (לֻקָּח)."

8. It is unlikely that the proliferation of this semiotic system in Ezekiel is due to confronting the highly developed semiotic system in Mesopotamia, because it is unlikely that Hebrew prophets had access to the inner workings of the Mesopotamian semiotic system. They were concerned primarily with their own tradition and their Jewish audience.

9. In Exodus 14:31, there is an intriguing statement that "Israel saw the great 'hand' [most translations render this as 'power,' 'deed,' or the like] which the LORD did [or, perhaps, 'by which he worked'] upon Egypt; the people feared the LORD and believed in the LORD and in Moses his servant." Whether or not we take the reference to God's hand literally, it is evident that Moses' gestures and those of the LORD were considered to be mutually indicative.

10. Textual variation and ambiguity in the context make it uncertain whether Moses raises one or both hands in this passage. See W. H. C. Propp, *Exodus 1–18* (Anchor Bible), New York: Doubleday, 1999, p. 614.

11. M. Wise, M. Abegg, and E. Cook, *The Dead Sea Scrolls: A New Translation*, San Francisco: Harper, 1996, p. 158 (trans. M. Abegg); cf. J. H. Charlesworth (Ed.), *The Dead Sea Scrolls: Hebrew, Aramaic, and Greek Texts with English Translations*, vol. 2, Tübingen: J. C. B. Mohr, 1995, p. 113 (trans. J. Duhaime, "and stretch out their hand(s) to the weapons").

12. L'Orange cites, in particular, the "filling of hands" (מלא יד) in the initiation of priests, the "strengthening of David's hand in God" by Jonathan in 1 Samuel 23:16, and king Joash's visit to Elisha in 2 Kings 13:14–19. See H. P. L'Orange, *Studies on the Iconography of Cosmic Kingship in the Ancient World*, New Rochelle, New York: Caratzas Brothers, 1982, pp. 161–2.

13. S. D. Ricks and J. J. Sroka, "King, Coronation, and Temple: Enthronement Ceremonies in History," in D. W. Parry (Ed.), *Temples of the Ancient World: Ritual and Symbolism*, Salt Lake City: Deseret, 1994, pp. 249–50, 253. This proposal is similar to that of Wyatt, who believes that this gesture was associated with the enthronement rituals of kingship, being used to ritually smite enemies in a temple ceremony following the reception of the divine weapons by the new king. See N. Wyatt, "Arms and the King," in M. Dietrich and I. Kottsieper (Eds.), *"Und Mose schrieb dieses Lied auf": Studien zum Alten Testament und zum Alten Orient*, Münster: Ugarit-Verlag, 1998, pp. 833–82.

14. For a summary of interpretations, see Propp, *Exodus 1–18*, pp. 203–4.

15. Another example of a gesture that is alluded to but not explicitly described is in the common oath formula, "Thus will God do to me and thus will he add," which likely involved touching the throat. On this, see P. Sanders, "So May God Do to Me!," *Biblica* 85, 2004, pp. 91–8; B. Conklin, *Oath Formulas in Biblical Hebrew*, Winona Lake: Eisenbrauns, 2011, pp. 22–3.

16. Jeremiah 31:32, which refers to this scene in Exodus 3 (in which the LORD covenants verbally to bring Israel out of Egypt), may contain a reference to this gesture: "not like the covenant which I made with their fathers in the day **I grasped their hand** to bring them out of the land of Egypt, which covenant of mine they broke, though I had become their husband, says the LORD." Israel's side of the covenant, which they broke, is precisely the commandment in Exodus 3:12 to worship (or serve, תעבדון) God on the mountain (cf. Exodus 32). Jeremiah employs the image of grasping the hand in a double sense, referring to both the covenant gesture and the metaphor of God taking Israel by the hand in order to lead them out of Egypt. For grasping the hand as a covenant gesture, see Z. W. Falk, "Gestures Expressing Affirmation," *Journal of Semitic Studies* 4, 1959, pp. 268–9; P. R. Ackroyd, "יד yad," in G. J. Botterweck and H. Ringgren (Eds.), *Theological Dictionary of the Old Testament*, Grand Rapids: Eerdmans, 1986, vol. 5, pp. 410–11.

17. It is not certain whether Moses is asking for his own benefit or, as he professes, for the benefit of the children of Israel who will doubt his having had the theophany. The reason Moses gives may be a pretext such as that of Manoah in Judges 13:17. Most interpreters assume that the name Moses seeks in Exodus 3:13 is the tetragrammaton, which is usually analyzed as a third person masculine singular verb from the root הוה/היה. However, in his response to Moses in verse 14, God does not give this name, but instead uses the verb אהיה, inflected in first person singular. This is, at best, quite a cryptic way of disclosing the name to Moses (though God refers to himself using the tetragrammaton later in verse 16). It is also possible that the name Moses sought was not this name at all, but another name the knowledge of which was restricted, such that Moses' knowing the name would be sure evidence of a personal encounter. In any case, the plain meaning of the initial response in verse 14, "I am who I am," sounds like a brusque way of avoiding the question. In the Hebrew Bible generally, as in Exodus 3:13–14, divine and semidivine beings are reluctant to disclose their names. Cf. Genesis 32:30 (Jacob asks a "man," who later turns out to be the LORD himself, what his name is and receives an evasive response, though the LORD gives him a blessing instead); Judges 13:17–18 (Manoah asks an angel what his name is; rather than disclosing the name, which is "too wondrous," the angel gives another, visual sign in verses 19–20).

18. Later, this staff is called "the staff of God" (Exodus 17:9). Elsewhere God provides his servant with a sword, such as that put in the hand of the king of Babylon in Ezekiel 30:25.

19. For the identification of Hebrew כידון as a Near Eastern sickle sword (instead of the traditional identification as a spear or javelin), see J. Carmignac, "Precisions apportees au vocabulaire de l'Hebreu biblique par la guerre des fils de lumiere contre les fils de tenebre," *Vetus Testamentum* 5, 1955, pp. 357–9; K. G. Kuhn, "Beiträge zum Verständnis der Kriegsrolle von Qumran," *Theologische Literaturzeitung* 81, 1956, pp. 25–30; G. Molin, "What is a *Kidon?*" *Journal of Semitic Studies* 1, 1956, pp. 334–7; Y. Yadin, *The Scroll of the War of the Sons of Light against the Sons of Darkness*, Oxford: Oxford University Press, 1962, pp. 124–31; O. Keel, *Wirkmächtige Siegeszeichen im Alten Testament*, Göttingen: Vandenhoeck & Ruprecht, 1974, pp. 21–6; L. Koehler and W. Baumgartner, *Hebräisches und Aramäisches Lexikon zum Alten Testament*, vol. 2, Leiden: Brill, 1974, p. 450. Keel (op. cit., pp. 86–7) suggests that the captain of the LORD's host who appears to Joshua in Joshua 5:13–15 may give the sword he holds in his hand to Joshua, and this may be the same sword that appears in Joshua 8:18, despite the fact that two different nouns for "sword" are used (חרב and כידון). Though far from certain, this interpretation would align these passages in Joshua with other ones in which God gives a weapon to his servant and subsequently commands the servant to use it in a gesture of destruction (Exodus 4:17; Ezekiel 30:25).

20. The giving of new names is another ritual motif that has traditionally been placed in a coronation context but is better viewed in a theophany context, at least for ancient Israel. This is explored in my Vanderbilt M.A. thesis, "The Giving of New Names in the Hebrew Bible," 2005.

5 "Human, all too human"

Royal name-making in wartime[*]

Jacob L. Wright

To Suzanne Last Stone

Adam, the progenitor who contains all human attributes,
recognizes in the infant soul of David his future epitome,
transformed from everyman to a quintessence: a superman,
if that term includes super-concentrated human failings.[1]

I.

Any serious discussion of war in the Jewish tradition cannot afford to neglect the part played by Israel's kings. They are, at least since the pivotal contribution of Maimonides' Code (*Mishneh Torah*), central to the discourse on "obligatory" versus "authorized" wars and the diverse legal issues subsumed under these categories.[2] Even if a modern democratic state is deemed to stand in sufficient continuity with the authority ascribed to the king,[3] one must appreciate the persistent appeal of the sources, which span more than a millennium, to a very particular form of government: a constitutional monarchy whose authority is clearly delimited and counterbalanced by other powers. My interest in the present paper relates to early developments in the Jewish tradition that paved the path for this separation of powers and that contributed to the longevity of the monarchy in halakhic discourse on war. Yet rather than treating war laws, I focus on *narrative*. Specifically, I seek to show how biblical authors demystify and demythologize the monarchy through story.[4] They undermine its conventional ideological underpinnings by illustrating, in a literary form accessible to a large audience, that Israel's greatest kings were "human, all too human." Where official inscriptions tend to draw on formulas, clichés and stereotypes to commemorate the great names that kings make for themselves in battle, the biblical authors provide their readers with glimpses from behind the scenes of the royal name-making enterprise – glimpses that are often unflattering to the kings themselves or that at least reveal the extent to which their battlefield success is product of collaborative efforts. The way in which the biblical narratives cut down kingship to human proportions represents the *literary* counterpart to the emergence of a Deuteronomic *law* that subordinates the monarchy to itself and thereby establishes the institution on a more enduring foundation. These narratives eventually also become a source for the creation of new law.

II.

The expression "make a name (for oneself)" has a long linguistic history. Already Ancient Near Eastern sources from the third millennium BCE use the Akkadian expression *šuman šakānum*, literally "to place/establish/set up a name," to describe various activities in which individuals "make a name" for themselves. The most basic of such activities is procreation, producing a namesake/progeny. That this method of name-making cannot be taken for granted is illustrated in the myth of Etana in which the first human king prays to the god Shamash pleading for a child: "Remove my reproach and establish for me a name!"[5]

Whereas making or perpetuating one's name through progeny was considered to be available to all (potent) males, the option of making a *great* name was reserved for the exceptional few. A common way in which elites made these great names was by establishing monuments.[6] Thus Absalom sets up a pillar in "the Valley of Kings" (2 Samuel 18:18), and we are told that his reason for doing so was his failure to sire a scion who could invoke and perpetuate his name.[7] Other options that were available to elites include major cultural contributions (such as Genesis 5:20–22), extraordinary erudition and wisdom (Proverbs 22:1, 1 Kings 10), or impressive building projects (1 Kings 6–7), as well as large donations (such as in 2 Kings 12:18).[8]

Yet the most popular path to a great name for men in the ANE appears to have been martial exploits and military service.[9] To cite a prominent example, Gilgamesh aspires to establish for himself a name by demonstrating his *intrepidity in battle* against "one whose *name* the lands keep repeating," the awe-inspiring Huwawa (or Humbaba). Gilgamesh declares: "Since a man cannot pass beyond the borders of life, I want to set off into the mountains, to make/establish a name for myself there [mu-ĝu₁₀ ga-am₃-ĝar]."[10] The close correspondence between military triumph, name-making, and monument-building can be witnessed in the way *šuman šakānum* occasionally functions metonymically as an expression of victory.[11]

As representatives and guardians (or "shepherds") of their peoples, kings seek to make on the battlefield a name for themselves that is known not only at home, within their own societies, but also abroad, among their neighbors and, if possible, in the outer reaches of civilization.[12] Such international renown serves two primary purposes. First, it benefits the security of their kingdoms insofar as it issues a warning to potential aggressors. Second, it serves the interests and needs of the throne itself: through feats of valor or exceptional success on campaigns, the king makes for himself an immortal name and secures a standing among the great rulers of history. Both purposes reflect the self-preservational character of name-making: the first, the preservation of the kingdom, and the second, the preservation of the dynasty.

Scholars often cast aspersions on the way rulers advertise success in word, image and behavior.[13] Yet instead of simply disparaging the motives of kings as egotistical and self-serving, one may seek to appreciate royal name-making from the perspective of performativity: in order to *be* a ruler, one must *behave* like one. Conversely, by performing the royal role, one accrues "symbolic capital" that is indispensable to effective rule.[14] This less moralistic stance is in line with Foucault's view that "sees the strategies of power used by kings and governments as embedded in and dependent upon the level of 'microrelations' of power, the local interactions and petty calculations of daily life."[15] It recognizes that prestige and status represent "the preconditions for developing the moral authority to influence group decisions, exert leadership, and wield power – or to resist the powers of others."[16] For any leader, but especially for an ancient monarch, a deficit of moral authority jeopardizes his or her control and increases the chance of failure. And such failure is not in the interest of a people who themselves recognize the need for reform and wish to mobilize for collective action.

Nevertheless, the fragility of Israel's and Judah's existence, and the tumultuous experiences of these states at the crossroads of imposing imperial powers, seriously undermined any claim of unmitigated autonomy on the part of native monarchs. Moreover, for biblical authors living after the subjugation of the kingdoms of Israel and Judah, native monarchic rule and military power were not always available options. It was therefore imperative to come to terms with an ancient tradition of kingship and conventional strategies of self-legitimization. The biblical authors do this in a way that presents the monarchy as a potentially beneficial, if not necessary, yet by all means fallible, institution. The king is portrayed as thoroughly human, indeed often as the *most* human of their characters.[17] By revealing how the ruler makes a name for himself, the biblical accounts undermine his grandiose titles and honorifics – and thereby the very idea of absolute, eternal royal power.[18] Yet by humanizing the monarchic institution, they intend to establish it on a more sustainable foundation, in the hope that it will survive to see another day.

III.

In their inscriptions and iconography, kings who ruled both great empires and much smaller states, such as Israel and Judah, present themselves as solid, stoic, immutable figures, committed to justice and fearless in the face of attack from their enemies round about. They make great efforts to evade the messy details of how they rose to power. Sometimes public knowledge of a conflict surrounding their right to rule obliges them to make reference to their disputed origins. But when doing so, they elide the less flattering facts by claiming that they were placed on the throne by a deity.[19] Other times rulers of petty states admit in their official inscriptions that they owe their office to the decision of the imperial throne. For example, Kilamuwa of Ya'diya/Samal (ca. 825 BCE) reports that he had to call on the King of Assyria for assistance against Danunian kings.[20]

Such admissions of dependency stand over against the more conventional royal ideology that presents the ruler as self-sufficient. To cite a notable example, the pharaohs of New Kingdom Egypt are often portrayed iconographically alone in their chariots, without drivers, the reigns tied around their waists (a method never actually practiced),[21] and towering above a multitude of enemies. A literary counterpart to this image is the lengthy song of triumph transmitted in the middle of the Qedesh Account of Ramses II (the "Kadesh Battle Poem").[22] In it, the Egyptian ruler begins, "No officer was with me, no charioteer/No soldier of the army, no shield bearer . . ." He goes on to describe how everyone abandoned him and how he was forced to sally forth against the enemy alone. In the end, after achieving extraordinary feats with the special assistance of his god Amun, both the enemy and his own army and officers praise his *name*. Similarly, in his Victory Stele, the Kushite ruler Piye (late eighth century BCE) recounts how his troops declared their allegiance with a series of self-effacing statements: "It is *your name* that gives us power . . . Your bread strengthens our bodies along the way. Your beer quenches our thirst. It is your bravery that gives us strength; for everyone trembles at the mention of your name. No army has success . . . Who is thy equal therein? Thou art a victorious king, achieving with his hands. . ."[23] In both accounts, the shadow of the king has almost completely eclipsed his army.

How are kings presented in biblical literature? On the one end of the spectrum, the royal ideology just described is not foreign to biblical literature. Thus, the "Royal Psalms" present the king as blameless, fighting alone, and benefitting from an exceptional union with the deity (see Psalms 2, 18, 20, 21, 45, 72, 101, 110, 132, 144). Research on these psalms has demonstrated their complexity and the ways in which they add nuances to earlier notions.[24] Yet even with their multiple layers, these psalms are still far removed from texts on the opposite end of the spectrum: narratives in Judges, Samuel and Kings that describe the actions of leaders and kings in the third person and portray them as fallible, very human figures who traverse long, politically embarrassing, and often bloody paths on their way to the throne. By providing behind-the-scenes glimpses of Israel's greatest rulers in action and by depicting their ambitions and failures, they complicate the grand claims in the psalms of the king's exceptionality, as one who fights his many adversaries solely with divine help. By revealing the king's success to be the result of collaborative work with his generals and armies, the narratives demythologize the royal name and demystify the institution.[25]

The demythologization defies the "hegemonic masculinities" presented in official royal inscriptions and iconography throughout the ANE.[26] More importantly, it provides a significant counterweight to those who, like the Chronicler, would re-mythologize the monarchic institution by erasing en bloc not only the unflattering account of David's rise to power but all the material related to the conflict regarding the establishment of the monarchy in the book of Samuel. In fact, the book of Chronicles avoids the history of the emergence of the monarchy altogether; instead, it takes for granted its role in Israelite society and makes the king the centerpiece of Israel's cyclical history.[27]

In order to illustrate how the biblical authors humanize kingship and challenge pretensions to self-sufficiency, I compare in the following section several biblically *transmitted* accounts that depict royal correspondence, on the one hand, to exemplars of confidential correspondence between kings and generals that have been *discovered* in archaeological excavations, on the other.

IV.

In the correspondence between a Hittite king (probably Tudhaliya IV) and an influential adviser to Tukulti-Ninurta I, heir to the Assyrian throne (1243–1207 BCE), the Hittite ruler writes about the plans of the young Assyrian ruler to undertake a campaign again Mitanni as soon as he assumes power, a move that was contrary to Hittite interests. Important here is the motivation the Hittite king places on the lips of Tukulti-Ninurta: "In this way I will establish a *good name* for myself" (*manwaza laman kuitki ijami*).[28] Apparently the mature Hittite ruler recognized the importance of a king manifesting his strength immediately upon accession to the throne. The campaign against Mitanni would not only demonstrate preparedness to protect and expand Assyrian influence but, if successful, it would also secure for Tukulti-Ninurta a prominent position among the international players of his day.

Biblical literature also portrays name-making through conquest as an important first achievement for rulers after their coronation. For example, immediately following the account of Saul's anointment and proclamation as king (1 Samuel 9–10), the book of Samuel describes his campaign to "rescue" Jabesh-Gilead from the hands of the Ammonites. By virtue of this feat, Saul wins the name of "savior" (מושיע, 11:3; see Judges 12:3).[29]

This account, in turn, may be compared to two letters sent to the Mari ruler Zimri-Lim (eighteenth century BCE). In the first, the king's general petitions him to come quickly and rescue the besieged city of Razama; otherwise the enemy may prematurely lift the siege, and Zimri-Lim would forfeit a good opportunity to be called by "the name of *savior*."[30] In the second letter, one of his servants writes:

> With respect to the king [of Yamhad], I have, in keeping with all that you wrote me, established a *great name* for my Lord (*šu-ma-am ra-<ba>-am be-lí aš-ku-un*). Hence his servants and the entire land are saying now: "Zimri-Lim is the one! He conquered the city of Azara and gave it Yarim-Lim." This news should make my Lord happy![31]

These two letters reflect the role played by Zimri-Lim's general and servant in public relations, political spin and propaganda – methods of rule and control that are particularly well documented in the Mari archives.[32]

For our present purposes it is important that one not forget the genre of these texts: rather than official inscriptions meant for public display, these are top-secret letters between a king and his right-hand men (his general and one of his representatives). It was, to be sure, in the interest of Zimri-Lim that no one outside his most trusted circle ever become privy to the correspondence. The public image that Zimri-Lim, like many other rulers, wished to present (in his official inscriptions, iconography, and other media) was that of a self-sufficient sovereign who stands head and shoulders above his subjects. In order to accumulate "symbolic capital," he needed to be the one who conquered these cities and therefore who earned the name of victor. The messy details of how he actually made his name should, of course, remain concealed.

The correspondence between Zimri-Lim and his general is strikingly similar to that between David and Joab. In the account of the Ammonite campaign, David's devoted general informs him that he had laid siege to Rabbah, the enemy capital. Because he had made considerable progress, the city was on the verge of capitulation. David should assemble the rest of the army and come finish the job, "otherwise I myself will take the city and it will be called by *my name!*" (2 Samuel 12:28). Joab's rationale of name-making strikes a chord with David, and in the end, the magnificent crown of the Ammonite king (or the deity Milcom) is placed on David's head. The act of making a name by conquering a city is of course not unique to this passage.[33] However, in contrast to the actual achievements earlier in his career, the name David makes for himself in the conquest of Rabbah was primarily the work of his competent right-hand man.

For the biblical author, there is nothing inherently wrong about David's actions here. They are indeed no different than those of other kings. The name he makes, like that of Zimri-Lim, is the result of collaborative action with his trusted general. He behaves like many other savvy leaders in history who arrived in the final moment of a momentous victory in order to take a lion's share of the credit and make a name for themselves. Just as David first made a name for himself after slaying Goliath with the help of Israel's women who hailed him as the one who "has slain his myriads," so too in the later stages of his rise to power, he, like Zimri-Lim, counts on devoted servants to protect and strengthen his name.[34]

Nevertheless, this narrative represents a truly remarkable phenomenon: whereas we know about the correspondence between Zimri-Lim and his general through modern research and discovery, we know about the correspondence between David and Joab because biblical authors "revealed" it to their readers. In contrast to a political exposé written by modern journalists, however, the work of these authors is literary construction. They created a narrative with an accessible and suggestive literary style that predestined it for a wide reception. More importantly, by unveiling the very human and fallible nature of the progenitor of the great Davidic dynasty, this narrative effectively shatters the superhuman masculine self-image that rulers in the ANE (including ancient Israel) were wont to present in their official inscriptions, iconography, state rituals, and monumental architecture.

One may compare this narrative to others in the ANE. Especially noteworthy in this respect is the Gilgamesh tradition, whose gripping tales of life, death, procreation, immortality, and ambition treat universal human concerns. Yet the standard twelve tablet Akkadian version, the Old Babylonian version, and the individual Sumerian poems cannot be said to critique the cult of kingship in the manner or to the degree that we witness in the biblical narrative. Indeed, the tragic account presents a deep transformation in Gilgamesh, yet he remains superhuman, two-thirds divine and only one-third human.

Another text relevant to the discussion is the "Cuthean Legend" of the deified ruler Naram-Sîn. This widely transmitted work (we have Old Babylonian, Neo-Assyrian, Neo-Babylonian and possibly Hittite versions) depicts this figure, who was known for his great conquests, suffering massive defeats. The cause of the catastrophe is his arrogant self-reliance: instead of heeding the divine oracles, he trusts solely on his own strength:

> What lion (ever) performed extispicy?
> What wolf (ever) consulted a dream-interpreter?
> I will go like a brigand according to my own inclination.
> I will cast aside that oracle of the god(s); I will be in control myself.[35]

Three years of cataclysmic defeat drive him to deep introspection and despair, as he doubts his worth as a ruler after bringing about great calamity upon his land and people (ll. 89–96). In the end, however, he is saved from complete ruination and he learns to act in accordance with the will of the gods. Insofar as this legend has a didactic purpose, it may have been used to warn future rulers against hubris: even if they are as powerful and valorous as Naram-Sîn, they will only bring about great suffering by defying the divine word communicated to them through prophets and other mantic functionaries.[36] If this suggestion is tenable, the legend may be compared to the Weidner Chronicle, which critiques past reigns of famous kings from the perspective of their solicitude for the Babylonian Marduk cult.[37]

While such texts do share features in common with the biblical narratives, I would suggest that the closest parallels are works of drama from early modernity, especially those composed by Shakespeare, that scrutinize political affairs and institutions at a time before newspapers began to publish exposés. What made Shakespeare great – and what sustains the wide interest in his work – is that he took the greatest rulers in the English imagination and revealed their all-too-human qualities.[38] Likewise, the authors of the book of Samuel create an epic account in which two of the most beloved kings in Israelite and Judahite memory, Saul and David, are the most human and fallible characters in their narratives.[39]

The episode of David making a name for himself as "conqueror" of Rabbah frames the Bathsheba affair. Together, they form one of the most penetrating critiques of royal power in the Western tradition. Instead of joining his royal peers in making a name for himself on the battlefield, David stays back in the capital sleeping with the wife of soldier Uriah. One may compare the account to a letter of Shamshi-Adad (eighteenth century BCE) to his son in Mari that contrasts lying among women with name-making on the battlefield.[40] Later David attempts to pass his child off as Uriah's namesake, and then finally kills Uriah and takes his wife under his own name.[41] The authors formulate this critique notably by revealing to their readers, as in 2 Samuel 12:28, the disturbing contents of *letters* sent by the king to his general in order to safeguard his good name (11:6, 14, 18–25).[42]

The aim of the authors of the book of Samuel is not to deny the legitimacy of the monarchy. Rather they seek to humanize it, cut it down to size, and subject it to the scrutiny of a common social code of conduct, just as the authors of Deuteronomy (17:14–20) bring it under the authority of a specific legal code of conduct.[43] In fact, such a move in many ways preserves royal rule (e.g. it paved the way for the more enduring model of constitutional monarchies with a long history in Europe). Moreover, because the king often embodies the hegemonic masculinity, the denial of his absolute authority necessarily challenges the identification of self-sufficiency as an essential element of manhood.

V.

As part of their work to challenge the self-sufficiency of the king, many biblical authors superimpose a "theological" layer on the king's success in making a name for himself.[44] With respect to Saul's name as a "savior," the authors of 1 Samuel 11 introduce an episode (vv. 12–13) that allows the king to attribute "salvation" (תשועה) to the deity.[45] Similarly, the interpolation of the covenantal promise to David (2 Samuel 7) shifts the king's success from his own virility and power to the deity. David's reproductive success is due to his God, who raises up for him offspring that will carry on his name. Instead of David making a name for himself, the deity proclaims "I will make *for you* a great name (שם גדול) like the name of the great ones of the earth" (v. 9). The principal way in which this international renown will be established is through conquest – by granting the king rest from all his enemies and making a place for Israel to dwell in peace.[46] By including this text, the authors provide their readers with a new lens through which to read the long list of David's conquests, and especially the explicit statement that "David made a name for himself" in the next chapter (8:13).[47] The redactional activity extends to the account of David's very first success, where a later hand has made David declare to Goliath: "You come with sword and shield, but I come in the *name* of YHWH Sebaoth" (1 Samuel 17:45). Significantly, these new layers do not wipe out the older traditions of military power and territorial sovereignty. Rather, they amplify them with a component that was for the biblical authors critical to Israel's survival in times when military power and territorial sovereignty were not available options.

The biblical authors adopted other strategies to undermine or complicate the masculine ambition to make a name for themselves. For example, the book of Judges employs women for this purpose. Rather than helping the warrior make a name for himself through their victory songs, as in David's career, women *deflect* honor away from men (e.g., 1:12–15; 4:4–9, 17–24; 5:24–31; 9:53–57; 11:34–40; chapters 14–16).[48] Similarly, the divine name contends with and counterbalances the names of warriors and kings. Thus, within the final form of Joshua, the deity is the hero who makes a name for himself. In the older parts of the book, the kings from far-off lands "hear" of Joshua's military feats (6:27, 9:1, 10:1, 11:1). A later author however constructed a new framework for these stories by prefacing them with accounts of how all the kings "hear" about the first great conquests by Israel's God (2:10–11, 5:1). From these passages one comes quickly to Exodus 9:16 and 15:3 and a wide array of texts related to the name of the divine warrior (Isaiah 63:12–14, Jeremiah 14:9, Habakkuk 3:2, Daniel 9:15, etc.), which anticipate the hypostatization of the divine name in later Jewish, Samaritan, and Gnostic works.[49]

It remains, in conclusion, to compare very briefly the demystification/demythologization of kingship in narrative, on the one hand, to the subordination of the king to the Deuteronomic code, on the other. Whereas the narrative cuts the monarchy down to size by revealing the reality behind the triumphant claim of kings, the Deuteronomic code goes much further: it assigns no military role whatsoever to the king (17:14–20, 20:1–20). Instead, it is "the priest" and "the officials" (שוטרים) who address the troops/people (20:2, 4). Likewise, "the commanders" (שרי צבאות) are appointed directly before battle (20:9) rather than belonging to a cadre of standing officers appointed by the king. In keeping with Numbers, the rest of Deuteronomy, Joshua, and Judges, the law refers to a force of citizen soldiers fighting their own wars rather than a standing professional force in the employ of a king. This is indeed one of the other prominent features in the Jewish tradition of war, and remains so today.[50] In order to understand how the king can become so central to the later Jewish tradition, one must remember that Deuteronomy, while leaving little room for the king on the battlefield, does not explicitly forbid him from taking part. Moreover, by reducing the monarchy to a very human and thus political institution, narrative paved the way for a re-emergence of the king in later discourse on war. This discourse encompasses both historiography (such as Chronicles and 1 and 2 Maccabees) and – inasmuch as narrative served as an important source for jurisprudence – law (in the halakhic tradition of Maimonides and those who followed him). Together, the demystification of the monarchy in biblical narrative and the subordination of the king to written law in biblical legal material paved the way for the re-emergence, in more recent Jewish jurisprudence, of non-monarchic structures of military command, as anticipated already by Deuteronomy.[51]

Notes

* This paper was completed with the help of a generous grant from the Memorial Foundation for Jewish Culture. I thank Hanspeter Schaudig (Heidelberg) for his invaluable suggestions.

1. R. Pinsky, *The Life of David*, New York: Schocken, p. 179, alluding to the *midrash*; see e.g. *Pirke Rabbi Eliezer* 19 and *Yalqut Shimoni* 1.41.

2. For Maimonides' ideas on the military role of the king, see G.J. Blidstein, *Political Concepts in Maimodean Halakha*, Ramat Gan: Bar-Ilan University Press, 1983 (Hebrew); idem, "Holy War in Maimonidean Law," in J. Kraemer (Ed.), *Perspectives on Maimonides: Philosophical and Historical Studies*, Oxford: Littman Library of Jewish Civilization, 1991, pp. 209–220. For the place of kingship in Jewish thought in general, see D. Polish, *Give Us a King: Legal-Religious Sources of Jewish Sovereignty*, Hoboken: Ktav, 1989; A. Ravitzky, "Kings and Laws in Medieval Jewish Thought (Nissim of Gerona vs. Isaac Abravanel)," in L. Landman (Ed.), *Scholars and Scholarship: The Interaction between Judaism and Other Cultures*, New York: Yeshiva University Press, 1990, pp. 67–90; D. Goodblatt, *The Monarchic Principle: Studies in Jewish Self-Government in Antiquity* (Texte und Studien zum Antiken Judentum 38), Tübingen: Mohr, 1994; A. Melamed, *Philosopher-King in Medieval and Renaissance Jewish Political Thought*, Albany: SUNY Press, 2003.

3. See A.I.H. Kook, *Mishpat Kohen*, Jerusalem: Mosad Harav Kook, 1985, pp. 336–338 (Hebrew).

4. As the reader will notice, I have been influenced strongly by H. White, "The Value of Narrativity in the Representation of Reality," *Critical Inquiry* 7, 1980, pp. 5–27. The way that law, in addition to narrative, can contribute to the demystification of institutions is demonstrated not least by Maimonides' *Laws of Kings and their Wars*, from his *Mishneh Torah: Book of Judges*. Even as they devote great attention to the king, they delimit and rationalize his authority, desacralizing and reducing it to a purely political institution. Nevertheless, Maimonides goes to great lengths to protect the special honors owed the king, without which they would have difficulty imposing their will (see on power and morale authority below).

5. *pil-ti ú-suḫ-ma šu-ma šuk-na-an-ni*, both in the Middle Assyrian (MA-IV 4') and Neo-Assyrian (II 140 and III 14) versions. See A. Zgoll, "'Einen Namen will ich mir Machen' – Die Sehnsucht nach Unsterblichkeit im Alten Orient," *Saeculum* 54, 2003, pp. 1–11, specifically p. 5.

6. K. Radner, *Die Macht des Namens: Altorientalische Strategien zur Selbsterhaltung* (Santag 8), Wiesbaden: Harrassowitz, 2005, pp. 114–166. Like procreation, monument-making is understood as a way of both *making* a name and *perpetuating* the one that a man already has. Forms of monuments included everything from un-carved stones, to images and inscriptions (especially of names), temples, garrisons (נצבים, cf. מצבות and 2 Samuel 8:13–14), and entire cities. The latter could either be constructed after conquest as a monument to triumph or renamed according to the name of a conqueror. The victor could demonstratively inscribe his name on a stele affixed to the municipal wall; see for example Ashurnasirpal II's actions in Tušḫa (RIMA II, A.0.101.1, p. 202, l. 2–12; pp. 242–243, l. 6–39); S. Richter, *The Deuteronomistic History and the Name Theology: lešakkēn šemô šām in the Bible and the Ancient Near East*, Berlin: De Gruyter, 2002, argues that the act of building memorials and inscribing names on monuments represents the earliest and most concrete expression of "making a name." The sense of "becoming famous" is grounded in this concrete plastic activity. In keeping with the close connection between setting up monuments and perpetuating one's name, the inscriptions on monuments often contain a curse petitioning that the gods punish anyone who would remove the name with the destruction of his progeny/seed.

7. Compare בן בעבור הזכיר שמי to *zākir šumim* as the designation for an heir, as in the OB stele of Dāduša of Ešnunna (xvii 6–8), newly published by B.K. Ismail and A. Cavigneaux, "Dādušas Siegestele IM 95200 aus Ešnunna. Die Inschrift," *Baghdader Mitteilungen* 34, 2003, pp. 129–156. In Akkadian and Hebrew, as well as many other languages, the words for (male) child, memory, name and monument are conceptually and often etymologically related. Karel van der Toorn argues that Absalom sets up the monument because he had no son to do it for him; the construction of a monument and the invocation of the name are traditional filial duties that go hand-in-hand; see his *Family Religion in Babylonia, Syria and Israel* (Studies in the History and Culture of the Ancient Near East 7), Leiden: E.J. Brill, 1996, p. 52.

8. For these aspects of name-making, see Radner, *Macht des Namens*, pp. 98–99; C. Wilcke, "Göttliche und menschliche Weisheit im Alten Orient: Magie und Wissenschaft, Mythos und Geschichte," in A. Assmann (Ed.) *Weisheit. Archäologie der literarischen Kommunikation 3*, Munich: Fink, 1991, pp. 259–270; idem, "Der Tod im Leben der Babylonier," in J. Assmann and R. Trauzettel (Eds.), *Tod, Jenseits und Identität. Perspektiven einer kulturwissenschaftlichen Thanatologie*, Freiburg: Karl Alber Verlag, 2002, p. 261. One of the prominent characteristics of masculinity in the self-presentation of ANE kings is the desire to attain and maintain what one's fathers had achieved, and ideally to go above and beyond it. Thus Rimush of Akkad (early twenty-third century) presents himself in his inscriptions as one who preserved what his great father, Sargon, had conquered; yet not being satisfied with this status quo, he strove for new conquests. In his inscriptions he places a noticeable stress on the uniqueness of his achievements; see S. Franke, *Königsinschriften und Königsideologie*, Munster: Lit, 1995, pp. 146–147. The

statement that a ruler outdid his predecessors became an essential characteristic of the ideal king and hence also developed with time into a *topos* in Mesopotamian literature, referring not only to conquests but also to building projects, erudition and other feats. For the West Semitic region, see esp. the inscription of the Sam'alite ruler Kilamuwa (ninth century BCE) referred to below.

9. A range of evidence reflects the attempt by scribes to demonstrate that *their* profession, not that of the soldier, offered the greatest opportunities for upward mobility; that such proof was needed shows that many disagreed. This competition between scribe and soldier provides an important backdrop for understanding the biblical and rabbinic transformation of the גבור from warrior to man of morals and Torah scholarship.

10. *Gilgamesh and Huwawa*, Version A, 4–7 and 32–33. See *The Electronic Text Corpus of Sumerian Literature*: www-etcsl.orient.ox.ac.uk/section1/tr1815.htm (accessed October 4, 2009). The passage is similar to the Old Babylonian version.

11. An example of this metonymy is found in a letter from the Jerusalemite ruler Abdi-Khepa (fourteenth century BCE) petitioning the Egyptian ruler to send him military assistance: "As the king has placed his name in Jerusalem forever [*ša-ka-an MU-šu i-na* KUR Ú-[*r*]*u-sa-limki a-na da-ri-iš*], he cannot abandon the lands of Jerusalem" (EA 287:60–63); see Richter, *Deuteronomistic History*, pp. 174–178, for further examples. Within biblical literature, this metonymy may be compared to such texts as 2 Samuel 8:13 and seems to inform the Deuteronomic "name theology" (לשום שמו שם / לשכן); in addition to Richter, see Y. Zakovitch, "To Cause His Name to Dwell There – To Put his Name There," *Tarbiz*, 41, 1971–72, pp. 338–340 (Hebrew).

12. See A. Malamat, "Campaigns to the Mediterranean by Iahdunlim and Other Early Mesopotamian Rulers," in T. Jacobsen (Ed.), *Studies in Honor of B. Landsberger*, Chicago: University of Chicago Press, (1965), pp. 365–373, for a discussion of the adventurous ambition of northern Mesopotamian rulers (from Sargon I to Shalmaneser III), which is mutually influenced by the Gilgamesh legends and is mirrored in Isaiah 37:24. Comparable to the Lewis & Clark expedition, or better, Sherman's "March to the Sea," these rulers boast of reaching the Mediterranean, offering of sacrifices, washing themselves and/or their weapons in the Sea, felling of massive (cedar and cypress/juniper) trees, and setting up monuments. They seek to place their name next to that of other great rulers, both in the tradition and in actual physical proximity (e.g. at Nahr al-Kalb in Lebanon where rulers from diverse lands carved inscriptions in the cliff).

13. See B. Hindess, *Discourses of Power: From Hobbes to Foucault*, Oxford: Blackwell, 1996. Characteristic of such disparagement of power is J. van Seters' consistently uncharitable reading (what he himself calls "cynical") of the David story in *The Biblical Saga of King David*, Winona Lake: Eisenbrauns, 2009.

14. P. Bourdieu, *La Distinction: Critique sociale de jugement*, Paris: Les Editions de Minuit, 1979. On the application of Judith Butler's performativity notion to royal behavior, see M. Gisborne, "A Curia of Kings: Sulla and Royal Imagery," in O. Hekster and R. Fowler (Eds.), *Imaginary Kings: Royal Images in the Ancient Near East, Greece and Rome* (Oriens et Occidens 11), Munich: Franz Steiner, 2005, pp. 105–124; and J.L. Wright, "Commensal Politics in Ancient Western Asia, Part II," *Zeitschrift für alttestamentliche Wissenschaft* 122, 2010, pp. 333–352, here pp. 345–351.

15. C. Bell, *Ritual Theory, Ritual Practice*, New York: Oxford University Press, 1992, p. 200.

16. M. Derrida and B. Hayden, *Feasts: Archaeological and Ethnographic Perspectives*, Washington, D.C.: Smithsonian Books, 2001, p. 15.

17. The British diplomat Alfred Duff Cooper, Viscount Norwich, insisted that the biblical account of King David must be factual because no people would invent a national hero so deeply flawed. See A.D. Cooper, *David*, London: J. Cape, 1943; see discussion in Pinsky, *Life of David*, p. 2.

18. The royal name is presented most often in the introduction to official inscriptions at great length; see B. Cifola, *Analysis of Variants in the Assyrian Royal Titulary from the Origins to Tiglath-Pileser III*, Napoli: Istituto Universitario Orientale, 1995, and Franke, *Königsinschriften*. For the masculine character of these epithets, see C.R. Chapman, *The Gendered Language of Warfare in the Israelite-Assyrian Encounter* (Harvard Semitic Monographs 62), Winona Lake: Eisenbrauns, 2004, pp. 22–33.

19. See, for example, the Tel Dan Stele, line 4: "And Hadad made me king." The Neo-Assyrian legend of Sargon of Agade presents its hero as an abandoned bastard who rises to paramount ruler thanks to the "love" of Ishtar. Similarly, in the Behistun Inscription, Darius claims to have assumed power and successfully quelled multiple rebellions by the "grace of Ahura Mazda" (beginning in 1.5, the statement is repeated over 35 times). For the Tel Dan Stele, see A. Lemaire, "The Tel Dan Stele as a Piece of Royal Historiography," *Journal for the Study of the Old Testament* 23, 1988, pp. 3–14. On the Sargon Legend, see B. Lewis, *The Sargon Legend: A Study of the Akkadian Text and the Tale of the Hero Who Was Exposed at Birth* (American Schools of Oriental Research Dissertation Series 4), Cambridge: ASOR, 1980. On the Behistun Inscription, see C.-H. Bae, "Comparative Studies of King Darius's Bisitun Inscription," Ph.D. dissertation, Harvard University, 2001.

20. Compare similar statements in the inscriptions of Zakkur of Hammath (KAI 202), Panammu II of Sam'al (KAI 215), Barrakib of Sam'al (KAI 216), Azitwadda of the Danunians (KAI II 3–4), and the Tell Dan Inscription. (KAI = H. Donner and W. Röllig, *Kanaanäische und aramäische Inschriften* (2nd ed.), Wiesbaden: Harrassowitz, 1966–69.) For the Iron Age Aramaic or Neo-Hittite evidence, see M. Hamilton, "The Past as Destiny: Historical Visions in Sam'al and Judah under Assyrian Hegemony," *Harvard Theological Review* 91, 1998, pp. 215–250. For the Southern Levant during the Late Bronze Age, the Amarna letters attest abundantly to this dependency on an imperial superpower; see the edition of W.L. Moran, *The Amarna Letters*, Baltimore: Johns Hopkins University Press, 1992.

21. See J.L. Wright, "Chariots: Evidence and Evolution," in A. Berlejung, G. Lehmann, J. Kamlah and M. Daviau (Eds.), *Encylopaedia of Material Culture in the Biblical World*, Tübingen: Mohr Siebeck, forthcoming 2011.

22. Translation found in M. Lichtheim, *Ancient Egyptian Literature: The New Kingdom* vol. II (3rd ed.), Berkeley: University of California Press, 2006, pp. 57–72.

23. M. Lichtheim, *Ancient Egyptian Literature: The Late Period* vol. III (3rd ed.), Berkeley: University of California Press, 2006, pp. 71–72.

24. See the articles and bibliography collected in P.D. Miller and P.W. Flint (Eds.), *The Book of Psalms. Composition and Reception* (Vetus Testamentum Sup. 99), Leiden – Boston: Brill, 2005.

25. For the "demystification" of monarchies, see the studies collected in J. Deploige and G. Deneckere (Eds.), *Mystifying the Monarch: Studies on Discourse, Power and History*, Amsterdam: Amsterdam University Press, 2006. The achievements of the authors of the book of Samuel are mirrored in the way David became a leading symbol of competing masculinities in Western art. Likewise, the account of his life influenced political thought in many medieval and early modern *specula principum*. To name just one, admittedly recherché, example, the *Fürstenspiegel* drafted by the sixteenth-century Prussian Duchess Anna Maria of Braunschweig-Calenberg-Göttingen for her son, Albert Frederick, sets forth David as the greatest model of both virtue and vice among "earthly sovereigns."

26. Unfortunately one cannot point to studies of hegemonic masculinities for the ANE that are comparable to the work of G.L. Mosse for the modern world; see his *Fallen Soldiers: Reshaping the Memory of the World Wars*, New York: Oxford, 1990, and idem, *Image of Man: The Creation of Modern Masculinity*, New York: Oxford, 1996. Chapman's work on biblical literature in, *Gendered Language of Warfare*, Winona Lake: Eisenbrauns, 2004, is a good point of departure for future work.

27. This remarkable feature of Chronicles has yet to receive the attention it deserves. See meanwhile G. Knoppers, *1 Chronicles 10–29: A New Translation with Introduction and Commentary* (Anchor Bible), New York: Doubleday, 2004, pp. 528–531.

28. A. Goetze (Ed.), *Keilschrifturkunden aus Boghazköi, 23. Historische Texte*, Berlin: Akademie-Verlag, 1928, text – 103 Rs. 14.

29. These chapters most likely originate from different hands, but we can nevertheless appreciate the way their transmitted editorial arrangement witnesses to the need of kings to display their military strength immediately upon assuming the throne; see J.L. Wright, "A Book-Oriented Approach to the Study of a Major War Theme," in B.E. Kelle and F.R. Ames (Eds.), *Writing and Reading War: Rhetoric, Gender, and Ethics in Biblical and Modern Contexts*, Atlanta: Society of Biblical Literature, 2008, pp. 33–56.

30. *šum šu-zu-ub-tim*; see *Archives royales de Mari, vol. 26*, Paris: P. Geuthner, 1950, text: 319, lines 27–30.

31. Unpublished tablet; see Radner, *Macht des Namens*, p. 95.

32. For an accessible and brief English treatment, see J. Sasson, *The Military Establishment at Mari* (Studia Pohl 3), Rome: Pontifical Biblical Institute, 1969, pp. 37–42.

33. Perhaps the most famous case is also from the biblical portrait of David: 2 Samuel 5:6–9 tells of the conquest of Jerusalem by David and his men, and concludes with the statement: "David occupied the stronghold and called it the 'City of David'." In the very next verses we are told that David's fame increased to such an extent that distant kings, like Hiram of Tyre, send him generous gifts (vv. 10–11). Closely connected to this name-making is David's act of taking numerous concubines and wives with whom he produces many sons to carry on his name (vv. 12–16). For other examples of conquerors renaming cities, see Jerusalem/Colonia Aelia Capitolina (Hadrian; the name plays on Hadrian's name and that of the god Jupiter Capitolinus); Sidon / Kār-Aššur-aḫḫê-iddina ("Harbor of Esarhaddon"); Nappigi / Līt-Aššur ("Victory of Assur," Salmaneser III). In a study of these and other ANE acts of name-changing, B. Pongratz-Leisten, "Toponyme als Ausdruck assyrischen Herrschaftsanspruchs," in B. Pongratz-Leisten, H. Kühne and P. Xella (Eds.), *Beiträge zu altorientalischen und mittelmeerischen Kulturen. FS W. Röllig* (Alter Orient Altes Testament 247), Neukirchen-Vluyn, 1997, pp. 325–344, notes that the toponyms often present the king and his god as the *sole* agents in the conquest of these cities – an observation that is suggestive for the David texts.

34. The difference is that the younger David actually performed on the battlefield while the older David was resting back in his palace at the time of the year kings go out to battle (2 Samuel 11:1).

35. First Millennium Standard Babylonian Version, lines 79–80; translation by J. Goodnick Westenholz, *Legends of the Kings of Akkade*, Winona Lake: Eisenbrauns, 1997, p. 317.

36. See, however, the different (and pacifistic?) "Admonition to Future Rulers" in the Standard Babylonian Version; admittedly, these lines (149–180) may be unrelated to the original point of the legend. The point about heeding oracles and hubris is repeatedly illustrated in biblical literature as well; see 1 Samuel 28:5–25, 2 Samuel 5:17–25, 1 Kings 22, etc.

37. See F. Blanco-Wissman, *"Er tat das Rechte": Beurteilungskriterien und Deuteronomismus in 1 Kön 12–2 Kön 25* (Abhandlungen zur Theologie des Alten und Neuen Testaments 93), Zurich: Theologischer Verlag Zurich, 2008. One should also mention here the long-standing motif of the *Unheilsherrscher* or "calamitous ruler," which is especially linked to the name of Nabonidus (the Cyrus Cylinder and the Nabonidus Verse Account); it continues into the Hellenistic period in the form of the Dynastic "prophecy" published by A.K. Grayson in his *Babylonian Historical-Literary Texts* (Toronto Semitic Studies 3), Toronto: University of Toronto Press, 1975, pp. 13–37.

38. See R.F. Hardin, *Civil Idolatry: Desacralizing and Monarchy in Spenser, Shakespeare, and Milton*, Cranbury, NJ: Associated University Press, 1992; R.H. Wells, *Shakespeare on*

Masculinity, Cambridge: Cambridge University Press, 2000. Given Shakespeare's extensive familiarity with biblical literature, these continuities between his work and the book of Samuel are likely due, at least in part, to direct influence; see S. Marx, *Shakespeare and the Bible*, Oxford: Oxford University Press, 2000.

39. To quote the poet Pinsky once again on David as an incomparable literary figure representing *human life*: "Nor to go down as a grizzled warrior like Beowulf charging into the cold twilight a final time to kill and die for his people. Lear may have been a beautiful boy once, but that is left to idle imagining – in the neverland where we are free to imagine Romeo and Juliet, had things gone differently, as a mellow old couple. Not for David the avenging self-destruction of Samson, nor the conclusive Pisgah vision of Moses, who is seen from childhood to old age but not in fulfillment. David's drama is that of a life entire. David in his faults and attainments, his losses and victories, embodies on a scale almost beyond imagining the action of *living a life*" (*Life of David*, pp. 178–179; italics in original). For a similar perspective in scholarly research on the David account, see J.W. Whedbee, "On Divine and Human Bonds: The Tragedy of the House of David," in G. Tucker, D. Peterson and R. Wilson (Eds.), *Canon, Theology, and Old Testament Interpretation: Essays in Honor of Brevard S. Childs*, Philadelphia: Fortress Press, 1988, pp. 147–165.

40. "Here your brother won a victory, but there you lie among women! Now, when you march with your army to Qatna, be a man [*lu-ú a-wi-la-at*]. As your brother has 'established a great name' [*šu-ma-am ra-bé-e-em iš-ta-ak-nu*], you also in your region 'establish a great name'" (*Archives royales de Mari, vol. 1. Correspondance de Šamši-Addu et de ses fils* [Ed. G. Dossin], Paris: P. Geuthner, 1950 – text: 69, rev. 8–16).

41. Even some leading rabbinic traditions exonerate David in this respect, claiming that Uriah had given Bathsheba a bill of divorce in keeping with the custom of soldiers going to war, the depicted scenario would seem to be proscribed by the Deuteronomic (levirate) provisions for fallen soldier in order that their names would not be "blotted out." See discussion of the Deuteronomic laws in J.L. Wright, "Making a Name for Oneself: Masculinity, Martial Valor and Procreation in Ancient Israel," *Journal for the Study of the Old Testament* 36, 2011, pp. 128–145.

42. Although the seventh-century BCE "Lachish Ostraca" witness to the use of writing as a medium of communication among commanders in wartime, the absence of an explicit reference to letters in the older account (2 Samuel 11:1, 12:26–31; see especially 12:27) raises the question why letters are mentioned in the episode with Uriah. The reason is likely only indirectly related to rise of literacy in eighth-century Judah and must be appreciated as being more immediately motivated by literary objectives; see J. Fokkelman, *Narrative Art and Poetry in the Books of Samuel, Volume One: King David*, Assen: Van Gorcum, 1990, p. 60. The most exhaustive study of correspondence in the account of David's Ammonite campaign was undertaken by T. Schaack, *Die Ungeduld des Papiers* (BZAW 262), Berlin: De Gruyter, 1998. It however does not consider the important "behind-the-scenes" aspect of the use of letters that I have described here. The same goes for other important and otherwise sensitive literary analyses such as R. Alter, *The Art of Biblical Narrative*, New York: Basic Books, 1981; M. Sternberg, *The Poetics of Biblical Narrative*, Bloomington: Indiana University Press, 1987; and R.C. Bailey, *David in Love and War*, Sheffield: Sheffield Academic Press, 1990.

43. B. Levinson, "The Reconceptualization of Kingship in Deuteronomy and the Deuteronomistic History's Transformation of Torah," *Vetus Testamentum* 51, 2001, pp. 511–534; idem, "The First Constitution: Rethinking the Origins of Rule of Law and Separation of Powers in Light of Deuteronomy," *Cardozo Law Review* 27, 2006, pp. 1853–1888. Compare also how the biblical authors portray kings submitting themselves to the authority of texts that they seek-and-find; see 2 Kings 22–23 and the book of Ezra-Nehemiah. See C. Grottanelli, *Kings and Prophets: Monarchic Power, Inspired Leadership and Sacred Text in Biblical Narrative*, New York: Oxford University Press, 1999;

J.L. Wright, "Seeking, Finding and Writing in Ezra-Nehemiah," in M. Boda and P. Reddit (Eds.), *The (Dis-)Unity of Ezra-Nehemiah*, Sheffield: Sheffield Phoenix Press, 2008, pp. 277–304; and most recently J. Ben-Dov, "Writing as Oracle and as Law: New Contexts for the Book-Find of King Josiah," in *Journal of Biblical Literature* 127, 2008, pp. 223–239.

44. For a similar phenomenon in royal inscriptions, see Franke, *Konigsinschriften*, p. 250. Nevertheless, the name of the king in official state inscriptions comes closest to the descriptions of the deity's name in biblical literature. A parade example of such name-glorification is found in the Victory Stele of Piye quoted above.

45. The discourse on "salvation" and "rescuing" in Judges and Samuel is highly developed and directly related to the institution of kingship; see Wright, "A Book-Oriented Approach."

46. The male ruler's potency of producing a namesake and claiming victory on the battlefield is closely related to the erection of steles, monuments, temples and other forms of monumental architecture to commemorate one's name. See the letter from Shamshi-Adad quoted in the introduction, which combines all three aspects (son, triumph, victory stele) under the rubric of being a man. According to ANE convention, a ruler undertook such building projects following successful military campaigns in tribute and honor to the deity. In keeping with this convention, the author of 2 Samuel 7 dates the promise to the time after David's great conquests (see v. 1). The king's declared intention is to build a house for the ark and *name* (vv. 13, 23, 26) of the deity. Yet the close association between the name of David (v. 9) and that of the deity is unmistakable and would have been intuitively perceived by ancient readers. In hundreds of building inscriptions throughout the ANE, a figure commemorates and perpetuates *his own name* by commissioning (or donating funds for) the construction of a temple to honor *the name of his divine patron*. See also the admonition in the Egyptian Instructions of Merikare (Papyrus St.Petersburg 1116A): "Construct [fine] monuments for the god, for it means the perpetuation of the name of whoever does it" (108–109). The most recent translation is that of R. B. Parkinson, *The Tale of Sinuhe and Other Ancient Egyptian Poems, 1940–1640 BC*, Oxford: Oxford University Press, 1997, pp. 212–234.

47. In Genesis 12 the deity commands Abram to abandon his country and his father's house for a new land where the deity would bless him and "magnify/enlarge [his] name." Aside from referring to the expansion of his name to "Abraham," the statement can mean both that he would become renowned and that his descendants would be numerous. What connects the promise to 2 Samuel 7 is the presentation of the deity as granting progeny and prosperity instead of these great men making names for themselves independently (the macho ideal of pulling oneself up by one's own bootstraps). The promise made to the patriarch necessarily precedes that made to the king because it *produces* Israel, while the second promise produces the royal line that should *protect* Israel from its enemies. Given this bifurcation, it is not surprising that Abraham's great name is established, in contrast to David's, in a non-martial, procreative manner. For a similar comparison between David and Abraham in relation to procreation and martial power, see the discussion of the *midrashim* related to King Og in Wright, "Making a Name for Oneself."

48. Furthermore, the book presents those who are fated for positions of leadership, such as Abimelech (genealogically) and Samson (by virtue of his physical might), as the most problematic figures. Power is also synergistic in nature, not only through human collaboration but also through the divine spirit that seizes the warrior directly before deeds of valor. In the case of Gideon, victory is rendered miraculous by transforming the hero from a great warrior into the least likely candidate (compare 6:15 with 6:12, 14, 27, 7:14, etc.) and reducing his forces both in size and military experience (7:2–7). Insofar as these texts often treat the body politic in terms of the human body, they are eminently relevant to the study of masculinity and manhood.

49. See J.E. Fossum, *The Name of God and the Angel of the Lord. Samaritan and Jewish Concepts of Intermediation and the Origin of Gnosticism* (Wissenschaftliche Untersuchungen zum Neuen Testament 36), Tübingen: JCB Mohr [Paul Siebeck], 1985.

50. As most European states have already abolished compulsory military service or are in the midst of doing so, Israel remains firmly committed to its citizen military force. On the origins and importance of citizen armies in the Hebrew Bible, see my study of war in ancient Israel, forthcoming in 2011 with Oxford University Press.

51. M. Lorberbaum, *Politics and the Limits of Law: Secularizing the Political in Medieval Jewish Thought*, Stanford: Stanford University Press, 2001. With respect to narrative as source for the creation of law, see S.L. Stone, "On the Interplay of Rules, 'Cases' and Concepts in Rabbinic Legal Literature: Another Look at the Aggadot of Ḥoni the Circle Drawer," *Dinei Israel* 24, 2007, pp. 125–155.

6 Civil war in the Bible

An unsolved problem

Amnon Shapira

Introduction – "prohibited wars" in the Bible

At an international conference held in Jerusalem in 1993 sponsored by the Ethicon Institute of California, Michael Walzer[1] claimed that Jewish political tradition knows only two categories of war: "Commanded War" (war that is divinely commanded be waged) and "Permitted War" (war that is permissible – using the terminology of Rabbinic literature), but lacks a third category of war which is improper or forbidden.[2] In response a number of essays were published, in which it was claimed that from the time of the Talmud (compiled in the third to the sixth centuries CE) through the present, *halakhah* (Jewish law) has indeed developed important principles of "Prohibited Wars."[3] On the basis of this discussion I devoted the fifth chapter of my book, *Democratic Values in the Hebrew Bible*, to a series of limitations I found in the Bible on conducting war.[4]

In the book I showed that, on the one hand, there is a systematic stance depicting a positive attitude to war throughout all the books of the Bible, especially in the early period of the conquest and settlement of the Land, as can be seen, for example, from the request of the Israelites for a king, and the agreement of Samuel and God to this request: ". . . we shall have a king over us . . . (who will) go out before us, and fight our battles" (1 Samuel 8:20). This particular instance is well known and requires no further expansion. But I wish to examine whether or not the opposite trend, of negating, preventing or limiting war, exists in the Bible as well.[5] After a comprehensive survey of biblical literature, I was able to give a positive answer to this question, and I divided the tens of examples that I found in the Bible into eight categories:

i)   requests for peace[6] and symbols of peace (such as the altar "over which a sword shall not be waved")[7] as moderating war;

ii) the paradox of agreement to war as a legal norm on the one hand, together with opposition in principle to any bloodshed on the other (such as the prohibition placed on David to build the Temple, because he had initiated many wars and shed much blood);[8]

iii) moral values that diminish the risk of war (such as the prohibition against breaching an earlier treaty with a foreign country);[9]

iv) a total ban on war against the peoples of certain neighboring lands, which had already been given by God to them (such as Moab and Ammon);[10]
v)   some of the laws of war (such as the prohibition against harming "a beautiful woman,"[11] or "destroying" trees in the course of a war);[12]
vi) the "ethical code" of war (such as the prohibition against harming the weak, that are not participating in the war);[13]
vii) the affinity that exists, according to the Bible, between military victory in war and the purity of motivation of the leadership and the people;[14] and
viii) moving from reality to utopia, the ultimate total elimination of all war from the world in the future ("nation shall not lift up sword against nation, neither shall they learn war any more").[15]

My conclusions from that comprehensive treatment of the subject there were as follows:

a) According to the Bible, the purpose of the Children of Israel on entering their land was to establish there a rural religious life for the people as a nation that maintained the laws of its Torah. When the period of conquering and settling the land came to an end, so also ended the period of war, and there were no plans for war as a political or theological objective.
b) From the sources in question it emerges that the Bible should not be regarded as a militaristic document that promotes the setting out to war and regards this as a norm. On the contrary, an attentive ear can hear in it the dominant voices claiming that even if there is an essential need for war, as part of the harsh human condition (primarily the wars to conquer and settle the land), it is best that it is restricted by a series of laws and rules. Therefore, it would seem, alongside the trend making certain types of war mandatory, there exists in the Bible a trend to limit war and even to eliminate it completely.
c) These conclusions, with all their theological significance, are totally different from what is known to us both from Ancient Near Eastern literature (in which there is full justification of war and of its being waged for ever), and from new theological interpretations of the Bible.

I have further claimed, with general reference to the moral aspect of war in the Bible, that, on the one hand, the Bible does not contain any message of pacifism (which has its origins in early Christianity)[16] and, on the other, neither does it contain any message of long-term "holy war"[17] of the *Jihad* type.[18] As regards Ancient Near Eastern literature: in all the anthologies of ancient laws that have so far been discovered (such as the Hammurabi Code, the laws of Neo-Babylonia, the laws of Eshnunna, the Hittite laws and the Lipit-Ishtar Code) not one single law has been found that limits soldiers in time of war (excluding a single case of moral claim as an early declaration before starting a war). To the best of my knowledge, the Bible is the first source in ancient world history that lays down a set of legal limitations that have a moral dimension relating to the conducting of war by an army. Therefore, despite the preliminary impression that emerges from the Bible, that it not only condones extended wars but even requires them, one can point to an opposite trend that exists in it simultaneously, of extensive moral limitations on war.

The problematic attitude of the Bible towards civil wars

When using the term "civil war" I am referring to war between two political camps among the Israelites, primarily between the Kingdom of Judah in the south and the Kingdom of Israel in the north. The Bible generally relates these internal wars, in which many thousands were killed on both sides, with few details and no criticism. This absence of criticism poses a very difficult theological problem. Below is a rough sampling that indicates the scope of the events described:

- "Now there was a long war between the house of Saul and the house of David; and David waxed stronger and stronger, but the house of Saul waxed weaker and weaker" (2 Samuel 3:1).
- "Now there was war between Rehoboam and Jeroboam all the days of his life" (1 Kings 15:6).
- "And there was war between Abijam [the son of Rehoboam] and Jeroboam" (1 Kings 15:7).
- "And there was war between Asa [king of Judah] and Baasa, king of Israel all their days" (1 Kings 15:16).
- "Now the rest of the acts of Joash [king of Israel], and all that he did, and his might[19] wherewith he fought against Amaziah king of Judah" (2 Kings 13:12).
- "For Pekah the son of Remaliah slew in Judah a hundred and twenty thousand in one day, all of them men of valor" (2 Chronicles 28:6).

A particularly difficult and extraordinary episode is when a king of Israel, in cooperation with a foreign king, fights against the king of Judah:

- " Then Rezin, king of Aram and Pekah son of Remaliah king of Israel came up to Jerusalem to war; and they besieged Ahaz" (2 Kings 16:5).

All this is in addition to Absalom's revolt, which was also a form of civil war, with its thousands of victims (2 Samuel 18:7); and the revolt of Sheba son of Bichri (2 Samuel 20). There were also cases of the total slaughter of all the members of one royal family by its opponents from Judah or from Israel, such as the murder of all the house of Jeroboam ("he left not to Jeroboam any that breathed," 1 Kings 15:29); the murder of the house of Baasha ("he left him not a single male," 1 Kings 16:11); the slaying of the royal family by Jehoram king of Judah ("he slew all his brethren with the sword, and also some of the princes of Israel," 2 Chronicles 21:4); the destruction of Tirzah ("and burned the king's house over him with fire," 1 Kings 16:18); the slaughter of seventy sons of the king and the sending of "their heads in baskets" to Jezreel on Ahab's order (2 Kings 10:7); the slaughter of all the house of Ahaziah king of Judah ("even two and forty men; neither left he any of them," 2 Kings 10:14) and more.

The above events teach us that the history of the First Temple Period, as described in the Bible, was fraught with extended internecine conflict between Judah and Israel in which a great number of people, thousands, it would seem, were killed on both sides. The fighting began in the days of Saul and David (around the end of the eleventh century BCE) and continued until the time of Pekah the son of Remaliah king of Israel (the second half of the eighth century BCE, just prior to the destruction of the northern kingdom); these civil wars, therefore, covered a period of approximately 250 years.[20]

The vast majority of these wars are described without any sort of moral criticism by either the prophets or the authors of the Bible, its writers and redactors. This is extremely surprising. These prophets, who unleashed blistering criticism against rulers and kings for a long line of moral transgressions – idol worship, exploitation, robbing the poor, shedding innocent blood (on the individual level) – for some reason ignored this gravest and most serious of phenomena from an ethical and moral point of view – the murder and slaughter of thousands of human beings in these internecine wars. What was the reason for this silence? In one place the death of no less that "five hundred thousand picked men" (2 Chronicles 13:17) who were killed in just one civil war between the men of Judah and the men of Israel is mentioned. Even assuming that the numbers are exaggerated, as they most certainly are, and need to be understood symbolically,[21] we still have to deal with the writers who wrote the stories and the redactors who edited the books, and inquire how it is that they copied these stories without even a hint of criticism.

Reservations regarding "civil wars"

There are, however, a few voices to be heard that express reservations regarding civil wars. However, these few voices criticize only the specific event in question, but not the concept of civil war itself for what it is, not civil wars in principle, as in the following examples:

> But the word of God came . . . saying: Speak unto Rehoboam . . . and unto all the house of Judah and Benjamin, and to the rest of the people, saying: Thus said the Lord: Ye shall not go up, nor fight against your brethren the children of Israel; return every man to his house; for this thing is of Me. So they hearkened unto the word of the Lord, and returned and went their way, according to the word of the Lord.
>
> (1 Kings 12:22–24)

This episode tells of a civil war that was prevented after the division of Israel and Judah, by the influence of the word of God, through the mouth of Shemaiah the prophet. However the opposition to the war was at a local, specific level and not as a matter of general principle.

> Then Abner called to Joab and said: Shall the sword devour for ever? . . .
> how long will it be before you bid your people return from the pursuit of
> their brethren? And Joab said: As God lives, if thou had not spoken, surely
> the men would have given up the pursuit of their brethren in the morning.
> So Joab blew the trumpet; and all the men stopped, and pursued Israel no
> more, nor did they fight any more.
>
> (2 Samuel 2:26–28)

In this story we see the stopping of a civil war that was already taking place.
There are scholars who interpret the rhetorical language used by Abner and Joab
as nothing more than military negotiations,[22] while others distinguish, rightly in
my opinion, signs of moral apprehension of civil war. These include Smith, who
regarded Abner's words as a direct expression of awareness of the "common blood"
of the "brethren" who were fighting each other.[23] The brotherhood (the expression
"brethren" occurs twice) between the two camps strengthened the feeling that
there was no point to this war ("Shall the sword devour for ever?").

> Then a wise woman called from the city [Abel-beth-maacah] . . . to Joab:
> . . . I am one of those who is peaceable and faithful in Israel; you seek to
> destroy a city which is a mother in Israel; why will you swallow up the
> inheritance of the Lord? Joab answered and said: Far be it from me, far be
> it that I should swallow up or destroy. That is not true . . . Give him up alone
> [Sheba son of Bichri] and I will withdraw from the city . . . And they cut off
> the head of Sheba son of Bichri . . . So he [Joab] blew the trumpet, and they
> dispersed from the city, every man to his home.
>
> (2 Samuel 20:16–22)

We have here another example of the prevention of civil war. This time the
argument is that "a city which is a mother in Israel" will be destroyed. This
expression of the wise woman is a *hapax legomenon* in the Bible, and also serves as
a "concentric structure" in the story of the revolt.[24]

The "concentric structure" (or "chiastic pattern") motive is important from a
literary and a theological point of view. Here N. Klaus, who sees in the story of
the revolt of Sheba the son of Bichri a complex centric structure whose climax is
in the verse: "you seek to destroy a city which is a mother in Israel." According
to the theory of the "centric structure," the peak is the heart of the story.[25] Hence
the abovementioned verse, which protests against the anticipated cruel outcome
of a civil war, clearly teaches the sensitivity of the Bible toward civil war, and its
opposition to civil war altogether.[26] This event is almost the only one in the Bible
where there is a dimension of principle opposition to internal warring.

Additionally, the double expression: " 'Far be it . . . far be it" spoken by Joab,
meant to express vigorous opposition to destroying a city of Israel, is also a *hapax
legomenon*, while the expression "the inheritance of the Lord" occurs very rarely.
This unique expression shows clearly that Joab's planned response to slay the
inhabitants of a city of Israel, was regarded in practice as extraordinary and that
the biblical author does not accept it:

The rebuking of Joab [by the wise woman] is based on an ancient law, that the besieger must first go to the gate of the city, to conduct negotiations and to call the city to make peace, and only afterwards [if negotiations fail] to engage in battle to the bitter end. If this was the case as regards enemy cities, how much more so was it proper to start by opening negotiations, when we speak of [. . .] those who are peaceable and faithful in Israel.[27]

From these examples it can be concluded that there are some voices that negate specific wars. These voices have support from some scholars. So D. Elgavish persistently claims that even if there was no prohibition in principle on civil wars, there was indeed a general phenomenon of restraint in the wars between Judah and Israel; restraint that was expressed primarily in two spheres: in the military sphere and in the political sphere. In the military sphere there is evidence of the infrequency of the wars; of wars against soldiers and not against settlements; of fighting using indirect strategies so as to reduce the damage caused. In the political sphere there is evidence of the moderating effect of public opinion on the war and of limited political objectives of wars.[28]

According to Elgavish, this restraint stems from the estimation (that does not always get the attention it merits in the commentaries and in research) that "the united monarchy of the People of Israel was divided into two states but not into two peoples,"[29] and he summarizes another of his studies as follows: the wars between Israel and Judah "had limited objectives that had been set in advance, and during the course of the wars both sides acted with considerable restraint. Israel and Judah had indeed been divided into two kingdoms, but the common sense of brotherhood among the people continued to accompany them in the wars as in peacetime."[30] Even if his conclusions are found to be reasonable, the phenomenon of civil war was still widespread, and the ongoing silence of the Bible on this subject continues to remain an enigma.

Civil wars: between the tribal period and the period of the monarchy

Though it can be claimed that all of the civil wars described in the Bible took place during the Monarchial Period, this claim needs to be examined in the light of the extensive war that is related at the end of the book of Judges (chapters 20–21), in the story of "the Concubine at Gibeah," regarded by many as a full-fledged civil war.[31]

It is worthwhile re-reading this tragic story, which is indeed described as a grim matter, but also as an exceptional and unanticipated event. The man, it will be recalled, refused the suggestion of his servant to spend the night in the town of Jebus, saying "We will not turn aside into the city of foreigners, who do not belong to the people of Israel" (Judges 19:12). It emerges from this casual remark that the social norms that were prevalent then in the cities of Israel were those of order and personal security. That the atrocity that was to occur was itself very exceptional is further accentuated by the comment: "And all who saw it said: Such a thing has never happened or been seen from the day that the people of Israel came up out of the land of Egypt until this day; consider it, take counsel, and speak" (Judges 19:30).[32]

The behavior of "all the community" in this case should be seen as positive, even exemplary. This was no "civil war," but rather an action meant to punish the criminal act committed by the men of Benjamin. The Israelites were emulating the actions of Moses who acted harshly against groups of sinners, causing the death of many people (such as in the story of the golden calf in Exodus 32). These acts are never described in the Bible negatively as a "civil war," but rather positively as the extermination of evil from among the Children of Israel. The same is true for the end of the book of Judges: despite the definition of this act as "civil war" that has been accepted in scholarship, this was no "civil war," but rather a general, national effort to punish the members of one of the tribes, the tribe of Benjamin, who had supported the atrocity committed against the concubine at Gibeah.

The story of the Concubine at Gibeah teaches us something about the unity of the people at this time. Nowhere else in the entire Bible do we see such constructive national unity as we do here. In the last two chapters of Judges (20–21) there occurs a concentration of collective terms referring to the people of Israel, rare in its power: "all the community," "the community as one person," "all of Israel," "as one person," "all the people," "all the people as one person," "the chiefs of all the people," "the assembly of the people of God," "the community" (×2), "every man of Israel" (×2), "tribes of Israel" (×2), "all the people of Israel" (×3), "all the tribes of Israel" (×3), "the people" (×7), "men of Israel" (×10), "people of Israel" (×17); a total of over sixty occurrences of epithets of a collective nature, which indicate explicitly that this was a general, national positive effort against one isolated and sinful tribe. So it is not right to refer to this event as a "civil war," and it should be referred to positively as a national punishment meted out on a recalcitrant tribe.[33] And so the story of the Concubine at Gibeah is not relevant to the subject in question, that of "civil wars."

Prisoners-of-war and slavery

The problem of the silence of the Bible on the question of civil war, acquires, it would seem, some reinforcement from the story of the prisoners in 2 Chronicles 28:5–15. The story describes a civil war which involved the capture and enslavement of the defeated men of Judah by the victorious northern Israelites. The writer demands that this should not be done, as emerges from the words of the prophet Oded and also from the reaction of the people of the Kingdom of Israel to his words:

> And now you intend to subjugate the people of Judah and Jerusalem, male and female, as your slaves? Now hear me therefore, and send back the captives from your kinsfolk who you have taken, for the fierce wrath of the Lord is upon you. And the men rose . . . and took the captives, and with the spoil clothed all that were naked among them; they clothed them, gave

them sandals, provided them with food and drink, and anointed them; and carried all the feeble among them on asses, and brought them to their kinsfolk at Jericho, the city of palm trees.

(2 Chronicles 28:10–15)

"The scale of this humanitarian act"[34] described here is especially prominent against the background of the cruelty which conquerors usually meted out to their enemies, as is described in the Bible and in other sources.[35] On the other hand, as is related here, after a civil war between Judah and Israel, the men of Israel waived their rights as victors in the war, and after having released all the prisoners also made sure to replenish anything that the prisoners had lost and returned them peaceably to their kinsfolk, the Judahites.[36]

The enslavement of Israelite captives by their brethren at the end of the First Temple Period is also mentioned in Jeremiah 34:6–22, though there it occurred as a result of the social situation and not of war, and the prophet opposes this behavior and attacks it vehemently.

This critical attitude of the Bible towards internal slavery is understandable, but it only reinforces our basic question: slavery is of course a negative phenomenon that should be rejected – but surely the killing of thousands in civil war is something far, far worse? We have already stated above that in another story this same book of Chronicles mentions the death of "five hundred thousand picked men" in civil war without expressing any criticism! While harsh criticism is laid in the case of the prisoners-of-war – that it is not right to capture prisoners of the men of Judah – the killing of thousands of them would seem to be of little account.[37] This dissonance remains a mystery, and I see it as one of the major enigmas of biblical theology.

Perhaps, as a supposition, I can offer the following thesis: "civil wars" in the Bible, which are wars of ruling dynasties that fought each other (such as the House of David versus the House of Saul) or of one part of the people against the other (primarily Judahites against the people of northern Israel) took place, as is related, during the Monarchial Period, and so it may be claimed that the wars are the direct result of the monarchy and of the rule of kings. Power itself leads to belligerence for its own sake ("power corrupts").

I have devoted much space to this subject in my book on Early Democracy in the Bible, particularly in Chapter 10, in which I developed the thesis that the centralized monarchical rule corrupts itself in the end and is condemned to self-extinction.[38] Though two events of civil bloodshed are described in the tribal period (the assassination of Abimelech and his seventy brothers, which included the killing of "about a thousand men and women" in the Tower of Shechem [Judges 9]; and the war of the men of Ephraim against the men of Gilead [Judges 12], an event whose tragic outcome was the "slaughter" of 42,000 men), these two events, atrocious though they might have been in themselves, were sporadic, once-only, local events.[39] The monarchy turned civil wars into a part of the monarchic system of government, which were waged systematically, consistently and extensively throughout almost all the years of the monarchy.

However the question remains open: one can perhaps understand the reasons for the actual occurrence of many civil wars in Iron-Age Israel, as this was the standard norm in the aggressive and violent culture of government in the ancient world, and the desire of Israel to liken itself to that world ("that we also may be like all the nations," in the context of the request for a king, 1 Samuel 8:20); but the fact that the Bible and its great prophets are silent on the moral implications of the issue leaves us with the question: why did they not negate these ongoing occurrences with the same raging anger with which they negated other, very much less severe, phenomena?

Notes

1. Who was defined by Aviezer Ravitzky as "The Senior Theorist of the Ethics of Warfare"; A. Ravitzky, *Freedom Inscribed – Diverse Voices of the Jewish Religious Thought*, Tel Aviv: Am Oved, 1999, p. 139 (Hebrew).
2. M. Walzer, "War and Peace in the Jewish Tradition," in T. Nadrin (Ed.), *The Ethics of War and Peace: Religious and Secular Perspectives*, Princeton: Princeton University Press: 1996, pp. 95–114.
3. For one example see A. Ravitzky, "Prohibited War in Jewish Tradition," in Nadrin, ibid., pp. 115–127. Some of the questions that are addressed in various halakhic sources are: Is there an enemy against whom one should not declare war? What are the purposes for which it is permissible to wage war? Is it permissible to wage war regardless of the number of potential victims?
4. A part of this article was based on my book: A. Shapira, *Democratic Values in the Hebrew Bible*, Tel Aviv: Hakibbutz Hameuchad, 2009, pp. 143–186 (Hebrew).
5. In recent years there has been a huge increase in the discussion and publications emanating from the "Yeshivot Hesder" in Israel (rabbinic seminaries that combine traditional religious Jewish studies with military service), especially in discussing ethical questions of war. A good example of such a book is: E. Bloom *et al.* (Eds.), *Values in the Trial of War: Ethics and War in the View of Judaism*, Jerusalem: The Mizrahi Family and Moreshet Publishers, 1985 (Hebrew), which includes chapters such as "War and Morality," "Military Command versus Values," and so on. The issue has also been discussed in rabbinic circles in the US: R. Kimelman, "Non-Violence in the Talmud," *Judaism* 17, 1968, pp. 316–334; D. Bleich, "Preemptive War in Jewish Law," *Tradition* 21, 1983, pp. 3–41. See also: T. R. Hobbs, *A Time for War: A Study of Warfare in the Old Testament*, Wilmington: Glazier, 1989; P. C. Craigie, *The Problem of War in the Old Testament*, Grand Rapids: Eerdmans, 1978.
6. See Deuteronomy 20:10.
7. Exodus 20:25.
8. 1 Chronicles 22:7–10.
9. As in the case of the Gibeonites (Joshua 9).
10. Deuteronomy 2:2–6; 9.
11. Deuteronomy 21:10–14.
12. Deuteronomy 20:9.
13. Deuteronomy 25:7–18.
14. Such as in the cases of Achan (Joshua 7:1) and of Ahab (1 Kings 21:19).
15. Isaiah 2; Micah 4.
16. As derives from "The Sermon on the Mount," in Matthew 5: 38–44.
17. According to G. von Rad, the "Holy War" (*Heilige Krieg*) was a cultic institution, accompanied by purification and other ritual sacred practices. See: G. von Rad, *Holy War in Ancient Israel* (trans. and Ed. M. J. Dawn), Grand Rapids: Eerdmans, 1991, pp. 41–51. Since a clear memory of this institution in the Bible has not remained,

von Rad speculated that the biblical stories about ancient wars (mainly from the settlement period), were written only after that "Holy War" was no longer practiced. This theory is important, but not sufficiently realized, and some scholars think that "most of the ideas on this matter are only speculation" – see J. Licht, "War," in B. Mazar and others (Eds.), *Encyclopaedia Biblica*, Vol. 4, Jerusalem: Bialik, 1962, p. 1061 (Hebrew).

18. See E. Tyan, "Djihad," in H. A. R. Gibb and others (Eds.), *The Encyclopaedia of Islam*, Vol. 2, Leiden: E. J. Brill, 1983, pp. 538–540.

19. The evaluation of the biblical text of the wars of Joash, the king of Israel, against the king of Judah, with the very positive expression: "heroism" (*gebūratô*), intensifies our question here.

20. See H. Tadmor, "Chronology," in B. Mazar and others (Eds.), *Encyclopaedia Biblica* Vol. 4, Jerusalem: Bialik, 1962, pp. 261–262 (Hebrew).

21. See M. Bar Ilan, *Genesis' Numerology*, Rehovot: Association for Jewish Astrology and Numerology, 2003; idem, *Biblical Numerology*, Rehovot: Association for Jewish Astrology and Numerology, 2005; as to the exaggerated number of the dead soldiers in wars see ibid., p. 102, n. 174.

22. A. Anderson, *2 Samuel* (WBC), Waco: Word, 1984, p. 45.

23. H. P. Smith, *Critical and Exegetical Commentary on the Books of Samuel* (ICC), Edinburgh: T&T Clark, 1969, p. 272.

24. "Chiastic patterns" (a-b-b-a) are well known in biblical research, as are triple chiastic patterns (a-b-c-c-b-a; for example, "sheds – blood – human, human – blood – shed" ("Whoever sheds human blood, for that human shall his blood be shed," Genesis 9:6). A larger chiastic structure is called a "concentric structure" (a-b-c-d-e-e-d-c-b-a). The important interpretive aspect of the "concentric structure" is that its center point, the peak of its literary structure, is also its ideological or theological center. In many cases, recognizing this literary strategy completely changes the understanding of the biblical text; as shown, for example, by J. P. Fokkelman in his various studies (such as *Narrative Art in Genesis: Specimens of Stylistic and Structural Analysis*, Amsterdam: Van Gorcum 1975).

25. A thesis that he developed in his doctoral dissertation, published as N. Klaus, *Pivot Patterns in the Former Prophets*, Sheffield: Sheffield Academic Press, 1999.

26. See N. Klaus, *2 Samuel* (Olam Ha-Tanakh), Tel Aviv: Sifrei Hemed, 2007, pp. 156–157 (Hebrew).

27. See M. Garsiel, *2 Samuel* (Olam Ha-Tanakh), Tel Aviv: Sifrei Hemed, 2007, p. 159 (Hebrew).

28. D. Elgavish, "Restraint in the Wars between Israel and Judah," in Z. H. Erlich and Y. Eshel (Eds.), *Judea and Samaria Research Studies: Proceedings of the 4th Annual Meeting – 1994*, Kedumim – Ariel: The College of Judea and Samaria, 1995, pp. 59–68 (Hebrew with English abstract).

29. Ibid., p. 65.

30. D. Elgavish, "War and Peace in the Relationships of Israel and Juda," M.A. thesis, Bar-Ilan University, Ramat Gan, 1978, p. 183.

31. See Shapira, *Democratic Values in the Hebrew Bible*, chapter 8: "'And in those days there was no king in Israel; everyone did as he pleased' (Judges 21:25) – Is This Anarchism?" pp. 240–260.

32. It is strange that this sharp expression, indicating the phenomenon as being extremely unusual, has not been seriously considered in scholarship.

33. As Yaira Amit wrote: "the tribal function described in the case of the Battle of Gibeah indicate that in the Judges' period, there had been public order . . . and there was law and order"; *The Book of Judges: The Art of Editing* (The Biblical Encyclopedia Library), Jerusalem – Tel Aviv: Bialik, 1992, pp. 312–313 (Hebrew). See also the English version: *The Book of Judges: The Art of Editing*, Leiden – Boston – Koln: Brill, 1998.

34. N. Avraam, *2 Chronicles* (Olam Ha-Tanakh), Tel Aviv: Sifrei Hemed, 1995, p. 218 (Hebrew).

88   *Amnon Shapira*

35. As an example see the way that David acted in the countries that he conquered: "He let out the people who lived there and set them to work with saws, iron threshing boards, and iron axes . . . David did this to all the cities of Ammon" (2 Samuel 12:31). For the harsh cruelties that Ashurnasirpal II (859–883 BCE) committed towards the peoples that he conquered, see H. Tadmor, "Mesopotamia," in B. Mazar (Ed.), *Encyclopaedia Biblica*, Vol. 5, Jerusalem: Bialik, 1958, pp. 88–89 (Hebrew). The unnecessary prisoners ("in the excess of the need") were executed in public. The number of these during the eighteen early years of his reign came to 30,000.

36. Mishnah *Sotah* 8:1 regards this event as depicted in 2 Chronicles 28 as a very positive example for future generations, and determined that "the priest anointed for war" should read this story aloud to the soldiers before every war as part of the ceremony described in Deuteronomy 20:2–4, and to point out that the nations of the world do not treat the people of Israel with the same brotherhood as the soldiers of Israel treated the soldiers of Judah in that war, and so they should do their uttermost to be victorious in battle.

37. If we compare the civil wars in the Bible to the American Civil War (1861–65), during which over 600,000 people were killed on both sides, my argument is twofold: the American Civil War was at least officially justified because of clear principles: both the relationship between the federal government and the southern states and a clear moral reason: the relationship to slavery. On the other hand, the silence of the Bible about the cause of most, perhaps all, of the inter-Israelite wars leads us to assume that there was no ethical or moral reason, but simple aggressiveness of the governments involved.

38. Shapira, *Democratic Values in the Hebrew Bible*, pp. 273–305.

39. As noted, the "Gibeah" war (Judges 20) was not a "civil war," but the punishment of a stubborn-rebellious tribe by the rest of the people.

7 Internecine wars in biblical Israel

Meir Bar-Ilan

One of the well-known "truths" of history is that every nation, at one time or another in its history, has suffered the horror of internal armed struggle. Such civil wars or any other type of internecine struggle between two branches of the same nation can be found easily in the historical annals of each and every nation, from the ancient Greeks through the Medieval English Wars of the Roses and all the way to such modern conflicts as the civil wars in the US, Spain and Lebanon. These and other such internal struggles are often characterized by members of nations, tribes and even families fighting their own flesh and blood.

However, in most written histories of the Jewish people, references to such internal struggles are rare. Very little has been written about wars between Jews, both in antiquity and in more recent times. Recent scholarship has practically ignored the subject, as if there is no evidence that such struggles ever took place.[1] This is strange in itself since, as we will see below, we do have quite a bit of evidence concerning this aspect of Jewish life in antiquity. It seems therefore that many of the historians who have written on this aspect of Jewish history are to an extent guilty of simply ignoring the facts.

It may be suspected that so far this aspect of Jewish history has been ignored, since the Jewish conception, so to speak, of Jewish historiography is based on the idea that the source of any disaster that befell the Jews must be external: be it Nebuchadnezzar, Titus, Hadrian or the Crusaders, they all were enemies of the Jews that caused pain and trouble. Disaster comes from the outside and thus there is no point in dwelling on Jewish self-killing. Salo Baron called this type of historiography "lachrymose"[2] and considered it to be typical of Jewish thought and thus a justification for the fact that Jewish historiography does not cover all aspects of Jewish life. In other words: it is better to mourn together and to encourage Jewish national unity than to give a balanced description of Jewish history, which includes a measure of self-criticism. A more moderate explanation is that writing about Jews who kill Jews seems not to be "politically correct" and historians are people who prefer to act according accepted norms and not to raise tough questions about "the spirit of Israel." Moreover, since already in antiquity the Jews, as a group, have often been accused, for religious reasons, of killing their own prophets,[3] modern historians have preferred not to raise such issues which, they feared, might cause trouble for contemporary Jewish communities; as such, the downplaying of this aspect of Jewish history could be considered a form of self-defense.

It is not my purpose to determine which of the above explanations is to be preferred. To me, it seems that all of them suffer from over-dogmatic thinking, as if they assume that all modern scholars of Jewish history were educated in the same school and share the same concerns. Furthermore, all of the above theories fail to acknowledge the sheer number of people, Jews and non-Jews alike, who are involved in modern Jewish historiography, representing many different schools of thought and methodologies. In my opinion, the main reason that the issue of Jewish internecine war has been all but ignored is far simpler: it is merely a result of the poor state of contemporary Jewish historiography. There is no conspiracy or bias involved; just not-quite mature historiography that is far from covering all aspects of Jewish life.

My suggestion here is that we put aside such theories and begin to discuss and to study the existing evidence that Jews, like any other nation, killed their brethren in bursts of internecine warfare. In this short paper I wish to begin by examining the evidence for such "civil wars" within the Hebrew Bible, in which one part of the nation of Israel fought the other. It should be added that the historical credibility of the biblical sources will not be discussed here. The sources used by the biblical authors, as well as their motivation, will stay in the shadows.

I. Before the monarchy

It is well known that the family life of many of the major characters of the biblical narrative is described as having been far from ideal. On the contrary, from the very beginning it is shown that "real life," as described in the Bible, is far from what we would consider "normative." First, Cain, one of the first children born in this world, kills his own brother Abel (Genesis 4:8). Later on, Esau attempts to kill his twin brother Jacob, who is forced to flee for his life (Genesis 27:41–45), and then the children of Jacob almost kill their brother Joseph, selling him into slavery instead (Genesis 37). Whatever the historical and literary sources of these stories may be, this is the way in which the biblical writers chose to present the origins of humanity in general and of the Israelite nation in particular. After such an "introduction," it is no wonder that the later history of Israel is filled with such struggles, many of which have escaped the attention of readers and scholars.

Moreover, in some cases of particularly severe religious sins the biblical narrators give full justification for killing the sinner. We can see this in the description of Moses' reaction to the golden calf (Exodus 32:27): "Thus said the Lord, God of Israel, put ye every man his sword upon his thigh, and go to and fro from gate to gate throughout the camp, and slay every man his brother, and every man his companion, and every man his neighbor." The same line of reasoning is applied in the case of Phinehas killing Zimri who had sexual relations with a Midianite woman in public, and because of that killing "the plague was stayed from the children of Israel" and Phinehas was praised with "a covenant of peace" (Numbers 25:7–13).

After Jephtah defeated the Ammonites he had to face accusations by the Ephraimites for not inviting them to join the war (Judges 12:1–6). This accusation led to a fight between Jephtah the Gileadite, from the tribe of Menasseh, and the Ephraimites, and the story ends with the killing 42,000 Ephraimites. Two questions arise from this episode:

1)   Did it happen as the text claims that it did?
2)   Were so many people really killed without any good reason?

Our assumption here is that the story is based on some actual event, even if it was embellished by the narrator. That is to say, it is highly probable that at some point during the pre-monarchial period, Menassites and Ephraimites fought and killed each other, even if not for the specific reason given by the narrator. Even if the specific story did not happen as told, it is based on a known reality of inter-tribal warfare. As for the second question, most modern historians assume that many of the numbers in the biblical text are somehow distorted and should thus not be considered historical.[4] According to the methodology presented here, the question of numbers should be treated apart from that of the historicity of the narrative itself. In many of the cases treated here, our assumption will be that there may well be a historical basis to the narratives themselves, even if the numbers are exaggerated. This rule of differentiation between the episode and the number of people involved will be used throughout this paper.

Judges 19–21 describes a case in which the town of Gibeah was destroyed and almost all the tribe of Benjamin exterminated because some of the townsmen had raped and killed the concubine of a Levite from Mount Ephraim. One may doubt the historicity of this story, especially in light of the similarities between this story and that of the "earlier" destruction of Sodom and Gomorrah (Genesis 19).[5] Without trying to explain these similarities and their meaning, as already done by many modern scholars, the differences between the stories should also be noted. The main difference between the fate of Gibeah and that of Sodom is that Sodom was devastated by the wrath of God in a miraculous way while Gibeah was destroyed by the wrath of men and the story is highly detailed with specific military tactics and numbers of those involved. In the first stage 400,000 Benjaminites killed 22,000 of the surrounding Israelite warriors. The next day 18,000 more were killed and only later 25,100 Benjaminites were killed, and so on throughout the narrative. This type of detail is exactly the opposite of what we see in the story of Sodom and Gomorrah. The main issue there, like in the Flood narrative in Genesis 6–7, is that of divine wrath – emphasizing the story's etiological nature. In the story of Gibeah the narrator focuses on the human nature of viciousness and how the city was destroyed by man, not by God. The story also shows similarities to that of the destruction of Shechem (Genesis 34) as well as to the siege of Troy: all three cities were annihilated because of a woman.[6] Moreover, the concept of demolishing a sinful city, albeit for the specific sin of idolatry, is stated in the Bible (Deuteronomy 13:1–19), illustrating the reality behind the story. Once again, the huge numbers of casualties should not be taken at face value but the bottom line is that the Gibeah story is evidence of internal Israelite warfare in the days before the establishment of the monarchy.

An additional case of fratricide that the biblical narrator describes in detail is that of Abimelech son of Jerubaal (Gideon). According to Judges 9:5, Abimelech "hired vain and light fellows" that killed his seventy brothers, sons of Jerubaal. Needless to say that seventy is a typological number that is not to be taken at face value. However our knowledge of many cases in other nations of royal heirs who killed their potential competitors gives credibility to the deeds of Abimelech. It seems that the pursuit of kingship can be used to justify any amount of killing.[7]

II. The monarchial age

Being a king means, inter alia, fighting against dissidents and rebels. Thus Saul attempted to kill David and David waged war against Ish-bosheth (2 Samuel 2:12–28), Sheba son of Bichri (2 Samuel 20) and his own son Absalom (2 Samuel 13).[8] No doubt, any king sees his crown as a justification for the killing of enemies of all sorts, including his own flesh and blood.

During the tenth to eighth centuries BCE two "twin" states ruled over the much of the Land of Israel: Israel and Judah. This is not the place to discuss the full range of issues concerning the relationship between the two kingdoms and their interaction with their various neighbors; what concerns us here is only the conflict between the two Israelite kingdoms. However, before we begin to deal with the two centuries of different kinds of wars between the two kingdoms, we wish to point out that there is only a single voice in the entire Bible that actually condemns all of this internecine bloodshed. Right at the beginning, just after telling how the northern tribes rebelled against Rehoboam son of Solomon and established the northern monarchy, the text reports the following:

> But the word of God came unto Shemaiah the man of God, saying: Speak unto Rehoboam the son of Solomon, king of Judah, and unto all the house of Judah and Benjamin, and to the rest of the people, saying: Thus said the Lord: Ye shall not go up, nor fight against your brethren the children of Israel; return every man to his house; for this thing is of me. So they hearkened unto the word of the Lord, and returned and went their way, according to the word of the Lord.
>
> (1 Kings 12:22–24)

In this case, divine intervention averted a war between the two kingdoms, but surprisingly enough, this seems to be the only case in which God, in this case through a prophet, stopped such bloodshed between Israelite brethren.[9] In most cases the people were not so lucky as to have a prophet such as Shemaiah the man of God to stop the war between the kingdoms.[10]

In the following section, we will discuss the wars between the two kingdoms not by their chronological order but rather according their military nature. These wars may be divided into three types, each arising under different circumstances:

1. battlefield wars;
2. sporadic clashes of uncertain character; and
3. raids for no reason.

1. Battlefield wars

The authors of the Bible, unlike their Greek counterparts, were not generous in supplying information about the political or geographical details of wars. Therefore there is no way to analyze each and every war in its own right. Instead, we shall view the various conflicts as a chain of wars between the same enemies. Three wars that took place in the battlefield are mentioned in the Bible, each is described in a different mode and the lack of clichés only add to the impression that the descriptions of the wars are more or less authentic.

a) Abijah – Jeroboam

King Abijah (as he is called in Chronicles, or Abijam, as he is known in Kings) son of Rehoboam ruled Judah for a short period of time, in the years immediately following the split between the kingdoms (c. 911–908 BCE). The book of Chronicles describes his reign as follows:

> In the eighteenth year of king Jeroboam began Abijah to reign over Judah ... And there was war between Abijah and Jeroboam. And Abijah joined battle with an army of valiant men of war, even four hundred thousand chosen men; and Jeroboam set the battle in array against him with eight hundred thousand chosen men, who were mighty man of valour ... But Jeroboam caused an ambushment to come about behind them; so they were before Judah, and the ambushment was behind them. And when Judah looked back, behold, the battle was before and behind them; and they cried unto the Lord ... Then the men of Judah gave a shout; and as the men of Judah shouted, it came to pass, that God smote Jeroboam and all Israel before Abijah and Judah ... And Abijah and his people slew them with great slaughter; so there fell down slain of Israel five hundred thousand chosen men ... And Abijah pursued after Jeroboam, and took cities from him, Bethel with the towns thereof, and Jeshanah with the towns thereof, and Ephrain with the towns thereof ...
>
> (2 Chronicles 13:1–19)

In this specific case it looks as if the author made a real effort to supply details, as if he took part in the drama, although the picture is still not terribly clear and needless to say the numbers given for the opposing forces and the victims are exaggerated. However, the fact that the battle ended in border changes between the kingdoms shows the importance of this conflict.[11]

For some unknown reason the author of Kings, unlike the Chronicler, preferred to only hint at this conflict: "And the rest of the acts of Abijam, and all that he did . . . And there was war between Abijam and Jeroboam" (2 Kings 15:7). From this opaque testimony one cannot guess at the details in the vivid description that appears in Chronicles and all one can do is to surmise why one author preferred to give a "full" description while the other mentioned the conflict only briefly, as if it was censored. This type of comparison between the books and trying to explain the source and motive of the Chronicler is far beyond the scope of this study, but it is hoped that future studies on the relationships between the two books will take into consideration the detailed descriptions of wars that appear in the "late" book as opposed its "predecessor."[12]

b) Amaziah – Jehoash

King Amaziah reigned over Judah in the early eighth century BCE and the author of Kings gives details about how he went to war against Israel without specifying the reason, except the historiographer's statement that the defeat of Amaziah was a divine punishment for worshipping the gods of Edom (2 Chronicles 25:20). However, the narrator did not explain the motivation of King Amaziah to go to battle against Jehoash in the first place, although the reason might be Israelite raiders that plundered and killed in Judea (see below, 3: Raids for no reason). It is stated as follows:

> Then Amaziah sent messengers to Jehoash, the son of Jehoahaz son of Jehu, king of Israel, saying: Come, let us look one another in the face. And Jehoash the king of Israel sent to Amaziah king of Judah, saying: The thistle that was in Lebanon sent to the cedar that was in Lebanon, saying: Give thy daughter to my son to wife; and there passed by the wild beasts that were in Lebanon, and trod down the thistle. Though thou hast indeed smitten Edom, and will thy heart lift thee up? Remain at home; for why shouldest though meddle with evil, that thou shouldest fall, even thou, and Judah with thee? But Amaziah would not hear. So Jehoash king of Israel went up; and he and Amaziah king of Judah looked one another in the face at Beth-shemesh, which belongeth to Judah. And Judah was put to the worse before Israel; and they fled every man to his tent. And Jehoash king of Israel took Amaziah king of Judah . . . and came to Jerusalem, and broke down the wall of Jerusalem from the gate of Ephraim unto the corner gate, four hundred cubits. And he took all the gold and silver, and all the vessels that were found in the house of the Lord, and in the treasures of the king's, the hostages also, and returned to Samaria.
>
> (2 Kings 14:8–14)

It should be added that there is no mention of victims, as if the battle was won without people being killed. No numbers of casualties are given (although details of the destroyed wall are specified) but still the unprecedented Aesopian-type fable which is included in the story,[13] shows not only his propinquity to the Judean king but also his desire to describe what happened in a manner which he thought would be of interest to his intended readers.

c) Pekah – Ahaz

No reasons are given for the attack of Pekah son of Remaliah (reigned c. 734–732 BCE) together with Rezin the king of Aram on Judah (2 Kings 15:37; 16:5). The author of Kings does not explain why there was a battle on the first place but from Isaiah 7:1–9 and from Ahaz' reaction (16:7–8), it is usually assumed that the two kings joined forces to enthrone a new king over Jerusalem, who would join their anti-Assyrian coalition.[14] In any event, the Chronicler's version skips all the background material and begins from the end:

> For Pekah the son of Remaliah slew in Judah a hundred and twenty thousand in one day, all of them valiant men; because they had forsaken the Lord, the God of their fathers. And Zichri, a mighty man of Ephraim, slew Maaseiah the King's son, and Azrikam the ruler of the house, and Elkanah that was next to the king. And the children of Israel carried away captive of their brethren two hundred thousand women, sons and daughters, and took also away much spoil to Samaria.
>
> (2 Chronicles 28:6–8)

Though details are not given it seems that the actual skirmish took place on the battlefield. No doubt the numbers are exaggerated but the story seems authentic. The three commanders that were killed show, apparently, that they ruled over one branch of the army while the other branch, under the king, stayed in Jerusalem, and those who stayed in Jerusalem were frightened for good reasons (Isaiah 7:4). The political situation as well as that on the battlefield is not clear but one thing is: both kingdoms attacked each other and the killing was mutual. The descriptions of the wars are very different from each other, showing that the narrator was not using clichés and this by itself can be considered a mark of authenticity. The defeat of the king of Judah and the tragedy of the death of the king's son (such as the death in battle of King Saul's sons) cannot be taken as a late invention, again adding to the feeling of the Chronicler's authenticity.[15]

2. Sporadic clashes of uncertain character

The authors of Kings and Chronicles mention many wars fought by the kings they describe, especially as part of the summary formulae given at the end of each king's reign. The authors do not supply details about these wars and their character is far from clear.

a) Rehoboam – Jeroboam

> And there was war between Rehoboam and Jeroboam continually.
>
> (1 Kings 14:30; 15:6 = 2 Chronicles 12:15)

These continual wars and their character will be discussed later but one wonders if these fighters ever heard the words of Shemaiah the man of God, as quoted above.

b) Asa – Baasa

King Asa ruled Judah ca. 908–867 BCE and it is stated as follows:

> And there was war between Asa and Baasa king of Israel all their days.
>
> (1 Kings 15:16)

In 2 Chronicles 16:1 it is stated: "In the six and thirtieth year of the reign of Asa, Baasa king of Israel went up against Judah, and built Ramah, that he might not suffer any to go out or come in to Asa king of Judah."[16] Though no specific war is mentioned Asa took this act of blockade as *Casus Belli* and asked Ben-Hadad king of Aram to attack Israel, forcing Baasa to retreat. In any event the reasons for these wars are not clear.[17]

In summarizing these "small" wars it should be noted that the authors did not try to explain what provoked these wars. On the contrary, the way they described the wars as a constant situation gives an impression that there was no need for a special occasion to go to war. It may be surmised that the authors had no political or military understanding or motivation and therefore their descriptions are so poor in detail. As far as I am aware, only David Elgavish has tried to explain the roots of these wars, and they can be summarized as follows:[18]

1. lack of a natural border;
2. areas with an agricultural potential;
3. demographic reasons; and
4. security reasons (such as achieving a strategic advantage).

I would like to add another reason for these "small" wars:

5. greed for plunder.

This reason, like those listed by Elgavish, is not specified in the Bible. However, as we know from such ancient texts as Homer,[19] plunder was a major motivation for war, and with human nature being what it is there is a good reason to think that just as in Homer's wars plunder played a major role, so did it in ancient Israel as well. Greed was a major motivation in ancient wars, more than in modern times. And beyond comparative analysis, one should read the following discussion about an episode that is described in the Bible that reaffirms the idea that plunder played a key role in wars in antiquity, in Israel as well as among the Greeks.

3. *Raids for no reason*

In 2 Chronicles 25:5–13 there is a story that is unlike any other in the Bible. The story is told with much attention to details, many of which are not known elsewhere and thus they all give the story a color of authenticity. The story begins with the preparations of King Amaziah of Judah to fight the Edomites, a war that is also mentioned, in much less detail, in 2 Kings 14:7. First he gathered 300,000 warriors from Judah and then he hired 100,000 mercenaries from Israel, for a hundred talents of silver. Then a man of God came to the king and rebuked him for his reliance on the northerners, and told him that God can help him without the help of the mercenaries. The king asked the man of God: "But what shall we do with for the hundred talents which I have given to the army of Israel?" and the man of God promised him that God will help him. Here is how things played out next:

> Then Amaziah separated them, to wit, the army that was come to him out of Ephraim, to go back home; wherefore their anger was greatly kindled against Judah, and they returned home in fierce anger . . . But the men of the army whom Amaziah sent back, that they should not go with him to battle, fell upon the cities of Judah, from Samaria even unto Beth-horon and smote of them three thousand, and took much spoil.
>
> (2 Chronicles 25:10, 13)

Thus, it is clear how these northern Israelites were quickly transformed from brothers in arms to enemies, just because their passion for war was not satiated. Needless to state that the numbers of the fighters seem to be highly exaggerated (and rounded off as well) and therefore unreliable.[20] Not only are the numbers corrupt but it seems that the name Shomron, usually translated "Samaria," is actually a corrupted form of "Shomer" or "Shemer," in the vicinity of Lod, not far from Beth-horon.[21] However, both the corruption of numerals and two (or more) variants of the same name are very frequent in the Bible and they cannot be taken as measures against the validity of the text. Two factors seem to attest the story's authenticity:

1. This is almost the only story about mercenaries in the Bible.[22] Other biblical sources say nothing concerning this phenomenon, though, at least in the Greek world, it was very common.
2. The story about the evil-doers doesn't serve any literary motive, and it gives the advice of the man of God negative consequences. Therefore it seems unlikely that the Chronicler would have invented such a story, making it seem highly authentic.

The Chronicler placed the story about Amaziah's challenge to Jehoash of Israel and the ensuing war between them (taken almost verbatim from 2 Kings 14:8–14) after the episode just mentioned and this seems very plausible. In doing so the narrator wanted to say that the Judean king and his people felt offended by the behavior of the Israelites in Judah and wanted to take revenge. In other words, the Israelite raiders were the political cause for the battle between Amaziah and Jehoash. At any event, this story tells of one very strong motive that people in antiquity had to kill others, including brother-Israelites: money (especially when one talks about mercenaries). As one may guess, people at the age of the fighters, 20–35, are not known for their ethics or morals in any culture, and young people tend to fight for any reason. It is almost human nature to fight others, and brethren are no exception.

Being aware of the pitfalls that await anyone who deals in comparative history, especially in the sphere of ideas, it seems appropriate to quote a well-known historian about the situation of battles in Medieval Europe. Concerning the internal wars in Europe, Robert Lopez writes as follows:

> In spite of its reputation, the age of feudalism used only very small armies, and if it delighted in innumerable skirmishes, it fought very few pitched battles
> . . .
>
> Some thousands of combatants, some hundreds of dead: these are the terms for evaluating the most bloody contests, those described in the most dramatic tones by the chroniclers.[23]

It seems that this observation was pretty well the case among Israel and Judah during the period of the two kingdoms: many clashes but with minor impact on the population as a whole.

Conclusions

The separation of Judah and Israel into two monarchies, small by any scale, yielded mutual killing for some two centuries, until the northern kingdom was destroyed and much of its population exiled far to the east. It looks like the biblical authors gave more attention to religious sins than to "plain" killing of innocent people.

The authors of the Bible were only partially aware of the problem inherent in internecine blood-shedding, although it seems the Chronicler was more interested in the subject than others, or at least revealed less a tendency to silence his sources. One cannot but surmise why the prophets, except Shemaiah, did not condemn this type of blood shedding.

The importance of the subject discussed above goes far beyond this study and it is hoped that in the future more studies will focus on this little-known aspect of Jewish social life in antiquity.

Notes

1. For two examples of studies which ignore such internecine struggles see S. Niditch, *War in the Hebrew Bible*, New York – Oxford: Oxford University Press, 1993, pp. 97–99; B.E. Kelle and F.R. Ames (Eds.), *Writing and Reading War: Rhetoric, Gender, and Ethics in Biblical and Modern Contexts* (SBL Symposium Series 42), Atlanta: Society of Biblical Literature, 2008.
2. S.W. Baron, *History and Jewish Historians*, Philadelphia: The Jewish Publication Society of America, 1964, pp. 63–64, 88, 96.
3. S.H. Blank, "The Death of Zechariah in Rabbinic Literature," *Hebrew Union College Annual* 12–13, 1937–38, pp. 327–346; B. Halpern-Amaru, "The Killing of the Prophets," *Hebrew Union College Annual* 54, 1983, pp. 153–180; I. Kalimi, "The Murders of the Messengers: Stephen versus Zechariah and the Ethical Values of 'New' versus 'Old' Testament," *Australian Biblical Review* 56, 2008, pp. 69–73; idem, "Murder in the

Jerusalem Temple – The Chronicler's story of Zechariah: Literary and Theological Features, Historical Credibility and Impact," *Revue Biblique* 117, 2010, pp. 200–209; M. Cook, "The New Testament: Confronting its Impact on Jewish-Christian Relations," in S. Scholz (Ed.), *Biblical Studies Alternatively – An Introductory Reader*, New Jersey: Prentice Hall, 2003, pp. 291–307.

 4. See H. Delbrück, *Numbers in History*, London: University of London Press, 1913; J.B. Segal, "Numerals in the Old Testament," *Journal of Semitic Studies* 10, 1965, pp. 2–20; S.W. Baron, *Ancient and Medieval Jewish History*, New Brunswick: Rutgers University Press, 1972, pp. 26–38; J.B. Payne, "The Validity of the Numbers in Chronicles," *Bibliotheca Sacra* 136, 1979, pp. 109–128; 206–220.

 5. The story has been analyzed once and again by many scholars from many standpoints and there is no need to mention them all. See, for instance: E. Leach, "Anthropological Approaches to the Study of the Bible During the Twentieth Century," in E. Leach and D.A. Aycock (Eds.), *Structuralist Interpretations of Biblical Myth*, Cambridge: Cambridge University Press, 1983, pp. 7–32. See also R. de Hoop, "Saul the Sodomite: Genesis 18–19 as the Opening Panel of a Polemic Triptych on King Saul," in E. Noort and E. Tigchelaar (Eds.), *Sodom's Sin: Genesis 18–19 and Its Interpretations*, Leiden: Brill, 2004, pp. 17–26.

 6. See A.A. Keefe, "Rapes of Women/Wars of Men," *Semeia* 61, 1993, pp. 79–97. See also H. Shalom-Guy, "Three-Way Intertextuality: Some Reflections of Abimelech's Death in Thebez in Biblical Narrative," *Journal for the Study of the Old Testament* 34, 2010, pp. 419–432.

 7. See K.M. Heffelfinger, "'My Father is King': Chiefly Politics and the Rise and Fall of Abimelech," *Journal for the Study of the Old Testament* 33, 2009, pp. 277–292.

 8. For various aspects of these killings see K.-P. Adam, "Law and Narrative: The Narratives of Saul and David Understood Within the Framework of a Legal Discussion on Homicide Law (Ex. 21:12–14)," *Zeitschrift für Altorientalische und Biblische Rechtsgeschichte* 14, 2008, pp. 311–335; K. Bodner, "Crime Scene Investigation: A Text Critical Mystery and the Strange Death of Ishbosheth," *Journal of Hebrew Scriptures* 7, 2007, article 13 (www.arts.ualberta.ca/JHS/Articles/article_74.pdf); W. Dietrich, "David, Amnon und Abschalom (2 Samuel 13): Literarische, textliche und historische Erwägungen zu den ambivalenten Beziehungen eines Vaters zu seinen Söhnen," *Textus* 23, 2007, pp. 115–143.

 9. See A. Frisch, "Shemaiah the Prophet versus King Rehoboam: Two Opposed Interpretations of the Schism (1 Kings XII 21–4)," *Vetus Testamentum* 38, 1988, pp. 466–468.

10. Another case in which fratricide is condemned is in Genesis 37:22: "And Reuben said unto them: 'Shed no blood; cast him into this pit that is in the wilderness, but lay no hand upon him'."

11. For more on the possible historical background of this story see R.W. Klein, "Abijah's Campaign Against the North (2 Chr 13) – What were the Chronicler's Sources?" *Zeitschrift für die Alttestamentliche Wissenschaft* 95, 1983, pp. 210–217; G.N. Knoppers, "'Battling against Yahweh': Israel's War against Judah in 2 Chr 13:2–20," *Revue Biblique* 100, 1993, pp. 511–532.

12. For one such discussion see S. Japhet, *I & II Chronicles – A Commentary* (OTL), Louisville: Westminster/John Knox, 1993, pp. 686–700.

13. In the Bible there are two "Aesopian" stories (Judges 9:8–15; 2 Kings 14:9 = 2 Chronicles 25:18) that reflect their originality on the one hand and their affiliation with the Ancient Near Eastern mode of thought on the other. See: W. Burkert, *The Orientalizing Revolution: Near Eastern Influence on Greek Culture in Early Archaic Age* (trans. by Margaret E. Pinder and W. Burkert), Cambridge – London: Harvard University Press, 1992, pp. 120–124.

14. For a survey and different views of this episode see B. Oded, "Ahaz's Appeal to Tiglath-Pileser III in the Context of the Assyrian Policy of Expansion," in M. Heltzer, A. Segal and D. Kaufman (Eds.), *Studies in the Archaeology and History of Ancient Israel in Honour of Moshe Dothan*, Haifa: Haifa University Press, 1993, pp. 63–71; L.R. Siddall, "Tiglath-Pileser III's Aid to Ahaz: A New Look at the Problems of the Biblical Accounts in Light of the Assyrian Sources," *Ancient Near Eastern Studies* 46, 2009, pp. 93–106.

15. It is worth noting the comments made by Japhet, *I & II Chronicles*, pp. 900–901. She sees this story as being different from other war-stories in Chronicles, lacking, for example, a reliance on divine intervention and such details as the locale of the battle and the numbers of troops on both sides. Her conclusion is that the story cannot be seen as a creation of the Chronicler, but as a report taken from an earlier source. The main purpose of the story, according the Japhet, "is the brotherhood of Israel and Judah . . . They are all 'the children of Israel' and 'the people of the Lord', and it is only their political circumstances, not any difference in national or religious identity, which estrange them."

16. In the parallel verse (1 Kings 15:17) the exact year (36) is missing and there is no reason for a later scribe to add such a detail. However, this year (that is: numerals) should not be taken for granted to calculate the exact date for the tendency of numerals to get corrupted as mentioned above.

17. D. Elgavish, "Objective of Baasha's War against Asa," in G. Galil and M. Weinfeld (Eds.), *Studies in Historical Geography and Biblical Historiography Presented to Zecharia Kallai*, Leiden – Boston – Köln: Brill, 2000, pp. 141–149.

18. D. Elgavish, "War and Peace in the Relationships between Israel and Judah," MA Thesis, Ramat-Gan: Bar-Ilan University, 1978, pp. 9–14, 31–33 (Hebrew).

19. N. Spiegel, *War and Peace in Ancient Greek Literature*, Jerusalem: Magnes 1986, pp. 25–38 (Hebrew).

20. The tendency to exaggerate numbers of fighters is clearly seen in the Bible. In 1 Kings 20:29 it is stated the Israelites smote 100,000 Arameans in one day. Needless to add that there was no way in which Judah could raise 300,000 fighters, a number that would reflect a population of more than 3,000,000 people.

21. A. Demsky, "The Genealogy of Asher (1 Chron. 7:30–40)," *Eretz-Israel* 24, 1993, pp. 68–73 (Hebrew).

22. The other one did not take place in Israel. See: 2 Samuel 10:6 (= 1 Chronicles 19:6). The role of mercenaries among the Greek nations is well known, but their role in the ancient Middle East is far from being clear. See: M. Trundle, *Greek Mercenaries: From the Late Archaic Period to Alexander*, London – New York: Routledge, 2004.

23. R.S. Lopez, *The Birth of Europe*, New York: M. Evans, 1962 (rep. 1967), p. 119.

Part II

Theoretical aspects of war in rabbinic thought

8 War and aesthetics in Jewish law

Joseph Isaac Lifshitz

1. Introduction

The ethics of war is one of the oldest subjects of moral debate, and dilemmas of justice in war have been studied and discussed from many perspectives. In this paper I will devote my attention to an important aspect of this question which has not received sufficient study: the aesthetics of war and the relationship of these aesthetics to the ethics of war. Much has been written about the horrors of war, and the sorrow of bloodshed and tears have often been described. We assume, at least in Western culture, that the making of war is no longer considered a virtuous activity. At the same time, human cultures seem to persistently develop an alternative narrative which, though sometimes concealed, extends a welcoming hand to war and warlike behavior. Proof of this statement is to be found, less in poetry and in literature as in the history of the aesthetics of arms. We see it when we examine articles of war, for instance the beauty of the sword or the gun, in military uniforms or in the intricate forms of warships. As much as Western culture may declare its hatred for war, the number of museums and illustrated albums which depict the colors, ornaments and shapes of war tell us a different story. In spite of our explicit disparagement of violence, there is perhaps after all a secret identification with war, physical force, and even bloodshed.

Of course, one may doubt if this is really so. Is the beautification of war an expression of identification with force, murder, and death – or is it merely an escape from it? After all, we might think that this beautification covers over and obscures the horror, ugliness and senselessness of wasted lives. And then again, the aesthetics of arms might simply be in the nature of the efficient design of articles of war. Perhaps the appearance of beauty is not deliberate, and not designed for the purpose of evading the ugly truth. Perhaps the efficient instrument has a beauty even when it's meant for killing, not unlike that of the shark or the tiger.

In this paper I will contend that in the aesthetics of war, identification with war really is decisive. While the aesthetics of arms, such as aircraft or tanks, is a product of efficient craftsmanship, it also stems from the place of war in human culture and from our identification with the warlike act, physical force and murder. I will contend further that because of this identification, the aesthetics of war presents an ethical problem.

I begin with a brief consideration of the foundations of aesthetics in human artifacts. My study then separately considers the aesthetics of war expressed by *halakhah* and by Jewish narrative sources, or, in other words, the aesthetics of war in law and language. *Halakhah*, it may be said at the outset, takes a very decisive and unambiguous view of war. From a Jewish legal perspective war is ugly, and that ugliness has extended halakhic ramifications. Narrative sources present a much more complex view. Though the biblical and aggadic narratives contain no direct propositions about the aesthetic value of war, such as those we find in halakhic rulings, we may nevertheless infer a view from some of the attributes which these narratives assign to God. Since the Bible describes God as a warrior, it may seem that war is granted aesthetic value. But I will show that despite the biblical descriptions of God as a warrior, the rabbinic aggadic literature consistently reinterprets these statements as merely symbolic. The approach of the Rabbis as commentators is thus consistent with their attitude as halakhists; they refuse to grant any aesthetic value to war.

2. Aesthetics and design

Questions about the aesthetics of war have been remarkably rare given the fact that so much effort has been devoted in the course of history to the aesthetics of arms, armor, military customs, aircrafts, tanks and even the act of war itself. There are several potential reasons why we endow articles of war with beauty, and I have mentioned some of them above. In this paper I will not be able fully to explore all of them. Rather I will focus on the cultural aspect of war, which I think sustains a direct connection to ethics.

As I have argued, the primary reason that human societies adorn war with aesthetics is the fact that war is perceived as virtuous. Arms receive their aesthetic features – even when these features are counter-productive to the function of those arms – because war and the warrior are considered virtuous.

I should warn the reader at this point that I will not be employing a traditional approach to aesthetics, but rather an approach conceived through modern ideas of design. In his work on perceptual psychology, James J. Gibson coined the term *affordance* – denoting the quality of an object, or an environment, which allows an individual to perform an action.[1] He used this term to express the idea that every object "enables" itself to man in a certain way. Donald Norman further developed Gibson's idea of *affordance* and altered it with a view to the world of design. For Norman *affordance* means the quality of a useful thing to easily "express" its function.[2] In order to understand Norman better, let us imagine an alien seeing a hammer for the first time. According to Norman, it can be assumed that the alien will know immediately where to hold the hammer and what to do with it. The same is true of a knife, a chair, a cup or any object endowed with *affordance*.

The reader will notice that the examples I've mentioned are of analogical objects, which are interpreted as images. Digital objects, such as numerical displays which appeal directly to abstract thought, possess a hidden form of *affordance*. According to Norman, the *affordance* of digital things presents a great challenge to designers for this reason. Be that as it may, for designers the main goal is to remove all unnecessary or extraneous features from the object; to strip it of any feature that would detract from its *affordance*. Good design means that the thing "speaks for itself," that it "affords" itself completely with no need for an instruction book. But Norman is aware that many things lack this quality, some for reasons of bad design, and some for the sake of beauty. After asking why we create beautiful things that aren't practical, or why we sometimes add features to objects which distract from their practical use, Norman determines that the aesthetical features of things are added to meet a human emotional need. Our emotions are therefore one important "use" which the object serves, albeit not as important as the practical use.[3]

Before disputing with Norman over the purely emotional value that he ascribes to aesthetics, I would like to present a challenge to his notion of *affordance*. I maintain that there isn't anything that "affords" itself without the help of human culture. The use of everyday things is always enabled by knowledge either in the forms of ideas or habitual praxis. For a culture that doesn't have praxis of cutting, a knife will not "afford" itself. For a culture that is used to squatting rather than sitting, a chair will not "afford" sitting; and for a culture that doesn't know about nails, the hammer will be of no obvious use.[4] *Affordance* never appears without a culture enabling the relationship between human artifact, in other words, without culture as a translator or medium, there is no *affordance*. The alien test will fail.[5]

With this in mind, we can understand why aesthetical properties cannot be explained as appealing to a merely emotional "use." Aesthetics serves as a cultural value. Beauty is an important feature indeed, but not only because it serves an emotional need, as Norman claims. Things are made pretty in order to serve as items of identity. The object becomes an extension of the owner. This is why efforts to beautify objects are unequal. We devote more time and energy to the beauty of some objects than, for instance, the sorts of objects that one uses to save oneself from a burning house, as functionally important as they may be. When a violin is decorated, it is not to enhance the quality of its tone, and when a religious item is adorned it is not purely to serve religious worship, but rather to mark or celebrate the place that these things serve in a particular culture.

The desire to decorate arms serves precisely this purpose – it emphasizes the fact that arms are an important cultural object. For a culture in which arms serve as objects of value they also serve as objects of personal identity, and hence as extensions of a man's power and personality. This is why the aesthetics of arms and of war in general presents an ethical problem. If man perceives war as an extension of himself, he understands all the horrors of war as his extension as well.

3. The halakhic approach

Until modern times, the sword was considered a sign and emblem of masculinity. It was not only for purposes of self-defense that every man of significance once carried a sword, while men of lower stations carried a knife. Personal identification with the sword was so great in antiquity that men were often buried with their swords.[6] There is no doubt that in most human cultures the sword has been considered an extremely important item signifying prestige and virtue. In marked contrast to this tendency, the majority of rabbinic opinions recorded in the Talmud argue that a sword represents, not prestige and virtue, but disgrace. In a discussion regarding the prohibition on carrying a load during the Sabbath, the rabbis argue over whether a sword may be considered the man's equivalent of what jewelry is for women. Rabbi Eliezer alone holds that it may, the other rabbis reject the analogy: jewelry is precious – the sword is a disgrace:

> A man may not go out [on the Sabbath] with a sword, nor with a bow, nor with a *teris*, nor with an *alah*, nor with a spear. And if he went out, he is liable to a sin-offering. Rabbi Eliezer says: They [the arms] are ornaments for him [for a man], but the sages say: They are nothing but a reproach, as it is written (in Isaiah 2:4): "and they shall beat their swords into plowshares, and their spears into pruning hooks; nation shall not lift up sword against nation, neither shall they learn war any more."
>
> (Mishnah, *Shabbat*, 6:4)[7]

In this dispute the law was decided according to the majority opinion of the rabbis.[8] Although the disagreement might seem to concern only a technical halakhic issue, it is in fact of great moral significance. The rabbis' decision to reject the definition of a sword as jewelry is not based on anthropological or psychological evidence, but on a direct appeal to a moral ideology. The messianic hope for a peaceful world is interpreted by the rabbis as an ideological premise about the real world and not merely a sweet dream or vision of the future. According to this ideology, a world that suffers from hatred, quarrels and wars is a negative world that ought to be changed. One may without difficulty infer an obligation to take action for the improvement of the world from this messianic hope, but the Rabbis take an even broader approach. They conclude that any object used for enhancing the negativity of the world is itself contaminated. The hope of a peaceful world has legal and hence practical ramifications.[9] The sword may no longer play the role of an object of identity. It may not express a man's masculinity. It is considered an ugly and disgraceful thing which, although sometimes necessary, can never serve as an article of pride.

Yet, one may not infer a pacifistic ideology from this halakhic approach. The rabbis indeed perceive arms as a disgrace, but they don't reject war altogether. War of course may be necessary at times, but they hold that its legitimacy should not lend it any other virtue besides necessity. War should be perceived as bitter medicine. Medicine may be taken at times of sickness, but shouldn't be mistaken for food.

According to the rabbis' opinion, as we have seen, war is not only ugly but also morally undesirable if waged beyond necessity. Even the exercise of war as sport is considered blameworthy. That is why the rabbis are critical of Abner son of Ner in their interpretation of the book of Samuel. They reason that the encounter between Abner and Joab was the theological cause of Abner's death:

And Abner son of Ner and the servants of Ish-bosheth son of Saul marched out from Mahanaim to Gibeon. And Joab son of Zeruiah, and the servants of David, went out and they met together by the pool of Gibeon: and they sat down, the one on one side of the pool, and the other on the other side of the pool. Abner said to Joab, Let the young men now arise, and play before us. And Joab said, Let them arise. They there arose and went over by number twelve of Benjamin, belonging to Ish-bosheth son of Saul, and twelve of the servants of David. And they caught every one his fellow by the head, and thrust his sword into his fellow's side; so they all fell down together: so that place was called Helkath-hazzurim, which is in Gibeon.

(2 Samuel 2:12–16)

Abner had suggested a war game of the sort that was very common at the time, but the rabbis disagree that a man of virtue should be involved in this type of activity. A person who respects life should not risk the life of others merely for amusement:

And Abner, why was he killed? Rabbi Joshua B. Levi explained: Abner was killed because he made sport of the blood of young men, as it proved by the text: "And Abner said to Joab: Let the young men, I pray thee, arise, and play before us."[10]

In addition to the passage quoted above, this source presents a very clear rabbinic opinion concerning war: It is a negative and ugly endeavor which should only be practiced in cases of emergency.

4. The aesthetics of war in the language of rabbinic literature

Despite the ideological morality of the rabbis, the Bible itself seems to have a different approach. For the most part, the biblical approach expresses itself through language rather than laws. The locutions of the Bible, especially phrases used in praising God, indicate a high regard for war in general and for the aesthetics of the warrior in particular. God is frequently depicted as a warrior, as a man of the sword. And thus the question arises: if this is God, why shouldn't man imitate this model according to *imitatio dei*?

To infer an attitude towards aesthetics from the linguistics of Jewish sources, not just a straightforward study or commentary on the text, may appear too modern. But it was in fact Nahmanides (Gerona 1194–1270) who first raised this argument about the aesthetics of war, in his commentary on Rabbi Eliezer's argument about comparing arms to jewelry. Nahmanides claimed that if the rabbis had considered the sword a disgrace, they wouldn't have praised the Torah as a sword.[11]

Nahmanides' argument seems very convincing, and indeed there are many biblical passages describing God as a warrior:

"The Lord shall go forth as a mighty man, he shall stir up ardor like a man of war."

(Isaiah 42:13)

"The sun and moon stood still in their habitation: at the light of your arrows as they speed, and at the shining of thy glittering spear."

(Habakkuk 3:11)

"[I have] raised up my sons, O Zion, against thy sons, O Javan, and made thee as the sword of a mighty man."

(Zechariah 9:13)

"Who is this King of glory? The Lord strong and mighty, the Lord mighty in battle."

(Psalms 24:8)

God is a warrior – a mighty and valiant fighter – and he carries a sword, arrows and spears. Although these forceful words are only poetic illustration, the fact remains that for the Bible, the virtues of war are a model of God. This is very far from the rabbinic teaching that war is a disgrace.

However, while all of this is true of the Bible, it isn't true for the rabbis who sublimated all descriptions of the warrior in the Bible. Though the biblical narrative does not hesitate to praise the warrior, careful study of the rabbis' biblical commentaries shows that they were less enthusiastic. Employing deconstructive hermeneutics, the rabbis consistently reinterpreted the basic meaning of the depiction of warrior into more transcendent attributes. The spear thus becomes a spear of light:

Great is the light of the Holy One. The sun and moon give light to the world, but from where do their lights derive? They snatch some sparks of celestial light. It is so stated: "at the light of your arrows as they speed, and at the shining of thy glittering spear" (Habakkuk 3:11). Great is the celestial light of which only one part in a hundred has been given to mortals.[12]

Not only spears are interpreted as light, so are swords:

"You are fairer than the children of Adam: grace is poured out on your lips: [therefore God has blessed thee for ever]. Gird your sword upon your thigh, O mighty one: [thy glory and thy majesty]" (Psalms 45:3–4). About whom do the children of Korah speak in this psalm? About Abraham: He was fairer than the children of the first Adam... You descended into the fiery furnace and experienced a lot of trials for my name. You arose and pursued the kings. But you have been proud of yourself in the world for all that you have done. From now on, you will seek to make my valor known. Gird on your sword: put your circumcision between your thighs. In that hour your glory and splendor shall be in the world.[13]

The efforts of the rabbis to sublimate the warrior and to extirpate the warlike flavor of the biblical narrative are continually evident. The rabbis are very deliberate about their approach to changing the literal meaning of the Bible into a spiritual or intellectual one. They do not refrain from giving corporeal descriptions of God, but these descriptions are never understood literally. They are always used for the sake of human imagination, as an aid to perceiving the transcendent. That is why descriptions of God as a warrior in aggadic texts should be understood metaphorically and not literally. God is described as a warrior not because God is a warrior but because man is. The rabbis also situate God's warrior attributes in the context of his other attributes – notably those of an old man, mercifulness and gracefulness – all designed to augment his fullness of being and to raise him above all beings.

> "The Lord the Warrior, the Lord is his name." Rabbi Yehuda says: this phrase is abundant in many places, in order to tell you that the Lord was revealed to them as a warrior armed with all sorts of arms. He was revealed to them as a mighty one girded with sword, as it says: "Gird thy sword upon thy thigh, O mighty warrior" (Psalms 45:4). He was revealed to them as a knight as it says: "He mounted a cherub and flew . . ." (Psalms 18:11). He was revealed to in arms and helmet like a mighty one, as it says: "For he put on righteousness as a breastplate, and a helmet of salvation upon his head" (Isaiah 59:17) [. . .] Does he need all these attributes? That is why it says: "The Lord the Warrior, the Lord is his name." When he fights, he uses his name and he doesn't need all these attributes. . . Why does it say "The Lord the Warrior"? Because he appeared on the [Red] Sea as a mighty one who fights in a war, as it says: "the Lord the Warrior." He appeared on Sinai as an old man full of mercy as it says: "and they saw the God of Israel."[14]

When God fights he doesn't need a sword, since he fights with his name and not with arms.[15] This is already sublimation. God is a warrior indeed, but he is an old man at the same time. To praise God with opposite attributes has, if not a cancelling effect, at least a sublimating one. The conclusion of the statement that God is not only a warrior but also an old man, is that he is not in fact a warrior. The rabbis also hold that the ability to fight enhances rather than qualifies God's gracefulness:

> When a king of flesh and blood goes to a war, and cities come to him and ask for their needs, they are told: he [the king] is full of anger of war. Come back and appeal for your needs after he returns victorious from the war. But with God it is not so, instead "The Lord the Warrior" when he fights with Egypt, "the Lord is his name": when he hears the cry of all the world's creatures, as it says, "O thou that hearest prayer, to thee shall all flesh come."
> (Psalms 65:3)[16]

God's ability to display two characteristics at once is an augmentation of his power, but also a sublimation of his corporeality. What is achieved is a sublimation of war. The tendency to sublimate war is indeed consistent throughout the Babylonian Talmud, and not only is God's character as warrior sublimated, so is man's. King David, portrayed by the Bible as a successful warrior, is perceived by the rabbis as a rabbi himself:

> One of the attendants spoke up: "I have seen a son of Jesse the Bethlehemite, that knows how to play, and a fine warrior, and a man of war, and prudent in speech, and a comely person, and the Lord is with him."
>
> (1 Samuel 16:18)

This phrase is explained in the Talmud as follows: "fine warrior – [the man] who knows how to answer well, a man of war – [the man] who knows how to argue in matters of Torah, a comely person – [the man] who is able to shed light on *halakhah*."[17] Rabbinic efforts to describe King David as a rabbi are not intended as the self-praise of rabbinic virtue but aim to sublimate war if not to eliminate its virtue altogether by undermining its aesthetics.

As we have seen, the rabbis were not keen on war or its virtues. But at the same time they did not forbid the use of arms. Maimonides puts the practice of war in a broader perspective:

> The actions are divided with regards to their ends into four classes: futile actions, frivolous actions, vain actions, or good and excellent actions ... A frivolous action is that action by which a low end is aimed at; I mean to say that something unnecessary and not very useful is aimed at therein, as when one dances not for exercise or as when one does things in order to make people laugh about those things. Such actions are indubitably called frivolous, but they differ according to the purpose and the perfection of the agents. For there are many things that are necessary or very useful according to some people, whereas according to others they are not at all needed; as in the case with regard to the different kinds of bodily exercise, which are necessary for the preservation of health according to the perceptions of those who know the art of medicine, and as is the case with regards to writing, which is very useful according to the men of knowledge. Thus those who accomplish acts exercising their body in the wish to be healthy, engaging in ball games, wrestling, boxing, and suspension of breathing, or those who engage in actions that are done with a view to writing, as for instance the cutting of reed pens and the making of paper, are in the opinion of the ignorant engaged in frivolous actions, whereas they are not frivolous according to the learned.[18]

The practice of war is virtuous if its aims are worthwhile, but is never virtuous as an end in itself; if so, it is frivolous or worse.

5. Evolution of the aesthetics of war

I began this paper by describing the aesthetics of war as if it was an unbroken historical phenomenon, but that is not the entire picture. Modern arms are no longer decorated as weapons once were, nor do modern soldiers wear ornate uniforms. The last war that paid tribute to the spirit of aesthetic magnificence, in which soldiers were attired in beautiful uniforms and girded with ornate swords and wore feathers in the helmets, was the First World War. By the Second World War the situation was quite different. Not only had the uniforms became simple with attention to the practical – arms, too, had given way to the new spirit. Classical aesthetics, it seems, had become obsolete together with many other traditional virtues. For the aesthetics of war, the First World War was a watershed event.[19]

The First World War had other effects as well. During the war large numbers of men became used to mass bloodshed. The battle of Verdun and its many dead might be considered an important historical crossroads in this regard. The battle began on 21 February 1916 and ended only at the close of the war with a toll of over one million casualties. The Germans attacked the French troops with heavy artillery and then advanced using flame-throwers for the first time. Their aim was to cause the French to bleed to death, and although they failed, unprecedented bloodshed resulted on both sides. The magnitude of the destruction of human life was so grave that the memory of this horror remained alive for many years.

But this wasn't the only factor underpinning cultural change. The twentieth century saw significant changes regarding aesthetics in general, which was by no means limited only to the aesthetics of war. A simpler and more realistic taste in aesthetics arose in the West, in opposition to the previous naïve sensibilities, which were now criticized as no more than beautiful colors and pleasing decoration. Hints of this change had begun to appear in the art of the nineteenth century, but gained widespread popular influence only in the twentieth. Although the change was gradual, there were political forces that helped push it along, such as both the socialist and Nazi movements. In both, the classical aesthetic was perceived as an instrument employed by the higher classes for the suppression of the lower classes, and was thus to be eschewed in favor of simpler design.

One version of the call to transform aesthetic sensibilities came in the form of a demand that realism replace the romantic notion of beauty. The proper role of art, according to this view, was to express the basic needs of the working classes, among which beauty was not included.[20] The nascent demand for realism was motivated in part by political ideology, but also reflected a cultural awareness of looming change and a desire for a cultural revolution which would strip away all the superfluous decoration used to mark objects of value. Political movements were undoubtedly an important factor in bringing about this change.[21]

But were political movements the entire reason for the change in aesthetic sensibilities witnessed in the Second World War? In all countries, but especially in Germany and Russia, this was indeed a war led largely by the proletariat rather than the nobility or the bourgeoisie. As already noted, regarding the history of aesthetics from the perspective of the battlefield does not provide the full picture. The pursuit of classical beauty dismissed in the twentieth century due to the ascendance of the practical in all aspects of life, a process by no means exclusive to the battlefield.

But to judge the transformation of aesthetics from the narrowest sense of what is held to constitute beauty would be a mistake. In addition to a revolution of the definition of beauty, the regard for beauty itself in human culture had undergone reevaluation. Especially in fine art many have observed an intentional decline in the pursuit of beauty. The place beauty had occupied in the work of art of the past came to be occupied instead by other types of ideals and by emotions. Art critics no longer judge art primarily as a medium for expressing beauty. As John Passmore observes, "we wouldn't have felt comfortable if we would have said that Goya's engravings and Hogarth's lithographs are beautiful."[22] Passmore goes on to opine that in our time only calendar producers and people that occupy coffee shops still care about beauty.[23]

I would argue, however, that the cause of the decline of old aesthetics is not solely the rise of the lower classes or a decline in the value ascribed to beauty. Change resulted more generally from the slow rise of a culture of abstraction. The place of beauty within our sense of the aesthetic underwent a major process of development. As Frank Sibley argues, aesthetics tries to makes sense of the complicated perception in which people see grace or charm in plastic art, hear insanity or sadness in music, or sense the glamour in patterns of colors.[24] Aesthetics derives from our culture and expresses it in all its complexity.

Men still collect guns and are forever enchanted by stories, films and computer games based on war. A survey from 1994 in the US shows that 25 percent of American adults own firearms.[25] We know that this high percentage does not reflect the need for security. We may assume that it reflects a desire for masculinity or power. This is a cultural phenomenon and it expresses a cultural idea, a particular aesthetic. As we can see, the story of aesthetics and war has not ended merely because today's arms are not decorated and military uniforms are not as colorful as they used to be. If the arms of today are not as pretty as they used to be, that is because they express a new sense of beauty. Tanks, aircrafts and guns are slick, sharp and sometime shiny, and may be described by the moniker *les beautés nouveaux*. But this new aesthetics of war should be judged with the same critical eye as exists in the Talmud with regard to the old aesthetics. We have to remember that it is this aesthetics, this sympathy for arms that is one of the deepest causes of war and violence.

One may ask if this process of decline in the aesthetics of war that I have described has any parallel in contemporary Jewish law. An answer to this question has to take into account one qualification – much of the new halakhic material concerning the subject of war ethics is affected less by the First World War and more by the events of the Second World War and by the establishment of the State of Israel. One may ask whether the watershed event which I described was an event in Jewish culture at all. Didn't Jews object to aesthetics of war in much earlier times? I think that signs of change in Jewish attitudes towards war may easily be found as well.

It was in the twentieth century that rabbis were asked, for the first time, if soldiers may carry arms during the Sabbath. Since there had not been an independent Jewish military force since the end of the Second Temple Period, this had never been a problem in practical *halakhah*. Unlike the cases dealt with by Talmudic or medieval rabbis, the question now was not just about armed civilians but also about soldiers who were obliged to carry their weapons in the line of duty. It is interesting to see how despite Talmudic law, twentieth-century rabbis decided to permit carrying arms, and their reasoning was based on practical observations rather than aesthetics. Rabbi Yechiel Michael Epstein was the first to rule that for a soldier, unlike for civilians, arms are a garment and shouldn't be thought of as an ornament at all.[26] In addition to this observation, Rabbi Yekutiel Yehuda Halberstam ruled that the purpose of a soldier's carrying arms is more as deterrent than for actual use, and therefore shouldn't be regarded mainly as a mortal object.[27] Rabbi Moshe Feinstein even distinguished between arms and armor. Armor, he ruled, is nothing but a garment for a soldier; not an ornament.[28] So even though Jewish tradition considered the aesthetic of war to be a negative property, it took this aesthetic into account. For the Jewish sages, war did have an aesthetic element, even though they understood its flaws and forbade perceiving the tools of war as an ornament. But during the twentieth century even that changed: in today's world, rabbis no longer even consider the possibility that arms might be used primarily as ornaments.

6. Conclusions

The rabbis' disparaging attitude towards arms may seem to suggest that their political theory is pacifistic, but that is not the case. Neither power nor violence are considered intrinsically negative.[29] Indeed, power is one of God's attributes.[30] And God is also violent when necessary, "O Lord God, to whom vengeance belongs" (Psalms 94:1). Notwithstanding the uneasiness of medieval scholars towards descriptions of God's corporeality in the Hebrew Bible, which occur relatively rarely, God's emotion is very often present. God loves and hates and he displays gracefulness and regret. He can become judgmental or wrathful and then forceful. God flooded the earth with water in the great deluge, destroyed Sodom and Gomorra, left the Israelites wandering in the desert of Sinai for forty years, and would not allow even his beloved prophet, Moses, to set foot in the Land of Israel.

The Bible's acceptance of violence is revealed not only in passages referring to the sword, but also in biblical locutions regarding God's actions and even in the law itself. One of the commandments of the Torah is to destroy the nation of Amalek. It is true that this commandment of genocide is now obsolete because the ancient tribe of Amalek no longer exists, yet the obligation to obliterate its name is still in force.[31] This obligation is meant to not only to commemorate a historical event, but serves as a reminder that evil is part of the human condition.

The Jew is obligated to remember that the world contains evil and to fight against it. Ignoring or capitulating to evil is tantamount to renouncing justice. But the quest for justice does not sanctify the sword. The Jewish tradition teaches that justice is an end which does not sanctify all and every means. The sword is perceived forever a necessary but ugly evil, one which must sometimes be employed to achieve a worthwhile end.

Notes

* I would like to thank Jonathan Yudelman for editing the English version of this paper.

1. J.J. Gibson, "The Theory of Affordances," in R. Shaw and J. Bransford (Eds.), *Perceiving, Acting and Knowing*, Hillsdale, NJ: Lawrence Erlbaum Associates, 1977, pp. 67–82; idem, *The Ecological Approach to Visual Perception*, Boston: Houghton Mifflin, 1979, pp. 127–143.

2. D.A. Norman, *The Psychology of Everyday Things*, New York: Basic Books, 1988, pp. 87–92. See more in idem, "Affordances, Conventions, and Design," *Interactions* 6, 1999, pp. 38–41.

3. Idem, *Emotional Design: Why We Love (Or Hate) Everyday Things*, New York: Basic Books, 2004, pp. 17–33.

4. In Heidegger's thought, practical knowledge is acquired through practical praxis, yet "readiness-to-hand" isn't possible outside the context of "presence-to-hand." See M. Heidegger, *Being and Time*, trans. J. Macquarrie and E. Robinson, New York: Harper and Row, 1962, pp. 91–122. See especially pp. 98–99: "Equipment can genuinely show itself only in dealing cut to its own measure (hammering with a hammer, for example); but in such dealings an entity of this kind is not *grasped* thematically as an occurring Thing, nor is the equipment-structure known as such even in the using. The hammering does not simply have knowledge about . . . the hammer's character as equipment, but it has appropriated this equipment in a way which could not possibly be more suitable. In dealings such as this, where something is put to use, our concern subordinates itself to the 'in-order-to' which is constitutive for the equipment we are employing at the time; the less we just stare at the hammer-Thing, and the more we size hold of it and use it, the more primordial does our relationship become, and the more unveiled is it encountered as that which it is – as equipment. The hammering itself uncovers the specific 'manipulativity' of the hammer. The kind of being which equipment possesses – in which it manifests itself in its own right – we call 'readiness-to-hand' . . . The ready-to-hand is not grasped theoretically at all, nor is it itself the sort of thing that circumspection takes proximally as a circumspective theme. The peculiarity of what is proximally ready-to-hand is that, in order to be ready-to-hand, it must, as it were, withdraw in order to be ready-to-hand quite authentically. That with which our everyday dealings proximally dwell is not the tools themselves. On the contrary, that with which we concern ourselves primarily is the work – that which is to be produced at the time; and this is accordingly ready-to-hand too. The work bears with it that referential totality within which the equipment is encountered."

5. For a similar claim see D. Ihde, *Postphenomenology: Essays in the Postmodern Context*, Evanston: Illinois Northwestern University Press, 1993, pp. 35–39.

6. E.S. Hartland, *Primitive Law*, Port Washington: Kennikat Press, 1924, reissued 1970, p. 88. For more about the history of the sword see R.E. Oakeshott, *The Archaeology of Weapons: Arms and Armour from Prehistory to Age of Chivalry*, London: Lutterworth Press, 1960.

7. *The Mishnah* (Everyman's Mishnah Series), trans. E. Levin, Ed. Bernard Susser, Jerusalem: Eliner Library, Department for Torah Education and Culture in the Diaspora of the World Zionist Organization, 1990, pp. 68–69.

8. Maimonides, *The Code of Maimonides, Book 3: The Book of Seasons*, The Sabbath 19:1, trans. S. Gandz and H. Klein, New Haven: Yale University Press, 1961, p. 116; Rabbi Joseph Caro, *Code of Hebrew Law Shulhan Aruk*, Orach Chaim, 301:7, trans. C.N. Denburg, Montreal: Jurisprudence Press, 1954–55. On ownership of arms in the Middle Ages see I.Z. Kahana, *Research on Responsa Literature* Jerusalem: Mossad Harav Kook, 1973, pp. 163–167 (Hebrew).

9. On hope in Jewish thought see A. Mittleman, *Hope in a Democratic Age*, New York: Oxford University Press, 2009, pp. 115–145.

10. *Midrash Rabbah, Leviticus*, 24.2, trans. H. Freedman and M. Simon, London: Soncino Press, 1939, p. 328.

11. Mosheh Ben Nahman, *Hasagot HaRamban to the Book of Commandments*, root 2, Ed. C.B. Chavel, Jerusalem: Mosad Harav Kook, 1981, pp. 44–45 (Hebrew).
12. Midrash Tankhuma, Numbers, Beha'alotcha, 3.10, trans. J.T. Townsend, Jersey City: Ktav Publishing House, 2003, p. 78.
13. Ibid., Genesis, Lekh Lekha, 3.22, p. 81.
14. *Mechilta D'Rabbi Ishmael*, Beshalah, the Shira tractate, Parsha 4, Ed. H.S. Horovitz and I.A. Rabin, Frankfurt am Main: J. Kauffmann Press, 1931 (Hebrew), p. 129, lines 4–17.
15. See *Midrash Rabbah*, Genesis, III.3, p. 20.
16. Mechilta D'Rabbi Ishmael.
17. BT *Sanhedrin*, 93b.
18. Maimonides, *The Guide of the Perplexed*, III: 25 (trans. S. Pines), Chicago: University of Chicago, 1963, p. 503.
19. The First World War generated a lively discussion on the subject of the aesthetics of war. Some were enthusiastic about the war and spoke for its beauty, others criticized it. The known protagonists to rave about the war were Max Scheler and Ernst Jünger. M. Scheler and M. Schiller *Der Genius Des Krieges Und Der Deutsche Krieg (1915)*, Whitefish: Kessinger, 2010; E. Jünger, *In Stahlgewitter* (46th ed.), Stuttgart: Klett-Cotta Verlag, 2007. On the critical side see H. Ball, *Flight Out of Time: A Dada Diary (Documents of Twentieth-Century Art)*, Ed. John Elderfield, trans. Ann Raimes, Berkeley – Los Angeles – London: University of California Press, 1996. Also see C. Schmidt, *Die Apokalypse des Subjekts*, Bielefeld: Aisthesis Verlag, 2003. I am grateful to Christoph Schmidt for these references.
20. F.D. Klingender, *Marxism and Modern Art*, London: Lawrence and Wishart, 1975, pp. 48–49.
21. I would like to thank Ofir Haivry for his insightful comments on the role of political movements in transforming early twentieth-century aesthetics.
22. J. Passmore, "The Dreariness of Aesthetics," in W. Elton (Ed.), *Aesthetics and Language*, Oxford: Blackwell, 1954, p. 50.
23. Loc. cit. On the other hand, see M. Mothersill, *Beauty Restored*, New York: Adams Bannister Cox, 1991, p. 257, who claims that despite the decline of beauty in the theories of art critics, it is always in the background.
24. F. Sibley, "Aesthetics and Nonaesthetics," *Philosophical Review* 74, 1965, p. 137.
25. P.J. Cook and J. Ludwig, *Guns in America: National Survey on Private Ownership and Use of Firearms*, National Institute of Justice, May 1997. Available at: www.ncjrs.gov/pdffiles/165476.pdf.
26. Y.M. Epstein, *Aruch Hashulchan*, Orach Chaim vol. III 301:52, Pietrikow: Yosef Tzvi Lew, 1905, p. 175 (Hebrew).
27. Y.Y. Halberstam, *Shut Divei Yatziv*, Orach Chaim, 148:3, Netanya: Machon Shefa Chaim, 1996, pp. 301–304 (Hebrew). See also the ruling of Rabbi Breish regarding Jewish soldiers in the Swiss army: M.Y. Breish, *Chelkat Yaakov*, vol. II, Orach Chaim, 96, Tel Aviv: Published by family of author, 1992, pp. 150–151 (Hebrew).
28. M. Feinstein, *Igrot Moshe*, vol. VIII 18 (on Shulcan Aruch Orach Chaim 301:7), Ed. Shabtai Avraham Hacohen Rappoport, Jerusalem: Published by family of author, 1996, p. 39 (Hebrew).
29. I am grateful to Shmuel Trigano for pointing this out to me.
30. One of God's names – Elohim – is understood as power. See F. Brown, S.R. Driver and C.A. Brigges (Eds.), *Hebrew and English Lexicon of the Old Testament*, Oxford: Oxford University Press, 1951, p. 43.
31. See J.J. Weinberg, *Seridei Esh* vol. II, 105, Jerusalem: Mossad Harav Kook, 1977, p. 253 (Hebrew); O. Yosef, *Book of Responsa Yabia Omer*, Orach Chaim vol. VIII, 54, 18, Jerusalem: Midrash Bnei Zion, 1995 (Hebrew).

9 The morality of war in rabbinic literature

The Call for Peace and the Limitation of the Siege

Yishai Kiel

Introduction

In recent decades many scholars have been involved in examining the attitude of Judaism to the question of war and to the moral issues associated with it.[1] Though these scholars indeed reflect a broad range of opinions and points of view, it is nevertheless evident that there is one basic problem that runs like a thread through the various discussions. This problem may be characterized as a basic tension that exists between the categories presently dominant in the fields of ethics and international law as regards the morality of war and the moral categories emerging from Jewish sources.

Modern thought on the subject of the morality of war is based to a great extent on the dominant doctrine, known as the "Just War Theory."[2] Side by side with realistic[3] and pacifist[4] worldviews on war it would seem that the "Just War Theory" is the model that has had the most powerful influence within the contemporary ethical and legal discussion. This theory is based in principle on a division of the morality of war into two main categories: the *"Jus ad bellum"* category which focuses on the question of the justification for initiating war, and the *"Jus in bello"* category which is concerned with morality in the course of the fighting.[5] Taking into account all its various components, a major attribute of the "Just War Theory" can be said to be its orientation toward reducing both the number and scope of wars. The theory postulates that going to war may indeed be unavoidable and even justified at times, but in general both the grounds for going to war (*Jus ad bellum*) and its scope and intensity (*Jus in bello*) should be significantly restricted.

It will be helpful to recall briefly some of the principles of the theory:

- Going to war should only be in self-defense or in defense of another community against aggression.
- Going to war must only be where there is a sincere intention of preventing aggression.
- Going to war should only be based on a decision of a government that faithfully and democratically represents the will of the public.
- War must be used only as a last resort in resolving the conflict.

- War should not be waged if the chances of victory are unrealistic and the aggression would not be coming to an end in any case.
- The reaction to aggression must be proportionate and be weighed up against other possible reactions.
- There are instruments of war that have particularly devastating effects and their use in any situation is totally forbidden.
- The use of force in the course of the fighting must be proportionate and be directed toward a specific purpose.
- All injury to the civilian, non-combatant population must be avoided.
- The basic human rights of enemy soldiers, when they no longer constitute a security threat, must be rigorously safeguarded.

There is no doubt that some of the principles of the "Just War Theory" are, for the most part, at odds with commonly accepted attitudes emerging from Jewish sources. This is true as regards the Bible, Talmudic sources and rabbinic literature throughout the ages. Without going into this complex matter in depth, it would seem that it will not be easy to bridge between the concept of the immunity of the non-combatant population and the biblical concept of the siege or the idea of annihilating the nation of Amalek.[6] The rabbinic categorization of wars into "Optional Wars," "Commanded Wars" and "Obligatory Wars" which does not include a category of "Forbidden Wars" is to a large extent likely to grate on the morally sensitive modern ear. The comments of Maimonides regarding the "king who fights other nations in order to enlarge Israel's borders and to increase his greatness and his renown"[7] or the realistic attitude of Rabbi Naphtali Zvi Yehudah Berlin who regards war as "a time to kill without any punishment at all – for that is how the world was made,"[8] only constitute further examples of this conflict of principles.

To be sure, the differences which we wish to point out between the "Just War Theory" and the various attitudes within rabbinic Judaism are more than the obvious difference that arises in any schematic comparison between modern views and those that were commonplace in the ancient world. The "Just War Theory," which is no doubt the dominant theory of moral warfare in the Western world, has its roots deep within ancient and medieval thought. The ancient Greeks had certain conventions of warfare, the breaking of which would lead to fierce condemnation and even punishment.[9] The Romans likewise believed that their wars were just, in the sense that they were allegedly waged only in defense of Rome or its allies.[10] During the first centuries of the Common Era these conventions developed into the pacifist attitudes about the legitimacy of war seen in Christian circles, and became the basis for the attitudes displayed by such as the Church Father Augustine and the scholastic Thomas Aquinas, who sought a precise definition of Just War.[11]

Nonetheless, despite its ancient roots, we first find systematic discussions on the moral restrictions of warfare, both of the reasons for going to war and of the limitations on conducting war, only as late as the sixteenth and seventeenth centuries. This development is connected to the work of several important theorists, among whom one might include Francisco de Vitoria, Francisco Suarez, Hugo Grotius and Emmerich de Vattel.[12]

As we have seen, the problem of the tension between the "Just War Theory" and certain Jewish concepts is indeed extensive, covering a wide range of sources from different periods in the history of Jewish thought. Various scholars have therefore sought to discuss this problem in general, by attempting to reveal the underlying principles of the "Jewish" attitude toward the morality of war. However, this "philosophical" approach to the problem in question is sometimes over-schematic in a way that does not properly distinguish between the different approaches and nuances in the various sources. This is particularly the case when we come to examine the Talmudic sages' views on the question of the morality of war. In this regard, there are many who seek to describe the stance of "rabbinic Judaism" on the issue of the morality of war, in light of well-defined rabbinic positions from the early medieval period onwards.[13] Though it is certainly possible to discern the existence of systematic rabbinic positions on the question of the morality of war in Jewish thought from the early medieval period onwards, it is doubtful whether these views can be foisted on the world of early rabbinic Judaism. An in-depth examination of the opinions of the sages relating to this question reveals a picture of the complex and multi-faceted world, which ought to be discussed on its own right and not merely as a pale image of later rabbinic views.

In coming to discuss the gap between the principles of the "Just War Theory" and the views emerging from rabbinic literature, we must pose the question of whether and to what extent the Sages were aware of the special moral problems connected with warfare. Did the problem of the absence from Jewish sources of a category of a "forbidden war" bother them in the same way that it bothers us today, or that it occupied the minds of various sages in other periods of history? The answer to this question must be based on a systematic and in-depth examination of the views of the Sages themselves on those issues that reveal the place of morality in war.

The morality of war in rabbinic literature

The rabbinic source in which we would most expect to find a discussion on the question of the morality of war is the eighth chapter of tractate Sotah, which is primarily devoted to halakhic considerations regarding the laws of war. The Mishnah, the Tosefta and the Babylonian and Jerusalem Talmuds devote a great deal of space within this chapter to the consideration of various halakhic questions connected to the laws of war. The moral viewpoint that we are concerned with is by its nature normative, although not legalistic in the full sense of the word, and so it is therefore natural that we first try to find what we are looking for in the area of normative halakhah among other laws of war.

However, perusal of this group of laws of war in the Mishnah and the Tosefta does not reveal any awareness of the existence of any moral difficulties connected to the state of warfare. What interests the Talmudic sages is not the moral context but various halakhic questions connected with the legal categorization of wars in terms of "optional," "commanded" and "obligatory" wars, the speeches given by the designated priest and the officers to the people, the definition of the different groups who return from the military campaign and the detailed laws relating to the fearful and the faint-hearted. It should be pointed out in this connection that the technical-halakhic preoccupation with the categorization of wars and the defining of those who are exempt from being drafted is not just typical of the Mishnah and the Tosefta, but also the Babylonian and the Jerusalem Talmuds do not stray significantly far from this framework and their discussions are centered on the existing Tannaitic categories.[14] It would seem that the sorting of the wars into "Optional Wars," "Commanded Wars" and "Obligatory Wars" brings to light the extensive gap that exists between the trend of decreasing and minimizing war that typifies the "Just War Theory" and the laws of war in rabbinic literature. M. Walzer, one of the prominent formulators of the "Just War Theory," expresses this feeling in the following words:

> The missing third category is the banned or forbidden war. It cannot be the case that all wars not required are permitted, for it is fairly clear that there were wars of which the rabbis disapproved. But the disapproval is usually explained with reference to conditions of various sorts imposed on the permitted wars, not with reference to wars that are never permitted.[15]

According to Walzer, the rabbinic sources relate only to two types of war – Optional Wars and Commanded Wars[16] – and these do not conform to the "Just War Theory," as he understands it. On the other hand the category of Forbidden Wars or methods of warfare that are categorically forbidden, do not occur at all in the rabbinic discourse. As opposed to the underlying assumptions of the "Just War Theory" that a war that is not a response to an attack is immoral and that certain methods of warfare are categorically banned, it would seem that rabbinic Judaism does not recognize these categories or indeed anything like them. While it is true that in certain cases the Talmudic sages did condemn the possibility of war and even limited the right of the king to declare war, nowhere whatsoever did they categorically forbid war or any specific means of warfare. This fundamental dissimilarity is perceived by Walzer and many others in terms of an unbridgeable gap between what is acceptable in contemporary discussion on the morality of war and the general approach reflected in rabbinic sources.

Contrary to Walzer's approach, a number of scholars are of the opinion that one can discern an affinity, at least in principle, between the moral approach of the Sages on the question of war and the moral approach emerging from the "Just War Theory."[17] In order to justify this claim of affinity between the two approaches, various passages in rabbinic literature that apparently intimate a moral approach which seeks to limit military activity in the spirit of the "Just War Theory" were discussed. However, some of the sources discussed do not, in truth, relate specifically to questions of the special moral approach dictated by the war situation, and others belong chronologically to a later period and do not reflect the approach of the sages of the Talmud. We shall mention here, therefore, the main sources from the Talmudic corpus, which are most commonly discussed in relation to the question of the morality of war.

1. Some scholars make the point that the limitation placed on the right of the king to wage an Optional War and his obligation to consult with the Sanhedrin and to inquire of the *Urim* and *Thummim* may be regarded as indications of the awareness of the Sages of the concept that fighting should be limited.[18] This requirement of the King was interpreted as the obligation to consult on moral issues prior to making a decision on going to war.[19] The required consideration on going to war is therefore a moral one, quite as much as it is a political or pragmatic consideration.[20] There are those who take this point even further and claim that the obligation to consult with the Sanhedrin on the moral issues refers not only to the morality of waging war (*Jus ad bellum*) but even to the way the war is to be conducted (*Jus in bello*).[21]

It should be pointed out in this connection that the consultation with the Sanhedrin could easily be interpreted in its constitutional context of sovereign authority and not necessarily in its moral context of limiting the fighting.[22] While it is true that the principle of "proper authority" constitutes a prerequisite for starting a war according to the "Just War Theory," this concept cannot be regarded as fundamental to traditional thought on warfare but is rather a constitutional question of sovereign authority which touches on other issues. An example of this principle can be found in the laws of war of the Roman army, which required the consent of the Senate in order to wage war, a condition whose purpose was clearly political and connected with the limiting of the powers of the Caesar.[23] The same is true in the US. The President is the Commander in Chief, but only the Congress can declare war. Therefore, one cannot use this Talmudic notion to deduce that the Sages felt that fighting should be limited.

2. Some scholars have pointed out the trend of various *midrashim* to negate the concrete obligation of certain biblical commandments relating to war, when they do not conform to moral sensitivities. In this connection, for example, it is taught that Sennacherib's relocation of the nations in his empire mingled ethnic groups to the extent that it became impossible to identify an Ammonite, thereby making the prohibition of Deut. 23:4 of not accepting an Ammonite into the congregation of the Lord unachievable and thus irrelevant.[24] This concept also abrogates, it would seem, the commandments relating to the complete extermination of the seven nations residing in the Land of Canaan and the people of Amalek. The abrogation of the biblical *herem* constitutes, according to this position, a decisive moral statement that is not prepared to come to terms with the concept of genocide.

It needs to be stated in this connection, however, that the first time this concept of "the mixing of the nations" was used in relation to the laws of war, is to be found in the words of Maimonides who points out, regarding the seven nations of the Land of Canaan that "their memory has long since been lost."[25] Also, the rabbinic principle of certain biblical commands that "never were and never will be," which is mentioned in various contexts in rabbinic literature,[26] is nowhere connected explicitly to the laws of war. It would seem therefore that this interpretive maneuver, although moral in nature, does not belong to the spiritual world of early rabbinic literature. As we shall seek to show below, only from the Middle Ages onwards do we find a clear rabbinic awareness of the question of the morality of war, and in all likelihood, it was this trend that also influenced Maimonides' assertion concerning the disappearance of the nations of Canaan.

3. There are those who have pointed out the trend toward the spiritualization of war in rabbinic literature by means of reinterpreting the battlefield in terms of the mental field of Torah study where the heroes are none other than great Talmudic sages whose victories are their victories (over each other) in the interpretation of *halakhah*.[27] In this connection it was suggested that the ascetic and heroic ethos of Torah study constitutes a moral equivalent of the ethos that developed for the most part on the battlefield.[28] Some scholars assumed therefore that this spiritualization of the laws of war was somehow connected with the unease of the Sages regarding the moral ramifications of war.[29]

In this regard it should be pointed out that the idea of "rabbinization" of biblical verses is a widespread phenomenon in rabbinic literature, which is connected with the attempt of the Sages to interpret the bible in a way that will bring it closer to their own world. There is absolutely no need to assume that it was moral opposition that motivated the Sages to interpret the Bible in this way. The absence of the reality of war from the world of the Sages on the one hand, and the intensive preoccupation with Torah study on the other was fertile soil for the emergence of a more spiritual worldview. But from this one cannot necessarily infer moral opposition by the Sages to warfare.

4. Certain scholars[30] sought to bring evidence of the moral awareness of the sages in the matter of warfare from the words of Shmuel, a third-century Babylonian rabbi, quoted in the Babylonian Talmud: "any[31] government that kills one in six people – is not punished."[32] While it is true that the Tosafist commentary interpreted this to mean those killed in an "Optional War,"[33] in which case one may discern from the words of the Talmud a concern for the number of casualties in war, this interpretation is itself far from clear-cut. Rabbi Shlomo Itzhaki (*Rashi*) alternatively interprets the phrase as referring to people "working in forced labor for the king."[34] In my opinion it is most likely that the reference is to the killing of people in accordance with the law, following Shmuel's principle that "the law of the government of the country is the law that prevails."[35]

5. There are those who see evidence of a negative view of war itself in the prohibition to carry a sword or other weapons on the Sabbath, as put forth in Mishnah Shabbat: "and the Sages said that weapons should always be regarded as pejorative objects as it is written 'and they shall beat their swords into plowshares . . .'."[36] It should be pointed out in this context that a possible historical interpretation of the Mishnah leads to the conclusion that while R. Eliezar who belonged to the School of Shammai and supported the armed struggle against Rome,[37] expresses in the Mishnah a positive opinion on the subject of carrying weapons on the Sabbath, claiming that they are a man's form of jewelry, the anonymous "rabbis" mentioned in the Mishnah, who apparently belonged to the School of Hillel, express primarily a negative opinion on the subject of carrying

weapons on the Sabbath. While this interpretation is not certain, it does provide a certain *Sitz im Leben* for the dispute and explains it as stemming from concrete historical and political attitudes, rather than general moral stances concerning the waging of war. Though it is true that the verses extolling peace in the Book of Isaiah lend some sort of pacifist dimension to the way the Sages relate to the subject of war, nevertheless one cannot necessarily detect here an approach that negates war itself.

It needs to be stressed that these examples in no way suggest that important moral insights connected with the ethics of war cannot be found in rabbinic sources. On the contrary, the emphasis on the sanctity of human life and the importance of saving life that exist in rabbinic literature are certainly sufficient to base the assumption that the killing involved in war is seen as despoiling the image of God incorporated in his creation. Relevant in this context are the frequently quoted words of Mishnah Sanhedrin: "This serves to inform us that whosoever destroys a single soul (!)[38] is imputed of having destroyed a whole world; and whosoever preserves a single soul (!) is merited with having preserved a whole world"[39] as are the words of Tosefta Yevamot: "R. Akiva says: anyone who sheds blood abrogates the image of God (i.e. since man is created in the image of God), as it is written he who sheds the blood of man, will have his own blood shed."[40] Certainly, whoever studied and transmitted these sources could not have easily agreed to the intentional slaughter of civilians in war.[41]

This having been said, through the examples given here we wish to indicate the ease with which some present-day writers enlist the words of the sages in contemporary moral disputes. Though moral insights that exist in rabbinic literature can illuminate one aspect or another of questions relating to the morality of war, this does not mean that the Sages contended with the special moral problems of warfare or with the problems that arose in later periods. Prudence obliges us to deal with the words of the Sages on their own terms in their unique contexts and to understand the various nuances and the differences that have occurred in the thinking of the Sages over the generations.

Were the Sages really aware of the special problematic nature of the morals of warfare, as some scholars assume, or was it a tendentious reading of the rabbinic sources that created this impression? In the following sections we shall attempt to answer this question by analyzing two central issues, the Call for Peace and the Limitation of the Siege, as test cases designed to evaluate the attitude of the Sages toward the special moral problems of warfare and the developments that occurred in their positions on this subject.

The Call for Peace

The Charter of the United Nations determines that war must be the last resort as a response to aggression, when all possibilities to settle the dispute by diplomatic means have been exhausted.[42] Although there is no overall agreement on the precise legal interpretation of this "Last Resort" principle[43] it would seem that diplomatic solutions are in general morally preferable over military solutions that for the most part involve bloodshed. Certain scholars are rightly of the opinion that there are echoes of this moral principle in rabbinic literature. Basing themselves on the concept of the "Call for Peace," the roots of which are already found in the Bible and which is systematically expanded on in rabbinic literature, they attempt to show that the concept of limiting hostilities by means of the "Last Resort" principle is an integral part of the Sages' moral landscape.[44] Within this framework we shall attempt to critically examine what the Sages have to say on the subject of the "Call for Peace," and to show the developments that occurred in this context.

According to a literal reading of Deuteronomy 20:10–15, the "Call for Peace" is actually directed to "all the remote cities" (Deuteronomy 20:15), though not applying to the nations of Canaan. This indeed was how these verses were understood by some of the commentators on the Torah, who interpreted it as follows: "Scripture is speaking of an optional war as stated in Deuteronomy, 'so shall you do to all the remote cities'."[45] This exegetical stance is based on *Sifre Deuteronomy*, which interprets the verses as relating to Optional Wars only: "'When you approach a city [to wage war against it]' (Deuteronomy 20:10) – Scripture is speaking of an optional war."[46]

However, the opinion of many of the post-Talmudic commentators is that the "Call for Peace" relates both to "Optional Wars" and to "Commanded Wars." So, for example, Nahmanides claims that: ". . . the call for Peace applies even in the case of Commanded Wars, for we are obligated to call for Peace even in the case of the Seven Nations of Canaan."[47] And similarly, Maimonides claims: "War must never be waged against any person in the world before calling for peace, whether in an Optional War or in a Commanded War."[48] It is possible that the expansion of the obligation to call for Peace to include Commanded Wars has its origins in the development of certain moral sensibilities among post-Talmudic rabbinic circles that were not at ease with the idea of limiting diplomacy to Optional Wars only.[49]

Recently, E. Zand has sought to point out the independent moral stance that emerges from Rashi's interpretations of various biblical verses. Thus for instance, regarding Gen. 15:1, when God appears to Abram and says to him: "Fear not, Abram; I am your shield," Rashi explains: "(a shield) from punishment, so that you will not be punished for all those souls that you have slain (in the battle against the Five Kings)."[50] In a similar vein, Rashi also interprets what is written in Deut. 2:26, regarding Moses' call for Peace to Sihon, king of the Amorites, explaining that Moses ostensibly defied God and challenged the morality of his commands. The moral stance displayed in Rashi's commentary, often deviates considerably from the *midrashim* on which he based his interpretation.[51] Rashi's sensitivity to the question of the morality of war places him therefore comfortably among the post-Talmudic tradition which seeks to "moralize" the Jewish laws of warfare.

However, even if this "moralized" interpretation in line with contemporary outlooks on warfare is valid with regard to the opinions of several medieval sages, this can hardly be termed the "rabbinic outlook" on the morality of war and even less so the outlook of "Judaism" as a whole. The unequivocal perspective emerging from the Tannaitic *midrashim* follows in fact the literal meaning of the text and limits the obligation to call for Peace strictly to Optional Wars. In the entire corpus of Tannaitic literature no attempt is made to extend the obligation to strive for peace through diplomacy as a moral imperative. Only in relatively late *midrashim* do we find, for the first time, expressions indicating the Sages' discomfort with the fact that the Call for Peace is not obligatory in the war against the nations of Canaan. We find such expressions, for example, in *Deuteronomy Rabbah*, the final redaction of which is dated to around the ninth century:

> The Holy One, Blessed be He, accepted all of Moses' decisions. How was this so? The Holy One, Blessed be He, did not instruct Moses to break the Tablets of the Law, but Moses went and broke them by himself. And how do we know that He agreed? Because it says: "which you have broken" [Ex.34:1] – you have done well breaking. Similarly, The Holy One, Blessed be He, instructed Moses to wage war against Sihon and Og, as it is written "and engage with him in battle" (Deut. 2:24), but Moses did not do this, but rather, "I sent messengers from the wilderness of Kedemoth to Sihon, king of Heshbon, with words of peace, saying . . ." (Deuteronomy 2:26). The Holy One, Blessed be He, said to Moses, I told you to fight him and you open peace negotiations!? Behold, I swear on your (i.e. my own) life, I accept your decision – any war they go out to fight, they must first open peace negotiations, as it is written "When you draw near to a city to fight against it, you must offer it terms of peace" (Deuteronomy 20:10).[52]

In this *midrash* the author emphasizes the fact that Moses' action in calling for peace to the king of the Amorites contradicted the specific commandment of God. Nevertheless, Moses' moral motivation is seen in a positive light by the author, and even God Himself is said to agree in the end with Moses, asserting that: "Any war they go out to fight, they must first open peace negotiations." What is written in Deuteronomy is therefore interpreted as God's retraction of his first command regarding the war against the Amorites and his acknowledgment, it would seem, of the justification of Moses' moral stance.

It would seem that this *midrash* seeks first and foremost to solve an exegetical problem. If, indeed, what is written in Deuteronomy refers specifically to an Optional War, why did Moses call for Peace to Sihon, king of the Amorites, particularly after God had specifically commanded to engage him in battle with no mention of a Call for Peace? The author of the *midrash* chose to solve this discrepancy by suggesting that God "changed his mind" as regards this matter, as a consequence of implied criticism from Moses. However, beyond the question of interpretation, the moral awareness of the author of the *midrash* to the problematic nature of declaring war without first trying a diplomatic approach, comes over clearly. This awareness comes to the fore particularly in view of Moses' actions that went against a divine command and their presentation as a criticism of a command of God. The *midrash* is therefore polemic in nature and stems, it would seem, from the moral anxiety over the aggressive treatment of the seven nations of Canaan.

A passage from *Midrash Tanhuma*, the final redaction of which dates from around the eighth century, goes even further in supporting Moses' moral stance in not agreeing to wage war without exhausting the possibility of calling for peace:

> "And this is the law of the sacrifice of peace-offerings" (Leviticus 7:11) – as it says: "Her ways are ways of pleasantness, and all her paths are peace" (Proverbs 3:17). Everything that is written in the Torah is written for the sake of peace. Even though wars are written in the Torah – they are written for the purpose of peace. You find that the Holy One, Blessed be He, abrogated his decree because of peace. When was this? When the Holy One, Blessed be He, said to Moses: "When you will besiege a city for a long time" (Deuteronomy 20:19) and the whole matter; the Holy One, Blessed be He, said to him that he must utterly destroy the nations of Canaan, as it is written: "You shall utterly destroy them . . ." (Deuteronomy 20:17). But Moses did not do this, but rather said: "now when I am going to strike them, I do not know who has sinned and who has not sinned, so I will approach them in peace," as it is written: "And I sent messengers out of the wilderness of Kedemoth . . . words of peace." (Deuteronomy 2:26). But since he saw that he did not come in peace toward him, he struck him, as it is written: "They have smitten him and his sons and his entire people" (Numbers 21:35). The Holy One, Blessed be He, said to Moses: I have said "You shall utterly destroy them . . ." (Deuteronomy 20:17), and you approached them in peace?! Behold, I swear on your (i.e. my own) life, that as you have spoken so will I do. As it is written: "When you draw near to a city to fight against it, offer it terms of peace" (Deuteronomy 20:10). For it is written: "Her ways are ways of pleasantness, and all her paths are peace" (Proverbs 3:17).[53]

In this version, Moses' moral reservation regarding the annihilation of the Amorites is depicted in rather bright colors: "now I am going to strike them but I do not know who has sinned and who has not sinned." Moses is thus presented as seeking to avoid harming the innocent. The principle of the immunity of non-combatants will be discussed below in detail, but already at this stage it can be pointed out that the "Call for Peace" and the "Principle of the Last Resort" are both ultimately designed to avoid the bloodshed concomitant with the state of war. Here too, the *midrash* concludes that God accepted Moses' criticism and reasserted the command to call for Peace prior to any war.

The critical moral outlook that we see in these late rabbinic *midrashim*, is not found in early rabbinic literature. Although early rabbinic *midrashim* praise Moses' call for Peace to Sihon king of the Amorites, Moses' actions are hardly presented as contradicting the divine command nor as carrying some decisive moral message. In this connection the version of *Sifre Numbers* is pertinent:

> Peace is a great value while dispute is despicable. Peace is so good that even in time of war peace is needed, as it is written: "When you draw near to a city to fight against it, offer it terms of peace" (Deuteronomy 20:10), as well

as: "I sent messengers out of the wilderness of Kedemoth to Sihon, king of
Heshbon . . . words of peace" (Deuteronomy 2:26).[54]

Moses' actions are not presented here as being subversive in any way as if
challenging an immoral command of God. On the contrary, Moses' actions are
presented as a direct continuation of the Torah's commandment that requires a
Call for Peace. This *midrash*, which is concerned with the virtues of peace, does
not seek to extend the halakhic obligation to make a Call for Peace, even if this
might be indirectly inferred from Moses' action in making a Call for Peace to one
of the kings of the nations of Canaan. Moses' call for Peace is presented here as
simply adhering to a commandment in the Book of Deuteronomy and not as an
attempt to expand this commandment.

A further example of noticeable moral development in the later *midrashim* can
be found in the following homily from *Deuteronomy Rabbah*:

> R. Shmuel bar Nahmani said: Joshua fulfilled this passage; what did Joshua
> do? He sent a message to every place that he was about to capture and he
> wrote in it: he who wants to make peace should come forward and make
> peace; and he who wants to run away should run away and he who wants
> to make war should come forward and fight. What did the Girgashites do?
> They turned around and went away, and the Holy One, Blessed be He, gave
> them a land as beautiful as their own – which is Africa. And Joshua made
> peace with the Gibeonites who came forward to make peace, but the thirty-
> one kings who came to fight with him were smote by the hand of the Holy
> One, Blessed be He. How do we know this? Because it is written: "and they
> smote them, until they left none remaining" (Joshua 11:8).[55]

Joshua's actions are understood here as a direct continuation of Moses' moral
criticism that appears earlier in the *midrash*, and are therefore connected with the
extension of the obligation to call for Peace. "Joshua fulfilled this," that is to say,
fulfilled the commandment of "offer it terms of peace" (Deuteronomy 20:10), which
the author of the *midrash* described above as a commandment that was reenacted
as a consequence of Moses' moral criticism. In other words, the author of the
midrash claims that even Joshua acted in line with Moses' moral criticism, and was
careful to call for Peace in all the wars he conducted.

This *midrash* appears in fact almost a half of a millennium earlier, in two
compilations from the Land of Israel from approximately the fourth century CE,
namely the Jerusalem Talmud and *Leviticus Rabbah*:

> Rabbi Shmuel bar Nahman said: Joshua sent three messages to the Land of
> Israel before entering the Land, saying: "whoever wants to leave should
> leave, whoever wants to make peace should make peace and whoever wants
> to make war should fight." The Girgashites, believing in God, left and went
> to Africa – "until I come and take you away to a land like your own land"
> (2 Kings 18:32 and Isaiah 36:17) which is Africa. The Gibeonites made peace

– "and how the inhabitants of Gibeon had made peace with Israel" (Joshua 10:1). Thirty-one kings made war and fell.[56]

Who is it that came to the Canaanites and told them that Israel was coming to their land? R. Yishmael Bar Nahman said: Joshua son of Nun sent three messages to them: "whoever wants to leave should leave, whoever wants to make peace should make peace and whoever wants to make war should fight." The Girgashites left and therefore they were given a land more beautiful than their own, as it is written: "until I come and take you away to a land like your own land" (2 Kings 18:32 and Isaiah 36:17), which is Africa. The Gibeonites made peace – "and how the inhabitants of Gibeon had made peace with Israel" (Joshua 10:1). Thirty-one kings made war and fell.[57]

Even though it also emerges from these earlier versions of the *midrash* that Joshua called for peace to the local inhabitants of Canaan, it should be noted that while the *Deuteronomy Rabbah* version links this to Moses' criticism, here in the Jerusalem Talmud and in *Leviticus Rabbah* there is a clear separation between the two issues. According to the earlier versions of the *midrash* Joshua's actions are not directly linked to the biblical injunction to call for Peace. Consequently, the idea relating to the extending of the Call for Peace to Optional Wars is not something that the authors of these *midrashim* were aware of. The actions of Joshua according to the Jerusalem Talmud and *Leviticus Rabbah* could be the result of military tactics and not necessarily of moral considerations. On the other hand, in the *Deuteronomy Rabbah* version we have the additional words of R. Shmuel bar Nahmani, linking the narrative to Moses' moral criticism. That is to say, that the actions of Joshua stemmed from the Torah commandment to call for Peace, after the correction of the commandment that Moses initiated and after the divine opinion concurred with Moses' correction. The actions of Joshua are presented clearly and explicitly as the first moral application of the new procedure to Call for Peace prior to any war. It is for this reason that in the *Deuteronomy Rabbah* version emphasis is placed on the fact that Joshua called for peace "to every place that he was about to capture" – an emphasis that is absent from the earlier *midrashim*.

There is no doubt that the author of *Deuteronomy Rabbah* was familiar with these homilies that existed and were available to him in the Jerusalem Talmud and in *Leviticus Rabbah*. Nevertheless, the innovativeness in the redaction of the later *midrash* cannot be ignored, in connecting Joshua's "peace messages" to the moral complexity connected with Moses' calling into question the morality of an explicit command of God.

In this context it is interesting to compare Moses' moral criticism of the divine commandment, as it occurs in *Midrash Tanhuma* and *Deuteronomy Rabbah*, to similar criticism attributed to King Saul in the Babylonian Talmud:

"And they fought in the stream-bed" (1 Samuel 15:5) – R. Mani said: they quarreled over dealings related to the stream-bed. When the Holy One, Blessed be He, said to Saul: "Now go and smite Amalek (and utterly destroy all that they have, and spare them not; but slay man and woman, infant and suckling, ox and sheep, camel and ass)" (1 Samuel 15:3). Saul replied: for the killing of a single soul the Torah demands the bringing of a decapitated heifer (Deuteronomy 21:1–9), what then can possibly be expected for the killing of so many souls? If a man sins, why should an animal be held responsible? If an adult sins, why should infants and sucklings be held responsible? A voice from Heaven was then heard telling him "Don't be so righteous!" and when Saul said to Doeg: "turn, and fall upon the priests (and Doeg the Edomite turned, and he fell upon the priests, and he slew on that day eighty-five persons who wore the linen ephod" (1 Samuel 22:18), a voice from Heaven was heard telling him "Don't be so wicked!"[58]

The Babylonian Talmud brings here a *midrash* which explicitly rejects the involvement of moral considerations in the framework of commandments relating to war. The sinfulness of Saul's action is described as a consequence of his merciful compunctions that (according to the *midrash*) are nothing but qualms of over-righteousness. The *midrash* therefore points to Saul's hypocrisy that in one place he exaggerates the moral issue and in another, orders the murder of innocent people.

It is interesting to note that the moral assertion made by Saul according to the Babylonian Talmud which stopped him from completely annihilating Amalek, is identical in essence to the assertion that *Midrash Tanhuma* places in Moses' mouth: "now I am going to strike them but I do not know who has sinned and who has not sinned." Moses' concern is therefore identical to Saul's, who did not want to harm the innocent. However, contrary to *Midrash Tanhuma*, the response of the *midrash* in the Babylonian Talmud to this assertion is not particularly positive. According to the Babylonian Talmud the concern for the innocent in war is a form of over-righteousness that does not, in truth, lead to a higher level of morality. So it turned out with Saul who claimed to be so concerned about Amalek but in the end slaughtered an entire city of innocent priests. As regards *Midrash Tanhuma*, on the other hand, the very fact that the assertion is ascribed there to Moses as opposed to Saul already shows the positive stance of the author of the *midrash*. Determining that God concurred with Moses constitutes the acceptance of his moral sensitivity and the turning of it into mandatory law. According to *Midrash Tanhuma*, then, every avenue must be exhausted in calling for peace in order to prevent war and unnecessary bloodshed.

From reviewing the sources that deal with the obligation to make a Call for Peace, it is possible to draw a number of conclusions on the question of the attitude of the Sages to the principle of the "Last Resort" and the limiting of the fighting on account of moral considerations. First of all, we have seen that within the framework of Tannaitic literature the Call for Peace is understood as being directed toward Optional Wars in accordance with the literal meaning of the biblical verses. The ideal of peace is indeed mentioned in many places in Tannaitic literature and even Moses' call for Peace to Sihon king of the Amorites is understood as a positive action in *Sifre Numbers*. However, the moral criticism and with it the controversial nature of Moses' actions are absent from the Tannaitic literature. Similarly, the conscience extension of the Torah's command-ments to make a Call for Peace in "Commanded Wars" as well, is absent at this stage.

Do we evince, then, a chronological change stemming from the late development of the concept of the Call for Peace in rabbinic literature? It might be assumed perhaps that the absence of this idea from Tannaitic literature is connected with the simple fact that the Tannaitic material is mostly concerned with *halakhah* and much less with *aggadah*. It would seem, however, that this change of approach is not merely a matter of genre according to which the Sages sought to restrict the discussion on these subjects to the world of *aggadah*. In light of the development that we have indicated from the earlier *midrashim* to the later, Medieval ones, it can be assumed that there is indeed a chronological development with respect of the Call for Peace. The fourth-century *midrashim* that have been discussed here from the Jerusalem Talmud and *Leviticus Rabbah*, which mention Joshua's Call for Peace, are not significantly different from the *midrash* cited in *Sifre Numbers* about Moses' call for Peace. In all these cases the Call for Peace is understood as a positive value, and as a natural and simple continuation of the biblical ideal. The absence of the controversial element of the divine command and the author's attempt to expand the application of that command show, however, that the moral basis of the idea of the Call for Peace is not fully developed in the early *midrashim* and does not express itself fully in moral terms until the later *midrashim* that were composed in post-Talmudic times.

The moral criticism and the decisive assertion that a Call for Peace must be made prior to every war was adopted, as we have said, by important commentators in the Middle Ages. It would seem that at this stage, expressed by the commentary of Maimonides, Nahmanides and certain Medieval *midrashim*, the Call for Peace underwent a process of "normatization" that turned the practice of proclaiming Peace into normative *halakhah*, a law obligating subsequent generations, both for "Optional" and "Commanded" wars. This process began, it would seem, already in *Midrash Tanhuma* and *Deuteronomy Rabbah*, whose interpretations of the verses in Deuteronomy were seen as evidence of God's admission of the moral precedence of the diplomatic process, even in situations of "Commanded Wars."

Limitation of the Siege

There is no doubt that the most important principle asserted within the framework of the "Just War Theory" is the principle of immunity of non-combatants. The extent of this immunity, however, is not entirely clear. It is unclear, for instance, whether it includes only those civilians who are not involved at all in the fighting or whether it includes even soldiers who are not playing a significant role in the war effort.[59] One way or another, it would seem that it is possible to find echoes of this important principle in the rules relating to the besiegement of a city in rabbinic law. Of these rules, one of the most important is the obligation to allow an escape route or safe exit for that part of the population that is not interested in fighting. A fully developed articulation of this halakhic obligation is found in Maimonides' "Laws of Kings and Wars":

> On surrounding a city in order to capture it, the city must not be surrounded on all its four sides, but only on three sides, and a place must be left to allow those who want to flee for their lives (to do so),[60] as it is written: "And they warred against Midian, as the Lord commanded Moses," (Numbers 31:7). Through tradition they have learned that this was what he had commanded.[61]

Certain scholars have sought to bring evidence from this *halakhah* that rabbinic preoccupation with matters of war is connected with their moral obligation to limit the fighting and injury of the non-combatant population. Though this interpretation of Maimonides is definitely legitimate,[62] the possibility exists that what is being discussed here is a technical command which has little to do with morals and more with military tactics. If an escape route is set aside for those who want to flee for their lives, this will undoubtedly affect the stance and morale of the enemy to the worse. I tend, nevertheless, to agree with "the moral explanation" since this law does not stand alone, but is one of a series of Maimonidian rulings designed to inculcate moral principles into warfare. Similar ideas that were seemingly taken directly from the words of Maimonides are found in *Midrash Hagadol* on Numbers:[63]

> "And they warred against Midian" (Numbers 31:7): What do we learn from the words "As God commanded Moses"? This teaches us that they only surrounded the city on three sides, and that they left the fourth side open without surrounding it, so that there would be somewhere for anyone fleeing for their lives to escape.[64]

But even if the orientation of Maimonides and the *Midrash HaGadol* in this context is indeed based on the moral issue and its purpose is to prevent the killing of non-combatants, it is difficult to point to the source of this ruling in early rabbinic literature. Though the homily is indeed based on *Sifre Numbers*, it can nevertheless be determined that the sense and context of the matter are clearly different:

> "And they warred against Midian" – they surrounded it on three sides.[65]
> R. Nathan says: he left them[66] a fourth side open, so that they would flee.[67]

A careful comparison between Maimonides' version and the version attested in *Sifre Numbers*, points to a significant ideological development that occurred in the transmission of the midrash. The *Sifre* does not address the "laws of besiegement" or any other religious imperative for that matter. Rather, the *Sifre* is only interested in the interpretation of the biblical verses, and hence in the actual measures taken by the Israelite soldiers in the Midianite war. This interpretive context is likewise maintained in *Midrash HaGadol* on Numbers, which is focused on the Midianite war and not on establishing the legal norms of besiegement. Viewed against this midrashic background, then, Maimonides' version represents an important shift from mere exegesis concerning the Midianite war, towards the extraction of legal and moral conclusions from the soldiers' behavior in battle.

As far as the version of *Midrash Tannai'im* on Deuteronomy is concerned, it is possible to discern an additional development, that is concerned with taking the *midrash* out of its original exegetical context in *Sifre Numbers* and transferring it to interpret the verses relating to the siege in Deuteronomy. The *Sifre*'s commentary does not relate to anything other than the actual behavior of the soldiers in the war of Midian in order to interpret the expression "And they warred," and in no way is concerned with the laws of besiegement. The transferring of this tradition to the verses relating to the laws of besiegement in Deuteronomy entails, therefore, an important change in the context of the *midrash*. The resituating of the *midrash* and its exegetical context, necessarily results in a shift from a description of the historical reality to a normative statement regarding the laws of besiegement. In *Midrash Tannaim* on Deuteronomy we read according to R. Nathan that: "They should leave the fourth side open, so that they could flee."[68] This is no longer a description of what happened in Midian, but rather a normative halakhic statement, stating what should always happen in situations of besiegement.[69]

The literary phenomena that have been discerned in the later *midrashim* and in the writings of several medieval authorities, express a significant ideological shift in the meaning and implications of our *midrash*. It is likely that the original meaning of the midrash as expressed in *Sifre Numbers* touches on the tactical question of how the Midianite war was conducted. In this context, there is no mention of a moral, or otherwise divine, commandment. Only in a later period the *midrash* was re-worded in order to give it a normative and halakhic orientation with a clear moral message. One can evince therefore a vivid chronological development in the moral orientation of the rabbinic discourse on the laws of warfare and besiegement. While the early *midrash* does not recognize any moral requirements as part the laws of besiegement, in post-Talmudic anthologies and in the works of Maimonides we find a well-established moral orientation that applies its moral assumptions to the halakhic norms of warfare.

Lately, Kahana has discovered another *midrash*, which possibly bears on the matter of rabbinic war ethics. The *Sifre Zuta* on Deuteronomy reads as follows: "R. Akiva says: ('You may destroy only the trees that you know do not produce food; you may cut them down for use in building siege-works against the town that makes war with you) until it falls' – until you conquer it on all four sides."[70] As can be proven from the context, this *midrash* is intended to encourage the soldiers to finish the siege as quickly and effectively as possible. This is evident from two adjacent homilies on the same verse, which permit the continuation of the siege on the Sabbath and exempt the warriors from the Passover sacrifice. As Kahana rightfully claims, this *midrash* is somewhat at odds with *Sifre Numbers*, which limits the siege to three sides alone. However, it would seem to me that we are dealing here with a tactical disagreement rather than a moral one. That is, what is the best way to conquer a city? Is it through hermetic besiegement or by letting people flee and thus discouraging the enemy? In fact, other homilies in *Sifre Zuta* on Deuteronomy also reflect similar tactical concerns, such as the instruction to place a siege at only one city at a time.[71]

Another *midrash* that bears on the question of limiting the siege appears in *Sifre Deuteronomy*. Regarding the "siege verses" in Deuteronomy 20, *Sifre Deuteronomy* expounds as follows: "to make war upon it – not to cause it to suffer starvation and not to cause it to suffer thirst and not to cause it to die of illness."[72] This could supposedly be understood in the spirit of moral limitations on warfare according to the modern concept of *Jus in bello*, in which certain means of conducting war are considered to be especially cruel and are thus forbidden. However, such a reading of the *midrash* is impossible. In this case, the very same *midrash* goes on to state that in certain cases, "even to cause it to suffer starvation and even to cause it to suffer thirst and even to cause it to die of illness."[73] The fact that the authors allow such means in the case of Obligatory Wars shows that the *midrash* is primarily concerned with halakhic categorization and not with making moral statements. The whole point of the "Just War Theory" is that even in cases of justified wars (Obligatory Wars?) there are severe moral limitations on the conduct of war. No awareness of such limitations can thus be found in this *midrash*.

It is proper to state in conclusion that I do not intend to present the viewpoint of Maimonides on these questions as being close in spirit to the regnant outlook that is accepted today among the proponents of the "Just War Theory." As Blidstein has already shown in a number of articles,[74] the purpose of war in Maimonides' philosophy is connected with the dissemination of the true religion and fighting the wars of God, which is closer in many ways to the outlook that is prevalent in fundamentalist Islamic trends. But at the same time, I want to make the point that on certain issues that have been discussed here, Maimonides does indeed show an awareness of the special moral problematic nature of warfare in a way that deviates from the early rabbinic sources.

Conclusions

In this article we sought to touch on certain aspects of the tension that exists between the "Just War Theory" that is prevalent today in the fields of ethics and international law and the moral orientation emanating from rabbinic literature. By analyzing certain sources from the extant rabbinic corpus we sought to examine the extent to which they reflect an awareness of the moral issues that today occupy our world in the field of warfare.

We started the discussion by pointing out the total absence of moral issues relating to warfare in the classical rabbinic statement regarding the laws of war in the eighth chapter of tractate *Sotah*, including the *Mishnah*, the *Tosefta*, and both Talmuds. Against the background of the systematic discussion that takes place on the subject of categorizing the wars and deciding who is exempt from conscription, this absence becomes all the more conspicuous. Additional references, furthermore, that are quite too often quoted from rabbinic literature which allegedly reflect the confrontation with questions that touch on the morality of warfare, turn out to have no connection with this issue at all.

In the core of the discussion we sought to deal systematically with a number of issues that indicate, in our opinion, important developments that occurred in rabbinic literature in this regard. From the analysis we conducted, it appears that while Tannaitic literature reveals no awareness of the moral problems that arise in the course of warfare, certain Amoraic traditions show the first signs of dealing with the problem of the morality of war. However, a vivid and systematic normative expression of these ideas is achieved only later, in post-Talmudic collections and medieval commentary.

In our treatment of the Call for Peace we attempted to show that the halakhic *midrashim* considered this obligation to be relevant only in the case of Permitted Wars, as befitting a literal reading of the biblical verses. The extension of the Call for Peace to obligatory wars first appears in the Jerusalem Talmud and in *Leviticus Rabbah*, although this extension is not considered binding and does not stem from a moral position. It is only in later *midrashim* such as the *Tanhuma* and *Deuteronomy Rabbah*, as well as in the writings of Maimonides and Nahmanides that the Call for Peace becomes a binding norm in all types of warfare and is accompanied by a significant moral message.

A similar phenomenon can be observed in the development of the laws of besiegement. In a tannaitic *midrash* we indeed find the opinion that the siege of Midian was limited to surrounding the city on three sides only. However, it is reasonable to assume that this opinion is based on the exegetical challenge of interpreting the verse: "And they warred against Midian" (Numbers 31:7) and on various strategic considerations. In certain post-Talmudic *midrashim* and in "The Laws of Kings and Wars" of Maimonides, however, this *midrashic* moral orientation becomes an obligatory legal norm. The normalization of the morality of war into the accepted halakhic standards is a special feature of Maimonides' established and systematic doctrine.

Notes

1. See for instance: Y. Shaviv, "The Torah's War against War," in *Batzir Avi'ezer: Studies Related to Society and Forbidden Work on the Sabbath*, Alon Shvut: Tzomet, 1989, pp. 111–126 (Hebrew); A. Ravitzky, *Freedom Inscribed: Diverse Voices of the Jewish Religious Thought*, Tel Aviv: Am Oved, 2000, pp. 139–158 (Hebrew); E. Bloom *et al.* (Eds.), *Values in the Trial of War: Ethics and War in the View of Judaism*, Jerusalem: The Mizrahi Family and Moreshet Publishers, 1985 (Hebrew); A. Lichtenstein, "Morality and War," *Techumin* 4, 1983, pp. 180–194 (Hebrew); E. Luz (Ed.), *Pacifism and Torah: Works by A.S. Tamares*, Jerusalem: Dinur Center, 1992 (Hebrew); R. Kimelman, "The Laws and Restrictions of War," in I.M. Gafni and A. Ravitzky (Eds.), *Sanctity of Life and Martyrdom*, Jerusalem: Zalman Shazar Center, 1992, pp. 233–254 (Hebrew); Y. Ahituv, "The Wars of Israel and the Sanctity of Life," in I.M. Gafni and A. Ravitzky (Eds.), *Sanctity of Life and Martyrdom*, Jerusalem: Zalman Shazar Center, 1992, pp. 255–276 (Hebrew); Y. Koren, "Morality in *Halakha*: Genocide, Divine Command and Halakhic Reasoning," *Akdamot* 18, 2007, pp. 41–54 (Hebrew); A. Shapira, *Democratic Values in the Hebrew Bible*, Tel Aviv: Hakibutz Hame'uhad, 2009, pp. 143–186 (Hebrew).

2. The literature on the "Just War Theory" is vast. In the current context, we shall only refer to several of the most important studies, which provide general surveys of the topic. See especially: M. Walzer, *Just and Unjust Wars*, New York: Basic, 1977; M. Walzer, *Arguing About War*, New Haven: Yale University Press, 2004; J.T. Johnson, *The Just War Tradition and the Restraint of War*, Princeton: Princeton University Press, 1981; B. Orend, *The Morality of War*, Toronto: Broadview Press, 2006.

3. On "realism" with regard to war ethics, see: J. MacMahan, "Realism, Morality and War," in T. Nardin (Ed.), *The Ethics of War and Peace: Religious and Secular Perspectives*, Princeton: Princeton University Press, 1996, pp. 78–92; D. Mapel, "Realism and the Ethics of War and Peace," in T. Nardin (Ed.), *The Ethics of War and Peace: Religious and Secular Perspectives*, Princeton: Princeton University Press, 1996, pp. 180–200.

4. On "Pacifism" in this regard, see especially: J. Teichman, *Pacifism and the Just War*, Oxford: Basil Blackwell, 1986; R. Holmes, *On War and Morality*, Princeton: Princeton University Press, 1989, pp.19–49; J. Narveson, "Pacifism: A Philosophical Analysis," in R. Wasserstrom (Ed.), *Morality and War*, Belmont: Wadsworth, 1970, pp. 63–77; J. Narveson, "Violence and War," in T. Regan (Ed.), *Matters of Life and Death*, Philadelphia: Temple University Press, 1980, pp. 109–147; for an updated and comprehensive survey of "realistic" and "pacifist" approaches to war ethics evident in Jewish sources, see: M. Hellinger, "War and Peace in Jewish Tradition: Between Idealism and Realism," in S. Avineri (Ed.), *War and Peace*, Jerusalem: Zalman Shazar Center, 2010, pp. 73–98.

5. To these categories, many add a third category of "*Jus post bellum*," dealing with the question of post-war justice, see for instance: Orend, *The Morality of War*, pp. 160–219.

6. It can hardly be denied that the attitude of Jewish sources to the question of war and peace is eclectic and complex. Within the Bible itself we find both realistic attitudes that consider war to be "the way of the world," together with idealistic and pacifist stances that revile war and praise peace. One could point out the commandment of total war against the nations of Canaan and Amalek on one hand, and the visions of universal peace along with the idea of all humans being created in God's image on the other. The various biblical views on war and peace belong of course to different sources that make up the mosaic that we call the Bible, and their development was connected to different milieus. What is important to us in this regard is that the various outlooks in the Bible continued to inspire generations of Jewish thought on these matters. In light of the basic ambivalence in the Bible, one should not be surprised to find similarly different and even opposing views on the morality of warfare within rabbinic literature as well. However, the fact that there are many different views within the biblical and Talmudic corpus, does not negate the fact that the main thrust of those views about warfare do seem to be diametrically opposed to the moral principles that are commonly accepted today. Emphasizing the anti-war voices that are expressed in the Bible is undoubtedly one way of dealing with the issue, but this is not enough to totally negate the basic conflict. For a discussion of the morality of war in the Bible, see especially: A. Shapira, *Democratic Values in the Hebrew Bible*, pp. 143–186; S. Niditch, *War in the Hebrew Bible: A Study in the Ethics of Violence*, New York: Oxford University Press, 1993; J.A. Wood, *Perspective on War in the Bible*, Macon, GA: Mercer University Press, 1998; N. Goodman, "Pacifism and Nonviolence: Another Jewish View," in J.P. Burns (Ed.), *War and Its Discontents: Pacifism and Quietism in the Abrahamic Traditions*, Washington D.C.: Georgetown University Press, 1996, pp. 67–73.

7. Maimonides, *Mishneh Torah*, The Laws of Kings and Wars, 5:1.

8. Commentary on Gen. 9:5–6 and Deut. 20:20; See: Rabbi Naphtali Zvi Yehudah Berlin, *Ha'amek Davar: A Commentary on the Torah*, commented and edited by M. Kupperman, Jerusalem: Luhot Frank, 2005 (Hebrew); On the latter's approach to the morality of war, see: Ahituv, "The Wars of Israel and the Sanctity of Life," pp. 255–276; Y. Kaufman, "A Time for War vs. A Time for Peace according to the Natziv,"

Merhavim 6, 1997, pp. 285–297 (Hebrew); N. Zohar, "Morality and War: A Critique of Bleich's Oracular Halakha," in D.H. Frank (Ed.), *Commandment and Morality: New Essays in Jewish Legal and Political Philosophy*, Albany: SUNY Press, 1995, pp. 245–258.

9. Thucydides, for instance, provides the following report concerning the Athenians: "On reconsideration, the Athenians thought it a savage and excessive decision to destroy a whole city rather than just the guilty." See: Thucydides, *The Peloponnesian War*, M. Hammond (trans.) with an Introduction and Notes by P.J. Rhodes, Oxford: Oxford University Press, 2009, Section 3.36, pp. 145–146; J. Ober, "Classical Greek Times," in M. Howard, G. Andreopoulos and M.R. Schulman (Eds.), *The Laws of War: Constraints on Warfare in the Western World*, New Haven: Yale University Press, 1994, pp. 12–26, 227–230; M.I. Finley, "The Fifth Century Athenian Empire: A Balance Sheet," in P. Low (Ed.), *The Athenian Empire*, Edinburgh: Edinburgh University Press, 2008, pp. 14–40; G. Herman, *Morality and Behavior in Democratic Athens*, Cambridge: Cambridge University Press, 2006.

10. A. Riggsby, *Caesar in Gaul and Rome: War in Words*, Austin: University of Texas Press, 2006, pp. 157–190; W.V. Harris, *War and Imperialism in Republican Rome*, Oxford, 1979, pp. 170–175; J. Rich, "Fear, Greed and Glory: The Causes of Roman War-Making in the Middle Republic," J. Rich and G. Shipley (Eds.), *War and Society in the Roman World*, London: Routledge, 1993, pp. 38–68.

11. J.H. Yoder, *The Politics of Jesus*, Grand Rapids: Eerdmans, 1972; R. Bainton, *Christian Attitudes towards War and Peace*, Nashville: Abingdon Press, 1960.

12. See for instance: R. Jeffery, *Hugo Grotius in International Thought*, New York and London: Palgrave Macmillan, 2006.

13. The tendency to project medieval rabbinic stances on early rabbinic literature is especially evident with regard to "Maimonidean" conceptions that are applied in the study of Talmudic sources. For other examples of this phenomenon, see for instance: Sh. Friedman, "How Much Anthropomorphism? Allowing the *Aggada* to Speak for Itself," *Sidra* 22, 2007, pp. 89–152 (Hebrew).

14. Several discussions in the Babylonian and Jerusalem Talmuds' eighth chapter of tractate Sotah, entitled "The Anointed for War," are devoted to biblical wars. Among the stories discussed in the Babylonian Talmud are David's battle with Goliath, the war against the Ammonites and the war against Midian. However, even in this exegetical context, there is no discussion of the moral problems of warfare in general.

15. Walzer, *Just and Unjust Wars*, p. 97.

16. Mishnah Sotah 8:7; JT Sotah 8:10, 23a; BT Sotah 44b.

17. Some of the prominent advocates of this approach are Shaviv, Ravitzky, Lichtenstein, Kimelman and Ahituv, mentioned in note 1 above.

18. Mishnah Sanhedrin 1:5, 2:4; BT Sanhedrin 16b; BT Berakhot 3b; *Midrash HaGadol* on Gen. 31:52.

19. Ravitzky, *Freedom Inscribed*; Kimelman, "The Laws and Restrictions of War."

20. Lichtenstein, "Morality and War."

21. Ravitzky, *Freedom Inscribed*, pp. 141–142; in his commentary on BT Sanhedrin 16b, Rabbi Shmuel Eliezer Idlish (1555–1631, known by his Hebrew acronym: *Maharsha*) wrote the following: "they took advice from the Sanhedrin how to act in war according to the Torah, in some affairs of war." Ravitzky would see this as referring to the receiving of moral instruction from the Sanhedrin "on the affairs of war and its conduct." However, *Maharsha* was not referring to the moral problem of warfare. He may have been referring to the problems of observing the laws of the Torah in the battlefield as interpreted by the sages. In any case, the Talmud does not address the issue of "moral advice."

22. See for instance: Kimelman, "The Laws and Restrictions of War," pp. 236–238.

23. See F.E. Adcock, *Roman Political Ideas and Practices*, Ann Arbor: University of Michigan Press, 1964.

24. See for instance: Mishnah Yadayim 4:4; Tosefta Yadayim 2:17; BT Berakhot 28a; BT Yoma 54a.
25. Maimonides, *Mishneh Torah*, The Laws of Kings and Wars, 5:4.
26. See for instance: BT Sanhedrin 71a.
27. Mekhilta deRabbi Ishmael 14:10; BT Bava Bathra 123a; BT Hagigah 14a; BT Megilah 15b.
28. W. James, "The Moral Equivalent of War," in J.J. McDermott (Ed.), *The Writings of William James: A Comprehensive Edition*, New York: Random House, 1968, pp. 660–671; M.L. Satlow, "'And On the Earth You Shall Sleep': Talmud Torah and Rabbinic Asceticism," *The Journal of Religion* 83:2, 2003, pp. 204–222.
29. Ravitzky, *Freedom Inscribed*, p. 155, and the sources cited in note 68.
30. Ravitzky, *Freedom Inscribed*, pp. 148–149.
31 Thus according to all manuscripts and the first printed edition; in the Vilna edition the word "any" [כל] is omitted.
32. BT Shevu'ot 35b.
33. Tosafot, ad loc.
34. Rashi, ad loc.
35. BT *Nedarim* 28a; BT *Gittin* 10b; BT *Bava Qama* 113a–b; BT *Bava Bathra* 54b–55a; and see recently: G. Herman, "The Exilarchate in the Sasanian Era," Ph.D. Theses, the Hebrew University, Jerusalem, 2005, pp. 231–232, and the sources mentioned in the footnotes.
36. Mishnah *Shabbat* 6:4, according to *genizah* fragment: Cambridge, CUL, T-S F2.32; there are no significant changes in the rest of the textual witnesses.
37. For the general approach of the house of Shammai towards the armed resistance to the Roman occupation, see: I. Ben-Shalom, *The School of Shammai and the Zealots' Struggle against Rome*, Jerusalem: Yad Ben Zvi, 1993.
38. Thus according to manuscripts Kaufman and Parma; it was only in later printed editions that the word "Israel" was added to the text.
39. Mishnah *Sanhedrin* 4:12.
40. Thus according to the Vienna manuscript.
41. It is interesting to examine in this regard, the criticism that is expressed by the Sages as regards the slaughter of the Priests of Nob and the murder of Amasa and Abner, for these acts of blood-shedding were associated with warfare in one way or another. See for instance: BT *Sanhedrin* 49a; BT *Sanhedrin* 20a; M. Greenberg, "Rabbinic Reflections on Defying Illegal Orders: Amasa, Abner and Joab," *Judaism* 19, 1970, pp. 30–37.
42. W. Reisman, and C. Antoniou (Eds.), *The Laws of War*, New York: Vintage, 1994, pp. 3–9.
43. See for instance: Orend, *The Morality of War*, pp. 57–58.
44. See for instance: Kimelman, "The Laws and Restrictions of War," pp. 246–248; Ravitzky, *Freedom Inscribed*, pp. 142–144.
45. Rashi on Deut. 20:10.
46. *Sifre Deuteronomy* 199, in L. Finkelstein (Ed.), New York: The Jewish Theological Seminary, 1993, p. 237; cf. *Midrash Tanna'im* on Deuteronomy 20:19, in D. Hoffman (Ed.), Berlin: Popperlauer, 1909, p. 121.
47. Nahmanides on Deuteronomy 20:10, in Ramban (Nahmanides), *Commentary on the Torah*, vol. 5, trans. from the Hebrew and annotated with index by C.B. Chavel, New York: Shilo, 1976, pp. 238–241.
48. Maimonides, *Mishneh Torah*, The Laws of Kings and Wars, 6:1, in Mishneh Torah: The Book of Adoration, Ed. according to the Bodleian (Oxford) Codex with an English Translation by M. Hyamson, Talmudic References and Hebrew Footnotes by C.M. Brecher, Jerusalem: Feldheim Publishers, 1981.

49. Though, many of the medieval commentators stressed the enslavement of those nations who accept the biblical "Call for Peace." See for instance: R. Bahya on Deuteronomy 20:10, in: *Rabbenu Bahya on the Torah*, vol. 3: Numbers-Deuteronomy, C.B. Chavel (Ed.), Jerusalem: Mossad Harav Kook, 1968, pp. 370–372 (Hebrew); *Sefer Ha'Hinnuch*, Mitzvah 527, in R. Pinhas Ha'Levi, *The Book of Education*, C. Wengrov (trans.), Jerusalem: Feldheim, pp. 138–143. However, according to the opinion of both Nahmanides and Rabbi Abraham ben David of Posquires (c. 112–1198, usually known by his acronym Ra'abad), nations who surrender and accept the seven Noahide laws are considered to be immune from enslavement, even if this is only done because of fear of that enslavement. As an explanation of Maimonides' "problematic" opinion that even those who do answer the Call for Peace may be enslaved, one can cite the ruling of Rabbi Avraham Yeshaya Karelitz, (1878–1953, popularly known by the name of his *magnum opus*, "Hazon Ish"), that those nations who had originally observed the seven Noahide laws may not be conquered in the first place. Based on these varied opinions, some scholars have emphasized the unease with which "Rabbinic Judaism" views the morals of biblical warfare. See Ravitzky, *Freedom Inscribed*, pp. 142–144. On Ra'abad, see: I. Twersky, *Raabad of Posquieres: A Twelfth-Century Talmudist*, Philadelphia: Jewish Publication Society of America, 1980.

50. Rashi on Gen. 15:1

51. E. Zand, "Did Rashi Embrace the Idea of Autonomous Morality in His Commentary on the Account of the Battle Against Sihon?," *Iggud* 1, 2008, pp. 103–124 (Hebrew).

52. *Deuteronomy Rabbah*, Parashat Shoftim 13, in *Midrash Devarim Rabbah*, edited from the Oxford Manuscript 147 with an Introduction and Notes by S. Lieberman, Jerusalem: Wahrmann, 1964, p. 101 (Hebrew).

53. *Midrash Tanhuma* on Leviticus 7:11, in *Midrash Tanhuma* (based on S. Buber edition), vol. 2: Exodus and Leviticus, trans. with introduction, indices, and brief notes by J.T. Townsend, Hoboken: Ktav, 1989, pp. 209–210.

54. *Sifre Numbers* 42.

55. *Deuteronomy Rabbah*, Parashat Shoftim 14, in *Midrash Devarim Rabbah*, Edited from the Oxford Manuscript 147 with an Introduction and Notes by S. Lieberman, Jerusalem: Wahrmann, 1964, p. 101 (Hebrew).

56. JT Shevi'it 6:1, 36c.

57. *Leviticus Rabbah* 17:6, in *Midrash Vayyikra Rabbah*, A Critical Edition by M. Margulies, London: Ararat, 1954, p. 386 (Hebrew).

58. BT *Yoma* 22b.

59. Orend, *The Morality of War*, pp. 106–110.

60. San Francisco MS: לברוח למי שרוצה; New York MS: לברוח ולמי שרוצה; Jerusalem MS: ולכל מי שרוצה לברוח; Printed editions: לבורח ולכל מי שירצה; It is possible perhaps that the varying textual traditions reflect differing opinions as to the extent of immunity that must be granted to the enemy.

61. Maimonides, *Mishneh Torah*, The Laws of Kings and Wars, 6:7.

62. The Radbaz, ad loc. writes: "and this expresses the Torah's ways, which paths are all peace," see the commentary of the Radbaz in Maimonides, *Mishneh Torah*, The Book of Judges, Sh. Frankel (Ed.), Jerusalem: Congregation Bnei Yosef, 1999, p. 263 (Hebrew).

63. On the literary sources and dating of *Midrash HaGadol*, see especially: *Midrash HaGadol* on the Pentateuch: Numbers, Z.M. Rabinowitz (Ed.), Jerusalem: Mosad Harav Kook, 1967, pp. 5–16; *Midrash HaGadol* on the Pentateuch: Deuteronomy, Sh. Fisch (Ed.), Jerusalem: Mosad Harav Kook, 1972, pp. 7–20. It can hardly be disputed that the author of *Midrash HaGadol* incorporated parts of Maimonides' *Mishneh Torah* into his compilation.

64. Rabinowitz, *Midrash HaGadol*, p. 538.

65. H.S. Horovitz (Ed.), *Siphre D'vei Rav,* Jerusalem: Wahrmann, 1966, p. 210, prefers the version that is attested in the printed edition: "four sides." However, all the manuscripts of the Sifre have the version: "three sides," see: Horovitz, p. 210, n. 13.

66. I followed the version accepted by Horovitz, *Sifre,* p. 210, which is attested in the Oxford and Berlin manuscripts of the *Sifre.* In the Vatican manuscript, however, we have: "leave them" in the imperative form, see Horovitz, p. 210, n. 14.

67. *Sifre Numbers* 157, in Horovitz, p. 210; cf. M. Kahana, "Prolegomena to a New Edition of the Sifre on Numbers," Ph.D. Dissertation, the Hebrew University, Jerusalem, 1982, pp. 72–73, n. 17.

68. *Midrash Tanna'im* on Deuteronomy 20:12, D. Hoffman (Ed.), Berlin: Poppelauer, 1909, p. 121.

69. See Horovitz's comments, p. 210; M. Kahana has suggested that the imperative version "leave them" in *Sifre Numbers* (according to the Vatican manuscript) suggests that R. Nathan's words in the *Sifre* were transferred from a midrash on Deuteronomy. I fail to understand, however, why this assumption is necessary. First, we have seen that several textual witnesses, although admittedly not as reliable as the Vatican manuscript, read "they left them" in the Sifre, in the past tense. But more importantly, the only attestation of this midrash as an interpretation of Deuteronomy appears in *Midrash Tanna'im.* Accept for this sole version, however, all rabbinic versions of the *midrash,* including *Midrash HaGadol* and Maimonides, address the verses in Numbers. Why not assume, then, that it is in fact the editor of *Midrash Tannaim* who attempted to reinterpret the *midrash* as a normative imperative, driven from the verses of Deuteronomy. Cf. Kahana, *Sifre Numbers,* pp. 72–73, n. 17

70. *Sifre Zuta* on Deuteronomy 21:1; see: M. Kahana, *Sifre Zuta on Deuteronomy: Citations from a New Tannaitic Midrash,* Jerusalem: Magnes, 2002, pp. 289–290.

71. *Sifre Zuta* on Deuteronomy 13:3; Kahana, *Sifre Zuta on Deuteronomy,* pp. 191–192.

72. *Sifre Deuteronomy* 199; in L. Finkelstein (Ed.), *Sifre on Deuteronomy,* New York: The Jewish Theological Seminary, 1993, p. 237.

73. *Sifre Deuteronomy* 200; Finkelstein, p. 237.

74. See for instance: Y. Blidstein, "Holy War in Maimonidean Law," in J. Kraemer (Ed.), *Perspectives on Maimonides,* Oxford: Oxford University Press, 1991, pp. 209–221.

10 Peace, secularism, and religion*

Avinoam Rosenak and Alick Isaacs

I. Introduction

In this article we outline the rise and fall of the vision of peace as a secular concept and consider its alternatives. Ultimately, these alternatives lie in a place where the post-modern critique of positivist secularism and religious mysticism overlap. Inherent in this place of overlap is a critique of the secularism of the nation-state as well as a critique of the fundamental notion of a universal humanism as grounds for co-existence. We shall trace the foundations of this critique in the reactions of twentieth-century thinkers to the national violence of the world wars. However we shall focus in particular on the expressions of the religious alternative to secular peace found in Jewish thought. Specifically we shall examine the non-humanist notion of co-existence embedded in the teachings of Rabbi Abraham Isaac Hakohen Kook (1865–1935) and consider the critique of the secular state provided by Rabbi Moses (Moshe) Avigdor Amiel (1882–1946).

Kant's Perpetual Peace

The notion of a secular peace between secular states is anchored in Kant's 1795 essay "Perpetual Peace: A Philosophical Sketch" ("*Zum ewigen Frieden: Ein philosophischer Entwurf.*" Kant's essay describes the rational, legal and moral principles on which peace may be established within and among states. In this approach, religion is seen as a divisive force, one of the ways in which nature creates differences among men; and "these [differences] may certainly occasion mutual hatred and provide pretexts for wars."[1] Accordingly, it is not religion and its metaphysical principles that can bring about the peace awaited by all; rather, it is the rationalist-secular way of thinking, which makes possible the existence of liberal religion. Not that this vision of peace denies religion a place; it allows for religion but requires it to assume, in Ernst Simon's terminology, a "Protestant" form.[2] Religion of this sort is a private religious matter, significant to its believers but confined to church and religious acts. Other areas of life become secularized, allowing for political and moral management guided by three liberal principles of the republican constitution: "firstly, the principle of *freedom* for all members of a society (as men); second, the principle of the *dependence* of everyone upon a single common legislation (as subjects); and thirdly, the principle of legal *equality* for everyone (as citizens)."[3] Peace thus becomes a subject of political rather than religious discourse, and religion – especially Catholicism, unique in its presuming to embrace all areas of life – is considered to be a factor that generates conflict and helps justify war.[4] (Religion is not alone in that regard; Kant notes other, political factors that tend to promote war: preserving the capacity to wage future wars; regarding the state as property; maintaining standing armies; using economic power to exert pressure and to threaten; one nation forcefully intervening in the governance of another; and international deployment of various sorts of violence.)

Critiques of Kant and the impact of the First World War

Having briefly recounted the Kantian vision of peace we will now turn to the examination of the post-modern critique of that vision, and the religious alternatives – specifically Catholic-like – made possible by that critique within Jewish and Zionist thought. These alternatives sharply criticize the violence inherent in the model of the secular-liberal state and strive to outline visions of all-embracing peace grounded in religion.

Kant's conviction was that the secularization of the collective identity of peoples in the form of the national State would allow modern society to begin the work of putting an end to perpetual war.[5] Basing his critique upon the negative model typically supplied by the Crusades, it seemed obvious that unflinching religious conviction bred violence that believers pursued with holy fervor. While the association of politics with religion was destructive, Kant believed that the secularization of collective values and interests and their encapsulation in the form of the state would allow for peaceful co-existence among all enlightened peoples. Kant proposed that the common ground upon which human beings might co-exist was rational, universal and therefore natural.[6] Just as the state regulated the lives of its citizens, Kant believed that a super-state structure comprising a "league of sovereigns" was necessary for regulating the interactions between states. While this body may not interfere with the sovereignty of any individual state, it would function as an adjudicator between states, regulating appropriate or legal inter-state practices and providing a context for the perpetual negotiation of disagreement within a liberal and non-violent discourse. Ultimately, the power of this body would rest upon the rational appreciation of the civilians and leaders of each state who recognize its value and choose to maintain the peace in service of the nobler interests and indeed inbred traits of humanity. Kant believed that this kind of political refinement was possible.

Kant's best reader (and perhaps his most vehement critic), Hegel, was skeptical about this vision. He maintained that leagues and coalitions, whatever their size and nobility, must by necessity pursue their own individuation. In so doing they cannot but generate conglomerate enmities of their own. As such, they are likely to emerge as larger bodies of aligned forces in war now capable of larger acts of destruction. He writes:

... Kant proposed a league of sovereigns to settle disputes between states, and the Holy Alliance was meant to be an institution more or less of this kind. But, the state is an individual, and negation is an essential component of individuality. Thus, even if a number of states join together as a family, this league, in its individuality, must generate opposition and create an enemy ... wars will nevertheless occur whenever they lie in the nature of the case [*sache*]; the seeds germinate once more, and talk falls silent in the face of the solemn recurrences of history.[7]

In Hegel's view it is an inevitable result of human individuality that human beings wage war against each other. Mechanisms that regulate power, whether they are secular or religious, are more likely to align in conflict than they are to remain protective – as Kant believed they must – of the peace.

The extraordinary and frightening experience of the First World War did more to validate Hegel's critique than the subsequent arguments of any theoretician might have without it. Without any sense of religious conviction or even moral outrage, soldiers in the war marched to their deaths in open celebration of their national pride. A good death was one died for the sake of one's country. The secularized nation state inspired a level of conviction that generated a self-sacrificial ritual that played out on the battlefield on a scale never before witnessed in human history.[8] The numbers killed in the war were unprecedented in military history. The modus operandi of marching across "No Man's Land" towards the enemy trench in a hopeless and utterly purposeless movement of assault offered little hope of survival. Reports from the field describe how soldiers barely ran. They simply walked to their deaths en masse as the enemy mowed them down – quite literally – with machine-gun fire. Years of combat ensued while millions of soldiers marched pointlessly to their deaths with neither strategic objective nor military gain in mind. Indeed during the course of the trench battles, the front lines moved no more than a mile or two in either direction over a period of two years.[9]

The First World War seemed to exemplify (more than any philosophical or political idea, essay or hypothesis might) the destructive power of the modern state. It utilized the full scale and depth of the civilian population and its resources to fuel this carnage for four years. State resources provided a constantly replenishing supply of weapons and young men willing to die.[10] It enabled the perpetuation of pointless conflict for four entire years. While the Second World War is clearly understood more readily in terms of ethics, right and wrong, it seems that here too the mesmerizing and overwhelming power of the state mechanism made possible the self-destructive devotion that were the fate of the combat soldiers on both sides. It must be clear that these were wars fought by secular nations in the name of a secular nationalism that aroused more hate and devotion than any religion had mustered in all of European history. The assumption that secular nationalism might provide an answer to humankind's perpetual propensity for war ought soon after to have crumbled.

Conflict and the post-modern critique

Recent scholarship has called into question the actual secularism of the nation state.[11] The notion that presumably secular wars might be described in terms of almost mystical national ideals for which combatants are prepared to martyr themselves draws attention to the failure of post-enlightenment culture to actually rid itself of metaphysics. Indeed, in the wake of the World Wars, the dominant thrust of European philosophy has been the debunking of modernist metaphysics.[12] Post-modernism is, at least in part, an attempt to expose the contingencies that attend upon the Western European notions of the objective and the universal while deconstruction and post-colonialism of the type espoused by Foucault, Derrida and Fanon have engaged in the challenge of exposing the failure of modern European thinkers to rid themselves of the violence of metaphysics.[13] While multiple intellectual and internal motivations were at play in this effort – not least of which was the desire to account for the meaning of language without resorting to an abstract and intellectually unsatisfying world of Platonic ideals – many thinkers such as Derrida, have called attention to the uncompromisingly violent characteristics of metaphysical thought. The shift that is often associated with the "linguistic turn" in Western philosophy is one of secularization; but it is one in which the notion of the secular itself is, once again, secularized.[14] The failure of the project of secularization itself is the object of this critique. Though secularism was successful in moving the structures of governance away from the sacred, modern political thought failed to move away from the unflinchingly certain and the universally absolute. Modernism bred a new form of certainty. Truth became a value in science while the scientific method which remained unexamined, blinded its adherents to its contingencies and choices, to its dependence upon convictions and belief systems none of which were subject to the scientific scrutiny readily applied to the presumably objective description of humanity and the physical world. The critique voiced by post-nationalists is that secular metaphysics is no less violent than religion and that the nation state is no less oppressive than the classical (or holy) Empire.[15]

Perhaps the most significant offshoot of this critique is the relativism – applied in post modern thought – to such values as truth and justice. Rather than understanding this as a disintegration of enlightenment values, we propose that this relativism is, in fact, a mode of co-existence that insists upon the necessity of competing views whose mutual role is to establish relationships between competing points of view on grounds that are not – and cannot be conceived as – "absolute." This approach is distinguished from pluralism or liberalism in that it does not simply allow for the coexistence of multiple truth claims. Rather, it demands a form of radical co-existence that – when absent – must be generated through the proliferation of multiple points of view through radical acts of interpretation. It is this proliferation that exposes the contingency of any single point of view and deconstructs it. The co-existence of voices, perceptions, and legitimately flawed hypotheses that this discourse requires culminates in the form of a complex network of contradictions and paradoxes that underline the mysterious or mystical dimension of human thought and insist upon the collaboration of contradictory elements in every attempt at positing a thesis, a vision or an ideal. It is within this context that the notion of the state with its absolute and idealized perceptions of its identity is softened and made sensitive to its inner moving parts. The state as a concept is deconstructed along with any other form of hegemonic narrative and is thus rendered less dangerous to its citizens and indeed to its enemies. Ultimately, one may argue that the post-modern insistence on multiple and contradictory narrative is designed to dismantle the dangers of metaphysics, undercut the constructions of certainty and expose inner weaknesses and contingencies in all their meekness. In this sense, "post" criticism is an attempt to issue a corrective to the belligerence of modernism and to rein in the passions that resulted in the most destructive wars in human history.

While most of the proponents of the post-modern critique can hardly be seen as "religious," it seems quite clear that the secularization of modern secularism – as the repetition implies – involves a return to the defiantly incomprehensible, the mystical and indeed the religious.[16] It is no coincidence that new-ageism entails a return to the life of questing and invites the journey on paths unlimited by vigorous convictions about the truth towards unknown ideals that can never be accomplished or contained. It is these phenomena that connect it to the traditional – perhaps pre-modern – visions of the religious life. This is one in which no firm truths are posited. They are perhaps assumed in good faith, but are also understood as belonging outside of the limits of human understanding.[17]

Our primary contention is that this notion of co-existence provides a model for a religious articulation of peace that is based upon the radical co-existence of mutually excluding points of view that must co-exist in a paradoxical unity. This unity is akin to the Jewish understanding of monotheism in which the complex and self-contradictory notion of God is united into a single being. Again, this paradoxical construction is akin to the biblical image of the co-existing wolf and lamb, which maintain their distinct natures and forms while still sharing an ultimate future of a rationale-defying peace between them.[18] It is this model that provides a meaningful alternative to the Kantian notion of humanistic rationalism as a foundation for shared and regulated living under the rule of law and it is this model that we wish to propose echoes as a central motif in the teaching of Rabbi Abraham Isaac Hakohen Kook. Though Kook was not a relativist, his sense of the absolute belonged exclusively to the realm of the sacred and the divine and enforced upon the human experience a form of radical co-existence that acknowledges the defiant mystery of God's unity. Similarly, the deconstruction of the state as social ideal capable of providing a solid and peaceful foundation for co-existence that is rooted in humanistic law is called into question by this critique. It is this dimension of the notion of secular peace that we wish to exemplify through the teachings of Rabbi Moses Amiel.

II. Rabbi Abraham Isaac Hakohen Kook

From among the wealth of intellectual models within religious Zionism, we can cite two different, if not opposing, approaches, each of which presents a penetrating critique of the liberal, secular-rationalist doctrine of the state and a far-reaching alternative to it. In addition, the two approaches offer different models of peace, each of which draws deeply on an all-embracing religious outlook. The first of these two approaches is that of Rabbi A.I.H. Kook, the founder of the modern Chief Rabbinate in Israel and the first occupant of the office of Chief Rabbi.

Immanence and "unity of opposites"

Notwithstanding his education in Lithuanian *yeshivot*,[19] Rabbi Kook's teachings are rooted in kabbalistic doctrine. His thinking grows out of the "Catholic" concept of the world described above, which contemplates an immanent divine presence in all areas of existence and infers from that universally applicable laws of conduct.[20] It follows, in his view, that the affinities and differences between Israel and the nations of the world are not merely a matter of consciousness and culture;[21] they are substantive and ontological.[22] Existence, in all its contradictions, is suffused with the divine presence[23] and those contradictions do not disturb the all-encompassing divine logic.[24] The divine presence instills vitality in the range of spiritual movements and historical processes. This dialectical logic forms the structure for "the doctrine of the unity of opposites" at the center of Rabbi Kook's thinking,[25] a doctrine based on the ideas of Rabbi Judah Loew of Prague (known as "Maharal")[26] and on kabbalistic and Hasidic literature in general.[27]

Israel and the nations

In Rabbi Kook's construct, Israel is the center of humanity and all existence, the kernel that encompasses and sustains all. Jews differ substantively from members of other nations, though that difference creates an affinity in that the nations embody in their own lives, in various ways, the seed implicit in Israel. He writes:

> All of the varied spiritual streams within the human world have a root within the community of Israel, for that community, in the spiritual sense unique to the highest and purest forms of yearning, is the center of humanity. For that reason, it is impossible for us to disregard any stream when we examine the spiritual force of the community of Israel, "the bride," "encompassing all."[28]

In this view, Israel is the center of humanity and the root of all the varied forms of spirituality in the world. For that reason, Jews are obliged to pay careful attention both to their own various streams – for they are the seed of cultural and spiritual activities among the nations of the world – and to the various streams among the nations, which embody those within Israel.[29] Given that variety, Rabbi Kook agues that "the community of Israel is the epitome of all existence . . . in its physicality and spirituality, its history and its faith. Jewish history is the ideal epitome of general history, and there is no movement in the world that does not find its model within Israel."[30]

Negation of negation

The premise of immanence, which sees divine providence in everything, negates negation. Rabbi Kook rejects ideologies whose narrow view of truth calls for rejection of other truths; he likewise rejects the compelled imposition of one truth. The whole embodies the divine infinite. "Every form of wisdom and every spiritual phenomenon in the world has a positive aspect and a negative aspect. The positive aspect is what gives the phenomenon its form and its extent, and the negative aspect is its blocking of other phenomena from extending into its space."[31] The positive is the ability of truth to be expressed in the world. The negative is the making of one position hostile to another as it attempts to conceal it. The ideal state is one in which a more expansive mode of thinking allows "the positive aspect" to become stronger while the "negative aspect grows weaker," to the point that "there is no negative aspect at all" and the "superior, pure wisdom" extends to everything and "augments everything with its positivity."[32] That, in Rabbi Kook's view, is the meaning of the heavenly voice calling out "These and those are the words of the living God,"[33] and "All of physical and spiritual existence, all its aspects, in its entirety, is it not the world of God?"[34]

The complexity of the dialectical personality

This dialectical approach entails tension and difficulty, and one who adopts it must have a mindset capable of oscillating between contradictory positions. On the one hand, he needs to take a particularist-subjective stance that clearly defines the bounds of its world. On the other hand, he must understand that this particularist stance is simply one facet of an objective truth that does not recognize the bounds of our familiar finite truths.[35] In Rabbi Kook's view, the *zaddiq* – a figure with which Rabbi Kook deeply identified[36] – is prepared to follow this path because "he unites within him all the opposites." He ascends to the higher worlds, in which there are no borders or fences, and he is equipped to embrace all the extremes with the power of kindness and mercy unconstrained by the attribute of judgment.[37] Rabbi Kook recognized the difficulty of living within dialectical tension and he was conscious of the duty to translate it into the realm of this-worldly subjective discourse (referred to in some mystical and Hasidic writing as the "garments").[38]

This dialectic is nicely conveyed in Rabbi Kook's explanation of how to manage a conflict that plays out simultaneously on multiple planes. It involves tension between change and tradition; between conflicting this-worldly opinions; between the concept of all-encompassing unity (suited to the *zaddiq* and the higher worlds) and the world as it exists, which includes mutually hostile opinions and positions. It requires one to live in a way that is faithful to the objective-higher dimension but also to the lower, subjective dimension ("the garments"), for both embody a truth that cannot be changed and must not be blurred. Rabbi Kook describes the complex dialectic as follows:

> We must always walk the road between difference and similarity and process opinions in such a way that it will be possible for each and every person to

find his unique spirit within those opinions while at the same time partaking of the quality of similarity, which brings everything together in a single unit.[39]

The vital return to corporeality: land and politics

Israel's return to its land, according to Rabbi Kook, is a process that is vital to fulfilling its potential for the entire world.[40] Israel's severance from its land, from its physical body[41] and its political body, had some advantages[42] but has now become a hindrance. Israel's return to its land is necessary for its own self-realization[43] but also for the nations of the world, who, as noted, are sustained by the spiritual kernel that is Israel. (Statements calling for the reversal of Israel's severance from the physical appear in Rabbi Kook's philosophical[44] and halakhic writings[45] alike.) Israel needs a state that will afford it physical and political strength[46] and a vital social order that will serve as a source of inspiration for all nations.[47]

Against violence and the "sin of the golden calf"

Israel's ability to influence the world and to return to its land without political struggle or violence both depend on its recognition of the weighty spiritual and cultural assignment it bears. It must not succumb to a form of the "sin of the golden calf"[48] that prevented it in the past from realizing its historical destiny. Kook argues that if Jews will "call on God's Name," they will not need weaponry to establish their state, for the other nations will recognize the vital nature of Israel's contribution.[49] Rabbi Kook's political vision with respect to the State of Israel thus excludes warfare, and that is why, in his view, Israel remained in exile until the state could be established without the use of force. Leaving politics behind – that is, being in exile – is negative but also has a positive aspect, for it allowed for Israel's spiritualization and its removal from "the dreadful sins involved in running a government in bad times." Now, however, "a time has come . . . when the world is improved and . . . it will be possible to conduct our state on a foundation of goodness, wisdom, uprightness, and clear divine illumination . . . It was not proper for Israel to be involved in government at a time when it entailed bloodshed and required a talent for wickedness."[50] Israel, then, must establish a state and a polity that do not require "the stormy spirit" of war but will, rather, "cause the divine sanctity spreading through the light of Israel to make its way calmly and moderately, in slow steps."[51]

Praise of war and disparagement of Christianity

Israel's redemption, to be sure, was taking place in the shadow of the Great War and against a background of terrible violence that represented, in Rabbi Kook's view, the Hegelian[52] epitome of the defining trait of the nations of the world.[53] But, paradoxically enough, Rabbi Kook saw something positive in a process that emphasized, in the context of world war, both the differences and the unity of the nations in general[54] and of Israel in particular.[55] These warlike statements appear against the background of his harsh criticism of Christianity as a system that fails to recognize the complexity of existence and offers a utopian and moralistic vision. In his view, Christianity is not sensitive to the contradictions and tensions that exist without exception throughout the world. He holds Christianity responsible for the unrestrained outbreaks of violence that grow out of its lack of complexity and its failure to understand the importance in the world of the body and the material.[56]

Heresy [that is, Christianity] began by declaring grace and love and asking how to tithe straw, how to tithe salt, how to repay good for bad and how to bless one who curses. But it culminated in sword and blood, cruelty and murder, endless bloody war, and profound hatred between nation and nation, tribe and tribe, man and man. It is as our rabbis said regarding the secret of the holy: the evil side [*sitra ahra*, lit., "the other side"] begins in unity and culminates in separation; the holy side begins in separation and culminates in unity.[57]

The Vision of Peace and its conditions

After the Great War's dust had settled, the reshaping of Europe and the transfer of the Land of Israel to the Jews should have made it possible "for humanity to unite in a single family, putting an end to all the skirmishing and all the bad qualities that result from divisions among nations and their boundaries."[58] That hoped-for peace – possessed of a utopian quality but also the object of the establishment of the State of Israel – depends, first of all, on the nations' recognition of Israel's role. That recognition, in turn, will bring about the nations' acceptance of Israel's vital contribution and the truth contained within it. Peace and the end of bloodshed, then, are achieved not through concessions and compromises but through a realistic insistence on each nation's unique role and on that of Israel in particular. Only this inner clarity will lead nations to recognize the damage caused by warfare. Hanan Porath has written of the way in which Rabbi Kook's disciples translated these ideas into contemporary discourse:

> Peace and the prevention of bloodshed will never come unless "all inhabitants of the world will recognize and know that to You every knee will bow and every tongue will swear loyalty." In a profound sense, there can be no peace without this element of "all inhabitants of the world will recognize." This does not mean that we need not make the effort, in the world in which we now find ourselves, to prevent bloodshed as much as possible, even at the cost of partial settlements. But in doing so, we must never compromise, Heaven forbid, the course that represents the redemption of the world.[59]

We see, then, that Rabbi Kook's teachings include a doctrine of peace that sees the speck of truth implicit in varied particularist truths; a doctrine of peace that sprouts within a religion that is "Catholic" in its perception of God's universal immanence and of the ubiquity of religious obligation; and a doctrine of peace based on a metaphysics grounded in the kabbalistic doctrine of the spheres and embodied in the "doctrine of the unity of opposites." The doctrine posits, on the one hand, a duty to transform all of humanity into a single family and to establish the State of Israel in a spirit of pacifism; on the other hand, it posits a need for the existence of war to prepare the way for the vision of the end of days. It sees a spark of something positive in Christianity;[60] but, in the same breath, it disparages Christianity's understanding of the world – an understanding that secularized the world and transformed it into a violent and war-like place lacking, from a Christian perspective, dense contact with the divine.

III. Rabbi Moses Avigdor Amiel[61]

The second rabbi whose position we wish to examine is Rabbi Moses Avigdor Amiel. Rabbi Amiel – a student of the Telz Yeshiva and disciple of Rabbi Hayyim Soloveitchik and Rabbi Hayyim Ozer Grozhinsky – came from a Lithuanian background with a quite different perspective than Rabbi Kook's immanent and kabbalistic approach. His writings include halakhic and meta-halakhic works (such as his treatise *Middot le-heqer ha-halakhah* [Principles of Halakhic Study])[62] as well as philosophical and contemplative works (such as *Li-nevukhei ha-tequfah*[63] and *Ha-zedeq ha-sozi'ali ve-ha-zedeq ha-mishpati u-musari shelanu*).[64] His library leaned toward philosophical works and he reacted to them in his own writings. In 1920 he was appointed rabbi of Antwerp. He immigrated to the Land of Israel in 1936 and served as Chief Rabbi of Tel Aviv.

Amiel was an important and active Zionist thinker who critically examined the ideas of Zionism's leaders and of his own party (The Religious Zionist Party – *Ha-Mizrachi*). He noted the spiritual dimensions concealed behind the "materialist" commitments of both Zionism and European nationalism. In his view, secular Zionism could be seen in part as derived from modern secular nationalism and therefore suffering from its flaws. Zionism needed to regroup, to recognize the spiritual dimensions it had unconsciously drawn from secular nationalism, and to reestablish itself on Judaism's distinct religious basis. Without this unique stance, Zionist culture might easily have become violent and callous about the value of human life. The Western commitment to human rights would have been a pale substitute for the deep set conviction to peace that lies at the heart of Jewish thought. In order to illustrate this point, we shall survey the ethical distinctions – most specifically in terms of attitudes to war and peace – that Amiel draws between Western and Jewish cultures.

Law, morality, and Torah

In distinguishing between law as practiced by other nations and Israel's Torah, Rabbi Amiel also noted the dissonance between "law" and "morality." Law is based on rules and the actions of society as a whole; underlying it is the desire for social order and a properly functioning state. Morality, in contrast, deals with worldviews – with the beliefs, intentions, and opinions of people (individually or collectively).[65]

European jurisprudence, Amiel argued, suffers from the subordination of morality to conventional social norms, which have the power to sway the view of the judge. It follows that concepts of good and evil are fluid,[66] and the "conscience in one's heart"[67] is often recast by accepted practice. Jewish law, in contrast, expresses eternal, divine morality, "the voice of God moving about within man";[68] it is not subject to society, to time, or to place.[69]

An aptitude for morality

Amiel also points to "Israel's unique aptitude" (with a nod to Rabbi Judah Halevi),[70] but that characteristic is not ontological. Israel is not a joining of being and essence (as it is for Rabbi Kook); rather, it is possessed of a unique quality in its moral-cultural sensitivity. For that reason – and in contrast to Halevi – Amiel has great fondness for converts: a convert's spiritual-moral decision elevates him to the highest possible level, and he becomes the elect within the Jewish group (as we shall see below).[71]

Between the collective and the individual

The uniqueness of Jewish morality lies in its enhanced sensitivity to the individual. Secular nationalism, in contrast, often harshly subordinates the individual to the collective – Amiel was thinking of Socialism and various twentieth-century totalitarian and ideological movements – and that attitude toward the individual is what differentiates the Jewish vision of the state from the secular-nationalist idea:

> For them [the nations of the world] the collective is primary, but they mean by that only the proletariat. They would be pleased if the others had never been created, and, faced with their having been created, they treat them as if they hadn't been. What all the nations of the world have in common is their shared belief that the individual is like clay in the hands of the collective potter, in whose discretion the individual is allowed to live or is put to death. For that reason, even the most enlightened and excellent governments find it just and proper, entertaining no doubts, to send individuals off to the battlefield, to kill or be killed in wars of necessity or discretion, defensive or offensive wars; and those who are unwilling to go are uniformly put to death. For it is conventionally agreed among them that the individual who does not fulfill his duty to the collective loses thereby his right to live on earth.[72]

The roots of this approach go back to ancient Greece. There, sons sent their parents to die in the mountains and weak children were exposed to death, all for the sake of social utility.[73] Western society was guided not by abstract Platonic ideals[74] as much as by a system of interest-based and egocentric ties grounded in fear of social anarchy.[75] As Amiel sees it, that is the basis of Western culture and of European religion and morality. But the morality in question is like a procrustean bed (used, in rabbinic lore, by the people of Sodom): "All the beds were of one size . . . and if the guest was larger than the bed, they would cut off his legs. Conversely, if he was too short, they would stretch his legs until they were severed from their place."[76] Abraham, in contrast to the practice in Sodom, "would provide a bed suited to the guest's size." But the advantages are not without their downsides: among the nations of the world, "justice is forgone in the interest of order"; in Judaism, order is forgone in the interest of justice."[77]

Affirming Zionism; negating territoriality

Amiel supported the psychological and political revolution embodied in the Zionist movement. In his view, it was necessary for Jews to take control of their own fate. He deemed it a duty to conquer the Land[78] and to participate actively in history and he believed that Zionism renewed the commandments "between man and his nation."[79] Those commandments are in addition to those "between man and his fellow" and "between man and God"; their fulfillment is obligatory even at the cost of one's life, if necessary; and one who gives his life in their fulfillment is considered holy.[80] Nevertheless, he belittled the Mizrahi (religious Zionist) movement as the "night watchman" for secular Zionism[81] and had serious reservations about Zionism's elevation of "place" over "time," contrary to his understanding of Judaism's priorities.[82] Suggesting that too much importance was being assigned to the Land[83] to the detriment of the Torah, he recalled the maxim that "our nation is no nation except through the Torah."[84] In his view, an exclusive focus on "the Land" linked Zionism to the Enlightenment movement with all its apostasy and assimilation.[85] Territorial nationalism "is felt by a donkey as well"; it is a feeding trough dressed up as a homeland that becomes primary and determines everything: "a feeding trough is small and a homeland is very large, but the difference is one of quantity, not quality."[86] Zionism did not come into the world to add another territorial and particularist state, defined in the way animals mark out their territories; rather, its goal is to call "to all the nations of the world that the Name of the Lord is upon you . . . and you will be the father of a multitude of nations."[87]

At the same time, of course, there is the commandment to settle the Land, central to the set of commandments "between Israel and its nation."[88] Fulfilling the commandment allows one to return to a life that brings body and soul together[89] – a blending denied in the past by Diaspora Jews' withdrawal from the material[90] and denied in the present by the Zionists' emphasis on the material.[91] Both states of imbalance are a form of idolatry.

Jean Jacques Rousseau set up a tension between his call to renounce society and culture and find happiness as an individual emulating the "noble savage" and his intense loyalty to the "social contract" to which each individual, overcoming egocentricity, freely commits himself.[92] A similar tension can be found in Amiel's writings. On the one hand, he attributes high importance to the commandments between man and his nation and recognizes a duty to sacrifice oneself for the greater good. On the other hand, he emphasizes the nature of Jewish law and moral justice, which have an anti-governmental streak and are sensitive to the individual even at the expense of the community and the nation.

International Zionism and anti-racism

In the light of Amiel's analysis, the distinction between the immanent violence in Western political culture and the inherent peacefulness in Judaism becomes clear. Amiel called on Zionism to avoid isolation and alienation from other nations,[93] arguing that "nationalism is the means and internationalism is the end."[94] Isolation and alienation from the "other" are rooted in hatred[95] and in the idolatrous notion that each nation and state had its own god.[96] Monotheistic Jewish nationalism,[97] in contrast, asserts a universal vision, looking beyond nationhood.[98] Assembling nations in separate states is a necessary but transient means; its purpose ultimately is to assemble all humanity under the wings of the all-embracing God.

Amiel was aware of the many statements and strains in Jewish literature and thought that seem to run counter to that view:[99] marriage with a non-Jew is forbidden; the Torah declares Israel to be God's "cherished possession";[100] the rabbis state that "we are the chosen stock" and "others are entirely removed from the category of man."[101] One often finds discrimination against gentiles; examples include the laws related to interest on a loan,[102] excess profit, court testimony, and purchase and sale. The lands of the non-Jewish nations are declared impure[103] as is the air above them,[104] and non-Jewish bread, oil, and wine are forbidden.[105] Moreover, the rabbis declare that "proselytes are as difficult for Israel as a rash,"[106] and "a Jew, though he has sinned, remains a Jew"[107] (that is, there can be no conversion from Judaism). On the face of it, at least, it would appear that "Judaism takes a national-racial perspective to the extreme."[108] Nevertheless, Amiel goes on to paint a very different picture of the Jewish faith:

> Judaism's worldview is pure, even extreme, internationalism.[109] When all is said and done, our history begins not with the patriarchs but with primeval Adam . . . Our Torah does not satisfy itself with nationalism alone; rather, it sees before it the world as a whole, and humanity as a whole precedes our ancestors. According to tradition, God courted all the nations, Torah in hand . . . before revealing it to Israel . . . All of our festivals, including the Sabbath, have not only a national aspect but also an aspect pertaining to mankind as a whole . . .; they are based not only on national historical events but also on nature, shared by all who live on earth . . . the spring festival . . . the harvest festival.
>
> Even the Sabbath is given two rationales in the Torah – the nationalist rationale of the Exodus from Egypt and the human rationale of "in six days the LORD made heaven and earth". . . Similarly, our New Year (Rosh Hashanah) celebrates primarily not our new year, which takes place at the

new moon of the month of Nisan, but their new year . . . When King Solomon built the Temple, he did not build it solely for his people; rather, he expressly prayed "Or if a foreigner who is not of Your people Israel. . . comes to pray toward this House, oh, hear in Your heavenly abode . . ."[110] Our prophets felt themselves to be prophets not only to the Israelites, and they knew their role to be "a prophet [to] the nations"[111] They felt the woes of each and every nation.[112]

Unlike racism, Amiel argued, Jewish nationalism means Israel takes on duties,[113] not privileges. The purpose of nationalism is the person (it was Pharaoh who first called Israel a "nation").[114] Notwithstanding the sources noted earlier, he maintains that Israel does not oust the rest of humanity from the category of "human." Very much the contrary: the Israelite nation establishes the linkage among all people under the rubric of "Have we not all one Father? Did not one God create us?" (Mal. 2:10).[115] Jewish nationalism is directed toward peace among nations, and in the Temple we prayed that "My house will be called a house of prayer for all peoples." If they do not heed our prayer and do not come to our house, we nevertheless sacrifice "seventy bulls, corresponding to the seventy nations."[116]

Israel cherishes proselytes, and the rabbis argued that "the Holy One blessed be He exiled Israel among the nations only so they would gain proselytes."[117] The statement about proselytes being as difficult as a rash is meant "in praise of proselytes, who are more punctilious in observing the commandments than are [native-born] Israelites, causing accusations against us [in the divine court]."[118] Maimonides' epistle to Obadiah the Proselyte[119] takes the normative view.[120] The proselyte is a member of the nation while the apostate is a stranger,[121] and it is not by happenstance that the Messiah will be the descendant of a Moabitess.

The culture of the sword vs. the culture of the pen

Amiel attacked the philosophical, secular and Christian ideas regarding the morality of war;[122] in all of them, he identified a strain of violence against the "other." Philosophy's monistic and narrow "knowledge of the truth" brings with it an ethics of aggression that imposes on the Other the "good" as defined by whoever is possessed of might or authority. That was how the Inquisition was justified, "for Christian morality . . . wanted to cram what pleased it into the Other . . . The Christians wanted to bring the souls of the others into Paradise, and if doing so required that they be burned alive, that did not matter."[123] "Moral" and violent monism of this sort appears as well in the secular approach, which Amiel sees as afflicted by the sin of eating from the "Tree of Knowledge," that is, as imprisoned within its technology and its pursuit of quality of life.[124] Secular, technological modernism makes a person's life more pleasant and comfortable but simultaneously produces killing machines that can subject humanity to greater disasters than those associated with the medieval Crusades.[125] Even worse, society's degree of comfort depends on the capacity to kill that is available to the rulers.[126] War is the impetus to technological creativity that pampers its beneficiaries, which in turn fans the warlike spirit as the cycle recurs.[127] That, in his view, is the logic underlying the great wars of the twentieth century.[128] The West ate from the Tree of Knowledge, but the Jewish idea of peace involves eating from the Tree of Life embodied in pursuit of law and righteousness[129] embracing mankind and nature.[130]

Amiel also contrasts Amalek and Israel. "Amalekism despises the weak; Judaism despises the mighty. Amalekism is concerned about the pursuers; the God of Israel is concerned about the pursued." Judaism does not believe in confronting force with force – "The accuser does not become the defender. We cannot extirpate evil from the world through the use of evil itself. We cannot eliminate terror from the world by terrorizing from the opposite side, and we therefore do not make war against physical might by the use of physical might." Rather, "war against the sword" should be waged "through the book. The book of paper or parchment . . . will prevail over all the swords." [131] This has always been Israel's way.[132] The nations of the world regarded this aspect of Jewish culture as so bizarre, Amiel suggests, that blood libels ensued on the premise that Jews must engage in some form of bloodshed.[133]

This does not mean, however, that Israel should never take up the sword:

> The Israelite nation has an extreme hatred for war, defensive war included. If they sometimes are compelled, having no choice in the matter, to apply the undisputed *halakhah* that "if one rises up to kill you, kill him first," they do so with profuse sorrow and grief, for they are the descendents of Jacob, who was more fearful of having to kill than of being killed.[134]

The loathing of war,[135] then, flows from fear of taking the lives of others, and war is used, if at all, only to avoid a worse war.[136] But spilling of innocent blood can never be the "price" paid for Israel's redemption, for we are dealing with the prohibition of "You shall not murder." "In my opinion," Amiel argues, "even if we knew that by doing so [that is, waging war], we would achieve the full redemption, we would be duty-bound firmly to defer that 'redemption' rather than be redeemed through blood."[137]

Zionism and secular socialism: a clash of worldviews

The governments of states and the law of the Torah represent two clashing worldviews. According to the Torah, "The collective contains nothing that is not in the individual"; accordingly, "each and every human individual is an entire world in himself. Socialist justice, however" – the polar opposite of the Torah – "is a successor to ancient idolatrous justice, which saw the individual person as important only insofar as his existence was useful to society."[138] Socialism, then, is based on the egotism of the group, the preservation of its might, and the fulfillment of its desires. The Torah's justice, in contrast, focuses on the individual, his troubles, and his will.[139] One seeking true equality, Amiel argues, should choose the Jewish approach, which differs from the socio-centrism that transforms the individual into an object serving the collective. Jewish equality is absolute, drawing no distinction between rich and poor: "you shall have one law."[140] Contrary to what political logic might suggest, the Torah commands "nor shall you show deference to a poor man in his dispute";[141] regarding the wealthy, it directs "you shall show no partiality."[142] Judaism grants absolute liberty to each individual; socialism, in contrast, enslaves individuals.[143] Socialism considers equality – and history and culture overall – through the narrow lens of "gut and bread alone"; in Judaism, meanwhile, the concept of the "image of God" inherent in man is the basis on which man assumes a higher standing.[144] Socialism promotes culture's decay into a barbarism holding that "the lower a person's standing on the ladder of development, the greater his ties to society."[145] Its governing principles are fear and egotism: "protect me and I will protect you" and "but for the fear of government, a man would consume his fellow man alive." Its family structure is similarly afflicted.[146]

Zionism, in contrast, can be expected to establish a system of governance based on the centrality of the individual. A Jewish ethics demands "honoring one's parents" even when doing so runs counter to social utility; and the Jewish duty to love mankind applies universally. As he recognizes, the approach is not without its weaknesses and can sometimes allow for "bad and difficult" events; an example is the biblical story of the Gibeah concubine, in which we see the application of the idea that the standing of the individual (in this case, the concubine) outweighs the large number of people who were killed.[147] Rabbi Amiel was aware of how the ideal challenges the actual social structure.

Jewish trends interfering with the Jewish state

This individualistic character of Jewish ethical doctrine rebuffs every form of governance and social order. Disorder is typical of Israel and it is embedded in the individualistic system of moral governance. The individual's lack of subordination to the collective generates an irresolvable tension when the efforts of "social governance" impose discipline on one and all.[148] In this spirit, Judaism requires the giving of charity to anyone who requests it, even a fraud or a loafer, "for it is better that the collective suffer in order to sustain those few people who are poor and not frauds."[149] As a result, and contrary to conventional sound economics, begging and idleness become more prevalent in Israel. The emphasis on individualism can also lead to gratuitous hatred growing out of the lack of inner discipline, as people refuse to yield to the group's leaders. "Each person judges his judges and builds himself a platform, without accepting the authority of the collective"; as a further result, factions become more numerous in Israel.[150]

This rebelliousness enabled Israel to survive the Exile ("in no way do we become self-effacing despite the majority standing against us") but makes it harder for it to maintain an independent state.[151] Amiel emphasizes how prophecy always took stands that challenged the accepted economic order and reasonable notions of security. In that regard, he cites its stance against those who accumulated wealth and oppressed the poor and its corresponding support for the lowly;[152] the commandment to observe the sabbatical year;[153] the abandonment of Israel's borders on each of the three annual festivals when the nation gathered in Jerusalem; the establishment of a single law for citizens and aliens alike;[154] and the exemption from military service, rather than the punishment or intimidation, of those who are fearful or tenderhearted.

Subservience to God as the solution to the moral paradox

There is an obvious tension, of which Rabbi Amiel was well aware, between a moral vision and a political, economic, and social reality. He argued that prophecy looked toward "the return to Zion" and the establishment of an improved "kingdom of Israel," yet it placed that reality under the rubric of "What I see for them is not yet, what I behold will not be soon" (Numbers 24:17), as something reserved for "the end of days."[155] The social, economic, moral, and political vision that anticipates a state in which "nation shall not take up sword against nation; they shall never again know war" and "the wolf shall dwell with the lamb" – conditions for realizing Jewish morality – requires "deferral of the kingdom of Israel to the end of days." That deferral "does not result, Heaven forbid, from lack of love for the Israelite nation that is deteriorating in its Exile and is oppressed by endless torments; rather, it is the consequence of 'our legal and moral justice,' which is one of our traits, a trait of our soul."[156] Amiel identifies a paradoxical "unity of opposites" in the words of the prophets and believes it something we should seize on. On the one hand, we should maintain an individualist morality that opposes all subjugation and all governance by the collective – an objective that accounts for Israel's continued exile from its land.[157] On the other hand, we should see within that vision a moral objective of absolute liberty that can be fulfilled through Israel's return to its land. "But how is it possible for these two opposites to coexist in a single subject, with the cause remaining in force but the effect – the bad result – not ensuing?"[158]

This paradox can be resolved only through the subservience of the individual to God: "This is the 'yoke of Torah,' which is superior to both the 'yoke of govern-ment' and the 'yoke of sound conduct.' Instead of the authority of the collective, there is the authority of the One who said 'they are My slaves, not slaves of slaves.'" The difference is that "even the authority of the collective is a sort of subservience and enslavement, while the authority of the One who said 'they are My slaves' is in no way enslavement, for there is no alien or external factor; there is only subservience to God, who is the essence and soul of man."[159] That subservience identifies man with the "spirit of the world," which establishes the moral ideal.

And yet, from a realistic perspective, the ability to establish a moral government requires "conditions in which 'the land shall be filled with devotion to the LORD as water covers the sea' and 'all your children shall be disciples of the LORD.'"[160] For it is clear that:

> When all is said and done, the world is the same all over, and it is impossible for one state to be an exception differing in the extreme from all others, like a small island in a great sea; for in that case, it would be fated to be uprooted

and eliminated from the world. It is impossible for one state to exist as a state of mercy alone when the entire world does not want to recognize even the quality of justice . . . It is impossible for one state to exist solely under the yoke of Torah when the entire world deals only with the yoke of government and the yoke of proper conduct . . . It is impossible for one state to exist under the attribute of kindness exceeding the law when the whole world fails to pay attention even to what is obligatory . . . And, of course, the latter days are still far removed from us. Still, every infinite ideal . . . has stages and degrees by which its summit can be approached, but all those stages must be directed toward the top of the ladder.[161]

Conclusions

The articles by Amiel and Kook that we have discussed seem to present two significant and separate critiques of Kant. They suggest an alternative to his political notions of the secular state on the one hand, and to his secularization of the grounds for universal knowledge on the other. Both Amiel and Kook point out the vitality of an approach to the problems of the secular state that is rooted in a religious metaphysical discourse.

We wish to suggest that the very secularism that is inherent in the notion of the state is not necessarily the best safeguard of civil liberties. Indeed it seems that religious thought might be drawn upon for articulating visions of Statehood and of co-existence that aspire to a higher degree of tolerance and acceptance than anything ever accomplished in liberal discourse.

However, perhaps more importantly, it seems clear that the almost axiomatic assumption that religion is an obstacle to compromise and therefore – by way of extension – that the opinions of religious people are an obstacle to peace must be reconsidered. The knee-jerk response that dominates so much of the international discourse about peace rejects religious thinkers and fails to appreciate how religious thought might contribute powerfully to the articulation of a peaceful vision for the future. We wish to suggest that a philosophy of peace that is mindful of religious metaphysics, if constructed with careful attention to the subtleties and depths of the Jewish tradition, might stand a chance of winning not only the support but perhaps even the enthusiasm of those who seek to build a Jewish life in the State of Israel full of theological and mystical meaning.

Notes

* Avinoam Rosenak's portion of this article was translated from the Hebrew by Joel Linsider. Except as noted, translations from Hebrew sources there contained are by the present translator.
1. I. Kant, "Perpetual Peace: A Philosophical Sketch," in H. Reiss (Ed.), *Kant's Political Writings* (2nd ed.; trans. H.B. Nisbet), Cambridge: Cambridge University Press, 1991, p. 114.
2. A.E. Simon, "Are we still Jews?," in A.E. Simon (Ed.) *Are We Still Jews?: Essays*, Tel Aviv: Sifriyat Ha-Poalim, Hebrew University School of Education and the Jewish Theological Seminary of America, 1983, pp. 9–46 (Hebrew).

3. Kant, "Perpetual Peace," p. 99.
4. Simon, "Are we still Jews?."
5. This principle is exemplified by Kant's insistence on the notion of peace as one that must exist between states. As such the nature of the state and the legality of its interactions with others is the subject of this entire treatise on peace. Ultimately, Kant (ibid., p. 135) argues, "There is no intelligible meaning in the rule of the law of nations as giving a right to make war."
6. Kant, ibid., p. 143, insists that the guarantee of perpetual peace is given, "by no less a power than the great artist nature in whose mechanical course is clearly exhibited a predetermined design to make harmony spring from human discord, even against the will of man."
7. G.W. Hegel, "Addition G" in *Outlines of The Philosophy of Right* (trans. T.M. Knox), Oxford and New York: Oxford University Press, 2008, p. 307.
8. This point has been argued vigorously by Richard Koenigsberg in his somewhat controversial (though convincing) study, *Nations Have the Right to Kill*, New York: The Library of Social Science, 2009, pp. 33–46.
9. M. Elksteins, *Rites of Spring: The Great War and the Birth of the Modern Age*, New York: Anchor Books, 1989, p. 144.
10. See J.J. Sheehan, *Where Have All the Soldiers Gone? The Transformation of Modern Europe*, Boston: Houghton Mifflin, 2008.
11. This argument has been made compellingly by W.T. Cavenaugh, "A Fire Strong Enough to Consume the House: The Wars of Religion and the Rise of the Nation State," in J. Milbank and S. Oliver (Eds.), *The Radical Orthodox Reader*, London – New York: Routledge, 2009, pp. 314–337.
12. See for example R. Rorty's description of this process in *Philosophy and the Mirror of Nature*, Princeton: Princeton University Press, 1979, p. 3.
13. See for example Jacques Derrida's classic essay, "Violence and Metaphysics: An Essay on the Thought of Emannuel Levinas," in *Writing and Difference* (trans. A. Bass), Chicago: University of Chicago Press, 1978, pp. 97–192. See also J. Perl, "Postmodern Disarmament," in S. Zabala (Ed.), *Weakening Philosophy*, Montreal: McGill-Queen's University Press, 2006, pp. 326–347.
14. This claim is articulated by Zabala in S. Zabala (Ed.), *The Future of Religion*, New York: Columbia University Press, 2005, p. 39.
15. Cavenaugh, "A Fire Strong Enough to Consume the House."
16. This is the thrust of John Caputo's analysis of Derrida's religion in *The Prayers and Tears of Jacques Derrida: Religion Without Religion*, Bloomington: Indiana University Press, 1997, pp. 117–160. See also R. Kearney, *The God Who May Be: A Hermeneutics of Religion*, Bloomington: Indiana University Press, 2001, p. 2.
17. Though this is a matter of some dispute, it seems more than tenable to align oneself with the conclusion (expressed vocally by Wittgenstein to Russell during the course of their post-war meeting in Vienna) that this is the ultimate and final "silence" implied in the finale of the *Tractatus*. See L. Wittgenstein, *Tractatus Logico-Philosophicus* (trans. D.F. Pears and B.F. McGuinness; With an introduction by Bertrand Russell), London: Routlege and Kegan Paul, 1961, p. 97.
18. See Isaiah 11, in which the prophetic notion of peace is most fully articulated. This chapter culminates in the celebrated account of wolves dwelling with lambs, leopards lying down with kids and the calf and the young lion fatling together. Isaiah's vision is not a manifesto that human power can set about concretizing in political reality. No policy can resolve the non-contemplative and non-conscious enmities that pervade nature. The effect of Isaiah's metaphor pushes peace outside the realm of the natural and beyond the aspirations of man.
19. Rabbi Naftali Zevi Yehudah Berlin (1816–93; known by the acronym *Neziv*), the head of the Volozhin Yeshiva, was an important teacher of Rabbi Kook. See A. Rosenak, *Rabbi Kook*, Jerusalem: Zalman Shazar Center, 2006, pp. 11–19 (Hebrew).

20. For discussion of this approach in contrast to normative sociological thinking, see A. Rosenak, "*Halakhah*, Thought, and the Idea of Holiness in the Writings of Rabbi Haim David Halevi," in R. Elior and P. Schafer (Eds.), *Creation and Re-Creation in Jewish Thought: Festschrift in Honor of Joseph Dan*, Tübingen: Mohr Siebeck, 2005, pp. 309–338.

21. This is the approach found in normative sociological thought; Maimonides was its primary exponent in the Middle Ages.

22. See I. Tishby, *The Wisdom of the Zohar* vol. 2, Jerusalem: Mosad Bialik, 1961, pp. 3–93 (Hebrew); Judah Halevi, *The Kuzari: An Argument for the Faith of Israel by Judah Halevi* (trans. H. Hirschfeld), New York: Schocken Books, 1964, part I, sections 26–48, 95.

23. Menahem Mendel of Chernobyl, *Me'or Einayim*, Jerusalem: Me'or Einayim Yeshivah, 1975, p. 13.

24. "The force of the contradiction is merely an illness that afflicts logic when limited by the special conditions of man's mind and attentiveness. As we assess the situation, we must sense the contradiction and use that sensation to arrive at a resolution. Above it, however, far above it, there is the supernal divine light, whose possibilities are unlimited and subject to no conditions whatever. It tolerates no impediment on account of the contradiction, and for it, there is no need to resolve it" (A.I.H. Kook, *Olat Re'ayah* vol. 1, Jerusalem: Mosad Harav Kook, 1989, p. 184).

25. On Rabbi Kook's doctrine of the unity of opposites, see Rosenak, *Rabbi Kook*, pp. 34–42; idem, *Prophetic Halakhah: The Philosophy of Halakhah in the Teachings of Rabbi Kook*, Jerusalem: Magnes Press, 2007, pp. 44–57 (Hebrew).

26. Maharal, *Gevurot ha-shem*, Benei-Berak: Yahadut Publication, 1980, ch. 5, p. 35; A. Neher, *The Teachings of Maharal*, Jerusalem: Reuben Mass, 2003 (Hebrew); A. Rosenak, "Unity of Opposites in the teachings of Maharal: A Study of his Writings and their Implications for Jewish Thought in the Twentieth and Twenty-first Centuries" (Hebrew; in preparation).

27. See, for example, T. Kaufman, *Know Him in All Your Ways: The Concept of the Divine and Worship through Corporeality in early Hasidism*, Ramat-Gan: Bar-Ilan University, 2009, pp. 250–395 (Hebrew).

28. A.I.H. Kook, *Eight Papers*, Hebron, Kiryat-Arba and Jerusalem: Pozner Publication, 1999, File 1 (1904–14), par. 26, p. 9 (Hebrew – henceforth cited by its Hebrew acronym "*SQ*").

29. "Every nation will receive the element of truthfulness in accord with the extent of its preparation." Accordingly, "their morality will adopt many hues, for each nation will impress its own mark on the understanding drawn from the light of the Torah, in accord with its natural and historically-determined decisions" (Kook, *Olat Re'ayah* 1, p. 316).

30. A.I.H. Kook, *Orot Ha-Qodesh* Jerusalem: Mosad Harav Kook, 1983, p. 129 (Hebrew).

31. *SQ* 1, par. 343, pp. 119–120.

32. Loc. cit.

33. BT *Eruvin* 13b.

34. *SQ* 1, par. 498, p. 160.

35. Loc. cit.

36. S. Cherlow, "The *Tzaddiq* is the Foundation of the World: Rav Kook's Esoteric Mission and Mystical Experience" (Ph.D. Dissertation), Ramat-Gan: Bar-Ilan University, 2003 (Hebrew with English abstract); S. Ben-Zvi, "Rabbi Kook's Self-Image: A New Reading in Light of Publication of *Eight Files*" (MA Thesis), Jerusalem: Hebrew University, 2003 (Hebrew with English abstract).

37. Kook, *Orot ha-qodesh*, 3, p. 307; *SQ* 1, par. 575, p. 182.

38. Loc. cit.

39. *SQ* 1, par. 24, p. 8.

40. A.I.H. Kook, "Israel's Destiny and Nationhood," in M.Y. Zuriel (Ed.), Otzrot Ha-Reayah [*An Anthology of Writings by Rabbi Kook*], Sha`alvim: M.Y. Zuriel, 1988, p. 693 (Hebrew).

41. A.I.H. Kook, *Orot,* Jerusalem: Mosad Harav Kook, 1982 (Hebrew), p. 80; *SQ* 3, par. 273, p. 100.

42. Idem, *The Sabbath of the Land,* Jerusalem: Mosad Harav Kook, 1979, p. 12 (Hebrew); see also: idem, *Eder Ha-Yaqar,* Jerusalem: Mosad Harav Kook, 1967, p. 128 (Hebrew). An interesting further "contribution" of the Jews' life in exile is the demise of the territorial concept of the divinity. See Kook, *Orot,* p. 115.

43. For numerous sources on this point; see Rosenak, *Prophetic Halakhah,* pp. 150–152.

44. A.I.H. Kook, *Arpelei Tohar,* Jerusalem: Rabbi Z.Y. Kook Publications, 1983, pp. 2–3 (Hebrew); *SQ* 2, par. 6, pp. 294–295; *Orot Ha-qodesh* 2, pp. 290–291; *Olat* 1, p. 39; *Letters of Rabbi A.I.H. Kook,* Jerusalem: Mosad Harav Kook, 1981, p. 58 (Hebrew); *Rabbi Kook's Articles* 1–2, Jerusalem: Mosad Harav Kook, 1984, pp. 94–99, 234–235, 401–411, etc. (Hebrew).

45. For example, in the context of preserving bodily cleanliness, A.I.H. Kook, *Mizvot re'ayah,* Jerusalem: Mosad Harav Kook, 1985 (Hebrew); idem, *Orah hayyim* 2:6, p. 17b; of the link between physical health and the ability to serve and know God, see *Orah hayyim* 6:1, p. 33a; of the sanctity of the body and the duty to bury a miscarried fetus see *Orah hayyim* 526:10, p. 81a; and of the duty to avoid demeaning the body see ibid., p. 81b.

46. Kook, *Orot,* pp. 80–81; *Letters* 1, p. 185.

47. Kook, *Orot,* p. 104; idem, "*Iqvei zon*" in *Eder Ha-Yakar* (note 42 above), p. 136.

48. "But for the sin of the golden calf, the nations dwelling in the Land of Israel would make peace with Israel and acknowledge them" (Kook, *Orot,* p. 14).

49. Kook, *Olat* 1, p. 233.

50. Kook, "Ha-milhamah," in *Orot,* Jerusalem: Mosad Harav Kook, 1982, par. 3, p. 14 (Hebrew).

51. *Olat* 1, pp. 233, 315–316.

52. On R. Kook's Hegelian thought, see S. Avineri, *The Zionist Idea,* Tel Aviv: Am Oved, 1980, pp. 216–226 (Hebrew).

53. *Letters* 2, p. 306.

54. *Orot,* 15; *SQ* 6, par. 152, p. 53.

55. *Orot,* p. 15; *SQ* 6, par. 165, pp. 57–58.

56. R. Kook's comments against "heresy" give voice as well to his concept of the close ties among "the act," "the spiritual idea," and "the soul of Israel." See A.I.H. Kook, *Orot ha-emunah,* Jerusalem: NP, 1985, p. 90 (Hebrew) and the parallel remarks in "*Shemen ra`anan,*" *Ozrot Hareayah,* M.Y. Zoriel (Ed.), Tel Aviv: Yeshivat Sha'alabim, 1988, vol. 4, p. 31 (Hebrew). For sharply critical comments about the damage caused by heresy's severance of thought (that is, *aggadah*) from act (*halakhah*) and its harmful effects, see *Orot ha-emunah,* pp. 11–14; A.I.H. Kook, *Ain Ayeh, Berakhot* 1, Jerusalem: Mosad Harav Kook, 1987, p. 64, sub-par. 162 (Hebrew); cf. a different view in sub-par. 161. On this issue, see E. Luz, "*Halakhah* and *Aggadah* in Rabbi Kook's teachings," *Journal of the Association for Jewish Studies* 11, 1986, Hebrew section, p. 8.

57. *SQ* 5, par. 177, pp. 280–281.

58. Kook, *Orot,* p. 151.

59. H. Porath, "Each Eye will See God's Return to Zion," *Petahim* 2, 32, 1975, p. 8 (Hebrew).

60. Hasidism, in Rabbi Kook's view, took from heresy its sting and the sparks that were within it. See *SQ* 7, par. 138, pp. 201–202. So, too, in an unpublished manuscript: "From the side of folly but excess love came one who wanted to confuse the world, broadening the area of the Torah's influence to a place in which it could

never be established because of the element of evil there. Only after many generations is it possible that it may be established through Israel's exaltedness" (my translation – A.R.).

61. This part of the article is a new and expanded version of A. Isaacs, "Zionism as an Apolitical Spiritual Revolution in the Teachings of Rabbi Moses Avigdor Amiel," in A. Sagi and D. Schwartz (Eds.), *A Century of Religious Zionism* vol. 1, Ramat-Gan: Bar-Ilan University Press, 2003, pp. 287–306 (Hebrew); idem, "A Socio-Cultural Inquiry into the Link between Jewish and General Culture in Light of the Teachings of Rabbi Moses Avigdor Amiel," in Y. Amir, (Ed.), *The Way of the Spirit: Festschrift in Honor of Eliezer Schweid* vol. 1, Jerusalem: Van Leer Institute and the Hebrew University, 2005, pp. 409–438 (Hebrew). Discussion of the topic has been expanded and enriched by E. Holzer, *Military Activism in Religious Zionist Thought*, Jerusalem: Shalom Hartman Institute, 2009 (Hebrew).

62. M.A. Amiel, *Principles of Halakhic Study*, Jerusalem: Mosad Harav Kook, 1939 (Hebrew).

63. M.A. Amiel, *To the Perplexed of the Age – Essays on the Essence of Judaism*, Jerusalem: Mosad Ha-Rav Kook, 1943 (Hebrew).

64. Idem, *Social Justice and our Legal and Moral Justice*, Tel Aviv: Torah Va-Avoda Movement, 1936 (Hebrew). See: *Encyclopedia Judaica* 2:846–847; Y.L.H. Fishman, "A Giant of Thought in *Halakhah* and *Aggadah*," in Y.L.H. Fishman (Ed.), *Festschrift Presented to Rabbi Moses Avigdor Amiel*, Jerusalem: Mosad Harav Kook, 1943, pp. 1–12; K.P. Tekhorsh, *Rabbi M.A. Amiel's Teachings on Halakhah and Aggadah*, Jerusalem: Religious Publication Society and Mosad Harav Kook, 1943 (Hebrew).

65. Amiel, *Social Justice and our Legal and Moral Justice*, p. 4.

66. "Yesterday's absolute justice becomes today's total evil" (ibid., p. 3).

67. Ibid., p. 4.

68. Ibid., p. 5.

69. Ibid., pp. 7–8; Amiel, *To the Perplexed*, pp. 113–114.

70. Amiel, *To the Perplexed*, p. 169; Halevi, *Ha-kuzari*, I:95.

71. *Ha-kuzari*, I:116.

72. Amiel, *Social Justice and our Legal and Moral Justice*, p. 54.

73. Ibid., p. 52.

74. This assessment might be taken to blur his distinction between Jewish and non-Jewish thought, for it suggests that the nations of the world fail to follow the ideas of their own philosophers – ideas that, if followed, might lead them to positions resembling more closely those suggested by Jewish thought. A full discussion of that issue is beyond the scope of the present article. On Rabbi Amiel's complex interaction with general philosophy – a philosophy that he rejects as non-Jewish thinking – see A. Rosenak, "General and Jewish Culture in the Thought of Rabbi M.A. Amiel: A Socio-Cultural Model," in Y. Amir (Ed.), *The Path of the Spirit: The Eliezer Schweid Jubilee*, Vol. I, (*Jerusalem Studies in Jewish Thought*, XVIII), Jerusalem: The Hebrew University of Jerusalem, pp. 409–438 (Hebrew).

75. Amiel, *Social Justice and our Legal and Moral Justice*, pp. 32, 92; idem, *To the Perplexed*, pp. 75, 92–97, 124.

76. Ibid., p. 71.

77. Loc. cit.

78. For example, he says the following about members of the religious kibbutz movement, participants in the enterprise of conquering the Land: "The great heroism of these Jewish heroes is incalculable – the heroism of these dear sons of Zion, more precious than gold, who give their lives for the sanctity of God's name and of the Land. All of us are obligated to honor them, to kneel before them" ("*Al ha-me'ora'ot ve-al ha-havlagah*," Ha-Zofe 27.8.1938, p. 3). He supported the Zionist *Yishuv* notwithstanding his strong opposition to Zionism's cultural atmosphere: "And yet, 'let the accuser be

silent and the defender take his place,' for even this form of nationalism contributes to the growth and progress of the Land of Israel. The actions themselves – settlement and building of the Land of Israel – are mighty actions" (*To the Perplexed*, p. 304). See also D. Schwartz, *Faith at the Crossroads*, Tel Aviv: Am Oved, 1996, pp. 255–256 (Hebrew).

79. M.A. Amiel, *The Sabbath Queen: Essays and Speeches on the Sabbath*, Tel Aviv: Mizrachi Publication, 1937, p. 22 (Hebrew).
80. See *To the Perplexed*, pp. 278–280.
81. M.A. Amiel, "On the Ideological Foundations of Mizrahi," Ha-Tor 3, 1935, p. 23 (Hebrew).
82. Amiel, *The Sabbath Queen*, p. 17. See also D. Schwarz, *The Land of Israel in Religion Zionist Thought*, Tel Aviv: Am Oved, 1997, pp. 160–169 (Hebrew). It is interesting to compare Amiel's feeling for time to its parallel in the teachings of Abraham Joshua Heschel. See A.J. Heschel, *The Sabbath: Its Meaning for Modern Man*, New York: Farrar, Straus and Giroux, 1951, pp. 3–10; D. Bundi, *How?* Jerusalem: Shalem Center, 2008, pp. 279–283.
83. Amiel saw within Zionism two separate and competing power centers – the secular and the religious – and was concerned that the latter was shrinking to the point of disappearance. See *Ha-yesodot ha-idiologiyyim shel ha-mizrahi*, p. 23.
84. M.A. Amiel, "More on the Ideological Foundations of Mizrahi," *Ha-tor* 16, 1935, p. 7 (Hebrew). See also *To the Perplexed*, p. 282; R. Sa`adyah Ga'on, *With Perfect Faith: The Foundation of Jewish Belief [Sefer ha-emunot ve-ha-de`ot]*, J. David Bleich (Ed.), New York: Ktav Publishing House, 1983, Part III ch. 7.
85. Amiel, *To the Perplexed*, pp. 282–285; "The Ideological Foundations of Mizrahi," p. 8; Z. Zohar, "'On the Basis of Judaism in its Entirety': Rabbi Amiel's Polemic against the Enlightenment, Secularism, Nationalism, Mizrahi, and Agudah," in N. Ilan (Ed.), *A Good Eye: Dialogue and Polemic in Israeli Culture*, Tel Aviv: Ha-Kibutz Ha-Meuchad Publications, 1999, pp. 313–348 (Hebrew). See also Schwartz, *The Land of Israel in Religion Zionist Thought*, p. 163.
86. Amiel, *Social Justice and our Legal and Moral Justice*, p. 111.
87. Idem, *To the Perplexed*, p. 243.
88. Ibid., p. 280.
89. M.A. Amiel, *Darkhei Mosheh* vol. 2, *Darkhei Ha-qinyanim*, Warsaw: Neta Krohberg Printers, 1931, "*Darkah Shel Torah*," p. 4.
90. Ibid., pp. 5, 12.
91. Ibid., pp. 12–13.
92. See the introduction by Hayyim Judah Roth to the Hebrew translation of Rousseau's *Social Contract*, Jerusalem: Magnes, 1984, p. vii.
93. "Zionism began . . . in the time of Abraham . . . of whom it is said, 'lover, indeed, of the people' (Deut. 33:3)," *To the Perplexed*, p. 289. See also Schwartz, *The Land of Israel in Religion Zionist Thought*, pp. 165–166.
94. Amiel, *To the Perplexed*, p. 238; Schwartz, *The Land of Israel in Religion Zionist Thought*, p. 165.
95. Amiel, *Ha-yesodot Ha-idiologiyot Shel Ha-mizrahi*, p. 9.
96. Amiel's statements on this matter are difficult. Secular Zionism, in his opinion, "flows from the source of nationalism in the spirit of the gentile nations – a nationalism whose foundation stone was laid by Bismarck and whose housewarming was celebrated by Hitler; a nationalism that is entirely idolatrous. Does it have any resemblance at all to the religion of Israel, which is entirely holy and entirely pure?" (*Zionism's Spiritual Problems*, Tel Aviv: The Mizrachi Organization, 1937, p. 41 [Hebrew]). Amiel here is writing in the 1930s, unaware of the horrors on the horizon.

97. This form of nationalism "draws its nurture from the one God, the Eternal One, whose house 'is a house of prayer for all nations.' Our nationalism is meant . . . to bring about internationalism and 'repair the world under the kinship of God'" (*To the Perplexed*, p. 287).

98. To prove his point here, Amiel relied on both Judah Halevi and Maimonides, despite the divergence between their views: "Both of them . . . try to show as well the revealed portion of the Torah . . . The *Guide*, which speaks to the perplexed among our people . . . offers general human thinking. R. Judah Halevi, in contrast . . . writing for the gentiles, offers authentic Jewish thinking" (*Darkhei Mosheh*, p. 11).

99. Amiel, *To the Perplexed*, p. 242.

100. Exodus 19:5; Deuteronomy 7:6; 14:2.

101. BT *Yevamot* 61a; BT *Bava mezi`a* 114b; BT *Keritot* 6b. Though writing in 1943, here, too, Amiel seems unaware of what was happening in Europe.

102. Deuteronomy 23:21. See also BT *Bava Mezi`a* 70b; *The Code of Maimonides, Book 13: The Book of Civil Laws, Creditor and Debtor* 5:1 (trans. J.J. Rabinowitz), New Haven and London: Yale University Press, 1949, p. 93. On the efforts of Amiel's contemporary Rabbi Simeon Shkop to deal with these issues, see A. Sagi, "A Study in Rabbi Simeon Shkop's Halakhic Thinking," *Da`at* 35, 1995, pp. 99–114, 102–104 (Hebrew).

103. BT *Shabbat* 14b–15a; JT *Pesahim* 6b; JT *Ketubbot* 50a.

104. BT Nazir 54b. See also Tosafot on BT Nazir 20a, s.v. leima be-ha; Tosafot on BT Nazir 15b, s.v. ve-a-avira litlot; *The Code of Maimonides, Book 10: The Book of Cleanliness*, Corpse Uncleanliness 11:1–2 (trans. H. Danby), New Haven: Yale University Press, 1954, pp. 43–44.

105. BT *Yevamot* 46b; BT *Avodah Zarah* 31a; *The Code of Maimonides, Book 5: The Book of Holiness, Forbidden Foods* 11:4–6 (trans. L.I. Rabinowitz and P. Grossman), New Haven and London: Yale University Press, 1965, pp. 208–209.

106. BT *Yevamot* 47b, 109b; BT *Qiddushin* 70b.

107. BT *Sanhedrin* 44a.

108. Amiel, *To the Perplexed*, pp. 235–236.

109. Amiel emphasizes the difference between Jewish internationalism, which flows from love of God's creatures and consciousness of God's unity, and the internationalism of the gentile nations, grounded, like their nationalism, in hatred of the Other and alienation from him. See Amiel, *Social Justice and our Legal and Moral Justice*, p. 114.

110. 1 Kings 8:41.

111. Jeremiah 1:5.

112. Amiel, *To the Perplexed*, pp. 236–237.

113. Ibid., p. 241

114. Ibid., p. 239.

115. "There is only one nation in the world, the nation of Israel, that highlights the first human and links its own ancestors to that first human as the specific is linked to the general" (ibid., p. 243).

116. Ibid., p. 111.

117. BT *Pesahim* 27b; Amiel, *To the Perplexed*, pp. 111, 133.

118. (*Tosafot* to BT *Qiddushin* 48a); Amiel, *To the Perplexed*, pp. 111, 133.

119. Maimonides, "Letter to Obadiah the Proselyte," in I. Twersky (Ed.), *A Maimonides Reader*, Springfield: Behrman House, 1972, pp. 475–476.

120. Amiel, *Social Justice and our Legal and Moral Justice*, p. 112.

121. Ibid., p. 113.

122. Mishnah *Sanhedrin* 4:5. Amiel places his criticism of Christian culture and secular-Western culture under a single rubric, but he also differentiates between them, favoring Inquisitional Christianity over the secularism that gave rise to the world wars. For all its horrors, the Inquisition involved a conflict "for the sake of Heaven."

In contrast, the conflict with factional and secular political thought no longer made use of a religious mask (*To the Perplexed*, pp. 137–138). Beneath the secular ideology, he thought, there festered the worst form of racism.

123. Amiel, *Social Justice and our Legal and Moral Justice*, p. 33.
124. *Darkhei Mosheh*, p. 22.
125. Amiel, *To the Perplexed*, p. 135.
126. On the contradictory nature of these trends, see ibid., p. 136.
127. Ibid., p. 137.
128. *Darkhei Mosheh*, pp. 19–20.
129. Ibid., p. 22.
130. Amiel, *The Sabbath Queen*, p. 24.
131. M.A. Amiel, *Discourses to my People*, Warsaw: Hacefira Publication, 1943, part 3, p. 134 (Hebrew).
132. In *Discourses*, pp. 135–136, he cites precedents in that regard going all the way back to Joseph's appearance before Pharaoh and continuing with Joshua confronting Amalek, Simeon the Just before Alexander of Macedon, and Rabban Yohanan ben Zakkai before Vespasian and Titus. After citing the *midrash* at BT *Yoma* 69a, he adds: "Simeon the Just waged war against Alexander of Macedon; we confront military garb with priestly garb." See further on the power of the book, ibid., p. 137.
133. "Not without due consideration did our enemies accuse us with blood libels, for their minds could not encompass how a nation could differ from all other nations and exist in the world without drawing blood. According their theory, they had no alternative but to suspect us of drawing blood in secret instead of openly as they do, spilling blood as water" (ibid., p. 137).
134. Ibid., pp. 138–139.
135. "For the sword has brought us, and brings to all the world, only the Ninth of Av [that is, mourning] and only graves" (ibid., p. 71).
136. "Because it [warfare] is extremely repugnant to us, and we engage in it only when necessary to end warfare" (ibid., p. 70).
137. M.A. Amiel, "The Prohibition of Murder with Respect to Arabs," *Tehumin* 10, 1989, p. 148 (Hebrew). According to Amiel, the negative Tree of Knowledge is the father of technology that is born or and nurtured by the desire for war. See *Darkhei Mosheh*, "*Darkah Shel Torah*," p. 22. On his attitude toward and critique of the policy of restraint in the face of Arab provocation, see his "On the Disturbances and on Restraint," *Ha-zofeh*, 28 Tammuz 5698 [summer 1938], p. 3 (Hebrew).
138. Amiel, *Social Justice and our Legal and Moral Justice*, p. 86; *To the Perplexed*, p. 94.
139. Amiel, *Social Justice and our Legal and Moral Justice*, pp. 91–92. "All of Judaism's principles . . . pertain to the individual will, until it becomes second nature within the Jewish nation, while all the principles of socialist justice are built exclusively on the collective will" (ibid., p. 87).
140. Leviticus 23:22.
141. Exodus 23:3.
142. Deuteronomy 16:19
143. Amiel, *Social Justice and our Legal and Moral Justice*, p. 87; *To the Perplexed*, p. 94.
144. Amiel, *Social Justice and our Legal and Moral Justice*, p. 89; *To the Perplexed*, p. 95.
145. Amiel, *To the Perplexed*, p. 95.
146. Ibid., p. 92.
147. "Indeed, the results were very bad. An unprecedented civil war raged. . . until they themselves saw that they had gone too far 'and they raised their voices and wept'" (Amiel, *To the Perplexed*, pp. 69–70).
148. Ibid., pp. 70–71.
149. Ibid., p. 72.

150. Loc. cit.
151. And this is "the downside of the foregoing trait . . . that every individual refuses to submit even to the will of his own collective, the Jewish collective itself" (Amiel, *To the Perplexed*, pp. 78–79).
152. Ibid., pp. 102–103.
153. Amiel, *To the Perplexed*, p. 214.
154. Ibid., p. 215.
155. Amiel, *Social Justice and our Legal and Moral Justice*, pp. 83–84.
156. Loc. cit.
157. On this approach, exile was something positive; see Amiel, "Exile and Redemption," *Ha-mizrahi* 49, 1920, p. 6 (Hebrew). In exile, he believes, Israel was liberated from the bonds of nationalism and became the people of the Torah. See also his "The Jewish Idea of Redemption," *Ha-boqer* 19, 1939, p. 2 (Hebrew).
158. Amiel, *Social Justice and our Legal and Moral Justice*, p. 84.
159. Ibid., p. 85.
160. Ibid.
161. Ibid.

11 Moral considerations relating to criticism of the Warsaw Ghetto Uprising

Rabbinic literature and the Just War Theory

Isaac Hershkowitz

1. Introduction

This article sets out to review a wide range of moral and ideological criticism by a number of rabbis relating to the Warsaw Ghetto Uprising and its transformation into a part of the Israeli ethos.[1] While these rabbis' personal background does play a significant role in the nature of their criticism and their ideological slant, they do raise moral points of major importance relating to coping with the question of the Uprising in the light of Jewish sources. In the course of this article I shall attempt to show if and to what extent it is possible to categorize this criticism in the light of the Just War Theory and thereby reach a sort of codex of the ethics of the limitations on war according to a selection of post-Holocaust rabbis.

The authorities whose criticism we will review are Rabbi Yeshayahu A. Steinberger, Rabbi Simcha Elberg, Rabbi Baruch Meidan and Rabbi Joel Teitelbaum. In this article I shall not deal with the positions of the rabbis who expressed support for the Uprising.

2. Just War Theory and the fighting in the Warsaw Ghetto

When we come to examine the Warsaw Ghetto Uprising, an ethical conflict arises regarding two of the principles that define a Just War. The first is the Principle of Proper Authority, and the second is the Principle of Probability. The Principle of Proper Authority demands that a war can only be waged after it has been approved by authorized institutions, in an orderly fashion, and the giving of adequate publicity of the intention to make war. These intensions should be made public both to the citizens of the attacking country and to the country being attacked.[2]

The Principle of Probability determines that only an armed struggle which has a chance of success is morally justified. Conversely, a hopeless struggle where blood will be shed is gratuitous since the position at its end is no better than that at its beginning, so whatever the case, it has no moral justification.[3]

However, for both these principles there exist reasonable reservations, as with regard to the case of the Warsaw Ghetto Uprising.

James Turner Johnson claims that while right intention, just cause and proper authority are deontological norms whose lack can never be justified, the question of the probability of the war is a prudential criterion and there are extreme cases in which their application is not consistent with the Just War principles.[4] A prime example of this is the question of the Warsaw Ghetto Uprising. Despite the extreme lack of probability of achieving military success in the Uprising, the right intention and just cause that motivated the fighters were so powerful and clear that they enabled the question of Probability to be overridden. Von Der Linden disagrees with him, claiming that in the Warsaw Uprising the dilemma is not how to rule between just cause and probability.[5] Probability is not rejected, and its virtue as a norm of deontological justice is not less than the other norms of a Just War. However, in contrast to Johnson, in his opinion the case of a struggle against a state that is seeking to humiliate its opponants, brings into play other principles of Just War. A human being's struggle for his self-respect, and for his right to die as a free agent and not as a slave and not to be murdered for ethnic reasons, is such that there is no room here for the Principle of Probability. These basic human rights position him in a different category vis-à-vis the norms of justice.[6]

Gilbert reinforces the point of the cancellation of the principle of Probability in extreme cases, such as that of the Warsaw Ghetto Uprising.[7] He claims that when it comes to anything relating to guerrilla warfare, the validity of the basic terms of Just War needs to be re-examined, but even more so there is a need to apply new principles in relation to guerrilla activities of a people under attack. Aggressive guerrilla activities, according to Gilbert, require the attackers to take into account the question of Probability and the cost in human life as a result of the type of warfare that they are initiating. Not taking into account the loss of innocent life (or even the lives of enemy fighters) in connection with aggressive guerrilla warfare is not, in his opinion, reasonable. But defensive guerrilla warfare, such as that of the Warsaw Ghetto Uprising, seeks to disrupt the enemy's designs to kill members of the Jewish People. Though it is true that the Probability of the enemy's defeat is extremely low, it is unreasonable to expect the rebels to offer themselves passively up for slaughter. Therefore, Gilbert claims, the Principle of Probability is totally irrelevant in the case of defensive guerrilla warfare.

Using this approach Von Der Linden solves the question of the required Proper Authority and determines that the special principles that govern a struggle of the type of the Warsaw Ghetto Uprising are such that make it impossible to apply the same rules as in a properly organized country. The existential fear of the Ghetto fighters justifies this change of principles. Conversely, politicians cannot make use of these criteria of war, and, in any case, from their viewpoint the fixed principles of Just War always apply, since they all hold a deontological status.

Rodin also seeks to determine that there is a substantial difference between a situation of war between countries and an "ethnic cleansing" campaign, to which different principles of justice apply.[8]

Similar claims have also been voiced on the Principle of Proper Authority. In a statement published by the Institute for American Values (2002), consequent upon the war in Iraq, a number of well-known scholars sought to outline to the fighters and their commanders a proper ethical framework for the war. This manifesto was publicized in different forums,[9] and received impressive coverage. As regards the question of Proper Authority, members of the Manifesto Committee pointed out that in cases where a struggle has an ethnic flavor and is directed against a civil population, there is no point, in any case, in determining the norm of Proper Authority. It was inconceivable, from their point of view, to negate an individual's right to fight for his life, even if this proves unsuccessful, and to instruct him go to his death like a lamb to the slaughter.

A similar claim was made by Fletcher and Ohlin, who made the distinction between a Polish peasant and a rebel in the Ghetto.[10] According to them, a Polish peasant at the height of the Nazi occupation, however galling his feelings might be due to his national pride, was not in fear of his life at the personal level. Therefore, despite the fact that he found himself deprived in many ways (subjugation of his sovereign rights, economic oppression and so forth), and despite the fact the regime he had to deal with was not "just" by definition, nevertheless his killing a German soldier or officer who was not directly threatening his life on his own initiative would be murder. Taking a life must be done within a general framework of a Just War which includes the approval of the authorizing body. On the other hand, there was a constant threat to the lives of the Jews in the Ghetto, or indeed, in any area under German rule during the Second World War. From his point of view any agent, fighter, or German government representative was a potential murderer. In any case, the taking of a German life was a means of self-defense, and there was no need for any higher authority or acquiring permission from it for the purpose of self-defense.

Statman relates directly to the question of the Warsaw Ghetto Uprising versus the Just War principle.[11] His important article provides us with a good summary of the question of self-defense (of individuals and of states) in the case of no reasonable hope of success. Statman formulates an assertion that includes in it all the elements required for the ethical definition of the Warsaw Ghetto Uprising. On the one hand there is the question of Probability which is normatively entrenched in the formulations of the Just War, and intuitively entrenched in the generally accepted principles of self-defense. But on the other hand, the fact that in certain cases the attacker seeks not only to take the life of the person under attack but also his property, and even his personal dignity, needs to be taken into consideration. The basic question that needs to be asked is whether the possibility of preserving a person's dignity is sufficient reason for his waging a hopeless attack, or whether the saving of his life (or at least the chance of saving it) is a moral prerequisite for the attack. Statman's claim is that it is necessary to weigh the overall considerations of the attacker (the nature of the attack being waged, whether it includes in it also elements of vitiating dignity and threatening life) and, in opposition to these, pose the rules of the reaction. That is to say, if the attackers are threatening to harm a person, and so take not only his life but also his dignity,[12] then the person being attacked is entitled to counter-attack and to use parallel and proportionate means to those used by the attacker. In this case, the defense of dignity also has a form of moral justification, which could serve as grounds for launching a counter-attack even in a case where the chances of success are very low.

At the foundation of Statman's claim is the assertion that the saving of human dignity should also be recognized as part of the calculation of the risks of the war. In other words, not only the saving of the life of the person being attacked is an expression of the possible success in the campaign, but also the saving of his dignity, his right to existence as a human being. Whatever the case, the Warsaw Ghetto Uprising was justified as what it was, and what it has been asserted to be, a struggle for the human dignity of the fighters. And this is so despite the fact that it did not achieve any other concrete aim beyond the matter of human dignity.

3. "Exile and military initiative is a contradiction in terms"

So far I have examined the questions of Probability and Proper Authority in the light of Western sources that are committed to universalistic, autonomous moral criteria, as expressed in Kantian philosophy, and whose design is linked to the liberal models of Just War. From here on my intention is to survey a series of halakhic and ideological sources that have the clear common denominator of total commitment to the Jewish law, as expressed in the sources of the Oral Law of the Torah. This being the case, it would seem that the basic moral assumptions are different, on many occasions going from one extreme to the other, and to a large extent the pretension to impose on these sources autonomous moral criteria is destined to fail. However, as I shall seek to show throughout this article, one may, on the one hand, use Western criteria to diagnose accepted moral positions, and, on the other, identify positions that are not moral in themselves, though they use exclusively moral rhetoric.

Rabbi Yeshaya Steinberger wrote two articles in the Israeli Chief Rabbinate's annual anthology *Shana Beshana*, in which he reviewed the background for the determining, by the Chief Rabbinate, of the Tenth of Tevet as the date on which the "General Kaddish" is said (for Holocaust victims whose date of death is unknown). He reviewed the connection between this date and that of Holocaust and Heroism Remembrance Day on the Twenty-Seventh of Nissan, the official appointed date for remembrance of the Holocaust, as legislated by the Israeli Parliament, the Knesset.[13] In his first article he reviewed the halakhic and ideological dispute that took place in the early days of the existence of the State of Israel, between the Chief Rabbinate and the legislators, concerning the proper date that would serve to commemorate the Holocaust. We are not concerned with this article here, but rather with Steinberger's second article, published in 1992. In this article Steinberger sought to provide an ideological background for the significance of remembrance in the world of halakhah, and to explain why the correct and proper date to serve as remembrance of the Holocaust is precisely the Tenth of Tevet and not the Twenty-Seventh of Nissan. On account of this discussion, Steinberger found himself having to cope frontally with the ethos that had developed in Israeli society about the Warsaw Ghetto Uprising, and with its religious meaning.

I have chosen to start with Steinberger's outlook precisely because of its deviance from the other works that will be discussed later. Steinberger is identified with the Religious-Zionist sector of Israeli society. He served as one of the heads of the *Yeshivat Hakotel* in Jerusalem (a "yeshivat hesder" whose students divide their time between religious studies and military service) and wrote numerous essays in Religious-Zionist rabbinic journals throughout the years.[14] Hence his basic position does not negate a situation in which Jews take up arms and defend themselves. However, his harsh criticism of the "sanctification" of the ethos of the Uprising stems from his religious outlook, but be that as it may, it is necessary to examine its basic moral and theological characteristics.

Steinberger's critical approach is revealed immediately with the exposition of his article. In relation to the National Holocaust Remembrance Day he says: "The day seeks to express a series of ideas that are based on a fallacious perspective of our national character. It is trying to connect the Holocaust with heroism, as if they came into the world hand in hand."[15] The series of fallacious ideas, according to Steinberger, are derived from erroneous notions of philosophy of history, morality and nationalism. We will now review these categories at length.

a. The "sanctification" of the Warsaw Ghetto Uprising

The first of the erroneous ideas mentioned above, according to Steinberger, relates to the question of the integrality of history, and derived from this is a misunderstanding of the essence of nationalism during the Exile (that is, throughout the two millennia since the destruction of the Second Temple). Making something of a Hegelian claim, he protests against the trend of those who wanted to highlight secular interpretations of the Holocaust: "They preferred to set the memorial day on an independent date having no previous historical significance since they refused to see the history of the Jewish people as one continuous whole."[16] As opposed to this, the intention of the Israeli Chief Rabbinate, in fixing the Tenth of Tevet as Holocaust Day, was exactly the opposite: "to emphasize the continuous chain of events from the Destruction of the Temple to the horrors of the Holocaust."[17] This claim becomes more pointed with him when he confronts the secular perplexity when dealing with the Holocaust. Since religious Judaism sees the Holocaust as part of the overall experience of Exile, then whatever the case, the Holocaust is "an event that does not shatter the principles of the religious Jew's faith."[18] On the contrary, there is plenty of evidence in the sources reflecting similar levels of threat and intimidation, as part of the overall exilic experience. However, humanistic secularism, which does not seek to find Divine immanence in human history in general or in Jewish history in particular, finds it extremely difficult to cope with the ramifications of the events of the Holocaust on humanity.[19] The secularists sought to design the memory of the Holocaust as the memory of heroism, of humanity, according to its humanistic model.[20]

This historiosophical process that Steinberger seeks to establish is rooted in a differentiation between the concepts of Exile and Redemption:

> The secret of the fate of the Jewish People, whose meaning is known only to He who directs history and dwells on high, though He revealed a morsel of it to His servants the prophets and to our sages. Although what is hidden is greater than what has been revealed, the one thing that is clear beyond any doubt is that Exile and Redemption are opposites [. . .] the contradiction is in the field of the working of Divine providence on the Jewish People in that most terrible period. The main characteristic of the Exile is not expressed in persecution or enslavement in themselves. It is expressed in the humiliation of the Jew and in the subjugation of his dignity as a man in the eyes of the gentile environment [. . .] the term "dignity" or "honor," as it is understood in gentile culture, cannot exist for the Jewish People in Exile, since "*Gaon Ya'acov*" (the Glory of Jacob), had then been cast into the dust; and we were the essence of Exile.[21]

According to Steinberger, the decree of Exile, which is of course a Divine decree, obliges the Jewish People to live in a state of humiliation, without honor. He does not go into the question of what means are required in order to achieve liberation from Exile, and whether this can be done by human means, by an awakening in the lower (human) world, or whether only a defined and focused Divine revelation can initiate the processes of Redemption. This matter was not relevant in the ghetto, and in any case does not affect the subject in question. The situation in the ghettos was one of humiliation and subjugation, which was the portion meted out to Jews in exile by its very essence. An artificial change in the character of the Jew in exile was, according to Steinberger, contrary to Divine will in the delineation of the course of history, which had decreed Exile upon the people of Israel. In any case, both the very initiating of the Uprising and the fixing of the Holocaust Remembrance Day on a special date ascribed to the Uprising, express a disregard of the Divine nature of the Exile and constitutes a contradiction to the essence of Jewish existence in the Exile.[22]

Steinberger does not say that there were no elements of heroism in the Exile, but rather seeks to emphasize passive heroism, the heroism of struggling and surviving, as the purpose of Jewish existence in exile.[23] On the other hand, he sees active heroism, that seeks to question the nature of life in exile, as totally invalid and unacceptable. Active heroism does indeed have a place of honor in the Jewish ethos, but only when carried out at a time of sovereignty in the Land of Israel. That is to say, official independence in the Land of Israel is sufficient reason, according to Steinberger, to take up arms and perform acts of active heroism in its defense. He accepts sovereignty and independence as proper considerations for maintaining a military organization and even for fostering a tradition of national heroism:

> If there were expressions of military heroism within the People of Israel, and indeed there were such, they occurred during periods of national

independence and not in exile. These were the acts of heroism of the troops of King David, and if we can make the comparison, there were acts of heroism by the fighters in the underground movements and the soldiers of the IDF. Their acts were those of a people fighting in its country and for its country. There is no historical precedent of the Jewish People going to war in exile. And so we have said that exile and military initiative are contradictions in terms.[24]

To sum up this historiosophical question – Steinberger seeks to focus discussion on the essence of the exile which is in opposition to active efforts to achieve redemption, and in any case the remembrance of the Holocaust must include a remembrance of the passive spiritual heroism of the survival, and not concentrate on the ethos of active heroism, that is not appropriate to the Holocaust.

b. Moral considerations in the criticism of the Warsaw Ghetto Uprising

Steinberger makes two moral protests in his article. One is against the creators of the ethos of the remembrance of the Holocaust in the State of Israel who favored the Twenty-Seventh of Nissan over the Tenth of Tevet as Holocaust Memorial Day. He claims that this act places a stamp of shame on all Jews who did not take up arms and defend themselves, and obliges them to struggle not only with their grim personal experiences but also with the criticism, covert and open, on their passive behavior during the Holocaust.[25]

Steinberger's major moral criticism is directed against the act of Uprising in the ghetto. Since it was clear to all that there was no real chance of reaching a favorable end by taking military action, there was a different purpose to the Uprising, that of preserving Jewish honor. However, Steinberger is of the opinion that this is foreign to the spirit of Judaism, and unacceptable from a moral point of view:

> The term "to die with honor," that has its origins in the heroic romanticism of the gentiles, is foreign to Judaism, even in times of peace. Therefore among Jews the duel was never accepted as a solution for quarrels of prestige. Even the committing of suicide on Masada documented by Josephus is never mentioned by our sages. This is a deafening silence, it would seem.[26] Judaism does not respect a person who takes his own life, unless this is done to save himself from committing a major sin.[27]

Steinberger's basic claim, in contrast to his historiosophical review précised above, is that dying with honor is improper in itself, and not only in contextual circumstances of one sort or another. It is not Exile that undermines the legitimacy of death with honor, but the moral foundations of the Torah. Death may serve as a means of escape only from personal anti-normative behavior, that is to say as a constraint from transgressing one of the Torah's commandments. Any other choice of unnatural death causes life to lose its value. However, if a person lives his life based on normative Torah principles, and an outside agent seeks to deprive him of his right to life, it is not legitimate for him to end his life on his own initiative. The correct moral decision in the Uprising, according to Steinberger, was to stay alive for as long as possible, without taking into consideration the question of the national and personal status of the victims in the face of their murderers. On the contrary, he reinforces his claim and asserts that considering how the murderer may regard his victim is itself a fallacious action, which in no way stands as justification for death:

> If it is done only in order to deprive the gentile oppressor of the satisfaction of humiliating his victim when murdering him, it is possible that the person committing suicide is committing a very serious offence.[28]

In summarizing Rabbi Steinberger's approach to the question of the Warsaw Ghetto Uprising and the fixing of Holocaust Day on the Twenty-Seventh of Nissan, we can make the following assertions:

a. The State of Israel that is fighting for its sovereignty in the Land of Israel, is entitled, and indeed obliged, to take up arms in order to repulse any aggressive enemy action. Moreover, it is possible that in relation to the State, considerations of honor and deterrence, and not only those of saving lives and self-defense, may be considered proper and valid. In this way Steinberger's moral stance comes into line with what is accepted in Just War Theory. Furthermore, he does not emphasize the subject of Probability in a war of this type, and it is possible that he would even permit the sovereign State to fight for its freedom and its honor even in a situation where anticipating a successful outcome is totally unreasonable.

b. While the Jewish People are in exile, that is to say, individual Jews are not part of the defined political collective, they do not have the moral right to take up arms for a purpose that is not the saving of life. In this way, Steinberger seeks to eliminate "honor" as a moral category in considerations of self-defense, and brings the discussion back to the classic norm of Probability, without taking into account the extreme circumstances of the Warsaw Ghetto Uprising and similar events.

c. "Dying with honor" is an unacceptable value in the light of Jewish tradition, and does not express heroism, but rather imbecility. Heroism in the context of Exile means survival, both material and spiritual. Hence, any taking up of arms that is not for a life-saving purpose is a purposeless, invalid act.

4. "This struggle is not entitled to be called an uprising"

Rabbi Steinberger's position brings up not a few unanswered questions regarding the nature of the exile, the attitude, in principle, of Judaism toward the taking up of arms, and the morality of a suicidal campaign. Another Talmudic scholar who reacted to the Uprising in a similar manner, though emphasizing different points, was Rabbi Simcha Elberg (1915–95).[29] Rabbi Elberg devoted three essays in his journal, *Hapardes*, to the question of the Warsaw Ghetto Uprising.[30] The first essay to be published was devoted to refuting the connection between Rabbi Menachem Ziemba and the Warsaw Ghetto Uprising.[31] His second essay was devoted to an attack on Holocaust Day as a day commemorating the Uprising, and the third essay provided a systematic explanation of his outlook and gave the reasoning for his opposition to the Uprising.

Despite his understanding of the ghetto fighters themselves, Elberg relates to the Uprising as to a "false petty-consolation." The Uprising was an expression of deep despair, and an attempt to shake off the shame of being brought as sheep to slaughter, but did not have any proper Torah-related motivation: "And so this Uprising was no more than an expression of depressive helplessness and the acme of hopelessness."[32]

Elberg's principal claim is that while there was a place for an uprising and for use of arms against the enemy if and when they were likely to lead to an effective outcome, the specific circumstances that had been created in the Warsaw Ghetto made that Uprising superfluous:

> All this heroic struggle in the last days of the ghetto, is in no way entitled from an historical point of view to be called an uprising. The historical justification for any uprising is connected and bound up with its hope, with its new perspective, and primarily with its message of redemption which releases all the shackles of slavery binding it. However, the Warsaw Ghetto Uprising was not capable of creating even the faintest of illusions that it would change the real, tragic situation and more than it extended life, it brought death more quickly.[33]

Elberg's principle assertion is that an uprising's ultimate purpose must be redemptive. The Jew may revolt if and when the purpose of the revolt is defined and it is within his power to save life. Rebellion for other purposes is not acceptable from the point of view of the Torah. One rebellion, in fact, that attempted to achieve freedom from exile, the Bar Kokhba Revolt, is regarded by Elberg as legitimate,[34] and contrary to the model depicted by Steinberger, he does not relate to the importance of Jewish sovereignty in the Land of Israel as an essential factor in defining the Revolt. From Elberg's point of view, even emancipation from the slavery of exile, and so even the Warsaw Uprising against the Nazi enemy, without any connection to immigration to Israel and defending the settlement there, is proper and legitimate. This is based on the assumption that the Revolt has the power to shake off the oppressive burden. However, a revolt for honor, for the "sanctity of death,"[35] is neither proper nor justifiable.[36] However, Elberg's description of the stoicism of the Jewish People reveals a further aspect of his philosophy regarding the ideological path the People should take, at least in times of distress such as those in the Warsaw Ghetto, which in any case raises a large number of questions:

In the People's constant silence, in its quiet expiry without showing any resistance to its being led inaudibly to slaughter, lies the excellent expression of the wonderful authentic essence of the Jewish People, who never based its historic existence on insurgence or revolution. It is precisely the quiet expiry of millions, in absolute silence, without the punch of an angry fist in the cruel face of the oppressor which more than conspicuously expresses the character of the Jewish People, whose chronicle of thousands of years is not based on bloody rebellions.[37]

Elberg's attitude to Bar Kokhba also changes in this article, as he asserts:

Bar Kokhba remains the only hero who led a revolt in the history of our people, and even so several of our holy sages did not show much sympathy for him [. . .] indeed in the Bar Kokhba Revolt his success is questioned since the outcome was extremely tragic. The Jewish People was small and then lost about half a million souls [. . .] Bar Kokhba fought to free the Land of Israel from the yoke of foreigners. But the Jewish People, which regarded exile as a punishment in the deepest sense, did not seek to free themselves of it by insurrection and revolution.[38]

This ideological change indicates, it would seem, that Elberg started by using an apologetic rhetoric, that was designed to soften somewhat the criticism that would be directed against his ideas (which had indeed happened a few decades earlier). Despite the preliminary positive stance toward the heroes of the Warsaw Revolt,[39] and also his taking of the popular stance toward Bar Kokhba, later on Elberg disagrees in principle to the use of insurgence as a method of attempting to escape from the decree of exile.[40]

With an outlook similar to that of Steinberger, Elberg also adopts a similar stance regarding Exile, maintaining that escaping from it is in effect escaping from the decree of God. But in the second section of his article Elberg goes one stage further, and also censures the revolt in the Land of Israel, the Bar Kokhba Revolt, that was clearly designed to reestablish Jewish sovereignty in Israel. In other words, the dispute between Steinberger and Elberg is rooted in their understanding of the concept of exile. For Steinberger it means territorial exile, and so the military activities of the Jewish Underground fighters and IDF soldiers are proper and desirable, even if the Underground acted at a time when the country was not under Jewish sovereignty. Whereas Elberg maintains that only a State whose existence has Divine ratification can justify the taking up of arms. Until this stage is realized, and as long as the Jewish nation is still in exile, even subversion to establish Jewish sovereignty in Israel is regarded by him as revolting against the Divine decree of Exile, and is in any case an activity that runs contrary to the spirit of the Torah.

In addition, their conceptions of the character of the Exile are slightly different. Steinberger saw the character of the Exile as one of humiliation and oppression, and be that as it may, a surfeit of humiliation and oppression does not contradict the character of Exile. Elberg expressed himself a little esoterically on the subject of the character of the Exile, although it is clear that he saw it as a place in which the Jews must make repentance. He did not emphasize the element of humiliation, but actually the idea of spiritual independence, as opposed to material stability, that falls within the purview of the redemption.[41]

5. "A proprietary act"

While there is a substantial similarity between the positions of Steinberger and Elberg, we shall now examine the ideas of two personages who present us with a totally different spiritual world. Rabbi Baruch Meidan, the author of series of books titled *Birkat Meir*, relates to the question of the Uprising in one of his works.[42] In this work he goes much further in emphasizing the need for passivity referred to by the abovementioned rabbis, though he defines an ideological paradigm into which he constructs his criticism. In his introduction he claims that the State of Israel was established by virtue of "a proprietary act," an action designed to repulse the spirit of God from the People of Israel. That is to say what forms the basis of the Zionist ethos is the thinking that the People of Israel have to perform significant, reality-changing, actions. This thinking, in Meidan's opinion, is an act of heresy, since it ignores the Divine Presence working in the real world. Meidan does not distinguish, for this purpose, between Exile and Redemption, but prefers to present the way of the world as one in which the Divine Presence works continuously, and man must (at least in terms of national behavior) remain totally passive in the light of this activity.

Following this introduction Meidan goes on to review the change that has taken place in the national consciousness, which has developed the disparaging attitude toward the "Diaspora Jew" as opposed to the "New Jew."[43] According to Meidan the Diaspora Jew is characterized as someone who reacts passively toward the real world by virtue of its unimportance to him. Humiliation holds no value for him and does not concern him, though it is humiliation that Steinberger and Elberg considered to be the essence of Exile. Yet Meidan does protest against the notion that gentiles' humiliation of Jews diminishes Jewish dignity.

The following is the image he uses to elucidate the passivity required:

> Until the establishment of the State, the Jew was the "Diaspora Jew" [. . .] and when he came to the nobleman to get his wages, the nobleman would require him to dance before him and kiss his feet in front of his fellow noblemen. And the Diaspora Jew would apparently be humiliated, licking the nobleman's feet while he would throw him a few coins. Afterwards the Jew would return home, and learn a page of Talmud [. . .]
>
> Did the Diaspora Jew feel inferior and humiliated while he had to dance in front of the nobleman [. . .] Not at all! From the time of the Giving of the Torah until the establishment of the State of Israel, the Jew regarded the gentile as today we regard dogs and cats. A man does not feel humiliated if he has to dance in front of the dog in order to save himself from being bitten.[44]

On the question of the nature of Exile, Meidan's assertion is the opposite of Steinberger's, but his conclusions (below) regarding the Uprising are very similar. While Steinberger regards the Exile as being based on humiliation, Meidan regards it as an opportunity for self-control over consciousness.[45] This opportunity is expressed in the overstated parable of the Jew and the nobleman. The Exile does not necessarily mean humiliation for the Jew (as with Steinberger), but provides him with the opportunity to prove perfectly his acceptance of Divine rule in the real world. In any case there is no distinction here between Exile and Redemption (primarily in the light of the obvious fact that in Meidan's opinion the establishment of the State of Israel has nothing to do with Redemption at all). The distinction is between a consciousness of "possessing" the real world and a consciousness of there being Divine control over it, what Meidan calls a "Divine Presence" consciousness.

What clearly follows from the above is harsh criticism of the Uprising as it occurred and particularly its "sanctification" and the turning of it into a cornerstone in the ethos of the New Jew. At the end of his work Meidan expressed himself as follows: "The Warsaw Ghetto Uprising is the educational base for the creation of the 'New' Jew, the opposite of the 'Diaspora' Jew – this is called 'a proprietary act'."[46] It should be pointed out that there are two ways of understanding Meidan's assertion concerning the act of taking possession described here. One is that the concept of man capable of acting to make a real change in the world, as the Warsaw Ghetto fighters thought, is a proprietary act, and whatever the case, education that follows this concept is problematic. However, it may be that the very thought that it is possible to create a New Jew is itself a forbidden proprietary act, and the attempt to fashion Jewish memory and feeling is a forbidden interference with the Divine Presence in Jewish History.

The distinction between the New Jew and the Diaspora Jew touches on the attitude to be taken towards Zionist ideals and their attempt to fashion the image of the Jew in a mold that ascribes him universal values, as opposed to the Diaspora Jew, who is measured only against the particularist values of Torah.

6. "The Torah obligates the Jew to avoid war"

Without any doubt, one of the most extreme philosophies in the world of Jewish thought in the twentieth century was that of Rabbi Joel Teitelbaum, the Satmar Rebbe (1888–1979).[47] Teitelbaum authored an impressive number of Torah-related books, though his name is always particularly connected to his famous anti-Zionist work, *Vayoel Moshe*.[48] In this work, that was written as a halakhic and theological response to the establishment of the State of Israel and the Zionist movement altogether, Teitelbaum asserts that the State of Israel is the work of Satan. By virtue of this assertion he decreed that any cooperation or benefit derived from the state are acts of absolute heresy, and are totally forbidden.

In writing his sequel to *Vayoel Moshe*, entitled *'Al HaGeulah V'al HaTemurah*,[49] Teitelbaum exacerbated and intensified his remarks, against the background of the Six Day War and the territorial expansion of the Israeli state. In the later work he refers a number of times to the question of the Warsaw Ghetto Uprising, and despite the extreme anti-Zionist nature of his political thought and despite the fact that the historical claim he makes against the Uprising is completely unfounded, the moral assumptions that lie at the base of his position require discussion. I will start by stating that Teitelbaum does not, on principle, accept that Jewish sovereignty over the Land of Israel prior to the coming of the Messiah has any legitimacy, and whatever the case may be, actions taken to defend this sovereignty are also unacceptable from a religious point of view.

Below are a number of quotations taken from the book *'Al HaGeulah V'al HaTemurah* that relate to the question of the Uprising:

> What the Zionist leaders explained to the Jewish People at the beginning of the rule of the accursed German enemy, may its name be blotted out, is well known: they declared war against it in the name of all Israel. And then every Jewish heart turned to water, so enormous was the fear and the terror, that of course this declaration had no purpose and no ability to save life [. . .] and by this dangerous step they aroused the wrath [of the Germans] even more strongly against Israel [. . .] from then on the troubles grew and multiplied from day to day until they caused the terrible loss.[50]

In the introduction to his book he relates to the subject and develops further the discussion on the immorality of the ghetto fighters:

> It is impossible to understand how they could have been so terribly cruel when they knew that so large a number of Jews were under their control and how it was possible for them to be so cruel as to abandon Jewish blood.[51]

The basic claim that Teitelbaum is presenting at this point is that since, on the one hand, the chance of being able to save lives in the Uprising was totally nonexistent and, on the other, the great danger that the Uprising would bring to all the residents of the ghetto, should have been enough to determine against it. However, his assertion that because of the Uprising killings and hostilities broke out against the Jews is totally unfounded, and perhaps one could even say contemptible, in its ignoring the deaths of millions of Jews in Poland and Slovakia, and in fact in the whole of Europe, apart from Hungary (the place that Teitelbaum was living at the time). However, his assertion stands on its own merits, that the lives of people must not be played with, and it is forbidden to initiate military action while there is the possibility that Jews could be harmed because of it.[52]

However, his opinion is intensified further by his introduction of an allegory relating to Jacob in the Book of Genesis, from which Teitelbaum develops an outlook that can almost be called pacifist. He begins the discussion with a quotation from Nahmanides, and then goes on to expound his own views:

> "When Jacob prepared himself against Esau with a gift, a prayer and made preparations for battle [. . .] this was an intimation for future generations that

everything that happened to our father with Esau would always happen to them again with Esau's descendants. And we should follow in the path of (Jacob) the righteous, and we should provide ourselves with the three things that he provided for himself – prayer, a gift, and saving oneself by way of battle, by fleeing and surviving."

And so you can see that even when going to war was necessary it finished "by fleeing and surviving." All effort possible should be made not to fight, even if this means taking flight, and a person is obligated not to fight, apart from when there is no other choice. Our father Jacob certainly had the power to overcome Esau and his men [. . .] but nevertheless did much prostrating and giving of gifts so that he would change his mind and not start fighting.[53]

While Nachmanides indeed uses the term "fleeing and surviving," the addition made by Teitelbaum is highly significant. He claims that Nachmanides means that war in itself is improper, so long as it is possible to escape from it in some way. It is clear that he is transferring the discussion from the individual sphere (Jacob, the patriach) to the national sphere, without any explicit source, but this point is emphasized and utilized again in the continuation of his book, as the basis for his thinking on the subject of war. War is the last option to be adopted, and the Jew's moral obligation is to flee for his life, and for lives of all other Jews, in any way that he can, and at any price. And this includes groveling and surrendering to the enemy.[54]

He wrote the following in an article that he attached to the end of the book:

In any event it is as clear as daylight that the Torah obliges us to make every effort in the world to negotiate peace and to avoid war [. . .] and even for all the profit in the world, could it be that the Torah would permit the abandoning of or causing the loss of Jewish lives? [. . .] and certainly the Holy Torah would not give permission to abandon Jewish lives for some bogus benefit or just for the love of victory.[55]

In connection with the State of Israel there is no doubt that Teitelbaum is intimating that any relinquishing of territory, surrendering of sovereignty or liquidation of the institutions of the State is an appropriate price to pay for safeguarding the lives of the Jews living in the country, and whatever the case if there exists a possibility that through a surrender and liquidation of this sort it is possible to establish peace, or at the very least save the lives of Jews – then there is a moral obligation of the highest order to do this. However, more important than this is the meaning of his words even beyond the context of Zionism. Teitelbaum declares that the threshold conditions for entering into war are extremely high. Contrary to the previously mentioned rabbis, he speaks explicitly of war that has in it an element of self-defense, and it emerges from his words that even a war in which there is a reasonable likelihood the Jewish forces will be victorious should be regarded negatively, and it would be best to avoid it at all costs. Teitelbaum regards the death of one soldier in a war that could have been prevented by giving up all the state's assets as an unacceptable sacrifice and that that soldier's blood is on the head of his commanders and the heads of the army.

This would be the place to examine whether Teitelbaum's positions (as well as Meidan's) are moral positions, or whether they are ideological positions, dressed up in moral clothing. While Steinberger and Elberg outlined a moral philosophy, which one can argue with, but whose internal logic is in general understandable, as are its moral assertions, Meidan and Teitelbaum seek to make a sharp particularistic distinction between the Jewish People and other nations.

According to the thinking of the latter two, the People of Israel should be deprived of its basic right of standing up for its own cause, even in extreme cases where there is the fear of losing its sovereignty, its honor and even perhaps its very life. Both Steinberger and Elberg accepted as a principle the assertion that in cases in which the uprising was likely to be successful, its outcome was likely to be the saving of life, or even the establishing of Jewish sovereignty in the Land of Israel – it should be seen as a reasonable activity from a moral point of view. Indeed, while their demand for passivity, as far as degrading the moral aspect of preserving a nation's honor, differs from the general thinking of Just War theorists, it can be seen as a formal interpretation of these moral values and even as a demand for a higher level of morality from the Jewish People because of particular considerations.

However, Teitelbaum's and Meidan's claims demand a complete negation of the moral right of the Jew to defend his life, even in cases in which is it obvious to every Just War theorist that self-defense both by the individual and by the nation is justified (for instance, cases in which it is reasonable that victory will be achieved and in which there is an authority taking responsibility for the act of war).

It seems to me that the moral criteria of Just War, as reviewed in the first part of this article, reflect universal norms and a consensus of opinion of the minimal requirements of justice for entering into war. These occasionally merit criticism because they tend to be overly moralistic and often do not take into account the needs of small, oppressed societies. However, they enable us to determine clearly the boundaries of what is a moral claim concerning the right to go to war. Hence it emerges that Meidan and Teitelbaum's positions deviate from the sphere of morality and cross into the sphere of ideology. The attempt to mold Jewish morals which are totally opposed to the accepted moral norms, not only regarding internal Jewish concerns, but also regarding external relations, seems to be unreasonable. Moreover, since both these two figures declare that they regard the establishment of a sovereign State of Israel, and indeed any banding together of Jews that is of a non-religious nature, as a sinful act, they can hardly be justifiably considered moral critics of war.

7. Summary

In this paper I have sought to review the moral and Torah-related positions of a number of rabbis who came out openly against the Warsaw Ghetto Uprising and the ethos of national remembrance of the Holocaust that developed as a

consequence. I have shown that despite the general common denominator of the
negation of Zionism by Meidan and Teitelbaum, even certain Torah scholars
of Zionist background did not necessarily accept the model of the Uprising as
appropriate, for a variety of different reasons.

In general we can say that there are two central issues that form the base of
the claims we have surveyed:

a. The concept of Exile, its meaning, function and influence on Jewish life in
    the individual and national spheres.
b. The question of the moral status of war – whether it is in essence morally
    unacceptable or whether it is a proper means of action in certain
    circumstances (the defense of Jewish sovereignty in the Land of Israel, the
    defense of the nation, defense against murder or as a last resort after all forms
    of surrender were not accepted by the enemy).

All of the rabbinic sources I studied criticized the Warsaw Ghetto Uprising,
yet not all did so from normative moral considerations. I have sought to show
how in more moderate models of criticism of the Warsaw Ghetto Uprising the
rabbis took positions similar to those prevalent in Just War Theory, and adopted
acceptable standards of criticism of war (even if not obliged to do so). They asked
questions of probability and success, as well as dealt with the need for sovereignty
and proper decision making. Thus, I believe Steinberger and Elberg are worthy
of being titled as moral critics of the Uprising, despite the fact that their critiques
did not comply with those of other Just War theoreticians.

On the other hand, Just War Theory enables us to criticize the more extreme
rabbinic positions. These positions negated the right of existence of Jewish
sovereignty in principle, for a variety of reasons, and thus considered the Uprising
to have been unjustified as well. Despite the fact that they used ostensible moral
considerations in their critiques, their basic ideological positions make it clear that
moral issues were hardly their chief motives.

Notes

1. Important background material for this paper can be found in D. Michman, "The
   Meaning of Jewish Resistance during the Holocaust: Some Theoretical Observations,"
   Dappim Leheker Tekufat Hashoa 12, 1995, pp. 7–41 (Hebrew). Michman differentiates
   between Standing, Bravery, Resistance, and Uprising, using their different definitions
   in several disciplines. He also gives a lengthy discourse on the founding of the heroic
   ethos of resistance in Israeli society and research. Also see: J. Tydor-Baumel, "Reactions
   to the Uprising among the Ultra-Orthodox," ibid., pp. 289–308 (Hebrew); H. Eshkoli
   (Wagman), "Religious Zionist Responses in Mandatory Palestine to the Warsaw Ghetto
   Uprising," *Holocaust and Genocide Studies* 11, 2, 1997, pp. 213–238. Baumel deals with
   several of the religious responses dealt with in this paper, yet she does not treat them
   typologically by means of ethical and historiosophic implications. Also see M. Prager,
   Sparks of Glory (trans. Mordecai Schreiber), New York: Shengold, 1974.
2. This is the third principle (out of six) of justifiably entering a war, *jus ad bellum*, as
   articulated in the *Stanford Encyclopedia of Philosophy*. This is how the Proper Authority

principle is described there: "A state may go to war only if the decision has been made by the appropriate authorities, according to the proper process, and made public, notably to its own citizens and to the enemy state(s). The 'appropriate authority' is usually specified in that country's constitution. States failing the requirements of minimal justice lack the legitimacy to go to war." See B. Orend, "War," E.N. Zalta (Ed.), The Stanford Encyclopedia of Philosophy (Fall 2008 Edition), (http://plato.stanford.edu/archives/fall2008/entries/war/).

3. This is the fifth principle of *jus ad bellum*. It is described ibid.: "A state may not resort to war if it can foresee that doing so will have no measurable impact on the situation. The aim here is to block mass violence which is going to be futile."
One must note the continued discussion in the encyclopedia, where it is stated that Probability is not anchored in international law, because of the hazard of deviation in favor of strong and aggressive states, which obviously stand a better chance in every international conflict. Hence, weak yet just nations might be bereft of the legitimacy to defend themselves. I will deal with this in relation to the Warsaw Uprising below.

4. J.T. Johnson, *Military and Contemporary Warfare*, New Haven: Yale University Press, 1994, p. 43.

5. H. Von Der Linden, "Just War Theory and U.S. Military Hegemony," in M.W. Brough, J.W. Lango and H. Von Der Linden (Eds.), *Rethinking the Just War Tradition*, New York: SUNY Press, 2007, pp. 56–57.

6. Coady asserted that S.S. officers and soldiers that operated against Jews in the Warsaw Ghetto and in other districts of occupied Europe (not while conducting regular military actions), had lost their self-defense prerogative. Since every Jew feared that an arrest or even a documentation inspection might lead to his being murdered on ethnic grounds, every German soldier posed an existential threat to him. Hence, slaughtering a non-armed German soldier, even when sleeping, was an act of self-defense and not murder. See C.A.J. Coady, *Morality and Political Violence*, New York: Cambridge University Press, 2008, p. 244.

7. P. Gilbert, *Terrorism, Security and Nationality: An Introductory Study in Applied Political Philosophy*, London – New York: Routledge, 1994, p. 18.

8. D. Rodin, *War and Self Defense*, Oxford: Oxford University Press, 2004, pp. 139–140.

9. See: www.americanvalues.org/html/wwff.html. This document is cited hundreds of times, and is brought wholly in many places. As an example see A. Etzioni and J.H. Marsh, "What We're Fighting For: A Letter from America," in A. Etzioni and J.H. Marsh (Eds.), *Rights vs. Public Safety After 9/11: America in the Age of Terrorism*, Lanham, Maryland: Rowman & Littlefield Publishers Inc., 2003, pp. 101–125, note 25.

10. G.P. Fletcher and J.D. Ohlin, "The Collective Dimension of War," in G.P. Fletcher & J.D. Ohlin (Eds.), *Defending Humanity: When Force is Justified and Why*, New York: Oxford University Press, 2008, pp. 180–181.

11. D. Statman, "On the Success Condition for Legitimate Self-Defence," *Ethics* 118, 2008, pp. 659–686.

12. Statman illustrates how honor was granted a moral value, and how invalidating honor is, in effect, invalidating humanness. Also see idem, "Humiliation, Dignity and Self-Respect," *Philosophical Psychology* 13, 4, 2000, pp. 523–540. In this paper Statman established the infrastructure of Kantian perspectives of honor as being inseparable from humanness.

13. Y.A. Steinberger, "The Tenth of Tevet: The Holocaust Memorial Day which became the General Day of Reciting the Kaddish," *Shana Beshana*, 1990, pp. 378–385 (Hebrew); idem, "The Tenth of Tevet as a Memorial Day for the Holocaust," *Shana Beshana*, 1991, pp. 311–320 (Hebrew). See also R. Stauber, "The Jewish Response during the Holocaust: The Educational Debate in Israel in the 1950s," *Shofar* 22, 4, 2005,

pp. 57–66, and A. Edrei's comprehensive essay: "Holocaust Memorial: a Paradigm of Competing Memories in the Religious and Secular Societies in Israel," in D. Mendels (Ed.), *On Memory*, Bern: Peter Lang, 2007, pp. 37–100. For another rabbinic criticism on the attitude toward the Warsaw Ghetto Uprising see: M. Sheshar, "Yom Hakadish Hakelali," *Turei Yeshurun* 8, 1967, pp. 3–4 (Hebrew).

14. Journals such as Shana Beshana; Kovetz Hatzionut Hadatit; Kotleinu; Mahanayyim; Or Hamizrach; Shema'atin, and others.

15. Steinberger, "The Tenth of Tevet as a Memorial Day for the Holocaust," p. 311.

16. Ibid.

17. Ibid., p. 312. For a similar position see M. Feinstein, *Iggerot Moshe*, Yoreh De'ah vol. 4, Jerusalem: Rabbi D. Feinstein, 1996, p. 289 (Hebrew).

18. Steinberger, "The Tenth of Tevet as a Memorial Day for the Holocaust," p. 315.

19. P.Y. Hakohen-Levin, "A Dangerous Illusion because of a Forgotten Principle," *Beit Ya'akov* 32, 1962, p. 2 (Hebrew).

20. As Steinberger, "The Tenth of Tevet as a Memorial Day for the Holocaust," wrote on p. 316: "Non-believers sometimes believed fully and sincerely in Man whoever and whenever he is [. . .] the Holocaust, which as is well known, did not distinguish between the assimilated Jew to the religious Jew, specifically destroyed the spiritual world of the assimilated [. . .] the non-religious Jew, who did not accept our ancient scriptures as relevant, was coerced to confront the Holocaust according to his tortuous path. This path brought him, among other things, to enforce his heresy, and forced him to save at least a small portion of his baseless outlook. This was done by approximating the bravery of the Ghetto rebels to the Holocaust, in an apologetic endeavor."

21. Ibid., p. 313. The gap between this notion and the one presented by Statman (above n. 11) is obvious.

22. On p. 317 Steinberger explained that the advantage of the Tenth of Tevet lies in the linkage it creates between the siege King Nebuchadnezzar cast on Jerusalem and the Holocaust, thus displaying a consecutiveness of agony bound with exilic being. He continues (p. 318) to speak of the historical impact of the first siege on Jerusalem, the first concrete experience of exile the Jewish nation had suffered, on generations of Jews, and of the similar impact the Holocaust has. By doing so he followed Rabbi Unterman's steps. Unterman, while serving as Chief Rabbi of Tel Aviv, on the Tenth of Tevet 5709 (January 11, 1949), justified the setting of it as the Holocaust Remembrance Day in light of the sequence of catastrophes. See Steinberger, "The Tenth of Tevet: The Holocaust Memorial Day which became the General Day of Reciting the Kaddish," 1990, p. 381.

23. See Steinberger, "The Tenth of Tevet as a Memorial Day for the Holocaust," p. 314, for several citations from Yisrael Zinger and H.N. Bialik, regarding the bravery of the Jews of the Diaspora, who did not allow the "filth" of the Diaspora to invade into their souls.

24. Ibid., pp. 314–315. This position creates a division between the "Self Defense" model (usually pertaining to individuals) to the "Just War" model (usually pertaining to sovereign states). Whereas a state has the right to defend itself, even when the probability to prevail in the conflict is low, according to Steinberger an individual does not have the right to do so. Perhaps what underlies this partition is an unconscious distinction between Jews in Israel under a sovereign Jewish regime, who receive, according to Steinberger, a national status, to the Jews in the Diaspora, who are dispersed and scattered. The collective amalgamating notion of the Jews in the Diaspora is mainly a religious one, and not a national one. This point of view was one of the foundations of Jewish Orthodoxy in Eastern and Central Europe. See Y. Salmon, "The Emergence of a Jewish Nationalist Consciousness in Europe During the 1860s and 1870s," *AJS Review* 16, 1–2, 1991, pp. 107–132 and idem, "Tradition and Modernity in Early

religious-Zionist Thought," *Tradition* 18, 1, 1979, pp. 79–98. See also D. Schwartz, "The Revolutionary Consciousness of the Religious Zionist Movement Since 1902," *Annual of Rabbinic Judaism* 3, 2000, pp. 175–184.

25. Steinberger, "The Tenth of Tevet as a Memorial Day for the Holocaust," pp. 312–313.
26. On this issue see the debate between Rabbis Moshe Zvi Neryah and Shlomo Goren regarding the heroism of the Masada rebels. See: S. Goren, "A Question and a Response on the Matter of the Heroes of Masada," *Or Hamizrach* 7, 3–4, 1960, pp. 22–27 (Hebrew). This paper gave halakhic approval of "the heroes of Masada." On the opposite side see, M.Z. Neryah, "The People of Masada's Suicide in Halakha," *Alei Mishmeret* 14, 1961, pp. 3–14 (Hebrew). On Masada and its significance in the creation of Jewish ethos, especially regarding the Holocaust and the rebellions see M. Brug, "From the Top of Masada to the Heart of the Ghetto: Myth as History," in D. Ohana and R.S. Westreich (Eds.), *Myth and Memory: Transfiguration of Israeli Consciousness*, Jerusalem: Van-Leer Institute and Hakibutz Hameuhad, 1998, pp. 203–227 (Hebrew).
27. Steinberger, "The Tenth of Tevet as a Memorial Day for the Holocaust," p. 313.
28. Steinberger, loc. cit.
29. Rabbi Simcha Elberg was chairman of the executive board of the Union of Orthodox Rabbis of the US and Canada for 25 years. He also served as editor of *Hapardes*, the rabbinic law journal published by the Union of Orthodox Rabbis, and was the author of multivolume books on rabbinic law and Talmudic concepts, as well as a historical bibliography of prewar Poland. He also served on the executive committee of Agudath Israel of America. On his meditations regarding the Holocaust see: G. Greenberg, "Myth and Catastrophe in Simha Elberg's Religious Thought," *Tradition* 26, 1, 1991, pp. 35–64.
30. *Hapardes* volumes 33, 7, 1959, pp. 2–3; 59, 7, 1985, p. 5; 63, 6, 1989, pp. 2–4.
31. The source of this linkage can be found throughout H. Seidman's *The Warsaw Ghetto Diaries*, Southfield, MI: Targum Press, 1997. Also see K. Caplan, "The Holocaust in Contemporary Israeli Haredi Popular Religion," *Modern Judaism* 22, 2, 2002, pp. 142–168 (especially notes 34–35).
32. S. Elberg, "The Warsaw Ghetto Uprising," *Hapardes* 63, 6, 1989, p. 2 (Hebrew).
33. Ibid. Elberg's linguistic distinction between a "struggle" and an "uprising" reflects a notion by which an uprising must be planned and organized, and with a concrete vision. Individual initiatives that lack intentions of actual salvation or reclaiming sovereignty are not eligible to be named an uprising. Perhaps this is Elberg's version of the Just War principle of Proper Authority.
34. Ibid., pp. 2–3.
35. Ibid., p. 3.
36. Compare to A. Etzioni, *Security First: For a Muscular, Moral Foreign Policy*, New Haven: Yale University Press, 2007, p. 95. Etzioni asserts that there is no "Good" war, only a "Just" war. Elberg, on the other hand, accepts the concept of a "Good" uprising, as long as it serves a profound religious motive, and not only a moral one.
37. Elberg, ibid., p. 3. The resemblance between Steinberger's ideas and Elberg's regarding Diaspora and medieval Catholic attitudes toward Judaism is striking. See: J. Cohen, *Living Letters of Law: Ideas of the Jew in Medieval Christianity*, Berkeley: University of California Press, 1999, pp. 23–66. Also see: B. Lewis, *Semites and Anti-Semites*, London: Weidenfeld & Nicolson, 1986, pp. 100–109; M. Friedman, "The Haredim and the Holocaust," *The Jerusalem Quarterly* 53, 1980, pp. 86–114.
38. Elberg, ibid.
39. See ibid., p. 2: "Those who by their heroism and courage rebelled." Also see S. Elberg, "A Holocaust Remembrance," *Hapardes* 66, 9, 1992, p. 2 (Hebrew), in which an editorial statement, attacking the Israeli formal Holocaust Remembrance Day, states:

"The attachment of the Holocaust and heroism is not acceptable by authentic Jews. In their eyes it is not the Warsaw Uprising that symbolizes Jewish heroism in those days, when [Hitler] endeavored to blind the eyes of Israel. This is stated without becoming involved with the question if it was bravery at all. And, following the Talmudic guidance 'do not judge your friend until you reach his state', we do not dare to touch this agonizing and bitter point."

40. See ibid. p. 4: "Throughout history Judaism saw the hand of Divine Providence. If the Jew could liberate himself from exile via an uprising, what purpose is there in this Exile? Who is he who does not know that our Exile has a profound goal, and it conducts to an important destiny."

41. Also compare to Raul Hilberg's views on Jewish History and character, as outlined by R.M. Marrus, "Jewish Resistance to the Holocaust," *Journal of Contemporary History* 30, 1, 1995, pp. 83–110.

42. B. Meidan, *Birkat Meir: Veyada'ata Vehashevotah*, Netivot: B. Meidan, 2003, pp. 364–365 (Hebrew).

43. Compare: O. Bartov, *Mirrors of Destruction: War, Genocide and Modern Identity*, New York: Oxford University Press, 2000, p. 128; idem, "Defining Enemies, Making Victims: Germans, Jews, and the Holocaust," in A. Weiner (Ed.), *Landscaping the Human Garden: Twentieth-Century Population*, Stanford: Stanford University Press, 2003, pp. 155–156.

44. Meidan, *Birkat Meir*, p. 364. As opposed to Steinberger and Elberg, who see the problem in the Zionist narrative of the uprising in the focus on honor and its moral merit, Meidan finds the problem in the misunderstanding of what honor is. He does not deny that self-esteem has a significant place in Judaism, yet he believes it shouldn't be surveyed in terms of Man and his surroundings, but in terms of Man and his spiritual level.

45. Compare to the Novhardok School's outlook on the soul's powers and struggles. See D. Stein, "The Limits of Religious Optimism: The 'Hazon Ish' and the Alter of Novardok on 'Bittahon'," *Tradition* 43, 2, 2010, pp. 31–48.

46. Meidan, *Birkat Meir*, p. 365.

47. On Teitelbaum's ideological and political outlook see: Z.J. Kaplan, "Rabbi Joel Teitelbaum, Zionism, and Hungarian Ultra-Orthodoxy," *Modern Judaism* 24, 2, 2004, pp. 165–178; A.L. Nadler, "Piety and Politics: The Case of the Satmar Rebbe," *Judaism* 31, 2, 1982, pp. 135–152.

48. J. Teitelbaum, *Vayoel Moshe*, New York: Yerushalayim, 1960 (Hebrew).

49. J. Teitelbaum, *'Al HaGeulah V'al HaTemurah*, New York: Sender Deutsch, 1967 (Hebrew).

50. Teitelbaum, *'Al HaGeulah*, pp. 87–88.

51. Ibid., p. 11.

52. Teitelbaum does not consider the Warsaw Ghetto Uprising to be the pivot of the Zionist-Jewish declaration of war against Germany. The historical event that is "granted" this title originates from the memoires of Rabbi H.D. Weissmandel. He recalled a statement given by Wissilceni, an S.S. officer stationed in Slovakia, who said that Hitler was outraged by the Jewish boycott on Nazi Germany declared by Rabbi Stephen S. Wise, president of the American Jewish Congress (1933), and thus decided to conduct an all-out war against International Jewry. Weissmandel, followed by Moshe Schonfeld, did not trace the lack of historical connection between the boycott and the Wansee conference, eight years later, and claimed that Hitler gathered all of the Nazi leaders immediately after hearing of the boycott and created the Final Solution. See M. Schonfeld, *The Holocaust Victims Accuse*, New York: Neturei Karta of U.S.A., 1977, p. 43. Also see H.M.D. Weissmandel, *Min Hameitzar*, New York: Emunah, 1944, pp. 15–16 (Hebrew). This fabrication is utilized by numerous organizations that support Holocaust denial and accuse the Jews of war crimes (against Germany?). See: "The Jewish Declaration of War on Nazi Germany," *The Barnes Review*, Jan./Feb. 2001,

pp. 41–45, which can be accessed at www.wintersonnenwende.com/scriptorium/english/archives/articles/jdecwar.html.

This article is fully cited in a Satmar oriented website, with slight alternations in the title (instead of "The Jewish Declaration of War on Nazi Germany" they write: "The Zionist Declaration of War on Nazi Germany"), see: www.jewsagainstzionism.com/zionism/jewishwar.cfm.

Additional anti-Semitic websites using these sources:

www.stormfront.org/forum/showthread.php?t=323991
www.white-history.com/hwr64iv.htm
www.slate.com/discuss/forums/thread/882215.aspx
www.radioislam.org/islam/english/jewishp/germany/crystalnight.htm
www.reallibertymedia.com/content/jewish-declaration-war-nazi-germany
www.liveleak.com/view?i=c4b_1218091404
my.opera.com/salventura/blog/a-fact-many-today-would-prefer-be-forgotten

A response to these allegations can be seen here:

http://goliath.ecnext.com/coms2/gi_0199-5461913/The-Jewish-Declaration-of-War.html

53. Teitelbaum, *'Al HaGeulah*, preface, pp. 10–11.
54. In this point Teitelbaum's discussion is diverted from the normative ethical discussion to an ideological sphere. His not accepting the violation of sovereignty as legitimate causes of *jus ad bellum*, without dealing with the probability of success in war, proves he does not treat the Zionist State as acceptable by religious standards, and thus does not seek to measure it in universal and legislative norms.
55. Teitelbaum, *'Al HaGeulah*, p. 194.

12 The law of obligatory war and Israeli reality

Kalman Neuman

Introduction: the definition of obligatory war

The classic Jewish texts on war were to a large degree formulated and codified in a time in which the Jewish people had no political independence and hence no ability to wage war.[1] To a great extent, therefore, the discussions of authorities on Jewish Law (*halakhah*) regarding the wars of the State of Israel are the first application of those laws to the "real world."[2] This paper will show how the reality of the State influenced the interpretation of the classic categories which govern the Jewish laws of war. To the extent that this is true, it is an illustration of a development of *halakhah* as a result of confrontation with new realities, in this case regarding public law.[3]

Defining a situation as subject to the laws of war (as opposed to a situation where the individual has the right to use force, such as saving a person from a pursuer) has a number of halakhic implications. First and foremost, such a definition empowers the legitimate political authority[4] to draft soldiers, whereas if the situation is not defined as warfare, an individual cannot be coerced to risk his life to save a third person (or people) in a life-endangering situation.[5] In addition, the blanket permit to wage war on the Sabbath (which entails activities otherwise forbidden) is more far-reaching than that which is extended to other life-saving actions.[6]

Talmudic and medieval *halakhah* distinguished between obligatory war (*milhemet mitzvah*) which does not require approval by the Sanhedrin, and optional, or authorized,[7] war (*milhemet hareshut*) which does (See Mishnah *Sotah* 8:7; *Sanhedrin* 1:5 and 2:4). Without authorization, engaging in a war which is not obligatory is considered a prohibited taking of human life.[8]

The category of the "optional war" has engendered analysis in some recent writings.[9] Although the Talmud (BT *Sanhedrin* 16a) seems to suggest that economic need alone is sufficient motivation to initiate such a war, and Maimonides even categorizes it as a war waged by the king "to extend the borders of Israel and to enhance his greatness and prestige," Blidstein and others have noted other Maimonidean texts which suggest that ultimately religious motivation is the only legitimate basis for a war waged by a Jewish king.[10] Other rabbinic authorities, without ascribing such restrictions, have suggested that there are other limitations on the possibility to declare such a war. Regardless of how the justifications for waging "optional war" are understood, the need for the consent of the Sanhedrin and the recourse to the oracle of *Urim ve-Tummim* make this question irrelevant to contemporary Jewish law. Any halakhic justification of war in the present day and age must be grounded in the definitions of obligatory war. Halakhic pronouncements relating to the wars of the State of Israel must therefore conform to the definitions of such wars.[11]

What, in fact, are obligatory wars? The Code of Maimonides lists three types: the war against the seven nations that inhabited Canaan at the time of the Exodus, the war against the people of Amalek and a war "to deliver Israel from the enemy attacking them."[12] The first two types are wars are connected to specific commandments of the Torah[13] which are clearly not applicable today.[14] This leaves us with the third category, which seems to be based on an extension of the principle of self-defense.[15] The contemporary reality of the State of Israel has engendered situations which required elucidation and elaboration of this legal principle.

The War of Independence

The war known to Israelis as the War of Independence or the War of Liberation and to others as the War of 1948 is usually divided by historians into two stages. The first ensued after UN General Assembly Resolution 181 (which called for the partition of Palestine/Eretz Israel into a Jewish state and an Arab State) was passed on 29 November 1947. This was a civil war between the local Jewish and Arab communities as a result of Arab rejection of partition. After the termination of the British Mandate and the declaration of the State of Israel on 15 May 1948 the war expanded in the wake of an invasion by neighboring Arab states. The first stage of the war brought about what are probably the first instances of recourse to the laws of war in halakhic decisions.

In a responsum of Chief Rabbi Isaac Herzog to Rabbi Werner of Tiberias written before April 1948, he related to the defense of the isolated Jewish neighborhood of Kiryat Shmuel.[16] First he analyzed the situation on the basis of the laws of individual self defense and concluded that if military experts think that there is an immediate danger of an attack it is permitted, if necessary, to build fortifications on the Sabbath. As an additional consideration Rabbi Herzog added that he saw the situation as war, in which it would be permitted even to initiate hostilities on Shabbat.

Why should this situation be defined as an obligatory war?

> . . . [T]he UN has given us part of the Land of Israel, and if we do not defend it properly we will lose the opportunity and will not have a place of refuge for our brethren in the Diaspora in case of distress, God forbid, (we have had enough in our recent experience, which should be sufficient for the wise). In addition, if this opportunity is missed it will (God forbid) cause the multitudes of Israel to lose hope and in the course of time this will cause most of our people to leave our holy religion and to assimilate . . .[17]

The definition of the situation as obligatory war was dealt with again by Rabbi Herzog in a responsum dated 25 Adar Bet 5708 (5 April 1948) regarding military activity on the Sabbath to members of the Ezra Orthodox youth group in Jerusalem. The rabbi explained that if the situation is defined in the context of the regular laws of preservation of life, then there may be limits on the possibility of initiating hostilities on the Sabbath, whereas if this was an obligatory war of self defense, no such limits would be in place. Rather than perceiving such initiation as preemption which would classify it as an "optional" war (and would be prohibited in the absence of a Sanhedrin), it was part of a war of self-defense because "they have already attacked us in order to destroy us and expel us from our holy land."[18]

Commenting on the second responsum (dated 27 Adar Sheini [7 April] two days after the letter was sent), Rabbi Meshullam Roth questioned the applicability of the category of obligatory war to offensive operations.[19] He also raised doubts if the battles could be seen as obligatory according to the view of Nachmanides, who defined conquest of the land of Israel as obligatory war. This, because it was not clear that territory conquered beyond the borders of the UN partition plan would remain part of the Jewish state. Because of these reservations, Rabbi Roth concluded that it was not halakhically legitimate to draft soldiers for combat duty and that conscripts could only be assigned non-combat roles.[20]

Rabbi Herzog responded that the notion of war as conquest was not his major consideration but rather that of the war of self-defense, which justifies conscription. Even regarding Jerusalem (which was not in the territory of the Jewish state according to the UN resolution), the goal of the Arabs was to cause the Jews to flee from the city and the aim of the battle against them is to insure a continued Jewish presence there, "which is akin to conquest of the land." This, says Rabbi Herzog, is necessary in order to insure the very existence of Judaism, adding that "a word to the wise is sufficient."[21] In an article on the halakhic status of the War of Independence (published posthumously in 1983) Rabbi Herzog reiterated this understanding:

> ... I say that this war is a war of self defense ... for Maimonides does not stipulate that it is only called an obligatory war if the enemy has come to destroy us, but it they wish to destroy or to expel us, it is not the case. It is indeed an obligatory war, because the Arab inhabitants of the land and their allies ... are attacking us, after we agreed to partition and did not attempt to conquer the land from them. Their intent is not to leave us a remnant in the land and instead to expel or destroy us ...
>
> Note that we are not dealing with this from the perspective of the requirement incumbent on all to save Jewish lives. From that point of view, if the enemy tells us that if we surrender to them we will not be harmed, the requirement to [fight in order to] save Jewish lives is not applicable. But when we are in the land of Israel after we have been permitted to establish our own state, then defending it is obligatory war. However, if they do not attack us and we nevertheless wish to extend our borders, then it has the status of an optional war.

Besides all we have said, this is clearly saving of Israel from an enemy, for there are hundreds of thousands of homeless refugees whose lives are in danger . . . this must be seen in the light of the obligation on the people of Israel . . . to fight so that the gates of the land will be open in order to save their brethren . . .In addition, this war is also for the future, for we know that there is a danger that there again could be an attempt to destroy part of the Jewish people, and if the Land of Israel was accessible during the destruction of that evil man, hundreds of thousands would be saved . . . [W]e already know from experience that there is a clear danger of this, and especially in the Middle East, where it is clear that if, God forbid, the Arabs take over all the Land of Israel, they will attack all Jews under their rule . . .[22]

From Rabbi Herzog's justification it is clear that categorizing the situation as obligatory war was not self evident. Why was this the case?

First, there probably was understandable reticence from using new halakhic tools. For Talmudists trained in a world without a Jewish state, when the Maimonidean depictions of war were thought of belonging to an undetermined (and perhaps eschatological) future, much like the laws of the Temple, the introduction of the halakhic category of war was a revolution in Jewish legal discourse and required specific justification.

Second, perceiving the situation as war was difficult not only for rabbis but for the Jewish population in general. A common perception saw the conflict as a continuation of the "events" of the Arab rebellion of the 1930s and not in terms of a full scale war. David Ben-Gurion was one of the few who realized that this would be different.[23]

There was a third difficulty in defining the situation as one of a war of self-defense, especially before 15 May 1948. The claim could be made that escalation of "disturbances" to war would be prevented if the Zionists would only forego the declaration of the state. This argument was made both by elements such as *Ihud*, which espoused a bi-national state[24] as well as by the extreme wing of the ultra-Orthodox anti-Zionists, known as Natorei Karta.[25] In order for a halakhist to justify the war, the concept of self defense had to be refined and expanded. Rabbi Herzog used two arguments in this context. He first established that UN resolution 181 had "given" the Jews a state, and thus responding to violence aimed at preventing its establishment was self-defense. Second, the condition of the Jewish people, especially after the Holocaust, made the establishment of the state a *sine qua non* for the continued existence of the Jewish people. This was clearly an extension of the classic category of "self-defense" – as it were, Israel has to defend itself not only from the enemies at hand but from those that will inevitably arise, as can be learned from millennia of Jewish history.

Similar arguments appear in another contemporary document, an open letter attributed to Rabbi S.Y. Zevin calling on *yeshiva* students to enlist in the army.[26] Rabbi Zevin called on the students to leave their studies and participate in an obligatory war of self defense. However, he added a stipulation:

I understand the spirit of the Natorei Karta who oppose a Jewish state and as a result consider the war as unnecessary. [They say that w]e must capitulate and that is the end of it . . . Fortunately, only a handful of people think so. All of the Jewish people . . . regardless of affiliation endorse and participate in this war of defense. All understand that there will be no prospect for the future of the Jewish community in the Land of Israel and for the remnants of the Jewish people in the Diaspora without an independent state in our land, which will absorb our brethren who are still bleeding and wandering around the nations . . . God himself knows . . . that we are not the attackers and we wish not war, we are not looking forward to battle and bloodshed . . .

Rabbi Zevin agrees that defining the situation as obligatory war is dependent on the assessment of the situation, which is influenced by larger considerations. He shares with Rabbi Herzog the definition of self defense as a war to defend the future of the Jewish people, even if at the moment the danger to Jewish lives could be deferred.

Rabbis Herzog and Zevin pointed to the UN resolution as the starting point of the war – the Arab rejection of partition defined the situation as one of self defense. However, for Rabbi Zvi Yehudah Kook the UN decision was not an event to be celebrated – indeed, the right to war was based on earlier events. In a celebrated speech given in May 1967, he recalled his reaction to the UN resolution:

. . . Nineteen years ago, in that famous evening in which we received the news of the agreement of the leaders of the nations for the establishment of the State of Israel, when everyone went to dance in the streets in rejoicing, I could not join the celebration. I sat alone in silence and could not resign myself to the awful news of the partition . . .[27]

For him, a resolution dividing the sacred Land of Israel could not be the legal basis for the right of the Jews to their State. In an essay published shortly after the declaration of the state which called for conscription to the army as a religious obligation,[28] he noted two reasons for this imperative. First, the command to save life even at the risk of endangering one's own life is even more binding when the existence of the Jewish people in their land is at stake. A second claim is based on the Nachmanidean obligation to conquer the land. For Rabbi Kook, this obligation remained unfulfilled for hundreds of years because of the metaphorical "walls" preventing settlement of the land which were "felled" by "the public announce-ment of kings and ministers acknowledging our divine right over the land and the establishment of a mandate in order to prepare the way for our return [to the land] beginning with the formation of our army brigade at the end of the first world war . . ." The basis for the legitimacy of the state, therefore, was the Balfour Declaration and the San Remo Conference of 1920 which recognized "the historical connection of the Jewish people with Palestine." The UN resolution of November 1947 is left unmentioned in Rabbi Kook's description, as he was a consistent and vocal opponent of partition. Therefore the war of 1948 was an obligatory war not because it defended the entity created by partition but because it implemented the commandment of the Torah to conquer the land. This was not the mainstream approach at the time, but it would become prominent as a result of circumstances twenty years hence.

Retaliatory raids as obligatory war

The question of the definition and extent of obligatory war is also treated in a well-known halakhic essay on the ethics of war by Rabbi Shaul Yisraeli, which was originally entitled "The Qibya Incident in the Light of the Halakha."[29] The attack by IDF units on 14–15 October 1953 on the village of Qibya just over the Jordanian border was retaliation for a terrorist attack at the Israeli village of Yehud in which a mother and two of her children were killed. The IDF operation left some 60 civilians including women and children dead.[30]

Rabbi Yisraeli's essay begins with a note:

> In Heshvan 5714 the criminal gangs carried out a brutal murder . . . It seemed that the gangs were organized and supported by the Arab population across the border . . . The attacked settlement decided not to continue to refrain from reacting before there would be more casualties, and one night attacked the Arab village Qibya, from where there was proof that the gangs received support of the local populace. The Arab village suffered casualties, including children and women. The "world" which had been indifferent to the murder of Jews, was "stunned" by the action at Qibya which was only retaliation, stemming from the anger of the border settlements and the inhabitants of the land in general. We are aware of the "morality" which typifies the behavior of the states which condemn us, we are not dependent on their protestations, and we will not learn from them values of justice. However, it is incumbent on us to clarify the proper response according to the Torah . . .[31]

The denial that the raid was carried out by the IDF is a repetition of the official version formulated by the Israeli Cabinet to try to ward off condemnation of Israel.[32] It is clear that many, if not all Israelis realized that this was an untruth, even if they were not aware of all the details of the military action.[33]

Rabbi Yisraeli's article has been often quoted and discussed in halakhic discussions of the status of non combatants.[34] I wish to focus on his treatment of the categories of obligatory and optional wars.

As already pointed out by Edrei,[35] the essay begins with an extensive discussion of the laws of the pursuer (*rodef*) which apply to all individuals and only then enters into an analysis of the situation based on the laws of war. Interestingly enough, the rabbi does not raise one obvious possibility of defining the situation as one of obligatory war. The "border wars" of 1949–56 could easily be seen as the continuation of the War of Independence and any military activity could be seen as part of the larger war, which had already been established as a war of self-defense.[36] Perhaps such an approach would not be appropriate in light of the Israeli view that the 1949 Armistice signified the end of the war (as opposed to the Arab claim that the war was continuous, with temporary pauses in belligerent actions).[37] Instead, the analysis of Rabbi Yisraeli offers three possibilities in the context of the definition of war: an innovative one based on the category of optional war, one expanding the traditional definition of self-defense to include preemption, and one based on a novel definition of obligatory war.

The first innovation is the suggestion that the very possibility for the nations of the world to legitimately wage war and to engage in the taking of human life is grounded in the notion of universal consent, from which we may conclude that forms of combat that are accepted within international norms are also permitted for a Jewish army, even when not included in the formal categories of obligatory war:

> As long as the practice of war is accepted among the nations, it is not prohibited by Jewish law, and consequently an optional war is permitted also for Israel.[38] Therefore the conclusion is that even in our days it is possible to engage in belligerent action . . . as long as this is the common practice among the nations. Therefore it must be evaluated regarding the case at hand (that of Qibya and similar cases) if such a response is common and accepted among the nations, it should be seen a tacit agreement on the part of all concerned, and therefore it is not to be seen as prohibited.[39]

The implementation of this definition is problematic. Edrei and Broyde see the passage as denying the very existence of unique Jewish laws of war, and claim that a halakhic army is subject only to the norms of international law (Broyde even suggesting that this explains the lack of discussions on military ethics in halakhic literature).[40] However, Blidstein and Gutel understand that the criterion would not be the dicta of international law, but rather the standards observed in practice by the international community.[41] I would add that the attitude to the international community in the preface to the essay would tend to support the second reading. In addition, the claim that Rabbi Yisraeli denies categorically the existence of a halakhic approach to warfare is not supported by the rest of the essay as discussed below, which itself suggests that there are halakhic categories to be applied, whether or not they are congruent with international norms.[42]

After raising the possibility of justifying the activity at Qibya on the basis of optional war, Rabbi Yisraeli offers another possible justification: defining the action as self-defense.[43] He discusses the attack in the context of preemption and says that even those rabbinic sources which do not include preemptive war as obligatory would certainly agree in this case, in which the enemy has already attacked and is simply enjoying a respite before the next attack.

However, Rabbi Yisraeli seems to think that this claim is not sufficiently substantiated to justify Qibya, and therefore he suggests another halakhic option. He introduces a radical interpretation of obligatory war, one based on revenge.

The justification for this type of war is derived from the commandment of the Torah to take revenge against Midian. Numbers 31:1–18 relates that Moses was commanded by God to take revenge on the Midianites and rebuked the commanders of the army who spared the women and children. Rabbi Yisraeli quotes the comment of Nahmanides on Numbers 31:6, which reconstructs a conversation between Moses and Phinehas, in which the latter thought that killing the males alone was in line with the God's commandments, while Moses was angry because there was a need to kill the women and children in order "to complete the retribution." Rabbi Yisraeli suggested that the war against the Midianites may be seen as establishing a different paradigm of obligatory war. This reading, which allows killing all of the enemy population, is clearly a broad extension of the war of self defense. Defining the war as one of revenge makes it possible to include intentional killing of noncombatants. Rabbi Yisraeli refrained from extrapolating a blanket permit for intentional killing of children (and added that there was no need to take care that the only casualties would be combatants), while he saw no reason to exclude the killing of adults – as this war is punitive and not limited to the parameters of self defense.[44]

This last speculation illustrates how Rabbi Yisraeli was willing to entertain different and innovative interpretations of the halakhic definitions of war in order to justify the action at Qibya, which was clearly a case of warfare not contemplated in the classic sources.[45]

After the Six Day War – the return of the war of conquest[46]

The question of the obligatory war reappeared in halakhic writing regarding the debate within Israel regarding the status of the territories taken by Israel in 1967. Much of the internal Israeli polemic on the future of the territories has revolved around the question of whether withdrawal would help achieve peace or would conversely provoke further violence. If it could be established convincingly that relinquishing the territories would avoid war and thus prevent loss of life, it would seem that halakhah would mandate such a move.[47] In contrast to this position, some of the religious opponents of withdrawal have claimed that Jewish law categorically prohibits withdrawal from territory even if such a move would result in preservation of life.[48] This position is based on extending the definition of obligatory war to include wars to conquer the Land of Israel.

We have already mentioned that Rabbi Z.Y. Kook had defined the 1948 war as obligatory because of the command to conquer the land as expressed by Nahmanides.[49] Rabbi Herzog saw this as a legally inferior claim and preferred to speak of the war in terms of self defense. To the best of my knowledge in the years 1949–67 no one suggested that Israel was halakhically obligated to initiate a war of conquest. However, after 1967 the case was increasingly made if there is an obligation to wage war, it trumps the halakhic rule which gives the preservation of life precedence over any halakhic obligation. Therefore, even if refusal to relinquish territory causes loss of life, the obligatory war of conquest prohibits such a withdrawal. An extensive exposition of this position was first made by Rabbi Y.M. Ehrenberg in a response to the National Religious Party ideologist S.Z. Shragai and has subsequently been explicated by many Religious Zionist rabbinic leaders.[50] Opponents of this ruling (which include proponents of withdrawal in addition to those opposed but on other grounds) have criticized this use of Nahmanides, whether challenging the interpretation of the opinion of the sage, or by suggesting that his opinion is not normative *halakhah*.[51]

In fact, the halakhic positions about the status of a war of conquest as an obligatory war usually dovetail with philosophical and religious understandings regarding the Land of Israel and the State of Israel. As is well known, the disciples of Rabbi Z.Y. Kook, who emphasized the sanctity and integrity of the land as part of the messianic aspect of the Zionist enterprise, have been in the forefront of opposition to territorial concessions. Many of them justify their unqualified opposition to territorial concessions on a particular interpretation of obligatory war. Here again we see how halakhic decisions reflect an interplay of extralegal considerations and legal formulations. This phenomenon is especially fascinating in the case of obligatory war, a legal category which has emerged from obscurity to the forefront of public discourse.

Notes

1. For an example, the reference to the question of preemptive war in the Talmud and in subsequent rabbinic literature did not have any practical application at the time. For a summary of the literature on this topic, almost all of which dates before the establishment of the State of Israel see J.D. Bleich, "Preemptive War in Jewish Law," *Contemporary Halakhic Problems* vol. 3, New York: Ktav, 1989, pp. 251–292. In the subsequent notes, I have attempted to refer to writings in English, when available.

2. See S.A. Cohen, "The Quest for a Corpus of Jewish Military Ethics in Modern Israel," *Journal of Israeli History* 26, 2007, pp. 35–66.

3. For a classic example of a case study of such a dynamic regarding ritual law see J. Katz, *The 'Shabbes Goy': A Study in Halachic Flexibility*, trans. Y. Lerner, Philadelphia: Jewish Publication Society, 1989.

4. The traditional sources all refer to a king as the legal authority. However, those halakhists who have attempted to apply the sources to modern reality have determined that in the absence of a king, the power to wage war reverts to the people, and any ruler accepted by popular consent has the halakhic status of a king. The *locus classicus* for this is Rabbi A.I.H. Kook, *Mishpat Cohen*, Jerusalem: Mossad Harav Kook, 1985, p. 337 (Hebrew).

5. See G.B. Levey, "Judaism and the Obligation to Die for the State," in M. Walzer (Ed.), *Law, Politics, and Morality in Judaism*, Princeton: Princeton University Press, 2006, pp. 182–208.

6. For a list of other halakhic implications of regarding a specific situation as war see Y. Kaufman, *The Army According to Halacha: Laws of War and of the Army*, Jerusalem: Kol Mevaser, 1994, pp. 2–5 (Hebrew).

7. This second definition is that defended by M. Broyde, *The Bounds of Wartime Military Conduct in Jewish Law: An Expansive Conception*, Herbert Berman Memorial Lecture 2004, Flushing, NY: Center for Jewish Studies, Queens College, CUNY, 2006, p. 14, n. 23.

8. See A. Ravitzky "Prohibited Wars" in Walzer (Ed.), *Law, Politics and Morality in Judaism*, pp. 173–174.

9. See N. Zohar, "Morality and War: A Critique of Bleich's Oracular Halakha," in D.H. Frank (Ed.), *Commandment and Community: New Essays in Jewish Legal and Political Philosophy*, Albany: SUNY Press, 1995, pp. 245–258 and the subsequent exchange with Bleich on pp. 259–267 and 269–273; idem, "Can a War Be Morally 'Optional'?," *Journal of Political Philosophy* 4, 1996, pp. 229–241; M. Walzer, "Commanded and Permitted Wars," in *Law Politics and Morality in Judaism*, pp. 149–168.

10. *The Code of Maimonides, Book 14, the Book of Judges*, trans. A. Hershman, New Haven: Yale University Press, 1949, Kings and Wars, 5,1 p. 217. G.J. Blidstein, *Political Concepts in Maimonidean Halacha*, Ramat Gan: Bar-Ilan University Press, 2001, pp. 230–245 (Hebrew); While Blidstein describes the tension between the legal approach which offers mundane justifications for war and the ideal approach which emphasizes its spiritual goals (p. 236), Rabbi Y. Amital decisively claimed that "according to Maimonides all wars . . . have as their major goal the struggle for promoting the belief in the unity of God, to break the arms of the wicked and to fill the world with righteousness." See Y. Amital, "The Wars of Israel According to Maimonides," *Tehumin* 5, 1987, 461 (Hebrew). See also Ravitzky, "Prohibited Wars," pp. 172–173. I thank Professor Josef Stern of the University of Chicago for sharing a draft of his paper on "Maimonides and War."

11. The interface of politics and the definition of obligatory war in contemporary *halakhah* has been noted by A. Klapper, "Warfare, Ethics and Jewish Law," *Meorot: A Forum of Modern Orthodox Discourse* 6, 2006, p. 5, n.22–23. However, his statement there regarding the Sanhedrin is not accepted by all authorities.

12. *The Code of Maimonides, Book 14, the Book of Judges*, Kings and Wars 5,1. This is the translation of A. Hershman, New Haven: Yale University Press, 1949, which in some matters regarding war (such as translating *milhemet mitzvah* as "a war for a religious cause") are unsatisfactory.

13. The commandments to wage war against the seven nations and against Amalek appear as positive commandments 187 and 188 in the enumeration of Maimonides. See *The Commandments: Sefer Ha-Mitzvoth of Maimonides: Volume One: The Positive Commandments*, trans. C.B. Chavel, London and New York: Soncino, 1967, pp. 200–203.

14. There have been claims that implacable enemies of the Jewish people are equivalent to Amalek and that contemporary wars against them are equivalent to the war against that nation, including the Torah commandment to kill all members of that nation. It has been suggested in the name of Rabbi Moshe Soloveitchik that Maimonides did not specify that the people of Amalek no longer exist (as he did regarding the seven nations), because the category of Amalek is still in force, as a commandment to engage in war against any people that seeks to destroy the Jewish people. This notion appears in a Hebrew essay by his son, Rabbi Joseph B. Soloveitchik which has been translated twice into English. See *Faith and Destiny: From Holocaust to the State of Israel*, trans. L. Kaplan, Hoboken: Ktav, 2000, pp. 93–95 and *Kol Dodi Dofek: Listen – My Beloved Knocks*, translated and annotated by D.Z. Gordon, Hoboken: Ktav, 2006, pp. 112–114. See also E. Horowitz, *Reckless Rites: Purim and the Legacy of Jewish Violence*, Princeton: Princeton University Press, 2006, pp. 144–146. This suggestion has been critically scrutinized by N. Lamm, "Amalek and the Seven Nations: A Case of Law vs. Morality," in L. Schiffman and J. Wolowelsky (Eds.), *War and Peace in the Jewish Tradition*, New York: Yeshiva University Press, 2007 pp. 201–238. I have elsewhere written that a careful reading of Rabbi Soloveitchik's statement does not confirm the notion of an identity between contemporary enemies of Israel and Amalek, to the extent that such an identity would justify killing individual "Amalekites." See K. Neuman, "To Blotto or to Blot Out," *Jerusalem Report*, July 10, 2006. In any case, these discussions are focused in the homiletical dimension and should not be seen as binding legal pronouncements.

Even if not applicable in modern times, the moral difficulty of the commandment to blot out the memory of Amalek has elicited different responses in Jewish tradition.

For one overview, see A. Sagi "The Punishment of Amalek in Jewish Tradition: Coping with the Moral Problem," *Harvard Theological Review* 8, 1994, pp. 323–346.

15. Surprisingly, the classic rabbinic literature does not feature extensive analyses of the legal justifications for the war of self-defense. I wish to thank Rabbi Yair Kahn of Yeshivat Har Etzion, who has discussed the question with me extensively and shared with me an unpublished paper of his on the topic. See also Klapper, "Warfare, Ethics and Jewish Law," p. 6.

16. The responsum was probably written in early March 1948 during a respite in the fighting in Tiberias. See N. Av, *The Battle for Tiberias*, Tel Aviv: Ministry of Defense, 1991, pp. 148–149 (Hebrew) who mentions Rabbi Werner as one of those who allowed the inhabitants to engage in fortification work on the Sabbath. The city fell to Jewish forces on April 18 after intensive fighting that started in mid-March. See B. Morris "Yosef Nahmani and the Arab Question in 1948," in *1948 and After* (rev. ed.), Oxford: Oxford University Press, 2004, pp. 171–180. It should be noted that already in 1938 Kiryat Shmuel had been attacked by Arabs and 5 inhabitants were killed (Av, *The Battle for Tiberias*, p. 26).

17. *Responsa Heichal Yitzhak Orach Haim*, Jerusalem: Committee for the Publication of the Works of Rabbi Herzog, 1972, no. 31, pp. 71–73 (Hebrew). The quotation is on p. 73.

18. Ibid. no. 37, pp. 93–95. The quotation is from p. 94.

19. Roth was a renowned halakhist, who was sympathetic to the Zionist cause. Herzog had also sent him other rulings to comment on, such as his instructions to the defenders of Kfar Etzion; *Heichal Yitzhak*, nos. 34–35.

20. The responsum was printed in Roth's *Kol Mevaser*, Jerusalem: Mossad Harav Kook, 1955, no. 47, pp. 124–125 (Hebrew). In the book of Rabbi Herzog's response, *Heichal Yitzhak*, it appears as no. 38 on p. 96 but the part doubting the status of the war as on obligatory one was not included, and the final paragraph quoted reads, "regarding all the other questions I agree to everything [you] wrote . . ." This deletion is despite the fact that no. 39 in *Heichal Yitzhak* contains the response of Rabbi Herzog to that claim. Perhaps the editors were somewhat embarrassed with the suggestion of Rabbi Roth that there would not be a draft to combat units.

21. *Heichal Yitzhak* no. 39, p. 99.

22. I. Herzog "On the Establishment of the State and Its Wars," *Tehumin* 4, 1983, pp. 21–23 (Hebrew).

23. On Ben-Gurion's view of the inevitability of war, see Yossi Goldstein's contribution in this volume.

24. See J. Heller, *From Brit Shalom to Ichud: Judah Leib Magnes and the Struggle for a Binational State in Palestine*, Jerusalem: Magnes, 2003 (Hebrew). Note the quote from Martin Buber on p. 378 blaming Israel for the outbreak of the war; T. Herman, "Ihud- A Peace Movement in a Test of Fire," in *State, Government and International Relations* 33, 1980, pp. 31–72, esp. p. 61ff (Hebrew). For a miscellany of quotes questioning the declaration of the State, see A. Ophir, "H-Hour," in A. Ophir (Ed.), *Fifty to Forty-Eight: Critical Moments in the History of the State of Israel*, Tel Aviv and Jerusalem: Hakibutz Hameuchad, 1999, pp. 15–33 (Hebrew).

25. For some comments on the extreme ultra-Orthodox opposition to the establishment of the state see the final section of Isaac Hershkowitz' article in this volume. The ultra-Orthodox mainstream, represented by *Agudat Yisrael*, did not oppose the establishment of the state but did not take an active part in the run-up to it. One of its leaders, Rabbi Yitzhak Meir Levin, was one of the signatories of Israel's Declaration of Independence.

26. One of the rabbis [S.Y. Zevin] "On the Question of the Conscription of Yeshiva Students" in A. Shapira (Ed.), *Draft According to the Halacha*, Jerusalem: Torah and Labor Guardians, 1993, pp. 217–220 (Hebrew).

27. "The 19th Psalm of the State of Israel," in Z.Y. Kook, *In the Paths of Israel (LNtivot Yisrael)*, Bet El: Me'Avnei Hamakom, 3rd printing, 2007, vol. 2, pp. 355–367 (Hebrew). The talk was first printed in the organ of the National Religious Party *Hatzofeh* a short time after the Six Day War.

28. *Regarding the Commandment of the Land*, n.p., Jerusalem, Iyar 5708 [May 1948]. It was later printed in *In the Paths of Israel [L'Ntivot Yisrael]*, vol. 1, pp. 168–183 (Hebrew). Regarding the circumstances of the publication of the booklet see S.Y.Cohen, "The Birth of the Booklet *Regarding the Commandment of the Land*," ibid. vol. 2, pp. 611–612 (Hebrew).

29. The article was published first in *Hatorah V'Hamedina [The Torah and the State]* 5–6 (5713–5714) which appeared in September 1954 and which was edited by Yisraeli himself. An expanded version was printed as chapter 16 in Yisraeli's book *Amud Ha-Yimini*, Tel Aviv: Moreshet, 1966, under the title of "Actions for the Security of the State in the Light of Halakha." The original (shorter) version (now under the title "Retaliatory Attacks in the Light of Halakha") appeared in *B'tzomet Hatorah V'hamedina* vol. 3, Alon Shevut: Tzomet, 1991, pp. 253–289. One can only conjecture as to the reason for the changes in title which obscured the connection to a specific event, despite the fact that the reference to Qibya in the introduction remained in all the versions. After submitting this paper, Yitzhak Avi Roness, who is writing a doctoral dissertation on Rabbi Yisraeli, was kind enough to send me his article, "Halakha, Ideology and Interpretation – Rabbi Shaul Yisraeli on The Status of Defensive War," *Jewish Law Association Studies* 20, 2010, pp. 184–195. Roness covers much of the ground that I do (comparing Rabbi Yisraeli to his contemporaries) and concludes that this issue illustrates "how a halakhic authority's ideological worldview can influence his halakhic decisions" (p. 195).

30. See B. Morris, *Israel's Border Wars 1949–1956*, Oxford: Clarendon Press, 1999, pp. 257–276. In an article on the raid by S. Tevet, "Who changed the General Command Order?" *Haaretz*, 9 September 1994, pp. b5–b6 (Hebrew), the author tries to discover who was responsible for the operational order which called for maximum taking of life without specifically excluding women or children.

31. Yisraeli, *Amud Ha-Yemini*, p. 162.

32. See State of Israel, *Documents on the Foreign Policy of Israel*, vol. 8, 1953, Ed. Y. Rosenthal, Jerusalem, 1995, pp. 774–776 (document 449). See also documents 432, 435, 444 and 446. In the official statement the raid was attributed to frontier settlers and attested that the Government of Israel deplored it "if innocent blood was spilled." Note, however, the hints of poet Natan Alterman in his popular weekly "seventh column" in the newspaper *Davar* on 23 October 1953 in which he questioned why Israel is trying to defend a "murky" action which should have been publically repudiated. See M. Naor, *The Eighth Column*, Tel Aviv: Hakibutz Hameuchad, 2006, pp. 294–295 (Hebrew). Note also the essay of Yeshayahu Leibowitz which was published on 15 December 1953 and takes for granted that the government (and the IDF) were responsible for the action. See Y. Leibowitz, "After Kibiyeh," in E. Goldman (Ed.), *Judaism, Human Values, and the Jewish State*, Cambridge, MA: Harvard University Press, 1995, pp. 185–190.

33. A careful analysis of Rabbi Yisraeli's essay requires distinction between a) what actually happened in Qibya; b) what R. Yisraeli believed had happened; and c) what he wrote had happened. The fact that he claims that the laws of war are applicable indicate that indeed he knew that it had been an authorized military operation and not a spontaneous rogue attack. Compare Y. Blidstein, "The Treatment of Hostile Civilian Populations: The Contemporary Halachic Discussion in Israel," *Israel Studies* 1, 1996, pp. 27–44, n. 3, who writes that "at the time of writing the article and its first publication the rabbi believed that the raid was carried out by members of the settlements that had been attacked by terrorists and not by the army or any authorized governmental body." As already mentioned, the misrepresentation of the event was copied in all reprintings

of the essay, before and after the death of Rabbi Yisraeli. In a correspondence with Rabbi Yisrael Sharir, Rabbi Yisraeli's student and son-in-law, he pointed out that his mentor was "a rabbi and not a historian" and the events of Qibya were an opportunity to analyze the entire question of non combatants in wartime.

34. See Blidstein, "The Treatment of Hostile Civilian Populations."

35. A. Edrei, "Law, Interpretation and Ideology: The Renewal of the Jewish Laws of War in the State of Israel" *Cardozo Law Review* 28, 2006, pp. 187–227, n. 62.

36. Indeed, Rabbi Yitzhak Kaufman quotes a conversation with Rabbi Zvi Yehuda Kook that a halakhic state of war has existed from the War of Independence up to the present. See Y. Kaufman, *The Army According to Halacha: Laws of War and of the Army* (2nd ed.), Jerusalem: Kol Mevaser, 1994, pp. 5–7 and n. 8. (Hebrew). That approach would allow viewing activities apart from the battlefield (such as espionage or activity to free hostages) as part of the war effort, with all this entails as far as the halakhic status of such actions. This is probably also the opinion of Rabbi Zevin, who wrote that the War of Independence, the Sinai War of 1956 and the Six Day War are all considered wars of self defense: "They, our neighbors, who began with an attack on our borders in order to realize their announced aim: to destroy Israel, both the people and the state. This was the situation in all three wars, such is the situation today, and there is no better example of an obligatory war." S.Y. Zevin, "War in the Light of the Halacha," in *In the Light of the Halacha* (new ed.), Jerusalem: Bet Hillel, 2004, p. 88 (Hebrew).

37. See, for example, the different perceptions of the situation that ensued after the signing of the armistice agreements in M. Bar-On, "Status Quo Before or After? Israel's Security Policy 1949–1957," in his *Smoking Borders: Studies in the Early History of the State of Israel, 1948–1967*, Jerusalem: Yad Ben Zvi, 2001, pp. 131–165 esp. 150.

38. Though it is not clear if he is referring to the people of Israel, i.e. the Jews as a nation, or the State of Israel.

39. Yisraeli, *Amud Ha-Yemini*, p. 196.

40. Edrei, "Law, Interpretation and Ideology," pp. 211–217; M. Broyde, "Only the Good Die Young," *Meorot: A Forum of Modern Orthodox Discourse* 6, 2006, pp. 1–2. Broyde sees this as the normative halakhic position and refers to other writings where he has expounded on this point.

41. Blidstein, "The Treatment of Hostile Civilian Populations," pp. 34–35; N. Gutel, "Combat in Areas Saturated With Civilian Population," *Tehumin* 23, 2003, p. 40 (Hebrew).

42. To the best of my knowledge no other halakhist has made the claim attributed to Rabbi Yisraeli, that it legal to wage war if is legitimated by international law, even when it cannot be defined within the rabbinic definitions of self-defense. Broyde claims that the opinion that "the government of Israel is not bound to uphold the obligations of war imposed on a Jewish Kingdom, but merely must conduct itself in accordance with the international law norms" is implicitly held by many halakhic authorities. See *The Bounds of Wartime Military Conduct in Jewish Law*, pp. 12–13 and n. 20. However, to the best of my understanding, this refers to *jus in bello* (which governs behavior in war) and not the conditions necessary for engaging in war *(jus ad bellum)*. The rabbinic authorities Broyde refers to grant that a situation defined as self defense exists, which legitimates the war as Obligatory, and only then do the international rules which govern *jus in bello* apply.

43. Note that in his halakhic discussion of the siege of Beirut during the first Lebanon War, Rabbi Yisraeli took for granted that if that war was not to be defined as an obligatory war, it could not be justified halakhically because "we have no permission to engage in such a war nowadays, because the king requires the agreement of the court of 71 [ie. The Sanhedrin, which does not exist in our time] for waging Optional war." See S. Yisraeli "The Siege of Beirut in Light of the Halacha" in his *Havat Binyamin* vol.1, Ed. N. Gutel, Kfar Darom: The Institute for Torah and Land, 5752 [1992], pp. 11–119, esp. p. 116. Cf. Edrei, "Law, Interpretation and Ideology."

44. Yisraeli, *Amud Ha-Yemini*, pp. 198–199. Note that this is the last justification suggested in the essay after which appears a summary of the conclusions. Gutel, "Combat in Areas Saturated With Civilian Population," p. 40 agrees that the source for the innovation of the category of war of revenge is obscure, especially as Yisraeli himself did not justify the incorporation of all the elements of the war of Midian into contemporary jurisprudence. In another essay written decades later regarding the military operation to rescue hostages in Entebbe, Yisraeli made a somewhat different use of the Midianite precedent. He argued that the basis for the obligatory war to save Israel from its enemies is "sanctification of God's name." Since the intentional targeting of Jews (as carried out by the terrorists at Entebbe) is a desecration of God's name, the operation is deemed an obligatory war. See Yisraeli, "Operation Jonathan in the Light of Halacha," in *Havat Binyamin*, pp. 126–133 esp. pp. 131–132 and Roness, "Halakha, Ideology and Interpretation."

45. I would accept the characterization of Yoske Ahituv who describes Rabbi Yisraeli as one who "endeavored in many different ways to find some halachic justification after the fact to the Qibya event." See "The Wars of Israel and the Sanctity of Life," in Y. Gafni and A. Ravitzky (Eds.), *Sanctity of Life and Martyrdom: Studies in Memory of Amir Yekutiel*, Jerusalem: Shazar Center, 1993, p. 270 (Hebrew).

46. The halakhic status of the 1967 war did not generate discussion. It was seen as a war of self-defense, regardless of who had fired the first shot, and irrespective of the question (which would subsequently be raised by historians) if an Arab attack was indeed imminent. The institution of a religious holiday to celebrate the victory was a reflection of that perception. See N. Rakover, *The Laws of Independence Day and Jerusalem Day*, Jerusalem: Ministry of Religions, 1973 (Hebrew).

47. It is not clear what proof of this would be sufficient from the point of view of Jewish law. In a famous pronouncement from 1967, the leader of the Modern Orthodox wing of American Jewry, Rabbi Joseph Baer Soloveitchik, insisted that any decision taken by the military and political leadership in Israel would be halakhically binding. For an English translation of the address (which was given in Yiddish) see www.aishdas.org/avodah/vol15/v15n040.shtml#10 (viewed 1 May 2010). On the other hand, former Chief Rabbi Ovadia Yosef, who has publicly stated many times that human life takes precedence over maintaining control over the entire Land of Israel, opposed the disengagement from Gaza in 2000 claiming that unilateral withdrawal would endanger Jewish lives.

48. In practice, most of the adherents of the position are confident that the conflict between the prohibition of withdrawal and the sanctity of life is only theoretical, and that territorial concessions will not bring peace but rather encourage further threats on Israel and its citizens.

49. The relevant text of Nahmanides is his list of commandments which, in his opinion, Maimonides had deleted from the list of 613 commandments. See C.D. Chavel, *The Book of Commandments of Maimonides with the Glosses of Nahmanides*, Jerusalem: Mossad Harav Kook, 1981, pp. 114–146 (Hebrew).

50. See Y.M. Ehrenberg, "The Prohibition of Transferring the Territories of the Land of Israel to non-Jews," *Tehumin* 10, 1899, pp. 26–33 (Hebrew); Ravitsky, "Prohibited Wars." A prominent proponent of the position which opposed withdrawal because of the command to wage wars of conquest is the late Chief Rabbi Avraham Shapiro. See E. Shochetman, *And He Established it for Jacob as a Law*, Jerusalem: Kol Mevaser, 1995, pp. 35–37 (Hebrew).

51. One distinguished authority who challenges the extension of obligatory war to include wars of conquest is Rabbi N. Rabinovitch, "The Opinion of Nahmanides Regarding Conquest of the Land," *Tehumin* 4, 1986, pp. 302–306 (Hebrew). See also Ravitsky, op. cit.

Part III

War and peace in modern Jewish thought and practice

13 "A victory of the Slavs means a deathblow to democracy"

The onset of World War I and the images of the warring sides among Jewish immigrants in New York, 1914–16

Gil Ribak

About a month after the onset of World War I, the New York conservative and popular Yiddish daily, the *Yidishes Tageblat* (Jewish Daily News) explained to its readers who the belligerent sides were: the Slavs were "a wild, barbaric and inferior race," which cohabited Europe together with the "Latin race" and the "Teutonic race," the latter being "much more important" than the Latin race. The editorial (probably written by one of the two coeditors, Gedalya Bublik or Leon Zolotkof) asserted that the Teutonic and Latin races did a lot for "humanity and progress," while wondering, "What have the Russians, the Poles, the Bulgarians, and the Serbs done for civilization?"[1]

At first glance, such an expression seems to match pseudo-scientific conceptions of race and culture that were prevalent before and after the turn of the twentieth century in Europe and the US, viewing the Germanic race as standing at the helm of human advancement.[2] Yet Jewish observers were not interested in racial ideas in and of themselves: they focused their condemnations on Russia and were less concerned with its allies, "Latin" France and "Germanic" Britain, which joined the Tsarist regime against Germany and the Habsburg Empire. As the following analysis demonstrates, World War I and the immediate dislocations and suffering it inflicted on Eastern European Jewry had coated some of the older images of Gentiles in a new, pseudoscientific terminology. The events abroad fitted well to preexisting notions among many Jewish immigrants regarding Eastern European nations, and especially the peasantry and its traits, which were classified in the more fashionable term as "Slavic."

The outbreak of "the Great War" was almost instantly followed by harrowing reports in the Yiddish press about the atrocities committed by Tsar Nicholas's soldiers: scorched-earth withdrawals, kidnappings, looting, torture, rape, and sadistic savagery. One account described how Cossacks played with a Jewish two-year-old: one of them tossed the child in the air, and the others caught him on their swords. Furthermore, the Russians also initiated a series of massive expulsions of hundreds of thousands of Jews from their homes in the western regions of the Pale of Settlement, ordering them to leave their homes, often at no more than twelve hours notice. The ominous newspaper reports from Europe were filled with the names of *shtetlekh* and cities from which many immigrants had come, and misery was the lot of many Jewish immigrants' parents, siblings, and offspring.[3] In a fever-pitch outburst of relief work activity, numerous *landsmanshaftn* (hometown associations), synagogues, and charitable societies organized benefits and bazaars, and provided monetary assistance as well as hundreds of volunteers to help solicitations and collections.[4]

As reports about Russian brutality were widely circulated, the bulk of Jewish immigrants in New York supported the Germans and Austrians (the Central Powers): their hostility was not directed at the Allied Powers (the "Entente," meaning Britain and France) per se, but rather at the hated Tsarist regime. Jews hailing from the Pale of Settlement could hardly forget the harassment, anti-Jewish decrees, university quotas, pogroms, the recent Beilis blood libel (1911–13), and the animosity of the Russian government.[5] The sweatshop bard, Yiddish poet Morris Rosenfeld wrote during the war, "The bleeding of Russia rejoices my heart/May the Devil do to her/What she did unto me." The *Tageblat* explained that Jews backed Germany, "because Russia bathes in Jewish blood." The left-leaning, independent *Varhayt* (Truth) reminded its readers that Russia "remains and will remain an antisemitic country," hence Jews decisively sided with the Central Powers. Louis Friedman, the father-in-law of Benjamin Koenigsberg, one of the key lay figures of Jewish orthodoxy in New York, wrote in the *Globe and Commercial Advertiser* (1915) that "even a cannibal" would have had mercy on defenseless women and children, but the Russians did not. Terms such as "Sober Russia" or "cultured, enlightened Russia," Friedman concluded, "would make a horse laugh."[6]

Apart from most immigrant Jews' deep loathing for the Russian regime, there were those who hailed from the Habsburg Empire (Hungary, Galicia, and Bukovina): they were typically enthusiastic Austrian patriots, and especially admired Emperor Franz Joseph, who was considered protector of the Jews. Helen Weinstein, who grew up in Krakow at the turn of the century, recalled how the local Jews were dedicated to the emperor and feared that after his death they would be left to the mercy of the "very antisemitic" Poles. Yiddish journalist Khone Gotesfeld, who also grew up in Galicia, remembered how Jews used to bless the "great friend of Jews" (the emperor) and believed that evil decrees came from the local Polish authorities. The Hungarian-Galician quarter (near East Houston Street) buzzed with prayers for the well-being of the Austrian emperor, curses against "Fonye" (a derogatory nickname for Russians derived from the nickname Vanya for Ivan) and a march down Second Avenue in support of Austria.[7]

The anxiety on the Jewish street intensified in the winter months of 1914–15 with the news about the Russian advance into Galicia and Bukovina and the ensuing devastation. Under such circumstances an openly pro-Entente (Allies) position – which was seen as pro-Russian – had become tremendously unpopular, as demonstrated in the case of Louis E. Miller. A leading figure in the Jewish labor movement and a pioneer of the Yiddish press in America, Miller edited the popular daily *Varhayt*. In August 1914 he published three editorials calling American Jews to assist the Allies. The newspaper's sales immediately plummeted by about 50,000 copies (close to a half of its daily circulation) following a spontaneous boycott against it. In dozens of Galician and Hungarian synagogues and *landsmanshaftn* (hometown associations) the "pro-Fonye" *Varhayt* was strongly attacked as irate readers snatched copies from newsstands and flung them to the gutters. A few thousand immigrants participated in protest demonstrations in front the *Varhayt* building on East Broadway. In January 1915 Miller was ousted from the newspaper he had founded in 1905 as the daily's owners sought to regain its popularity, and his subsequent journalistic ventures were unsuccessful.[8]

Many of the attacks by Jewish intellectuals and in the Yiddish press were not merely aimed at the Tsarist regime: the Slavic peoples in general were portrayed at times as backward and bloodthirsty. A coeditor of the orthodox Yiddish daily *Morgen zhurnal* (Morning Journal), Yankev Magidov, remarked that the chief editor Peter (Perets) Wiernik harbored unrelenting anti-Russian feelings. More than a decade before the war Wiernik wrote, "Left to himself, the Russian is a most helpless human being," and "the unhappy medium between the Asiatic and the European." In August 1914 Wiernik claimed that although antisemitism was quite developed in "Das Land der Dichter und Denker" (the land of poets and thinkers, i.e. Germany), "You still cannot deny that the German is better than the Russian in that regard." In another editorial, the *Morgen zhurnal* chastised Britain, which had "no business allying itself with the Asiatic barbarian." In the same vein, the *Tageblat* warned that, "A victory for the Slavs means a deathblow for science, for democracy, for liberal ideas."[9]

One of the fiercest anti-Russian intellectuals was Shmuel M. Melamed. Originally a Yeshiva student from Lithuania, Melamed attained a Ph.D. in Germany, and became a prolific writer in a host of German and later American newspapers, as well as Hebrew newspapers (he would also become active in the Zionist movement in America). Melamed arrived in America in 1914, and wrote in various Yiddish and English publications: The post-Miller *Varhayt* was more than happy to win back its readership with Melamed's articles, which detailed how the cultivated Germans must defeat the "rotten Slavs" and "people of the prairies" (i.e. Russians). One of the images Melamed evoked was that of the Russian *muzhik* (peasant) who drinks and beats up his wife.[10]

The position of the Jewish radical intelligentsia in New York was more ambivalent. Many of them were immersed in Russian culture and had close relations with likeminded Russian revolutionaries. Labor firebrand Elizabeth Hasanovitz exemplified that approach when she wrote (toward the end of World War I), "How hateful the word Russia sounded," but hastened to explain, "Not as a country, but as an autocratic government." Yet the overall tendency

רוסלאנד! דער שוואַרצער בער, טראַמפעלט איבער דיא ערמאָ־דעטע, גע
פייניגטע אידישע מענער, פֿרויען און קינדער אין זעטיגט זיך מיט זייער פֿלייש א'
שטילט זיין דורשט מיט זייער בלוט...

Figure 1 *Forverts*: "Russia! The black bear tramples on the murdered, tortured Jewish men,
    women and children, feeding itself on their flesh, and quenches its thirst with their
    blood."

leaned toward an anti-Russian sentiment. A towering figure among Jewish immigrants and Jewish socialism was Abraham Cahan, the influential editor of the *Forverts* (Jewish Daily Forward). His position, nevertheless, resembled that of the conservative rivals. When war broke out, Cahan enlightened his readers that even though each Slavic nation has its own language and customs, "they are all very similar to one another." Cahan added that, "In truth, the Germanic peoples are more advanced, stronger and more energetic than the Slavs." A week later Cahan argued that, "all civilized people sympathize with Germany, every victorious battle against Russia is a source of joy." In April 1915 the *Forverts* showed (Figure 1) a cartoon of a blood dripping, vicious-looking bear, identified as "Russia," trampling on dying women and babies, as the caption read: "Russia! The black bear tramples on the murdered, tortured Jewish men, women and children, feeding itself on their flesh, and quenches its thirst with their blood." Even a neutralist such as Chaim Zhitlovsky, a champion of Yiddishism and Diaspora nationalism, who was deeply rooted in Russian politics and culture, wrote (in November 1914) that if the war were only between Russia and Germany, "we would all be on Germany's side." He determined that the war pitted "a European constitution against Asiatic despotism," and personal freedom against "barbarian oppression." But since Britain and France also fought against Germany, he remained neutral.[11]

To be sure, a handful of Jewish socialists, such as the former secretary of the United Hebrew Trades (UHT), writer Yankev Milkh, the journalist M. Baranov, and socialist Zionist leaders Ber Borokhov and Nachman Syrkin went beyond neutralism and openly supported the Allies. Yet their stance remained fairly isolated and reveals the anti-Russian mood among immigrant Jews: historian Elias Cherikover (who later became the main chronicler of postwar pogroms in Ukraine) warned against the "Russo-phobia" on the Jewish street, while A. Litvak (pen-name of Chaim-Yankl Helfand), a leading figure in the Jewish Socialist Federation (JSF), lambasted "anti-Slavism," arguing there was no more antisemitism in the nature of the Slavic race than in the nature of the Germanic race. Litvak cautioned that, "We begin to look on people amongst whom we live and work as wolves, as inferior creatures."[12]

Anti-Slav sentiments were also tied to heightened appreciation of the Germans. In the summer of 1915, when the German army retook Austrian Galicia and also conquered the large Jewish centers in Warsaw, Bialystok, and Kovno, the Yiddish newspapers struggled to exceed one another in celebrating the German and Austrian victories: when Lviv (Lemberg) was recaptured, the *Morgen zhurnal* congratulated Galician Jews, who were liberated "from the rule of the Asiatic barbarian." Abraham Cahan, who returned from Eastern Europe in May 1915, declared at a socialist mass meeting in Carnegie Hall, "The German of today is a better man than he ever was." The *Forverts* extolled the German rule in Warsaw and showed a picture of a Hasidic rebbe in Lodz under a humorous caption: "Now he is a daytsh": Hasidim were the bitter opponents of the *maskilim* (proponents of Jewish enlightenment), who were often called daytshn. By cleverly fusing a familiar Jewish type (daytsh) to the new occupiers, the *Forverts* relayed to its readers a homey, soothing image of the German, which was diametrically opposed to that of the bloodthirsty Russian/Cossack. In 1916 a Jewish dentist on Suffolk Street, Dr. B. Schwartz, published his practice in an ad titled "Germany strikes all the enemies of the Jews," which claimed that "God sent Germany to punish Russia and Romania" for their cruelty toward Jews.[13]

The positive representations of Germans manifested themselves in various ways: in April 1915 the UHT and the International Ladies' Garment Workers' Union (ILGWU) cosponsored with the pro-German elements of the American Federation of Labor (AFL) in New York a mass meeting at Cooper Union. The meeting, in which socialist Congressman Meyer London and New York State Assemblyman Abraham Shiplacoff spoke, called to consider a general strike in the arms and food-producing industries. In June 1915 many Jewish socialists, as well as banker Jacob Schiff and Samuel Untermeyer (a wealthy attorney associated with Tammany), joined the United German Societies of New York City in sponsoring a peace mass meeting at Madison Square Garden that called on the US to impose a trade and arms embargo on the Entente. That appeal corresponded to the German embargo campaign in America, which was financed in part by the German government.[14]

With such an atmosphere it was little wonder that the Yiddish humorist weekly, *Der groyser kundes* (The Big Stick) remarked in 1914, "The German soldiers are positively the best in the world: they are 'made in Germany'." In January 1915 *Varhayt* published an unnamed feuilleton which mentioned how in the past, "who if not the Brooklyn daytshukes [a pejorative for Germans]" used to pull the beards of Jews on the East New York (Brooklyn) cars and harass Jewish women and girls. But since the war began, "the old hatred is taken back," and one could not find "two other races that would live so peacefully, truly sleep under one blanket, as the Jews and Germans." By early 1916 the Yiddish writer and news editor of the independent daily *Der Tog* (Day), Alexander Zeldin, complained about what he saw as exaggerated appreciation of the Germans on the Jewish street: "many people believe the Germans are from a race of titans or half Gods."[15]

The events that unfolded on the eastern front had a direct effect on the image of other Slavs, especially the Poles. As the war broke out the anti-Jewish boycott in Poland continued, and some Poles began circulating false rumors that Jews were German spies, thus aggravating the brutality of the Russian military toward the Jewish population. Yiddish folklorist and playwright S. An-ski (Shloyme Zaynvl Rapoport), who traveled with the Russian army throughout Poland, remarked that, "poisonous slander had penetrated every . . . stratum of the Polish people." When the Russians expelled tens of thousands of Jews, cheering Poles stood alongside the roads, telling Russian soldiers "May God protect you from Germans and *zhids* [kikes]." Moreover, during the war there were Poles who also took part in anti-Jewish violence.[16]

News of these events was widely published by Jewish emissaries from Europe and in the Yiddish papers. In January 1915 Zionist leader Shmaryah Levin published an article in the *New York Times* where he accused the Poles of "treachery and duplicity" and blamed them for the murder of more than a thousand Jews and the expulsion of tens of thousands. A *Jewish* representative of the Polish National Committee, Arthur Hausner, arrived in New York in 1915, and participated in a mass meeting at Cooper Union, where he called American Jews to support Poland's independence and urged rapprochement based on anti-Russian feelings: he was hooted off the platform, as many in the audience ran up to the stage, shaking their fists and shouting invectives. It seemed that many in the audience were about to storm the podium. In 1916, Ukrainian-born Shmuel-Zvi Zetser, a critic who translated to Yiddish classical Jewish texts, dissected the roots of Polish antisemitism and characterized the Poles as people who had "the greatest measure of . . . vain, foolish arrogance." The editor of the Zionist weekly *Ha-toren* (The Mast), Y. D. Berkovitch (Sholem Aleichem's son-in-law), expressed a similar view, writing in the same year, "If there is a people in the world, which has shown us its despicable cruelty, all of its wild rage . . . it is the Polish people."[17]

In order to gain a better understanding of Jewish immigrants' conceptions of the warring sides, one must look at their Eastern European origins and cultural background. Until the last third of the nineteenth century, most Eastern European Jews still resided in *shtetlekh* (small to mid-size market towns) that provided surrounding villages with commercial services. Despite frequent and varied economic relations between Jews and Gentiles, social mingling remained fairly uncommon. Jews differed from the rest of the population in their domicile, clothing, language (Yiddish) and other aspects of appearance (beards and sidelocks for men, covered hair for married women). As a result of the Jews' economic situation, the Gentiles most Jews normally encountered and interacted with until the late-nineteenth century were mostly (occasionally drunk) peasantry (whether Belarusian, Polish, Romanian, Ukrainian, etc.), the Polish *Porets* (lord, landowner), and the Russian or Austrian officialdom.[18]

The basic image of the Gentile in Jewish folklore was that of a peasant, portrayed as inherently Jew-hating, strong, coarse, drunk, illiterate, dumb, and sexually promiscuous. That attitude yielded songs such as "*oy, oy, oy/shiker iz a goy/shiker iz er/trinken muz er/vayl er iz a goy*" (drunk is a Gentile/drunk is he/drink must he/because he is a Gentile); sayings such as "a Gentile remains a Gentile"; "when the Gentiles have a feast they beat up Jews"; "when the Jew is hungry he sings; when the Gentile is hungry he beats up his wife"; and "the Jew is small and Vasil (a common Ukrainian name) is big."[19] Furthermore, Yiddish speakers used *lehavdl* (differentiation) language – a separate set of words to depict the life cycle of Gentiles: future anarchist Yisroel Binimetsky (later Beneqvit), who grew up in a Ukrainian *shtetl* in the 1870s recalled how the local Jews refrained from using the regular verb *shtarbn* (to die) when talking about the death of non-Jews; instead, they applied the word *peygern* (denotes the death of an animal). The Gentiles did not eat but "devoured," and their family members were "fatheru, motheru, sisteru" (mocking Ukrainian pronunciation). There were also contemptuous names for Gentiles, especially peasants, such as "*Zhlob*" (a boor or yokel), "*Doverakher*" (literally "other thing," figuratively meaning something impure such as a pig or a scoundrel), "*shkots*," "*orl*" (a more contemptuous term than goy, referring to the uncircumcised), "*poperilo*," "*kaporenik*" (figuratively someone who is worthless), or just "Ivan."[20]

Many memoirs and accounts by people from various regions and dissimilar political and cultural trajectories still invoked that basic image: the Yiddish poet Yoysef Rolnik, who grew up in the 1880s in a small village near Minsk, described the peasants as crude: they swam in the local river in "a primitive way, kicking their thick feet"; and their women used to ride horses "spread-legged, like men." Future garment worker Avrum Pinkhes Unger, who grew up in the Polish town of Strykov in the 1880s and 1890s recollected how during local fairs peasants sometimes got drunk, and thinking a Jew cheated them, began shouting "beat up the Jews" and fights broke out. The Yiddish author I.J. Singer, who grew up in a Polish *shtetl* at the turn of the twentieth century, described how during Christian holidays thousands of peasants swarmed into town; right after the religious ceremonies, the peasants "got drunk, danced, and beat each other up."[21] The image of the peasant was so closely associated with rudeness and dullness, that as late as 1952 Yiddish linguist and folklorist, Hirsh Abramovitch, argued that one should not use the word *poyer* (peasant) when referring to Jewish farmers or agricultural workers: "my pen does not let me write down the word poyer" when discussing Jews. The image of the peasant was deeply rooted in the Yiddish language and folklore, where the words *poyer* or *muzhik* denoted rusticity and small-mindedness.[22]

Peasantry was not the only stratum of society encountered by Eastern European Jewry. Polish lords (*pritsim*) were often associated with brutal and capricious behavior: the very term *porets* is derived from the Hebrew verb "to transgress." Jewish estate-managers (*arendators*) for *in absentia* Polish gentry, merchants who arranged the sale of those lords' produce, and whole communities who received permission by a local lord to live on his land, had various contacts with Polish landed gentry. Since Jews managed the lords' estates and collected their taxes among the peasantry (which was often not Polish), they were identified with the hated gentry and from time to time incurred the serfs' wrath. In some cases Polish noblemen defended the Jewish communities against peasant aggression and even vouched for "their" Jews in legal disputes against non-Jews. Historians have revealed the dual image of the *pritsim* in the Hebrew and Yiddish literature: there were signs of Jewish empathy with the stratum that was an economic ally and protector, and was seen at times as a carrier of higher culture than the surrounding peasantry.[23]

On the other hand, there were also feelings of revulsion and alienation for what Jews saw as brutal and licentious behavior of Polish lords, who habitually treated their Jewish lessees with utter contempt if not violence: Yiddish writers often described the lord as wanton, capricious, and cruel. Yekhezkel Kotik, who became a Yiddish and Hebrew writer and a communal reformer in Warsaw, depicted in his memoirs the conduct of the Polish lords in his native Kamenets (Byelorussia) in the mid-nineteenth century. The *porets* used to flog "his" Jews, humiliate them, and set his dogs on them: and "if the Jewish estate manager had, God forbid, beautiful daughters, it was a terrible misfortune" and the parents prayed they would not attract the *porets*, who might have his way with them. Countless Jewish folktales characterized the *porets* as mean, capricious, and tyrannical. One *porets* ordered a Jew to teach a dog to speak or face decapitation. Another tale presented a *porets* who visited his estate with his new wife and commanded his Jewish manager to cover the entire path from the train station to the estate with green fabric.[24]

Whereas Jews were hardly attracted to the Polish, Ukrainian, or Byelorussian peasant culture around them, and were ambivalent (at best) toward Polish lords, respect for Germans and German culture was noticeable among Yiddish-speaking Jews by the mid-nineteenth century, if not earlier. By that time the terms "*daytsh*" or "*daytshish*" (German) were common when referring to almost any new custom or social phenomenon. German culture and manners, channeled through German and Eastern European *maskilim*, as well as Jewish bankers and merchants in Galicia and cities across the pale like Warsaw, Odessa, Berdichev, and Zamoshtsh, were the symbols of modernity, and the *daytsh* was a bearer of higher culture and science with a universal appeal. In 1892 one of the leading Hebraists in America, Wolf (Ze'ev) Schur, whom a rival Jewish journalist called "dirty," responded to the insult in a letter to a friend: "I'm not a Russian Jew who just left the ghetto . . . and in my house reigns cleanliness like that of the Germans." Shmarya Levin wrote in his memoir, "I admired the strict order of German life in general; I admired the German drive for education and knowledge . . . I admired even more the German language and literature, with which I became more familiarized than the Russian."[25]

Similarly, clothing manufacturer Louis Borgenicht, who grew up in Galicia in the 1860s and 1870s, wrote "I had been reared to look upon 'German' as the stamp of excellence in trade, science, thought." Growing up in Vitebsk (1870s) the young Chaim Zhitlovsky noticed that his father and neighbors had a clearly distinct attitude toward Germans. Zhitlovsky's father felt deep respect toward Germans: "The German nature had made a tremendous impression on him." The father was particularly impressed by the German's "absolute honesty," where "a word is a word!" and even a simple German such as a local locksmith was "clean and well-dressed." In contrast, one looked at the Russian masses as "animals and beasts." Young Zhitlovsky's surroundings were "laden with hatred toward the Russian landowners and state officials who fleeced us, took our children as soldiers, persecuted . . . and treated us like dogs." Russians were derisively nicknamed "*Fonye*," usually combined with another pejorative: "murderous *Fonye*," or "lice *Fonye*."[26]

Unquestionably, as most of the 2.4 million East European Jews who immigrated to America between 1881 and 1924 had made their way through Germany, heading to one of the major European ports, the image of the cultured German had dimmed. Brushed against German border officials, policemen, train conductors, innkeepers, ship crewmembers and ordinary Germans, pushed aside on crowded streets, called "damn Jews" and "Russian pigs," and treated as the scum of the earth, Jewish immigrants found there was more to Germany than high culture and cleanliness. The emergence of political and pseudo-biological antisemitism in Germany after its unification (in 1871) also contributed its share to the travails of transient Jewish immigrants in Imperial Germany.[27] Still, the Germans were still seen as the personification of a higher culture, a more elevated Gentile world that was a sea of difference from Eastern European peasantry.

Conclusions

The onset of the Great War offers a unique setting in which to examine Jewish perceptions of Gentiles in a trans-Atlantic framework: this case study demonstrates how the historical juncture of war had deepened preexisting images rather than reversing or invalidating them. Nevertheless, the war did have the effect of recasting some of the older stereotypes and categories in a new, pseudoscientific vocabulary in light of the new world crisis. The events in Eastern Europe and the harsh conditions on the eastern front availed themselves to an existing conceptual framework among many Jewish immigrants that juxtaposed peasantry with Germans, the latter being the representatives of a higher culture. The Tsarist regime had long been hated, but the conflict enabled Jewish observers to attribute Jewish society's distinctions between different strata in the Gentile society to the Central Powers and their "Slavic" enemies.

One should not assume, however, that such images were rigid and unchanging. Later on, after the Tsarist regime collapsed in March 1917 and the U.S. entered the war on the Allied side (in April of the same year), the configuration changed: when the Germans were seen as the villains, it was easy to invoke other elements from the Jewish collective memory, portraying Germans as the creators of modern antisemitism, whose ingrained Teutonic cruelty had never ceased to guide them, even in their mistreatment of Jewish emigrants en route to America. That transformation affected even those who had been the most pro-German: a friend of the influential socialist activist and journalist Tsivyen (penname of Ben-tsien Hofman) described him as "in love with German culture." By August 1917, nonetheless, that very Tsivyen wrote about the "barbaric, bloodthirsty Germans that have to be wiped from the face of the earth so humanity may live in peace."[28] Yet at the same time the continued horrors in Eastern Europe, especially during the Russian civil war and the Soviet–Polish war, kept fanning the older images of the violent, volatile Slavic peasantry.[29] Those developments would continue to strain Jewish relations with immigrants from those countries (especially Poles) in America well into the interwar period.

Notes

1. *Yidishes Tageblat* (hereafter *YT*), 3 August 1914, p. 3. See also ibid. 27 July 1914, p. 4; 30 July 1914, p. 4. On that daily and the New York Yiddish press during World War I in general see Y. Khaykin, *Yidishe bleter in amerike*, New York: Published by the author, 1946, pp. 104–12, 241–7.

2. See B.D. Baum, *The Rise and Fall of the Caucasian Race: A Political History of Racial Identity*, New York: New York University Press, 2006, pp. 118–21; E.L. Goldstein, *The Price of Whiteness: Jews, Race, and American Identity*, Princeton: Princeton University Press, 2006, pp. 75–6, 95–8; D.A. Rich, "Russia," in R.F. Hamilton and H.H. Herwig (Eds.), *The Origins of World War I*, Cambridge: Cambridge University Press, 2003, pp. 204–5. H.H. Herwig, "Germany," ibid. pp. 163–4. J. Higham, *Strangers in the Land: Patterns of American Nativism 1860–1925* (second ed.), New York: Atheneum, 1978, pp. 131–57.

3. *Forverts*, 6 August 1915, p. 4; J. Jacobs (Ed.), *American Jewish Year Book* 5676, Philadelphia: The Jewish Publication Society, 1915–16, pp. 225–7, 244–6, 269. On the dissemination of information in New York about the suffering of Russian Jews see the letter from Ber Borokhov to S. Niger, 25 October, 1914, in: M. Mintz (Ed.), *The Letters of Ber Borokhov*, Tel Aviv: Am Oved, 1989, p. 613 (Hebrew). Yiddish folklorist and playwright S. An-ski (Shloyme Zaynvl Rapoport) described the Russian soldiers' cruelty (including the Cossack story) in "Khurbm galitsye," *Gezamlte shriftn* vol. 4, Warsaw: Farlag An-ski, 1925, pp. 10–14. Also see E. Lohr, *Nationalizing the Russian Empire: The Campaign against Enemy Aliens During World War I*, Cambridge: Harvard University Press, 2003, pp. 137–50.

4. *YT*, 8 September 1915, p. 4; *Forverts*, 24 April 1915, p. 12; M. Engelman, *Four Years of Relief and War Work by the Jews of America, 1914–1918*, New York: Shoen, 1918; D. Soyer, *Jewish Immigrant Associations and American Identity in New York 1880–1939*, Detroit: Wayne State University Press, 1997 (reprinted 2001), pp. 161–89; M. McCune, *"The Whole Wide World Without Limits": International Relief, Gender Politics, and American Jewish Women, 1890–1913*, Detroit: Wayne State University Press, 2005, pp. 43–77.

5. J. Frankel, *Prophecy and Politics: Socialism, Nationalism, and the Russian Jews 1862–1917*, New York: Cambridge University Press, 1981, pp. 134–7, 473–99, 509–12; B. Nathans, *Beyond the Pale: The Jewish Encounter with Late Imperial Russia*, Berkeley: University of California Press, 2002, pp. 268–71; E. Lifshutz, "Repercussions of the Beiles Trial in the United States," *Zion* 28, 1963, pp. 206–22 (Hebrew).

6. Rosenfeld is cited in Z. Szajkowski, *Jews, Wars, and Communism: The Attitude of American Jews in World War I, the Russian Revolutions of 1917, and Communism (1914–1945)*, New York: Ktav, 1972, vol. 1, p. 3. *YT*, 12 August 1914, p. 4. *Varhayt*, 30 July 1914, p. 4. *The Globe and Commercial Advertiser*, 26 April 1915, p. 3. See also *Morgen Zhurnal* (hereafter *MZ*) 3 August 1914, p. 4; 5 August 1914, p. 4; and the recollection of socialist journalist A. Held, *Oral History Collection of the Labor Movement* (YIVO), box #2, pp. 14–15; J. Rappaport, *Hands Across the Sea: Jewish Immigrants and World War I*, Lanham, MD: Hamilton Books, 2005, pp. 20–31; idem, "The American Yiddish Press and the European Conflict," *Jewish Social Studies* 19, 1957, pp. 113–28.

7. H. Weinstein, tape I-65, *NYC Immigrant Labor History Project* (Tamiment Institute, New York University). K. Gotesfeld, *Vos ikh gedenk fun mayn lebn*, New York: Fareynikte galitsyaner yidn in amerike, 1960, pp. 41–2. *Varhayt*, 29 July 1914, p. 4. *Forverts*, 31 July 1914, p. 4. *MZ*, 3 August 1914, p. 4. On the Jewish high regard for Franz Joseph see also the memoirs of Galician-born clothing manufacturer L. Borgenicht, *The Happiest Man: The Life of Louis Borgenicht as Told to Harold Friedman*, New York: Putnam's Sons, 1942, p. 33. A different etymology for "Fonye" is in N. Cohen, "On the Origin of the Name 'Fonye'," *Yeda-'Am* 10, 1964, p. 19 (Hebrew with English abstract).

8. At first Miller lambasted Russian antisemitism – *Varhayt*, 30 July 1914, p. 4. Then came the incriminating editorials, ibid., 8 August 1914, p. 4; 10 August 1914, p. 4; 25 August 1914, p. 4. The most comprehensive treatment of the Miller affair in 1914 is in Khaykin, *Yidishe bleter in amerike*, pp. 218–31. Also see D. Shub, *Fun di amolike yorn*, New York: Cyco, 1970, pp. 421–2; Rappaport, *Hands across the Sea*, pp. 30–1; T. Tadmor-Shimoni, "From Cosmopolitan Socialism to Jewish Cultural Nationalism – The Case of Louis Miller," *Yahadut Zémanenu – Contemporary Jewry* 8, 1993, pp. 23–38 (Hebrew with English abstract). On the *Varhayt*'s circulation see N.W. Ayer and Sons, *American Newspaper Annual and Directory*, Philadelphia: N.W. Ayer and Sons, 1914 , p. 1265.

9. Y. Magidov, *Der shpigl fun der ist sayd*, New York: by the author, 1923, pp. 41–4. P. Wiernik, "The Jew in Russia," in C.S. Bernheimer (Ed.), *The Russian Jew in the United States*, Philadelphia: John C. Winston, 1905, p. 21. *MZ* 3 August 1914, p. 4; 9 September 1914, p. 4; 2 October 1914, pp. 1, 4; 16 November 1915, p. 4. *YT*, 3 August 1914, p. 4. See also the cartoon in the Yiddish satirical weekly, *Der groyser kundes* (Big Stick), which showed two disheveled, unshaved, drunk Russian soldiers whose "war plan" is to desert – 20 November 1914, p. 7.

10. See Melamed's article in *Varhayt*, 11 January 1915, p. 4. See also his editorial in the *American Jewish Chronicle*, 20 October 1916, p. 723. On Melamed's connection with Germany's Information Bureau in New York see the Senate Sub-Committee of the Committee on Judiciary, *Hearings on Brewing and Liquor Interests and German and Bolshevik Propaganda*, 66th Congress, 1st Session (1919), vol. 2, pp. 1448–9. On his literary career see Z. Reyzin, *Leksikon fun der yidisher literatur, prese un filologye* vol. 2, Vilna: Kletskin, 1927, pp. 436–7.

11. E. Hasanovitz, *One of Them: Chapters from a Passionate Autobiography*, New York: Houghton Mifflin, 1918, p. 160. Cahan (and his colleague H. Burgin, who expressed a similar view) wrote in *Forverts*, 31 July 1914, p. 4; 7 August 1914, p. 4; 20 August 1914, p. 4. The cartoon of the murderous bear is from *Forverts*, 28 April 1915, p. 2. C. Zhitlovsky, *Gezamlte shriftn* vol. 8, Warsaw: Brzoza, 1929, pp. 37–8, 51. See also A. Veslof's opinion in the anarchist *Fraye arbeter shtime*, 21 November 1914, p. 5.

12. Borokhov wrote in *Varhayt*, 8 January 1915, p. 4. Other Jewish radicals are quoted in Rappaport, *Hands Across the Sea*, pp. 28–30. Cherikover wrote in *Tog*, 20 January 1916, p. 4; 27 July 1916, p. 4. Litvak wrote in the JSF's organ, *Di naye velt*, 7 January 1916, p. 5. For the neutralist position see L.B. Boudin, *Socialism and War*, New York: New Review Publishing, 1916, pp. 198–212; See also the anarchist periodical *Mother Earth*, August 1914, p. 178; November 1914, p. 281; and the Yiddish anarchist newspaper *Fraye arbeter shtime*, 26 December 1914, p. 4; M. Mintz, *New Times – New Tunes: Ber Borokhov, 1914–1917*, Tel Aviv: Am Oved, 1988, pp. 37–8, 49, 270–9 (Hebrew).

13. *MZ*, 24 June 24, 1915, p. 4. Cahan is quoted in the *New York Times*, 2 May 1915, p. 5: *Forverts*, 11 August 1915, pp. 4–5. The ad was published in *YT*, 15 December 1916, p. 8. See a similar ad in the humorist *Groyser kundes* (Big Stick), 13 October 1914, p. 10. Linguist Hirsh Abramovitch recounted how "almost" all the Jews in Vilna were elated by the German conquest of the city (September 1915) in *Farshvundene geshtaltn: zikhroynes un siluetn*, Buenos Aires: Tsentral farband fun poylishe yidn in argentine, 1958, pp. 262–4, 297–8. See also V.G. Liulevicius, *War Land on the Eastern Front: Culture, National Identity, and the German Occupation in World War I*, Cambridge, UK: Cambridge University Press, 2000, pp. 17–21.

14. Szajkowski, *Jews, Wars, and Communism*, vol. 1, pp. 66–7; See the reports in *Tog*, 4 April 1915, p. 8; 16 April 1915, p. 1; *Varhayt*, 18 April 1915, p. 1; *Forverts*, 16 August 1916, p. 4. See also Hillel Rogoff's article in the *Tsukunft*, November 1916, p. 903. Rappaport, *Hands Across the Sea*, pp. 48–9. See also F.C. Luebke, *Bonds of Loyalty: German-Americans and World War I*, Dekalb: Northern Illinois University Press, 1974.

15. *Groyser kundes*, 7 August 1914, p. 8; *Varhayt*, 14 January 1915, p. 8; *Tog*, 14 April 1916, p. 4.

16. An-ski, "Khurbm galitsye," pp. 6–9, 24–9. I. Gutman, "Jews – Poles – Antisemitism," in I. Bartal and I. Gutman (Eds.), *The Broken Chain: Polish Jewry through the Ages. II. Society, Culture, Nationalism*, Jerusalem: Merkaz Zalman Shazar, 2001, pp. 612–17 (Hebrew); V. Shulman, "In di yorn fun der ershter velt-milkhome," in A. Menes (Ed.), *Di yidn in poyln*, New York: By a committee, 1946, pp. 751–8; E. Mendelsohn, *The Jews of East Central Europe Between the World Wars*, Bloomington: Indiana University Press, 1983, p. 21.

17. *New York Times*, 8 January 1915, p. 3 (the Yiddish version was published in *Varhayt* a day earlier). The Hausner episode was covered in *Varhayt*, 19 April 1915, p. 4; 30 April 1915, p. 1; *YT*, 30 April 1915, p. 1. Hausner called the audience "pogromists" – See Bernstein's respective letters (16 March 1915 and 6 May 1915) to Josef Hoffman and to Dr. Kaplansky, *Herman Bernstein Papers* (YIVO), folders #168, #176. See also *Tog*, 16 November 1914, p. 4. Zetser wrote in *Tsukunft*, November 1916, p. 943. *Ha-toren*, 28 July 1916, pp. 1–2. A. Kapiszewski, "Polish-Jewish Conflicts in the United States at the Beginning of World War I," *Polish American Studies* 48, 1991, pp. 63–78.

18. A. Polonsky, "Introduction – The Shtetl: Myth and Reality," *Polin* 17, 2004, pp. 5–10. G. Hundert, "The Implications of Jewish Economic Activities for Christian-Jewish Relations in the Polish Commonwealth," in C. Abramsky, M. Jachimczyk and A. Polonsky (Eds.), *The Jews in Poland*, Oxford: Basil Blackwell, 1986, pp. 55–63. A vivid description of market days may be seen in the memoir of Galician-born Louis Borgenicht, *The Happiest Man*, pp. 42–3. Also see W.P. Zenner, "Middlemen Minority Theories and the Jews: Historical Survey and Assessment," *Working Papers in Yiddish and East European Jewish Studies* 31, 1978, pp. 1–30; S. Kassow, "Shtetl," in G. Hundert (Ed.), *The YIVO Encyclopedia of Jews in Eastern Europe* vol. 2, YIVO and Yale University Press, 2008, pp. 1732–6; E. Hoffman, *Shtetl: The Life and Death of a Small Town and the World of Polish Jews*, New York: Houghton Mifflin, 1997, pp. 73–109.

19. The most illuminating studies of Jewish folklore are in Yiddish. The quotes are from I.L. Cahan, *Der yid: vegn zikh un vegn andere in zayne shprikhverter un rednsortn*, New York: YIVO, 1933, pp. 25–32; N. Stutchkov, *Der oytser fun der yidisher shprakh*, New York: YIVO, 1950, pp. 167–8; Y. Mark, "A zamlung volksfarglaykhen," *Yidishe shprakh* 5, 1945, pp. 99–140; A. Funkenstein, "The Dialectics of Assimilation," *Jewish Social Studies* 1, 1995, pp. 1–13. See also B. Borokhov, "Di oyfgaben fun der yidisher filologye," in Sh. Niger (Ed.), *Der pinkes*, Vilna: B.A. Kletskin, 1912–13, p. 11; D. Sadan, *A Bowl of Raisins, or, A Thousand and One Jokes*, Tel Aviv: Mordecai Newman, 1950, pp. 395–411 (Hebrew); I. Bernshteyn, *Yudishe shprikhverter un rednsarten*, 1908, reprinted Wiesbaden: Fourier, 1988, p. 53; H. Schwarzbaum, "Jews and Gentiles in Folklore," *Yeda-'Am* 15, 1971, pp. 55–61 (Hebrew with English abstract).

20. I.A. Beneqvit, *Durkhgelebt un durkhgetrakht* vol. 1, New York: Kultur federatsye, 1934, pp. 104–5. See also M.R. Cohen, *A Dreamer's Journey*, Glenco: Free Press, 1949, pp. 27–8, 219; M. Weinreich, *History of the Yiddish Language* (trans. J.A. Fishman), Chicago: University of Chicago Press, 1980, pp. 193–4. I. Bartal, "Non-Jews and Gentile Society in East-European Hebrew and Yiddish literature, 1856–1914," Ph.D. Dissertation, Jerusalem: Hebrew University, 1980, pp. 257–9 (Hebrew).

21. Y. Rolnik, *Zikhroynes*, New York: With the help of the David Ignatoff Fund, 1954, pp. 19, 33. A.P. Unger, *Mayn heymshtetl strykov*, New York: Arbeter Ring, 1957, pp. 49–50. I.J. Singer, *Fun a velt vos iz nishtu mer*, New York: Matones, 1946, p. 208. See also M. Kushner, *Lebn un kamf fun a kloakmakher*, New York: Published by a committee from local 9, International Ladies' Garment Workers' Union, 1960, p. 56; B. Tsukerman, *Zikhroynes* vol. 1, New York: Yidisher kemfer, 1962, pp. 22–3, 47–8.

22. H. Abramovitch, "Onvayzungen un bamerkungen," *Yidishe shprakh* 12, 1952, pp. 122–3; Stutchkov, *Der oytser*, p. 214. See the negative portrayal of Polish and

Lithuanian peasants aboard a ship to America, *Yudisher emigrant*, 28 January 1909, p. 10; A. Drori, "Mokraja-Kaligurka," *He-avar* 19, 1972, pp. 231–2 (Hebrew with English abstract).

23. A very positive depiction of Polish nobles is in the Hebrew novel *Ayit Tsavua* ("The Hypocrite," 1858–64) by Abraham Mapu, in *The Complete Works of Abraham Mapu*, Tel Aviv: Dvir, 1959, pp. 373–6 (Hebrew pagination). See also I. Bartal, "The Porets and the Arendar: The Depiction of Poles in Jewish Literature," *The Polish Review* 32, 1987, pp. 357–9; M.J. Rosman, "Jewish Perceptions of Insecurity and Powerlessness in 16th–18th Century Poland," *Polin* 1, 1986, pp. 19–27; idem, *The Lords' Jews: Magnate-Jewish Relations in the Polish-Lithuanian Commonwealth During the Eighteenth Century*, Cambridge: Harvard University Press, 1990, pp. ix–xi, 206–212; G.D. Hundert, *Jews in Poland-Lithuania in the Eighteenth Century: A Genealogy of Modernity*, Berkeley: University of California Press, 2004, pp. 38–44; W.J. Cahnman, *Jews & Gentiles: A Historical Sociology of their Relations*, New Brunswick: Transaction, 2004, pp. 80–5.

24. Y. Kotik, *Mayne zikhroynes* vol. 1, Warsaw: A. Gitlin, 1913, pp. 10–14, 20; D. Assaf (Ed.), *Journey To a Nineteenth-Century Shtetl: The Memoirs of Yekhezkel Kotik*, Detroit: Wayne State University Press, 2002, pp. 78–9, 114–15. The story with the dog is by Shoshana Goldenberg from Lithuania, story #913 (Israeli Folktale Archives, Haifa University). The green fabric is by Dvora Lipkind-Fus who heard it from her mother in a *shtetl* near Vilna (translated to the Hebrew by Israel Rosenthal), account #652 (ibid.). See also accounts #291, #331, #688, #714, #773, #1913, #4340 (ibid.). A late-eighteenth-century portrayal of *pritsim* as ignorant and immoral is by S. Maimon, *An Autobiography* (translated from the German by J.C. Murray 1888), reprinted Urbana: University of Illinois Press, 2001, p. 81. See the stories about *pritsim* in A. Katz's folktales, *Yeda-'Am* 2, 1953, pp. 61–4 (Hebrew with English abstract) and in those by D. Rubin, *Yeda-'Am* 14, 1969, p. 80 (Hebrew with English abstract).

25. Schur's letter to Yosef Yehuda Leib Sossnitz (31 March 1892) is printed in E.R. Malachi (Ed.), *Igrot Sofrim*, New York: By Dr. Simon Miller, 1931, pp. 120–1 (Hebrew). See also S. Levin, *Memories of my Life* vol. 3, (trans. Z. Vislevsky), Tel Aviv: Dvir, 1935, pp. 15–16 (Hebrew); I. Bartal, "The Image of Germany and German Jewry in East European Jewish Society During the 19th Century," in Isadore Twersky (Ed.), *Danzig, Between East and West: Aspects of Modern Jewish History*, Cambridge: Harvard University Press, 1985, pp. 3–17.

26. Borgenicht, *The Happiest Man*, p. 305. C. Zhitlovsky, *Zikhroynes fun mayn lebn* vol. 1, New York: Zhitlovsky's Jubilee Committee, 1935, pp. 160–1, 166–7. There are many other examples: For example, see the letter by someone who identified as "Not a German" in *Kol mevaser*, 19 November 1870, p. 343 (Yiddish); A.Y. Paperna, *Kol ha-ktavim*, edited by I. Zmora, Tel Aviv: Machbarot le-Sifrut, 1952, pp. 318–19 (Hebrew); A. Reyzin, *Epizodn fun mayn lebn* vol. 1, Vilna: Kletskin, 1929, pp. 7–8; Rolnik, *Zikhroynes*, p. 109.

27. News reports and memoirs about such encounters with hostile Germans abound: *Ha-magid*, 4 September 1884, p. 301; *Ha-tsefirah*, 5 November 1891, p. 942; *Yudisher emigrant*, 27 November 1908, pp. 12–13; B. Vaynshteyn, *Fertsik yor in der yidisher arbeter bavegung*, New York: Veker, 1924, pp. 15–16; Y. Kopelov, *Amol in amerike*, Warsaw: Brzoza, 1928, pp. 15–18; M. Weisgal, *So Far: An Autobiography*, New York: Random House, 1971, p. 19. M. Antin, *The Promised Land*, 1912, new ed., New York: Penguin, 1997, pp. 138–9; P. Nadell, "The Journey to America by Steam: The Jews of Eastern Europe in Transition," *American Jewish History* 71, 1981, pp. 269–84; Z. Szajkowski, "Sufferings of Jewish Emigrants to America in Transit to America through Germany," *Jewish Social Studies* 39, 1977, pp. 105–16; G. Alroey, *The Quiet Revolution: Jewish Emigration from the Russian Empire, 1875–1924*, Jerusalem: Merkaz Zalman Shazar, 2008, pp. 150–91 (Hebrew). On German policy toward transient immigrants see J. Wertheimer, *Unwelcome*

Strangers: East European Jews in Imperial Germany, New York: Oxford University Press, 1987, pp. 50–1, 176–81.

28. The friend is Dovid Shub, *Fun di amolike yorn*, p. 450. Tsivyen wrote in the organ of the Workmen's Circle, *Der fraynd*, August 1917, p. 9.

29. See, for example, the words of Sholem Ash and A. Glanz-Leyeles (respectively) against the Poles in *MZ*, 12 December 1918, p. 1; *Tog*, 30 May 1919, p. 6. See also A. Kapiszewski, *Conflicts Across the Atlantic: Essays on Polish-Jewish Relation in the United States During World War I and in the Interwar Period*, Krakow: Ksiegarnia Akademicka, 2004, pp. 137–226.

14 Ben Gurion and the onset of war

Yossi Goldstein

In the autumn of 1946, David Ben Gurion reached the conclusion that war between the *Yishuv* (the Jewish Settlement in the Land of Israel) and the Arabs living in the area was inevitable.[1] For the next year and a half he devoted most of his thought, his time and his efforts to preparing for the day when the *Yishuv* would face this situation. And then, on May 12, 1948, *Minhelet HaAm* (The National Council), the body that ruled the *Yishuv*, was forced to decide on the question of whether to declare the establishment of the State of Israel two days later, on the day the last British soldier would leave the country. The Council's alternative was to accept an American proposal, behind which was an Arab initiative, that would postpone for the meanwhile the declaration of the new state, in return for which the US would put pressure on the Arabs to freeze their intentions to make war.[2] Ben Gurion decided to reject the American initiative and gave those members of the Council who leaned towards supporting the US proposal no choice whatsoever, that is to say coerced them into rejecting the initiative, and within two days declared the establishment of the State of Israel. On the very next day, as everyone expected, the regular armies of five Arab states invaded the country, joining the local Palestinian militias which had been attacking Jewish settlements since the passing of the UN resolution to partition the country into separate Jewish and Arab states, and full-scale war broke out. Israel's War of Independence had commenced.

In the discussion below we will try to understand and analyze the leader of the *Yishuv's* thought processes, his political philosophy and ideology, so that we can try to understand his motivation in rejecting the American proposal, despite the fact that it was very clear to him that such a rejection would mean the outbreak of war.

I.

Ben Gurion believed in three basic justifications for Zionism and the establishment of a Jewish state. First, he believed deeply in "the historical connection between the People of Israel and the Land of Israel."[3] According to his thinking:

> It is an historical fact that the Jewish People's homeland is the Land of Israel; it was here that the Jews lived as a nation; it was here that they had lived in

national independence, sometimes fully, sometimes less; it was here that their national works came into being, works that were to leave their stamp on the whole of Jewish history and, to a large extent, on the history of mankind.[4]

Second, he understood anti-Semitism as a permanent, perpetual phenomenon:

That the People of Israel have suffered terrible distress and have undergone appalling tribulations is the key and fundamental fact – not the hell of Hitler, not the present destruction of European Jewry, not the pogroms of Czarist Russia, since these are not fundamental, but rather random phenomena dependent on time. I am speaking of the tribulations and distress of the People of Israel as a constant phenomenon inherent in the very fact of our being in exile, a phenomenon which has occurred in all countries and at all times without any exceptions – even in places where there is no Hitler, even in places where there are no pogroms, even in places where there are no persecutions and no banning of Jews. It is manifested nevertheless by i) a lack of independence: there is no place in the world where the Jews have sovereign independence; ii) a lack of a homeland: there is no place in the world where Jews, as Jews, have a homeland of their own; and iii) everywhere Jews are a minority. The combination of these three things is what makes the Jewish People different from other nations in the world and this is a basic and major fact on which Zionism as a platform is based.[5]

And not just this. As far as Ben Gurion was concerned, the Holocaust proved the undeniable necessity of establishing the state, without which, as was unequivocally made clear by the Second World War, the Jewish People could not survive:

I do not know if any person can express the horror of the Holocaust. Trivial words will be nothing more than a profanation of the pain. So I myself will not attempt to recount the destruction and ruination . . . It is not only that six million Jews were destroyed with satanic malice aforethought – something that had never occurred previously, even in our own history, but that it completely undermined and destroyed the foundation on which Jewish history in the Exile has been based to the present day. The ground has been removed from under the very existence of the people and if we do not quickly find something that our national existence can hold on to, who knows if we will be able to survive."[6]

Ben Gurion's third basic assumption was his belief that Zionism without *Aliyah* (the immigration of the Jewish People to the Land of Israel) was untenable:

The war for *Aliyah* – a war we are conducting every minute of our lives – is our main war and this war which will determine our existence and our future. The (British) Mandate without *Aliyah* empties Zionism of meaning . . . making the chance of establishment of a Jewish state a dead letter, if prior to the establishment of the State, the country is closed to Jewish immigration.[7]

II.

Ben Gurion, therefore, saw in the unequivocal connection of the Jews to the Land of Israel, in the existence of anti-Semitism as a perpetual phenomenon and in the need for *Aliyah*, the main reasons for the establishment of a Jewish state and the justification of Zionism. Despite all this, it was clear to him that the Arab block states would do everything they could to prevent the establishment of a Jewish national home in the land. In the thinking of the leader of the *Yishuv*, there was no logic in this, for a number of reasons: their frequent claim that there was not enough room in the country for two peoples lacked any factual base:

> At the end of the Second Temple Period some four million Jews were living in the Land of Israel. Could it be that now the country is incapable of containing a few more million? There is no doubt whatsoever that it could! Today the Land of Israel is half desolate and devastated.[8]

A further Arab claim that the main intention of the Zionists in establishing a state was to oust them from the country also lacked any foundation:

> The calumny of our planning to oust the Arab population . . . has been examined and has been proved to be false . . . the Jews came to the country not to improve the condition of the Arab population but to build their national home here. Jewish settlement is not a means of achieving the Zionist objective – it is the objective itself: to solve the question of the Jewish People and to resettle them anew in their ancient homeland. However, the nature of Jewish settlement is such that it entails Jewish production activities which have brought to the country and to all its inhabitants the benefit of the results of the *Aliyah* and the settlement . . . the Jewish settlement has been a blessing for all those living in the country and has helped to improve the quality of life of the Arab population.[9]

And more than this:

> The Jews are not returning to Arab Palestine. In realizing their right to return to Zion they are creating a new "Land of Israel" – a new economy, a new agriculture and new industries. They are establishing a new Jewish Knesset that stands on its own feet and is not dependent on the Arab population nor appropriates anything from them. The Jews are not settling in Arab villages – they are building new villages; they are not living in Arab cities, they are founding new cities. They are plowing and sowing their fields with their own hands, and in the same way they are planting their trees, building their houses and setting up factories – and we are claiming the right of the Jewish people

to continue this enterprise. It might be possible to wrest this right from us by physical force – but in no circumstances would it be possible for the Jewish People to renounce it. The Land of Israel is our homeland by right and in law, and we do not recognize its exclusive ownership by the Arabs.[10]

This, therefore, was the reason that the resolution of the United Nations General Assembly on November 29, 1947 that was passed in the by a large majority and supported by the two rival superpowers – the US and the USSR – the decision on the partition of the Land of Israel into two sovereign states, was seen by Ben Gurion as an act of historical justice:

> To re-establish the sovereign state of the Jewish People in part of its ancient homeland is an act of historic justice which atones, at least in part, for unparalleled atrocities suffered by the Jewish People in our generation and in preceding generations for more than one thousand eight hundred years. It is a great moral victory for the United Nations ideal . . . the Jewish People will remember with gratitude the efforts of the two great superpowers – the United States of America and the Union of Soviet Socialist Republics – as well as all the other states, small and large who brought this about . . . the Jewish People that never succumbed to despair even during the bleakest hours in its history and never lost its faith in itself or in the conscience of mankind, shall not fail, in this great hour, to grasp the historic opportunity and responsibility that it has been given. Judah, renewed, will take up its honorable place in the United Nations as a factor for peace, prosperity and progress in the Holy Land, in the Near East and in the world as a whole.[11]

III.

The Arabs, of course, did not agree with Ben Gurion's assumptions. They regarded the country as belonging exclusively to them and Zionism as an imperialistic provocation seeking to oust them from their land. This was the reason why, therefore, they made the decision to fight against the establishment of the Jewish state to the bitter end. Fighting a war for the country from their point of view, was, and remained the only option. This was also the reason that Ben Gurion made the unequivocal decision:

> We have to see the danger for what it is – and the thwarting of this danger must play a central role in Zionist concerns, in Zionist planning and in Zionist activity as a whole. It requires there be a change in all Zionist strategy, external and internal and the concentration of all our efforts and abilities toward this primary objective – security. We must recruit the means and the manpower in the *Yishuv* and among the Jewish People as a whole to repulse this danger – which it is possible to do. In the same way as there is no doubt that the danger exists – I have no doubt of the possibility of staving it off. And the concern for security involves, first and foremost, the organization of

a Jewish armed force, its training and equipping. But this is not all: we are obliged to defend all our positions in the country and, indeed, expand them. Without expansion – continuous and very fast growth by enlarging our enterprise and significantly increasing the size of the *Yishuv* – there is no way of ensuring our security.[12]

It is no wonder then, that the putting together of a defense force, according to Ben Gurion, was the primary task of Zionism at that time:

> I only want to stress now the obligation of the *Yishuv*, of the Zionist Movement, and of the Jewish People, to see the full scope of the problem of security in all its severity and in all its urgency, and to see the danger likely to befall the *Yishuv* in the country. This perhaps may not be today or tomorrow – the Arab countries are not yet ready to make their move – but we are about to see major changes, a transformation, and we must not wait until the danger is fully developed. We must act immediately with our maximum technical and financial ability. This, in my opinion, is the first task of Zionism at this time. I will not start listing the essential and extremely severe matters that need to be dealt with – there are two or three – but the problem of security is central, since it is here that there is a threat to the basis of our existence. What is required now is a new approach to the problem, greater means are required, a reorganization of our forces and a preparedness of a totally new order.[13]

And indeed, in December 1946 Ben Gurion was appointed to be in charge of the management of the security of the *Yishuv*, at the same time serving as chairman of the Executive of the Jewish Agency. He began to implement the major changes that were required in his opinion for the building of an army. In the course of June 1947 he appointed Yisrael Galili as head of the National Command of the pre-State defense force, the *Haganah*, Yaacov Drori as its chief of staff, and Yigael Yadin (then Sukenik) as head of its Operations Division. Simultaneously he began to implement changes in the frameworks that carried out the activities of the *Haganah*, and gave their powers to the "General Staff" and to "the National Command." He designed all these moves with one single purpose in mind: the founding of a full-fledged army:

> We want to establish a Jewish army. For us it is more essential than for any other people whatsoever or for any other country whatsoever in the world; we have more enemies than any other people and require more self-defense than anyone else in the world. We want to establish a Jewish army and to have its beginnings in this country.[14]

From Ben Gurion's point of view the establishment of the army was part of the general struggle for the Land of Israel:

> This struggle to establish a Jewish army is not yet finished. In the same way as we are working toward the establishment of a Jewish state and are not

waiting for the world to declare our right and make us a gift: "Here take your country," but are rather acquiring it foot by foot, tree by tree, house by house – so also with the creation of a Jewish army: we will not wait until they declare our right to have one. In the same way as we acquired the land foot by foot and planted each tree and built each house, it wasn't for the foot of land or the tree or the house, but for the vision called "homeland" – a vision that includes our own economy, culture and administration as well as Jewish independence recognized in international law – so also will we build an army: first one unit, then a second and then a third. Our intention is to build an organized Jewish army, with all its units, its organization, its flag, its language, its High Command."[15]

IV.

It would seem that Ben Gurion's mode of thought was clear and simple: the Jews needed to establish a state of their own in the Land of Israel. They had no other option. They were willing to live in their country alongside the Arab population, but the Arabs were opposed to this and would do everything, using any means possible, including military means, to prevent them living in their country. War, therefore, from Ben Gurion's viewpoint, was inevitable. Therefore the Jewish *Yishuv* would have to live by the sword, to establish an army and to prepare for war. The next anticipated step was war that would be declared by the Palestinian Arabs in the country and the Arab countries abroad.

V.

Was the *Yishuv* prepared for this unavoidable war? The unequivocal response to this question by the *Yishuv*'s leader, in charge of its security, was positive! In the same dramatic meeting, mentioned above, on May 12, 1948, he did indeed claim so, in these words:

> Sooner or later the Arab armies will invade the country and the only question that we have before us now is: Do we see a realistic possibility of resisting this invasion, or not? And if we have to summarize the answer in one sentence, it would be: by increasing the manpower, by recruiting and training at home and abroad and with the possibility of increasing military equipment (partly by manufacture in the country and partly, a larger part, by bringing what we have bought to the country) – we can resist the invasion and even overcome the enemy, not without casualties and distress, and the *Yishuv* should be prepared for this.
>   In this matter – this is what I mean. What I am saying is: the situation is difficult and there are many dangers. And this is not what is being heard. Only the positive side of the things that I talk about is being heard – the negative side is ignored. But people should not be so optimistic – though that is how the *Yishuv* is. However, despite all this, with moral fortitude and

the conditions to deploy adequate directed manpower together with the increased equipment – we have every possibility, though with many distressing casualties, of achieving victory.[16]

Notes

1. The various details on the life of Ben Gurion are taken from S. Tevet, *Kin'at David: The Life of David Ben-Gurion*, vols. 1–4, Jerusalem and Tel Aviv: Shoken, 1976–2004 (Hebrew).
2. It is disputed whether there was a discussion on this matter at this meeting. In the minutes of the meeting (Minutes of *Minhelet HaAm*, 12 May 1948, State Archives (SA)), there are only vague hints relating to the vote on the subject. Zev Sharf, the Secretary of the Council at the time, wrote about this explicitly and we accept his explanation. See Z. Sharf, *Three Days, 12–14 May 1948*, Tel Aviv: Am Oved, 1965 (Hebrew). I. Ilam, "The Declaration of Independence, the Drama, the Myth and the Historical Truth," *Kivunim Hadashim* 12, 2005, pp. 92–119 (Hebrew); Also compare: M. Sarid, "The Declaration of the State – The Historical Truth about the Fateful Vote," *Kivunim Hadashim* 13, 2006, pp. 155–157 (Hebrew); Y. Goldstein, "The Reply of a Lazy Historian," *Kivunim Hadashim* 13, 2006, pp. 157–169 (Hebrew); idem, "Why was Ben Gurion Interested in Rewriting History?" *Ha'aretz*, 14 May 2006 (Hebrew).
3. From a speech Ben Gurion delivered at a seminar of the Histadrut labor organization in Rehovot, in Nissan 5701 (March 1941), from Ben Gurion's archives at Sedeh Boker (BGA).
4. Ibid.
5. Ibid.
6. Ben Gurion speaking at the World Zionist Conference in London on 2 August 1945, BGA.
7. D. Ben Gurion, "Our Task at this Hour," a speech written (in Hebrew) on 18 March 1938, apparently never actually delivered; BGA.
8. D. Ben Gurion, "Towards the Future," *HaToren*, 25 June 1915 (Hebrew).
9. D. Ben Gurion, "The Book of Evil," *Ha'aretz*, 18 May 1939 (Hebrew).
10. Ben Gurion speaking at the St. James' Conference, London, 11 February 1939; Public Record Office, London; Foreign Office 371/23223.
11. From the front page of *Davar*, 30 November 1947 (Hebrew).
12. Ben Gurion speaking at the 22nd Zionist Conference, 18 December 1946, Stenographic Report, Jerusalem, Zionist Archives.
13. Ibid.
14. *Davar*, 30 May 1948.
15. Ben Gurion speaking at a gathering of recruits, Passover 5703 [April 1943], BGA.
16. Minutes of the Meeting of *Minhelet Ha'Am* (the National Council), 12 May 1948, SA.

15 The journey after – of one who saw the horrors of war

A study of Orpaz's *The Voyage of Daniel*

Ziva Feldman

A discussion of Orpaz's literary work *The Voyage of Daniel*,[1] requires us to take a look at his philosophical essay, *The Pilgrim*,[2] on the assumption that they mirror each other. Hence, in this discussion I shall attempt to examine the following points:

1   How Orpaz's *The Voyage of Daniel*, relates to the painful problem of shellshock, using Daniel as the principal character of the story.
2.   Since Orpaz's essay, *The Pilgrim*, relates to a pilgrim who has no holy place to reach, as opposed to the religious pilgrim; to what extent can Daniel be seen as Orpaz's secular pilgrim figure who sets out on a journey after a grain of sand?

The story of *The Voyage of Daniel* is the story of an Israeli soldier, who comes home and tries to cope with the reality of the situation after a war. The novel opens with the words: "Daniel Dror came back from the war extremely tired. He slept for two days . . . his hands folded behind his head, not moving."[3] Daniel's behavior is typical shellshock behavior, alienated from his mother and from friends, seeing only the black hole in the stomach of the dead soldier. This can be seen as a description of the post-traumatic state of a solder who has experienced death in battle. "The more the trauma is acute and the longer it lasts, the more it will distort the victim's mental processes, forcing him to adopt desperate strategic survival strategies to deal with the inhuman reality . . . these strategies may take the form of mental warps such as dichotomization, alienation, amnesia and so forth."[4] This is in fact a state of traumatic stress "in which a person is helpless in the face of an external threat on his life and does not have the resources (internal or external) to cope. As a consequence of this condition his personality is changed, the primary change being the undermining of faith in the regularity of the laws of nature that exist in the world and the self . . ."[5] And so Daniel attempts to cut himself off from the grim experience that keeps coming back to him, creating symptoms that make the post-traumatic syndrome even worse. Many times this brings about a withdrawal from involvement with others and distancing himself from those close to him. Judith Lewis Herman goes further and claims that "traumatic events undermine even basic human relationships. They tear to shreds relationships with family and friends, relationships with girlfriends and love, relationships with the community . . . and turn them into an existential crisis."[6] Daniel cannot continue his relationship with his girlfriend, and also cannot live in the same house with his mother and her ludicrous boyfriend, who tries to take the place of his father. He cuts himself off and when anyone addresses him his replies have no connection with the questions being asked. When his mother says to him: "We have given the matter a lot of thought, so that you can start being yourself again, Danny. So that you can start being yourself again."[7] Daniel replies: "Pretty Polly," and their response immediately sets him off bird squawking. He cuts himself off from his mother and asks: "and now I want you to leave me alone . . . I want to go to pot in peace."[8] He wants to go to pot in peace among the meandering sand dunes.

Daniel often hallucinates and dreams. His dreams are a translation of his own existential reality. In his dreams everything becomes mixed up – the sand with the man and the black hole:

> Light-flooded expanses of glittering sand and above the light – darkness. Solders with sloping helmets are trying, while jumping about funnily, to get a stretcher into a pit. The pit is too short and cannot take the stretcher . . . and this game is shaking up the man on the stretcher, who is sitting on it and holding on to it so as not to fall off. The man is dressed in white cloth pants and has a big hole under his chest . . .[9]

People in a post-traumatic condition suffer from nightmares: "Any attempt to moderate the effects of post-traumatic stress disturbances is without doubt an inadequate, if human, endeavor to save people from the full force of their nightmares and from undergoing the repeated experience of the trauma that is paralyzing them, phenomena that are the aftermath of the memories of atrocities of battle . . ."[10] Kot refers to this experience as a black hole,[11] a post-traumatic expression parallel to what Daniel experienced. In other words, one can relate metaphorically to the "black hole" in Daniel's dreams as the traumatic fear that paralyzes all sufferers, because of his memories of his terrifying experience. Daniel experienced the "black hole" in his hallucinations and in his dreams, day and night. It is this mental state which makes him leave on his pilgrimage.

Having said this, the question of whether Daniel's journey to the sea and the grain of sand is the journey of the *secular pilgrim* needs to be examined. The sea calls to Daniel and he goes to it on a journey of self-observation, on the thin line between reality and fantasy, between certainty and absence. Here the sea should be understood as the place to which people in states of suicidal depression go, and it is where they are searched for, to try to save them. Orpaz gives expression to this in directing Daniel's journey to the sea:

> There are types of fish that on a particular day, are drawn by the power of some ancient memory, uproot themselves from the river and return to the sea. Daniel seems to be someone returning to the sea. Hidden feelings are

set in motion in his body. His metamorphosis was slow, but keenly felt . . . new power flowed into his limbs . . . though not fully, since he was not yet completely weaned of the stress of the memories by day and the dreams by night. But these also underwent significant change.[12]

The beginning of the journey is through the power of the ancient memory that draws him to the sea, from which the process of change will start. This is not a search after holiness, but a search after the internal essence of the self-observer. The secular pilgrim is a pilgrim without a holy place: "His pilgrimage is a mental activity, a certain thirst, unease, rebellion, a pilgrimage that is an end in itself." [13] Thus *"death, eternity, God – these are different names for one unknown."*[14] Daniel also says things using this formula: "So they are also capable perhaps of giving this thing a name. Perhaps there are those who call it God. It is foolish in my opinion to call this thing God, just because it lacks a name. . ."[15] This unknown is translated into uncertainty in the modern world, wherein lies the vitality of the "secular pilgrim." So Orpaz says: "The journey of the secular pilgrim is in its innermost essence the journey of the observer"[16] – the observation in this novel is an internal journey, and in this there is an ironic aspect involved primarily with the status of the Absent. "The secular pilgrim is a typical existentialistic model,"[17] expressing a journey of far-outness from the world. So Daniel tries "to introduce the extraordinary into a flat world, as well as the absurd, as a result of this same flatness."[18]

Orpaz claims that in contemporary fiction the feeling is that the significant thing that takes places between the main characters is something outside the story itself, something that is not comprehended – something that does not exist, that is "without manifestation, without definition, beyond law."[19] The person conducts a one-way dialogue with this Absent Thing. This is the stance of the person in the face of the Absence; it is what turns him, in this way, into a secular pilgrim. In the light of this, Daniel's departure to the sea is not in its essence a negative flight, since it is part of the process of introducing himself to reality and the attempt to understand it. This comes at the end of the novel where it is written: "His hand hovered lightly on the door handle."[20] That is to say, he cannot return absolutely to the reality that existed prior to the war, but there is an attempt to return and to touch. Thus the pilgrim does not return absolutely and he, like Sisyphus, will try to roll the boulder again to the top of the mountain. He will seek significance in the Absence which can be very present for him, as observing the place of one who is not there. Daniel looks at the empty chair that was his father's, and at the bridge where they once walked together. He sees his father's empty seat and so feels his presence. This presence is the Nothingness that can be seen, as compared with God who is not present and is entirely absent, just as Beckett expressed it in *Waiting for Godot*. Therefore, the father, as educator and instructor, is compared with God and Absence. This can be found in Hebrew fiction in Judith Hendel's novel, The Psychologist's Madness. This Absence is a mystery which does have a presence "within the story and is indefinable outside of it, it is what draws the story to it and what activates its characters."[21]

The secular pilgrim is a rebel. From this point of view Daniel is also rebelling against the insufferable existential condition of war. This is done through realistic-yet-fanciful writing to describe the modern lonely world of individuals. Orpaz says: I write about separate individuals, about one individual man and another individual man . . . a collection of individuals."[22] Daniel leaves on a journey as a "secular pilgrim" searching for the essence of things in a grain of sand, as a microcosm that can include everything and within it all the beginnings in the genesis of the world. Therefore his journey can be regarded as a dialogue, together with Blake's poem that says: "To see a world in a grain of sand, And a heaven in a wild flower. Hold infinity in the palm of your hand, And eternity in an hour."[23] Daniel also learns to see into a grain of sand: "His hand was stretched out in front of his eyes with a few grains of sands still on it. He covered his eyes with one of them and it grew and got bigger. And as it continued to grow it opened up toward the light . . ."[24] This looking into a grain of sand is what allowed him existence in Nothingness.

The journey of observation begins with the nausea that seizes Daniel from the situation in which he finds himself: "the wide black hole in the stomach of the man who has been put to sleep . . . it is I who did it. It is I who dispatched the bullet in him. On the other hand, it was nighttime and I didn't see the man, I could only see shadows . . ."[25] This is exactly the state of existential uncertainty in which Daniel exists when dreaming of battle, which will lead to the feeling of nausea: "Daniel went . . . and vomited a lot . . ."[26] In Sartre's *La nausée* too the feeling of nausea is the beginning of a voyage of self-discovery, as Sartre writes in his book.[27] The nausea leads to awareness of the ego and to the empty understanding of our existence. War is the place for nausea, so Sartre writes this after a war which saw the collapse of all ideologies and ideals. This is literature which is involved in looking at the black hole of the wound, which brings nausea on. This is Daniel's heroism: he was a first class soldier who was stunned and as a result went into shellshock. Out of the heroism comes the black hole that causes nausea, which is what haunts him and causes him to leave on his journey as a secular pilgrim. In Sartre's *La nausée* there is disappointment with all connections with life and the universe. Daniel's nausea begins at the point that he realizes that the place from which he drew his milk, his mother's breasts, has passed into the hands of a nauseating, ludicrous stranger.

Sartre does not see this as a religious discovery but rather as a "philosophical discovery that is, in a certain way, a sort of opposite of a religious discovery . . . a discovery which starts with an expression of astonishment at a stone gown and comes to a climax at an encounter with the trunk of a chestnut tree . . . which can be called disrobing the universe, changing the appearance of the face of the world for the purpose of shattering illusions."[28] The discovery occurs through the creation of a direct connection with nature. If, with Sartre, illusions are shattered through observing a stone gown and a chestnut tree, with Daniel it is through observing a grain of sand and a palm tree. The palm, as part of the Israeli landscape, is in his hallucinations, which are his memories from the war. So it can be said of Daniel: "and he sees the man under the palm tree with a sort of problem, his hands resting on the sand, and an unpretentious silence on his face. And the man is attentive to the life which is flowing from his sleepy limbs into the sand and from there to the grass and the stone, to the palm tree and the wing of the eagle."[29] Again we have the observation of Nothingness and Absence. In this case, the Nothingness of the dead man.

Daniel turns to a grain of sand, to the sea and to the palm tree and receives from them signs that he should continue his journey. So Daniel knows that the sea is speaking to him and through it he will also understand his god, and this way aspires to reach the secrets of Creation and to understand the things themselves. This penetration into the sea is in fact a form of re-entering the womb and so he is hurt, because the sea is not yet ready to accept him. This can be understood from the burning he gets when he first dips in the sea, and from the clam that he refuses to eat, saying at the same time: "The sea has spit you up and to the sea I will return you . . . it is a sign that the clam has given me . . . and the signs are so many, and in me have formed a sort of expectation, a sort of expectation."[30] So he says in the continuation: "And I look into the grain of sand and see in it a sort of mirror held opposite my face, and I am amazed and cry out: 'Wow – it's me! it's me, it's me!' ."[31] Therefore, finding the Nothingness allows one only to hold the grain of sand, and to be held by it.

The light may be seen as a parallel to the grain of sand in its significance. When the grain of sand becomes self and has the power to hold him, the light suddenly breaks through and is the same spark of hope which exists in the Nothingness. The light is something concrete, which occurs also in Kafka before death. Towards the end of *Before the Law* when Kafka is not allowed to go through the gate of the law he sees a spark of light, dawn suddenly appears. This also can be found in *Metamorphosis* when, at the end of the story, tranquility arrives and dawn breaks through. This is a point of light that enables one not to despair and to keep rolling the boulder. The grain of sand is the pith, the Essence without which Daniel will fall into the abyss and will remain with his nauseating black wound:

> A grain of sand . . . suddenly he sees the faces of all the people, the loving, the charming, the satisfied, those with evil intentions, the aggressive, the shy, the hopeless, the bitter, all with the sweat of life on their faces. 'For tomorrow all of you are dead' is the shout he hears from inside himself. He looks at the palm of his hand. After all this, the grain of sand is there. And it has grown and become bigger, and as it added to its size it opened up to the light, like the crystal of the diamond, and the light flowed into it and it broke into pieces.[32]

Orpaz claims that the secular pilgrim is a tragic character. A tragic character is a character who cannot rise above the pain and move forward. It is impossible to regard Brecht's Mother Courage as a tragic figure, because, if we follow Aristotle, she arose above her losses and went forward. The secular pilgrim is not an anti-hero; he is a hero because he "bears the burden of his life within a world of chaos."[33] He is aware of his own distress, that he is carrying the boulder to the top of the mountain to no purpose and to no place, therefore the tragic circle is the circle of the significance of the universe. Daniel tries to go back, but does not know if he will succeed, or will just try over and over again. This is a constant state of hopeless yearning. Therefore this is a tragic character who is a mixture of longing and fear. It is a character who comes close to the occult and to religious ritual in an illogical world, in which Daniel does not think according to regular norms.

The secular pilgrim chooses an isolated place for himself – which will be the place to undergo the experience he anticipates. This is Daniel's place. The place which is his journey and his trial. There is a struggle here between the expectation of something irrational and the refusal of the spirit to surrender its freedom. Therefore the secular pilgrim, Daniel that is, wins and is beaten only in that he, in practice, creates significance for his own existence. This is an introduction to Sisyphusian research as the ultimate experience. Therefore, the standing of the secular pilgrim is like that of the caveman in terms of its ritual and the paucity of details on his biographical past. In this novel we meet a man scarred in the middle of his life, and we know very little about his past. He is "cast out and pursued, while he himself pursues, searches and masquerades, rebels and ties himself up – and in all of this, swapping and changing, longings and fear."[34] There is no solution to the struggle; the ending is not complete and the conflict remains open. This is a clash over an abyss and the abyss is the Absence. The story of Daniel does not reach a solution but neither does it lead to destruction and ruin, which enables him to continue on his Sisyphusian trail. The pilgrim will continue to be cursed, despite the fact that "for the moment the emptiness is filled with the feeling of significance and light."[35] This is how he appears at the end of the novel:

> All that night Daniel wandered the streets. Sometimes he found himself on the way to the sea, but he came back from there. He paid attention to the houses, to the windows, the balconies . . . Daniel shouted softly, after that he proffered his face to the dawn wind that had just now begun to blow from the sea.[36]

Notes

1. Y. Orpaz, *The Voyage of Daniel*, Tel Aviv: Am Oved, 1986 (Hebrew).
2. Y. Orpaz, *The Pilgrim*, Tel Aviv: Hakibbutz Hameuchad, 1982 (Hebrew).
3. Orpaz, *The Voyage of Daniel*, p. 9.
4. J.L. Herman, *Trauma and Recovery*, Tel Aviv: Am Oved, 1994, p. 9 (Hebrew).
5. S. Noy, *Traumatic Stress Situation*, Tel Aviv: Shoken, 2000 (Hebrew).
6. Herman, *Trauma and Recovery*, p. 71.
7. Orpaz, *The Voyage of Daniel*, p. 23.
8. Orpaz, *The Voyage of Daniel*, p. 13.
9. Orpaz, *The Voyage of Daniel*, p. 15.
10. J. Kot, *The Human Memory*, Tel Aviv: Matar, 2007, p. 51 (Hebrew).
11. Ibid., p. 52.
12. Orpaz, *The Voyage of Daniel*, p. 75.
13. Orpaz, *The Pilgrim*, p.13.

14. Ibid., p. 42.
15. Orpaz, *The Voyage of Daniel*, p. 62.
16. Orpaz, *The Pilgrim*, p. 42.
17. O. Bartana, *Fantasy in Israeli Literature*, Tel Aviv: Hakibbutz Hameuchad, 1987, p. 143 (Hebrew).
18. O. Bartana, *End of Century and Beginning of Century*, Tel Aviv: Eked, 2001, p. 163 (Hebrew).
19. Orpaz, *The Pilgrim*, p. 7.
20. Orpaz, *The Voyage of Daniel*, p. 209.
21. Ibid., p. 209.
22. Orpaz, interview on Israel Radio channel 1, 26.2.06.
23. W. Blake, "Auguries of Innocence," in J. Bronowski (Ed.), *A Selection of Poems and Letters*, London: Penguin Books, 1958, p. 67.
24. Orpaz, *The Voyage of Daniel*, p. 136.
25. Ibid., p. 28.
26. Ibid., p. 28.
27. J.-P. Sartre, *La nausée* (trans. H. Lazar), Tel Aviv: Siman Kriya, 1978 (Hebrew).
28. M. Brinker, *Jean-P. Sartre*, Tel Aviv: Ministry of Defense, 1992, p. 40 (Hebrew).
29. Orpaz, *The Voyage of Daniel*, pp. 205–206.
30. Ibid., p. 135.
31. Ibid., p. 130.
32. Ibid., p. 205.
33. Orpaz, *The Pilgrim*, p. 714.
34. Orpaz, *The Pilgrim*, p. 78.
35. Orpaz, *The Pilgrim*, p. 78.
36. Orpaz, *The Voyage of Daniel*, p. 208.

Part IV

Israel, war, ethics and the media

16 War, religion, and Israel's foreign press corps

Yoel Cohen

An important characteristic of Israel's international image is the considerable quantity of coverage which Israel receives in the foreign media. Hess, examining foreign news coverage on US television (ABC, CBS, and NBC) and US newspapers (the *New York Times, Chicago Tribune*, and *Los Angeles Times*) for the 1988–92 period, found that Israel comprised 10.2 percent of television foreign coverage and 4.7 percent of newspaper foreign coverage. The Middle East as a region accounted for 9 percent of foreign news coverage in newspapers and 8.2 percent in the case of television.[1]

Different factors have been offered to explain news interest. Psychological factors for foreign news interest are manifold. Adams hypothesized that foreign news interest was dominated by a relatively small number of countries with the result that news flow reflects political and economic eliteness and dominance.[2] Hall argued that news values be explained in terms of structural ideological meanings.[3] Rosengren sights correlations between reader interest and the physical distance between countries.[4] Galtung and Ruge postulated that negativism or social breakdown and conflict, cultural proximity and elitism explain news interest.[5] Hester and Zaharapoulos developed the cultural proximity thesis that news interest could be conceptualised in terms of cultural proximity between the audience and the foreign country subject of the news.[6]

War is a major ingredient of foreign news reporting. Much foreign news in the international media comprises wars, conflict and diplomacy. Hess found that 24.5 percent of foreign correspondents which he surveyed replied that armed conflict was the key type of event they covered, 26.6 percent replied diplomacy, and 17.4 percent replied economics.[7] A major increase in foreign news interest in Israel occurred with the Six Day War. The dramatic nature of news in Israel has made conflict and war a factor in explaining foreign news reporting from Israel.

War is the corollary of religion in foreign media coverage because religion is almost not at all a subject of foreign media coverage. Proximity or "closeness" may be defined in various contexts: in addition to geographical proximity, and political and economic proximity, cultural proximity may also be seen in religious terms. There is little research on religion as a subject of international news, most research on religion having been carried out in the domestic context.[8] The Israeli case is useful in examining the place of religion in international news flows because religion news in the Holyland would, it might be postulated, be more pronounced than in most other countries. Even though Israel is the Holyland; war is the major story with little interest in the "Holyland" per se as a subagent of news. It will be argued that a closer look suggests that religion influences the intensity and type of coverage of the conflict – seemingly double standards underlie the coverage of the Israeli-Palestinian conflict.

The overwhelming quantity of international coverage is done by foreign correspondents – even if the coverage is not done directly by correspondents of the specific news organizations but by the correspondents of news agencies. No more than 100 journalists, for example, provide most of the information in the US media about Israel. In small countries, most of that country's media are represented in Israel by a handful of reporters who speak the country's language. It gives foreign correspondents a very important role in agenda setting Israel's external image, and raises important questions about that community of journalists.

While research on foreign news has long been interested in gatekeeping and selection criteria to explain the construction of reality, much of the limited research about foreign correspondents has been concerned about organizational questions, both within news organizations, such as knowledge and training level of journalists, and patterns of relations between reporters and news sources. Ghorpade, Hess, Mowlana and Nair studied organizational aspects of the work and patterns of news sources of foreign correspondents based in Washington, Morrison and Tumber those of foreign correspondents in London, Pedelty studied foreign correspondents in El Salvador, Slaatta examined Norwegian correspondents covering the EEC, Tiffen looked at the foreign press corps in South East Asia, and Knight investigated the foreign correspondents of the Australian media in South East Asia.[9] In an early study Kruglak examined the foreign correspondents of the US media around the world, a study which has been updated more recently by Hess and by Shanor.[10] Another focus of enquiry has been patterns of the distribution of foreign correspondents.[11] Cohen examined patterns of the distribution of foreign press corps around the world.[12] In a two-directional study Kliesch examined foreign press corps in South East Asia, and the distribution of the foreign correspondents of the media of key South East Asian countries.[13]

While the subject of foreign media coverage of Israel and of the Arab-Israeli conflict has received considerable attention,[14] there has been almost no systematic research about the permanent foreign press corps in Israel.

This article seeks to determine the relative places of war and religion as factors for foreign news interest in Israel. In order to generate data about war and religion as categories in foreign news reporting from the Jewish State, foreign correspondents were surveyed in 2009 by the author to verify determinants of news interest. The survey resulted in 160 filled questionnaires, covering about 40 percent of the foreign press corps. Data about foreign correspondents was gathered from the Foreign Press Association in Israel. While the foreign correspondents survey is the main means of collecting data, a secondary source comprises a content analysis carried out by the author of all copy sent from the Associated Press office in Israel during a twenty-one year period from 1968 to 1988, broken down both according to quantities of reports and by their subject matter. The month of March was used as the sample for each year, given that there were no major significant, unusual developments in that period. The inter-coder reliability coefficient was .88.

The growth of the foreign press corps

Some 350 foreign news organizations were represented in Israel full-time or part-time in 2010. The foreign press corps in Israel has shown a gradual growth over the years since 1967 and the dramatic Six Day War in which Israel trebled its territory and captured the Golan Heights, the West Bank, Gaza and the Sinai Desert. The number of foreign news organizations represented in Israel increased from 32 journalists in 1957 (the first year when records were kept in the form of a membership list of the Foreign Press Association of Israel, established in that year) to over 400 in 2010, which was a slight reduction from the turn of the millennium, both as a result of fewer dramatic newsworthy developments, and of the impression that foreign publics have tired of the seemingly never ending Israeli-Arab dispute.

Even before the 1967 war the foreign press corps was not inconsiderable in size. But while many foreign news organizations today are represented by full-time staff from abroad posted in Israel for a number of years, prior to 1967 these organizations were either unrepresented or had part-time local stringers. Only the *New York Times* and Agence France Presse had full-time staffers from abroad. Even Reuters and AP got by each with a local Israeli representative. The 1947–49 War of Independence and the creation of the state was an important post-Second World War news story, coming so soon after the Holocaust. The interest continued as the infant Jewish state grappled with the economic and social problems and tasks of early statehood. The 1956 Suez war generated wide interest particularly in the US, Britain and France. The Eichmann trial brought many correspondents to cover the trial. But in each case, foreign news organizations which sent correspondents from abroad pulled them out afterwards, leaving only local Israelis on a contract, non-full-time basis. After the 1967 war – the fast-changing drama of which fitted so closely to the media clock – a succession of events, mostly related to the Arab-Israeli conflict, provided "periodic justification" for foreign editors abroad to maintain a staff presence in Israel.

Compared to foreign press corps in other countries, Israel in 1995 was found to have the tenth largest foreign press corps in the world. By comparison, the largest was the US (944 foreign news organizations) followed by Brussels, the headquarters of the European Economic Community.[15] Today 35 foreign countries are represented in the foreign press corps in Israel. By comparison, 80 foreign countries are represented in the foreign press corps in the US. The foreign press corps in seven other countries (including six West European ones) have 50–65 foreign countries represented in their foreign press corps. Whereas Israel has the tenth largest foreign press corps in the world it has only the fourteenth most geographically diverse foreign press corps. Israel has the largest foreign press corps in the Middle East. The next largest foreign press corps in 1995 were those in Cyprus (120 foreign news organizations), which has been used as a regional base for the international media's covering the Middle East region as a whole, and in Egypt (115). Hamilton and Jenner (2004) argued that a there has been a change in the flow of foreign correspondents with alternative sources of foreign news replacing resident foreign correspondents.[16] While it is true both that there has been an increase in other forms of foreign coverage such as "parachute" foreign correspondents who fly in to cover a breaking crisis and leave after the crisis or news interest in it abated,[17] and that there are – and have always been in the Israeli case – many locally-based Israelis working as foreign correspondents, the overall increase in the size of the foreign press corps in Israel, including an increase in resident foreign correspondent posted to Israel, raises questions about whether the term "foreign correspondence" should be redefined.[18] Broken down according to types of medium, 48 percent of foreign news organizations represented in Israel in 2007 are newspapers, 15 percent radio stations, 17 percent magazines (including Jewish weekly newspapers), 10 percent television stations, 7 percent foreign news agencies, 2 percent photo syndication agencies, and 1 percent cyberspace/online news services.

War and terrorism

Correspondents' self-evaluations of their news interest found that war and terrorism are overwhelmingly the major factors. Correspondents surveyed confirmed that the centrality of the conflict story – a category embracing war, terrorism, Arab-Israeli conflict, the diplomatic peace process, the Israeli military, defense policy, that war and terrorism – is the major factor determining this interest. Of correspondents surveyed, 70 percent said that war was "very important" and a further 24 percent said it was "somewhat important" to explain the news interest. 78 percent said that terrorism was very important; a further 19 percent said it was somewhat important. The Israeli-Palestinian process was regarded as very important by 78 percent; a further 22 percent said it was somewhat important.

In times of conflict, the volume of coverage increases by far. Conflict is characterized by the arrival of visiting correspondents who fly in either to cover a particular breaking story such as a war or have come for a brief period to update about the country. Correspondents surveyed by the author estimated that on average 23 reports a week are filed at times of crisis in contrast to 10 reports a week during "quiet periods." During the first week of the major wars of 1967, 1973 and 1982, the content analysis of Associated Press found that it sent 147, 190 and 113 items respectively from its Israel bureau, and concerned with the war in its various aspects. For example, in the twelve months after the beginning of the *Intifada* (the Palestinian uprising) in 1986 a total of 2,438 visiting reporters – three times the figure for visiting reporters over the previous twelve months –

flew to Israel, 225 alone flew in the first three weeks after the beginning of the *Intifada*. 1,600 reporters visiting reporters flew in to cover the visit of Egyptian President Anwar Sadat to Jerusalem. Some 1,500 reporters, mostly from Catholic countries, flew into cover the visit of Pope John Paul II in 2000.

The difference between the pre-1967 and post-1967 periods is also illustrated by the lateral growth in the sizes of the bureaus of the major news agencies and major Western television networks. Increases in foreign news interest have occurred periodically since 1967 both as the Arab-Israeli conflict brought further war, related episodes such as terrorism and the *Intifada* and such diplomatic developments as bilateral peace agreements between Israel and neighboring Arab states. The former include the 1973 and 1982 wars, the 1991 and 2004 Gulf Wars, major terrorist incidents such as the 1972 Munich Olympics, the aerial hijackings preceding the 1970 Jordanian civil war, the Entebbe hijacking, the assassination of Prime Minister Yitzhak Rabin, and the death of Palestinian leader Yassir Arafat. In 1974, the year after the 1973 war, there were 220 foreign news organizations represented, an increase from 169 in 1973. In 1989, the end of the first year of the *Intifada*, 270 foreign news organizations were represented in Israel, an increase from 248 in 1988.

The Arab-Israeli conflict and peace diplomacy were also the dominating themes in contacts between official news sources and correspondents. The main news sources were the IDF Spokesman, the Foreign Ministry and the Prime Minister's Office. Eighteen percent of foreign correspondents surveyed had daily contact with the Prime Minister's Office, and a further 19 percent had weekly contact. 16 percent had daily contact with the IDF and a further 18 percent weekly contact. While only 9 percent of foreign correspondents had daily contact with the Foreign Ministry, 31 percent reported weekly contact. The difference between the Foreign Ministry and the IDF Spokesman may be explained by the fact that on a daily basis there were few daily changes in Israel-related diplomacy, unlike the Army, which reports daily military occurrences. Only 27 percent had less than monthly contact with the Foreign Ministry – the lowest figure for correspondent-government ministry contacts for the "less than a month" category. Noteworthy was that in 1989 – during the first *Intifada* – there was greater frequency of daily contact between foreign correspondents and the Foreign Ministry than with the IDF Spokesman – 40 percent and 21 percent respectively.

The level of contact with key Israeli government departments associated with the conflict and peace process was mirrored by foreign correspondents' contacts with the Palestinian Authority. 12 percent and 24 percent of correspondents had daily or weekly contacts with the Palestinian Authority: only 25 percent reportedly less than monthly contact.

Religion and Holyland news

There is a need to define religion news in foreign affairs. Examining religion in American television nightly news, Buddenbaum defined the entire Arab-Jewish conflict as a Muslim–Jewish religious struggle.[19] In the age of television, religion news has found a place in international news flows, notably where religion becomes linked to international or domestic conflict such as the al-Qaida attack on the World Trade Center on September 11, 2001, the seizure of the US embassy by Muslim students in Tehran in 1979–80, the mass suicide of David Koresh and the Davidian sect in Waco, Texas and the assassination of Israeli Prime Minister Rabin. The Israeli-Palestinian struggle for control of Judea and Samaria is a subject of foreign news. Yigal Amir said that he murdered Rabin in order to stop the handover of the biblical Promised Land to non-Jewish control. However, it is argued that a more narrower definition of religion news is required given that the Buddenbaum definition is too all-embracing, and does not enable a clearer differentiation between religion news on the one hand and political news, defense news and economic news on the other. Hoover, for example, has argued that something is religious if it is essentially religious (1998).[20]

The potential for foreign news with a Holyland motif originates with the connections which Judaism, Christianity and Islam have with the Holyland. Jewish connections to the Holyland go back to the biblical era of the land of Canaan. In Jewish thought, early Jewish statehood extended from the twelfth century BCE to 70 CE and included the First and Second Temple periods. The religious connection to the Land of Israel continued throughout the Dispersion as Jewish communities continued to look towards Jerusalem as the focus of prayer, and aspired to a return of Jewish statehood, albeit, in part, as a solution to antisemitism. In 1948 the Jewish state was established, and in the 1967 war the Old City of Jerusalem, including the Temple Mount and the Western Wall, were captured by Israel. The media influences relations between Jews in the Diaspora and Israel because the media are an important source of information about Israel.

Christianity had its origins in Bethlehem, Nazareth and Jerusalem. According to Christian beliefs, Jesus was born in Bethlehem, spent most of his life in Nazareth, and was crucified in Jerusalem. For Islam, *Haram al Sharif* ("The Noble Shrine" – known to non-Muslims as the Temple Mount) is one of the three *kibleh*s in Islam to which Muslims direct their prayer. It was from Haram al Sharif that Mohammed ascended, or, according to certain interpretations dreamed that he ascended, to Allah to receive the tenets of Islam.

Given the rivalry for control over holy sites the conflict element also possesses a religion news dimension. Indeed, a string of events and developments both within a single religion, such as secular–religious tensions within the Jewish population or intra-Christian tensions, and inter-religious tensions between Christians and Muslims, or Jews and Muslims, have drawn foreign media interest. Most notable of the inter-religious conflict spots are the Jewish–Muslim conflict over Temple Mount/*Haram al Sharif*, Christian–Muslim tensions regarding the status of Christian property in areas controlled by the Palestinian Authority, and Muslim attempts to build a mosque near the site of the Church of the Annunciation in Nazareth. Intra-Christian tensions are reflected in the tensions between different Christian communities for control of the Church of the Holy Sepulcher in Jerusalem. There is also limited religion news interest among the foreign media in subjects such as the religious political parties which have been key members of Israel's coalition style of government since the state's inception over sixty years ago and in secular-religious tensions over Sabbath public observance. Other issues which are covered widely in the Israeli media like the recruitment of ultra-orthodox students to the army and the budgeting of *yeshivot* (academies of higher religious learning), draw no interest among the foreign media.

The survey found that notwithstanding that the three monotheistic faiths, Judaism, Christianity and Islam, have close historical and religious ties to the Land of Israel, "the Holyland" as a factor for news interest was rated low by foreign correspondents, considerably lower than, for example, war and terrorism. Only 21 percent of respondents rated the Holyland as a very important factor to explain news interest in Israel in contrast to 78 percent and 70 percent of respondents who said terrorism and war respectively are very important factors, and 39 percent who said that Arab states' challenges to Israel were "very important."

As a factor to explain the news interest in Israel, the Holyland was also higher for US media correspondents (67 percent very important and 17 percent somewhat important) than Western European media correspondents (13 percent very important and 67 percent somewhat important). This reflects the higher level of religious practice among Christian believers in the US today and a declining trend in Western Europe. Similarly, Christian audience interest as a factor for news interest was higher among the US media correspondents (39 percent very important and 33 percent somewhat important) than among Western European correspondents media (20 percent and 30 percent very important and somewhat important). The term "Holyland" is more appropriate in media terms to the Christian media than to the Jewish or Islamic media. Christian media follow the activities of the Christian communities in Israel and the Palestinian-controlled areas, the Christian holidays, and the status of the Christian holy places.

Jewish audience interest was regarded as a higher factor for news interest by the US media correspondents than by the Western European media correspondents, reflecting the large Jewish population in the US, in particular in the New York area – which is also the headquarters for some key US news organizations. 39 percent and 28 percent of US correspondents rated Jewish audience interest very important and somewhat important respectively. By contrast, only 11 percent and 32 percent of Western European correspondents rated Jewish audience interest as very important and somewhat important. The news from Israel is an important staple ingredient in news content of the Jewish Diaspora media. The Jewish Diaspora media perceive Israel as the Jewish homeland, or "*Eretz Yisrael*," with audiences less interested in religion news per se. Even if such news is also covered, and does enrich their Jewish identity, it is done together with all the rest of the news coming out of Israel, including defense, politics, and culture news.

The status of *Haram al Sharif*, or the Temple Mount, generates acute news interest among Arab audiences. A few of the stations, such as ART from Saudi Arabia, broadcast Friday prayers and the nightfall service each night during the month of Ramadan from there. Interest comes to a climax on the last Friday or the twenty-seventh day of Ramadan, when, according to Muslim tradition, Mohammed made his ascent to Allah. There was no significant difference in Muslim audience interest between the US and Western European groups of correspondents.

Any suggestion of a lack of coverage of the Holyland cannot be explained by any lack of knowledge among foreign correspondents about the land. In spite of the limited news interest in religion news, correspondents surveyed said they were well-informed about religion. The self-evaluation of knowledge of correspondents about Judaism and Islam was high, particularly in the former. Of the correspondents, 57 percent described their knowledge of Judaism as good, and 35 percent as adequate; 10 percent described their knowledge of Islam as good, 55 percent as adequate, and 35 percent as inadequate. The high self-evaluation for Judaism may be explained by the fact that two-thirds of the foreign press corps are, in fact, Israeli nationals, and many of those who are not are Jewish immigrants to Israel, who work as foreign correspondents. These correspondents have worked as journalists for an average of 22 years, as foreign correspondents for 9.7 years, and lived in Israel for an average of 15 years.

The lack of interest between journalists and officials is mutual. Reflecting the lack of news interest in the Holyland, correspondents do not turn to official religion sources. Correspondents were asked to rate their access to official news sources on a daily, weekly, monthly, and less than monthly basis. The Ministry of Religious Affairs was one of the least turned to government departments – 0 percent of correspondents reported daily contact with the Religious Affairs ministry, 2 percent weekly contact, 18 percent monthly contact, and 80 percent less than monthly contact. Even in contrast to other official sources of domestic Israeli news stories – such as the Finance Ministry and the Justice Ministry – contact with the Religious Affairs Ministry was remarkably low.

A lack of Holyland motif reflects broader questions on the overall efficiency or inefficiency of the country's external public media relations.[21] Both because of – as well as in spite of – the lack of interest in the Holyland among foreign correspondents, it is surprising that Israeli policy-makers fail to engage in more proactive work in projecting the Holyland theme. Policymakers in successive Israeli governments have not articulated a specific religion-related message or information program beyond a generalized message of Jewish statehood. A lack of official initiative to generate contacts with foreign correspondents on religion-related themes may be explained as resulting from a number of factors. Over the years there has been a built-in dilemma within Israel's official elite about projecting the Holyland. True, on the one hand, the Jewish state draws part of its legitimacy – and title to territory – from the fact that it is situated in the ancient Holyland of the Jewish people, the land of the Bible. The access which the government provides for different faiths to their places of worship builds support for the country abroad and among adherents of those faiths. Yet, Israeli officials are torn between building upon the Holyland motif and their desire to project Israel as a modern, democratic state. Moreover, the Holyland motif runs counter to international calls for Israel to withdraw from the biblical territories of Judea and Samaria and to calls for the creation of a Palestinian state in those territories. This was particularly true for the Labor Party, which was in power continuously up to 1977 and which regarded excessive usage of motifs of Holyland as weakening its post-1967 policy of relinquishing territory for peace. Even the nationalist Likud did not envelop its expansionist policy of settling the area into a specifically Holyland message, with the exception of East Jerusalem and its holy places, but has rather focused upon the strategic reasons for opposing territorial withdrawal. Settler groups in the West Bank, possessing little faith in what they regarded as Western public opinion hostile to their case, have seen little purpose in seeking out the foreign media in their search for political legitimacy. Furthermore, Jewish religious political parties – who generally have held the religious affairs portfolio in the coalition-style government in the country – are hesitant to exploit for PR goals the access given to the holy places of other non-Jewish religions lest this be interpreted as theological legitimacy of other religions.

The lack of PR initiative was mirrored in foreign correspondents' contacts with other non-official Israeli organizations and non-Jewish faiths, with the exception of the Latin Patriarchate. The Palestinian *Wakf*, which administers the Islamic holy places on *Haram al-Sharif*, focuses its media PR activities towards the Arab media; its officials believe that the Temple Mount situation is newsworthy enough so that journalists make contact with the *Wakf* on their own initiative. The Greek Patriarchate focused only on the Greek media. The Latin Patriarchate has a media liaison and conducts press conferences before Easter and Christmas – which are usually attended by between 20 and 40 journalists including some foreign correspondents (notably from the Italian, French, Belgium, and German media) as well as Israeli and Palestinian media. Given the lack of political certainty which the non-Jewish communities inevitably feel about their status, it was surprising that media relations are so low key. Most of the activities of the Reform and Conservative Jewish movements – which are struggling for formal official recognition in Israel – are directed at Jewish Diaspora media correspondents among the foreign press corps rather than the mainstream foreign correspondents.

Religious affiliation as a news interest factor

Some Christian fundamentalist groups, drawing upon a literal interpretation of biblical prophecy, look to events in the Middle East today as part of the process that will lead to the Second Coming of Christ. But few correspondents saw any validity in this as a factor to explain news interest in Israel: only 3 percent and 27 percent said that emotional fear and curiosity about the supernatural was very important and somewhat important respectively to explain news interest in Israel.

Foreign news about Israel is to some extent seen by Christian and Western audiences through a "biblical" prism of right and wrong through which to "judge" foreign news from Israel. 28 percent and 39 percent said that "moral failings of the Jewish State" were very important and somewhat important respectively to explain the news interest. The Hess study on US foreign correspondents found that 29 percent of television reporting and 20 percent of press reporting from Israel comprised "human rights" reporting.[22] Reflecting the high value accorded to human rights in Western European countries, Western European media correspondents gave higher ratings for the news interest in Israel to such factors or stories as Rabin's assassination and the Israeli-Palestinian peace process than did the US media. 79 percent and 22 percent of Western European media correspondents said the Rabin assassination was very important and somewhat important respectively as a news factor in contrast to 15 percent and 35 percent of US correspondents respectively. The Israeli-Palestinian peace process was also incrementally a little higher as a news factor for the Western European media correspondents over the US media correspondents. This was also expressed in perceived moral failings of the Jewish state (for example, the deaths of Arab civilians in Israeli military operations): 29 percent and 51 percent of Western European media correspondents said this was very important and somewhat important in contrast to 10 percent and 35 percent of US media correspondents respectively.

In a more general sense, the Holyland acts as a latent "trigger" drawing general interest among Christian, Jewish and Muslim audiences abroad to other categories of foreign news emanating from Israel, rather than being a news motif in itself. Notwithstanding the limited interest in religion and Holyland, some people explain the news interest as resulting from the Judeo-Christian tradition. Thomas Friedman, Pultizer prize-winning columnist and former *New York Times* bureau chief in Israel, claimed that Christian roots in the Holyland are a factor in the intensive news interest in the country. There is evidence to support the cultural-cum-religious proximity thesis. 21 percent and 40 percent of foreign correspondents said that the Holyland was a very important variable or somewhat important variable to explain the news interest in Israel.

Yet, citing the Judeo-Christian tradition as an explanation for Israel's international newsworthiness fails to explain why prior to the dramatic 1967 Six Day War Israel appeared far less on the foreign news pages and had far fewer foreign correspondents – 150, nearly all of whom were part-timers, locals who worked in the Israeli media. And, while the wars and violence confirm Galtung and Ruge's theory that drama was one of three major criteria determining which foreign events become defined as news and which get dropped, the pre-1967 and post 1967 experience suggests that the Judeo-Christian connection as foreign news should be redefined in terms of latent and actual news interest. The Judeo-Christian connection contributes to creating the intrinsic or potential news interest but this only becomes actualized by the blood and drama of war, conflict and terrorism. As Galtung and Ruge, in examining factors for news interest, postulate, "It is not enough for an event to be culturally meaningful. This defines only a vast set of possible news candidates. Within this set, the more unexpected have highest chances of being actualised as news. It is the unexpected within the meaningful and the consonant which is brought to one's attention."[23]

Conclusions

If a solution to the Arab-Israeli conflict occurs in the longer-term, there will be a general decline in reporting from Israel – including of religious affairs – as foreign correspondents pack their bags for more newsworthy pastures. It was the Six Day War and terrorism that pushed Israel into the headlines and it is peace in the event that it occurs which will bring about the decline of coverage. To be truthful, correspondents surveyed thought this unlikely to occur. Asked "whether the news interest by your news organization in Israel had increased or decreased as a result of the above diplomatic developments in the Arab-Israeli peace process," only 6 percent of foreign correspondents said it had decreased, while 59 percent said it had increased and 35 percent had said that there was no change.

One cost of the linkage of religion to the Arab-Israeli conflict was that audiences were inclined to understand the Jewish religion itself in Israel through the prism of that conflict. It means that the richness of the Jewish tradition in its manifold features and multi-layered value system gets narrowed and distorted. Features and values comprising conflict are emphasized, whereas other features and values lacking a seeming conflict dimension fail to get covered. This should raise important questions not only for religious leaders such as rabbis and teachers who see themselves as advocates of the Jewish religion, but also for official diplomatic representatives of the Jewish state.

Notes

1. S. Hess, *International News & Foreign Correspondents*, Washington DC: The Brookings Institution, 1996.
2. J.B. Adams, "A Qualitative Analyisis of Domestic and Foreign Networks on the AP-TAWire," *Gazette* 10, 1964, pp. 285–295.
3. S. Hall, "The Rediscovery of Ideology: Return of the Repressed in Media Studies," in M. Gurevitch, T. Bennett, J. Curran and J. Woollacott (Eds.), *Culture, Society & the Media*, London: Methuen, 1982, pp. 56–90.
4. K. Rosengren, "International News: Methods, Data, Theory," *International Journal of Peace Research* 11, 1974, pp. 74–80.
5. J. Galtung and M. Ruge, "The Structure of Foreign News," *International Journal of Peace Research* 1, 1965, pp. 65–91.
6. A. Hester, "An Analysis of News Flow from Developed and Developing Nations," *Gazette* 7, 1971, pp. 29–43; T. Zaharopoulos, "Cultural Proximity in International News

Coverage: 1988 US Presidential Election in the Greek Press," *Journalism Quarterly* 67, 1990, pp. 1990–1994.

7. Hess, *International News & Foreign Correspondents*, pp. 120–122.

8. See, for example, R. Abelman and S. Hoover, *Religious Television: Controversies & Conclusions*, Norwood: Ablex, 1990; J. Ferre, (Ed.), *Channels of Belief: Religion & American Commercial Television*, Ames: Iowa State University Press, 1990; *Media Coverage of Religion, Spirituality, & Values*, Garrett-Medill Center for Religion and the News Media, Evanston: Northwestern University, 1999; S. Hoover, *Religion in the News*, Thousand Oaks: Sage, 1998. For a discussion of media and religion in Israel, see Y. Cohen, *God, Jews & the Media: Religion & Israel's Media*, New York & London: Routledge, 2012.

9. S. Ghorpade, "Sources and Access: How Foreign Correspondents Rate Washington DC," *Journal of Communication* 34, 1984, pp. 32–40; S. Hess, *Through Their Eyes: Foreign Correspondents in the United States*, Washington DC: The Brookings Institution, 2005; H. Mowlana, "Who Covers America?," *The Journal of Communication* 25, 1975, pp. 86–91; M. Nair, "The Foreign Media Correspondent: Dateline Washington DC," *Gazette* 48, 1991, pp. 59–64; D. Morrison and H. Tumber, "The Foreign Correspondent: Dateline London," *Media, Culture & Society* 7, 1985, pp. 445–470; M. Pedelty, *War Stories: The Culture of Foreign Correspondents*, New York & London: Routledge, 1995; T. Slaatta, (2001), "Transnational Politics and News Production. Norwegian Correspondents on the Brussels Beat," in S. Hjarvard (Ed.), *News in a Globalised Society*, Goteborg: Nordicum, pp. 129–148; R. Tiffen, *The News from Southeast Asia: The Sociology of Newsmaking*, Singapore: Institute of Southeast Asian Studies, 1978; A. Knight, "Re-inventing the Wheel: Australian Foreign Correspondents in Southeast Asia," *Media Asia* 22, 1995, pp. 9–17.

10. T. Kruglak, *The Foreign Correspondents: A Study of the Men & Women Reporting for the American Information Media in Western Europe*, Geneva: Librairie E. Droz, 1955; Hess, *International News & Foreign Correspondents*; D. Shanor, *News from Abroad*, New York: Columbia University Press, 2003.

11. J.R. Wilhelm, "The World Press Corps Dwindles: A Fifth World Survey of Foreign Correspondents," paper read at the Association for Education in Journalism Convention, Carbondale, Illinois, August 1972.

12. Y. Cohen, "Foreign Press Corps as an Indicator of International News Interest," *Gazette* 56, 1995, pp. 89–99.

13. R. Kliesch, "News Media Presence and Southeast Asia," *Journalism Quarterly* 57, 1980, pp. 255–261.

14. For example W. Adams (Ed.), *Television Coverage of the Middle East*, New Jersey: Ablex, 1981; Y. Cohen, "Focus on Israel: Twenty-Five Years of Foreign Media Reporting," *Encyclopaedia Judaica*, decennial edition 1983–92, Jerusalem: Keter, pp. 46–56, 1994; Y. Kamalipur (Ed.), *The US Media and the Middle East: Image & Perception*, Westport: Praeger, 1995; J. Lederman, *Battle Lines*, New York: Henry Holt, 1992; E. Said, *Covering Islam*, New York: Pantheon, 1981; M. Yegar, *The Growth of the Israeli Foreign Information Policy Apparatus*, Herzliya: Lahav, 1986, (Hebrew). D. Goren, A.A .Cohen and D. Caspi, "Reporting of the Yom-Kippur War from Israel," *Journalism Quarterly* 52, 1975, pp. 199–206, examined the visiting correspondents who came to Israel cover the 1973 Yom Kippur war.

15. Cohen, "Foreign Press Corps as an Indicator of International News Interest."

16. J.M. Hamilton and E. Jenner, "Redefining Foreign Correspondence," *Journalism* 5, 2004, pp. 301–321.

17. See E. Erickson and J.M. Hamilton, "Foreign Reporting Enhanced by Parachute Journalism," *Newspaper Research Journal* 27, 2006, pp. 33–47.

18. Hamilton and Jenner, "Redefining Foreign Correspondence," p. 36.

19. J. Buddenbaum, "Network News Coverage of Religion" in J. Ferret (Ed.), *Channels of Belief: Religion & American Commercial Television*, Ames: Iowa State University Press, 1990, pp. 57–78.
20. Hoover, *Religion in the News*, pp. 14–16.
21. E. Gilboa, "Public Diplomacy: The Missing Component in Israel's Foreign Policy," *Israel Affairs* 12/4, 2006, pp. 715–747.
22. Hess, *International News & Foreign Correspondents*, pp. 119–121.
23. Galtung and Ruge, "The Structure of Foreign News," p. 65.

17 The *New York Times'* justification of its coverage of the Gaza War

An apologia

Carol Lea Clark

"Waves of Israeli airstrikes destroyed Hamas security facilities in Gaza on Saturday in a crushing response to the group's rocket fire, killing more than 225 – the highest one-day toll in the Israeli-Palestinian conflict in decades."[1] So began the *New York Times'* twenty-two day coverage of "Operation Cast Lead," or the Gaza War as it is called in the American media, when in December of 2008 Israel bombed and later invaded the Gaza Strip. This first sentence, quoted above, indicates the balancing act the *New York Times* would attempt in its coverage of the war. The first part of the sentence could be labeled pro-Israeli because it clearly says that the Israeli air strikes were in response to Hamas's rocket fire. The second half of the sentence could be considered pro-Palestinian because it points out that the 225 killed in Gaza is the "highest one-day" casualty count in decades.

Examining the extensive day-to-day coverage, often two to four articles a day, that appeared in the *Times*, it is evident that the newspaper was not consistent in attributing blame or censure. "Striking Deep Into Israel, Hamas Employs an Upgraded Arsenal," for example, is an article that discusses rocket damage to a school in Beersheba, Israel. It reads, "By firing rockets deep into Israeli territory, the militant Palestinian group Hamas has in recent days displayed an arsenal that has been upgraded with weapons parts smuggled into Gaza since it seized control of the territory 18 months ago."[2] This story stressed that Hamas had improved the technology of their rockets until they could strike into Israeli towns, including hitting a school. Though no children were injured, the story makes clear that families in Beersheba, an Israeli town, have valid fears that the rockets Hamas was firing could cause damage and injuries or deaths in their community. "Warnings Not Enough for Gaza Families," in contrast, depicts a Gaza father distraught over the bodies of his children. It reads,

> The Samouni family knew they were in danger. They had been calling the Red Cross for two days, they said, begging to be taken out of Zeitoun, a poor area in eastern Gaza City that is considered a stronghold of Hamas. No rescuers came ... At 6 a.m. on Monday, when a missile fired by an Israeli warplane struck ... there was nowhere to run. Eleven members of the

extended Samouni family were killed and 26 wounded, according to witnesses and hospital officials, with five children age four and under among the dead.[3]

Here members of a Gaza family, including children died, with the point being that non-combatants were being killed in the Israeli air strikes.

To evaluate the *New York Times*' coverage, it is important to remember that the primary readership of the newspaper is in the US, though people around the world may read the online edition. Americans' grasp of Israel's history and geography may be somewhat hazy, and they may not realize that administration of the Gaza Strip was given to Palestinians in 1994 as a result of the Oslo Accords, that all of the Israeli settlements and military bases in the Strip were evacuated in the summer of 2005, and that on the eve of "Cast Lead" there were no Israeli forces inside the Gaza Strip.[4] Americans may not, at the beginning of the war, have remembered that Gaza borders the Mediterranean and Egypt and that the size is small by American standards, some 25 miles long and four to seven miles wide, and is not contiguous with the West Bank. They may also not have been aware that Hamas is in control of Gaza, rather than the Palestinian Authority. In consequence, during the first days of the war, the *Times* printed maps of the Gaza strip showing its size and location, as well as providing other background information.

Analyzing the *New York Times*' coverage is important because the newspaper serves as a gatekeeper to news coverage in the US, as regional newspapers often carry its articles. The newspaper community, though, is far from monolithic, and regional papers do not always follow the *Times*' lead.[5] Moreover, major newspapers tend to choose their articles through a process of selection and exclusion that is a kind of bias, and they decide to cover stories that are salient to their overall mission or orientation. According to Bartimaroudis and Ban, the *Times*, in comparison to European newspapers, is more ethnocentric, covering primarily stories related to US's interest and policies. Content in a European newspaper such as the *Guardian*, in contrast, is driven by news as it unfolds internationally.

Quantitative textual analysis of the *New York Times*' coverage of the Gaza War to determine the actual percentages of pro-Israeli versus pro-Palestinian articles is beyond the scope of this paper. Instead, the focus of this article is upon the perception of bias in the *New York Times*' coverage of the Gaza War by readers and the reaction of the *Times*' editors to that perception. Not long after the war began, readers, bloggers, and media watchdogs began to question the impartiality of the *Times*' coverage. On January 2, 2009, 6 days into the 22 days of the *Times*' coverage, Jill Abramson, the managing editor for news, already felt compelled to answer a number of questions from readers about biased coverage. These are some examples:

- Q. "Why is the *New York Times* so anti-Israel? I have stopped buying the *Times* and I experience joy every time I hear that the old grey lady is in financial trouble. In fact, my happy day is when there are pink slips handed out to your pro-terrorist reporters. The reporter you have in Gaza is a working member of the Hamas propaganda machine. Do you think that this is not going to hurt your paper's reputation? You have lost me as a reader."

- "Q. How come the *Times* only writes about Gaza hardships when there is [also] immense suffering from the Israeli side due to the rocket attacks?
- "Q. When will your newspaper begin to offer a balanced analysis of the Israeli-Palestinian conflict? Although you are not as bad as the *New York Post*, you are still pretty bad."
- "Q. In the current Israeli invasion of Gaza, what effort is the *New York Times* making to consult and cite sharply critical analysts from the Arab world and Europe, as well as the usual Israeli and Washington sources?[6]

The intensity of the critiques in these readers' questions should not be a surprise, considering how high emotions run regarding the Israeli-Palestinian conflict. Abramson says that no other topic arouses so much controversy.[7] Nicholas Lemann, dean of the graduate school of journalism at Columbia University said, "It isn't just a war. It's a media war. Public opinions outside the region are very important, and they're shaped by the press coverage."[8]

Following her examples of reader questions, Abramson responds to these accusations of bias regarding the *Times*' coverage of Gaza by saying that "we scrupulously avoid taking sides" and believe it is the responsibility of the newspaper to "fully document the motives, histories, politics, and perspectives of everyone in the conflict." Abramson says that the *Times* is careful to provide a back story because "there is usually a chain of actions and reactions that stretches back over time." In the recent Gaza fighting,

> ... we wrote both of Israel's actions – the air and ground campaigns and the resulting casualties and hardship – but also what provoked them – the sustained firing of rockets by Hamas into Israeli territory and the terror that was inflicted on many Israeli communities.[9]

Here the *Times*, through Abramson's voice, is asserting its belief in and its commitment to being unbiased, at least in the *Times* editors' perception of what unbiased means. Remember Bartimaroudis and Ban's assertion that the *Times* tends to cover international stories that involve US interests. If that is true, even if the *Times*' individual articles about the war are unbiased, the fact that the newspaper chose to cover the war and in such detail, is a kind of bias by inclusion since it is providing that coverage because of U.S. interests in the region. The US continues to be a committed ally to Israel, so criticism of Israel's actions affects American credibility. Moreover, US corporations and individuals are invested heavily in Israel.

Then, on January 11, 2009, Clark Hoyt, the public editor of the *Times*, weighs in on the continued reader complaints about bias by publishing a column called "Standing Between Enemies" regarding criticisms about the *Times*' coverage of the war. As public editor, Hoyt was hired to function "outside of the reporting and editing structure of the newspaper." He answers reader questions and comments about *New York Times* articles, but the opinions and conclusions he expresses are "his own" and "not necessarily that of the *Times*."[10] However, this particular one of Hoyt's column reads as if he is within the structure of the paper because he is essentially justifying the *Times*' coverage of the war. He writes, "Bombs and rockets are flying between Israel and Palestinians in Gaza, and once again, the *Times* is caught in a familiar crossfire, accused from all sides of unfair and inaccurate coverage."[11] His tone may be somewhat defensive, but, as public editor, Hoyt may have received hundreds of emails and letters saying something like these two contrasting views:

- "To describe the *Times*' reporting as inadequate and favorable to Israel is an understatement."
- "Why do you not print any articles of the suffering of the people in Israel?" "Where are the pro-Israel articles?"[12]

It was not as if this was the first time that the *Times* had been criticized for biased coverage regarding the Israeli/Palestinian conflict. For example, former New York City Mayor Ed Koch, in 2006 accused both the *New York Times* and the BBC of consistently carrying "news stories and editorials that are slanted against Israel and sympathetic to the Palestinian Authority and Hamas."[13]

The *Times*' defensive attitude regarding criticism of media bias begs the question of why readers would expect the *Times* to be unbiased considering public distrust of media in the twenty-first century. Peter R.R. White suggests "the media itself . . . claims a special epistemological status for its texts, asserting that, at least in principle, the news report is factual, disinterested, impersonal and objective." Meanwhile, readers partially accept this media stance, relying on the media for their understanding of events, yet "viewing journalistic discourse with suspicion, as often inaccurate, commercialized, sensationalist and biased."[14] This contradiction – that readers rely on a newspaper such as the *Times* to learn about international events but at the same time believe that the *Times*, like other media, is irredeemably biased – is a recipe for hostility on one side (the readers) and defensiveness on the other (the media).

In 2004, Daniel Okrent, the public editor of the *Times* before Hoyt, wrote a column addressing accusations of bias in the *Times*' coverage, though not specifically that of the Israeli-Palestinian conflict. His column asks in its title, "Is the *New York Times* a Liberal Newspaper?" When he answers his own question, "Of course it is," it becomes clear that the question was rhetorical. He continued, "If you think *The Times* plays it down the middle on any [issue], you've been reading the paper with your eyes closed."[15] If one is going to evaluate the news bias of the *Times*, he says, it should be in the context that the newspaper's primary audience, which is, according to Okrent, urban, Northeastern, culturally seen-it-all, and liberal. If the *Times* is going to be unbiased on an issue, the two sides it presents, if there are two, are going to be skewed to the left and have a sophisticated urban twist as well.

Apparently, the *Times*' readership, though united demographically by liberalism, does not speak with one voice when it comes to being pro-Israeli or pro-Palestinian. Seemingly, one can be urban and liberal and be pro-Israeli, and one can equally be urban and liberal and be pro-Palestinian, at least if one reads the *New York Times*. The determination of one's perception of bias related to the *Times*' stance on Gaza may depend on the individual's own political position – Israeli sympathizers see the newspaper as pro-Palestinian and Palestinian sympathizers view it as pro-Israeli. Remember the reader comment Abramson quoted: "I have stopped buying *The Times* and I experience joy every time I hear that the old grey lady is in financial trouble." Unless this reader is borrowing someone else's copy of the newspaper, he or she is criticizing the *Times*' coverage without reading it, and this person is not the only one. Once a person decides the *Times* (or any other newspaper) is biased, that person is unlikely to read future articles about politically charged topics with an eye toward changing that opinion. This conclusion is supported by political scientists Brendan Nyhan and Jason Reifler whose research indicates that "false or unsubstantiated beliefs about politics" will not be altered by subsequent news items.[16] Readers, once offended by the *Times*' coverage of an issue, are unlikely to offer the newspaper a second chance.

Hoyt's column, "Standing Between Enemies," which I would like to consider here at some length, is an apologia – a classical rhetorical genre that may be defined as an attempt either to apologize for or to defend actions – or both. Hoyt, in his column, feels a need to address readers (or former readers) who consider the *Times*' coverage to be biased, and defend the newspapers actions. Apologia is an ancient rhetorical genre and one of the most enduring. Ware and Linkugel explain, "The recurrent theme of accusation followed by apology is so prevalent in our record of public address as to be, in the words of Kenneth Burke, one of those 'situations typical and recurrent enough for [individuals] to feel the need of having a name for them'."[17] These are three famous examples of modern American apologias:

- Richard Nixon's 1952 "Checkers" speech in response to charges of political corruption stemming from a previously undisclosed fund.
- Senator Edward Kennedy's statement after the Chappaquiddick incident.
- President Bill Clinton's speech admitting his inappropriate sexual relationship with Monica Lewinsky.

An apologia is in response not only to accusations of wrongdoing but also to attacks on a person's morals, motives, or reputation, and it is not necessarily an admission of guilt or culpability. Apologias exhibit an assortment of styles including "appeals to traditional cultural values, invective, references to a greater divinity, reliance upon legitimate bases of power, factual accounts of an issue, and inductively reasoned organization.[18] Disputes generating apologia can be brief, one-time events, or long term, entrenched controversies. Moreover, apologia can be divided into five categories, according to the posture of the speech or document. Essentially, these categories are a catalog of options or strategies available to rhetors when they wish to issue an apologia.

1. Acknowledge the charge and respond with an admission of guilt (or fault, responsibility, etc.) and ask for forgiveness or absolution.
2. Seek acquittal. Acknowledge the charge and respond directly to it with a declaration of "not guilty" or "I didn't do it."
3. Attempt an explanation. Acknowledge the charge and offer an account of what took place. The objective is to make the audience members less likely to want to condemn the action based on their new knowledge of the circumstances. Explanatory apologias usually are ambivalent on the charge of wrongdoing; there is no specific declaration of innocence or admission of guilt.
4. Seek vindication. This is another indirect response to the charge. In most cases of vindication, the charge never is directly acknowledged or given any legitimacy by the accused. Vindication is accomplished through various strategies of indirection (such as attacking the source of the charge as a way of discrediting the charges without addressing them directly).
5. Justification. In adopting this posture, the rhetor seeks a major redefinition or transformation of how the entire situation is conceptualized. The objective is to change the act (or acts) in question into something justifiable or even praiseworthy.[19]

At first blush, one might say that Hoyt's column takes posture number two, "seeks acquittal" by responding directly that the *Times* was not biased in its coverage. He agrees with Abramson – seeing a backwards vote of confidence regarding *Times* reporting, given that "every identifiable faction in this fractured collision of peoples and injustices believes so firmly that we are taking a side – someone else's."[20] Thus, Abrahamson and Hoyt are saying, the *Times* simply is not guilty of the accusation of bias and, indeed, the number of accusations of bias on both sides indicates the *Times'* neutrality.

However, Hoyt's column takes the issue of the backward vote of confidence a bit further, writing:

> It can be risky for editors and reporters to think that if everyone in a dispute is angry with them, then they must be doing something right. Sometimes they are so wrong the anger is justified. But in the case of the complex, intractable struggle between Israel and the Palestinians, even the best, most evenhanded reporting will not satisfy those passionately on one side or the other.[21]

He is saying here that when everyone, even people on both sides are saying you are wrong, it is possible that, indeed, you are in error. Hoyt's position might, then, seem to be closer to position number three, attempting an explanation. He denies that the *Times* was in error, claiming that the struggle is so problematic that even the most impartial reporting will garner criticism. And in his first sentence, he says that receiving criticism from all sides is a "familiar place," one where they have been before and will be again.

In making his explanation for the crossfire directed at the *Times*, Hoyt paraphrases a quote from David K. Shipler, a former *Times* correspondent who won a Pulitzer Prize for his book *Arab and Jew: Wounded Spirits in a Promised Land*: "each side firmly believes it is the victim in the struggle." Likewise, sympathetic readers on both sides believe their chosen side is the victim. In reality, according to Shipler, "Both sides are both victims and perpetrators at the same time."[22] Sympathizers of one side or the other are unlikely to understand that.

The only way to report fairly in a situation in which both sides believe they are the victims, Hoyt agrees with Shipler, is fair-minded coverage that "shatters that paradigm" – the belief that either side is simply a victim rather than both victim and perpetrator.[23] The *Times'* coverage attempts to do this by presenting articles in which there is no easy attribution of blame – or there is an attribution of blame to both sides. One article, for example, is called "A Gaza War Full of Traps and Trickery" described tricks played by both Palestinians and Israelis. Hamas soldiers, wearing civilian clothes, "emerge from tunnels to shoot automatic weapons or antitank missiles, then disappear back inside, hoping to lure the Israeli soldiers with their fire." And, Israelis are tricksters, also. "Israeli intelligence officers are telephoning Gazans and, in good Arabic, pretending to be sympathetic Egyptians, Saudis, Jordanians or Libyans . . . After expressing horror at the Israeli war and asking about the family, the callers ask . . . if there are fighters in the building or the neighborhood."[24] Both sides, according to the article, aren't fighting fair but are resorting to subterfuge.

Using a different technique to shatter the paradigm, the reporter in another article addresses the reader, saying, "Your unit . . . has taken mortar fire from the crowded refugee camp nearby. You prepare to return fire, and perhaps you notice – or perhaps you don't, even though it's on your map – that there is a United Nations school just there, full of displaced Gazans." The reporter asks readers to put themselves inside the mind of the Israeli soldier:

> International law allows you to protect your soldiers and return fire, but also demands that you ensure that there is no excessive harm to civilians. Do you remember all that in the chaos? You pick GPS-guided mortars . . . and fire back. In the end, you kill some Hamas fighters but also, the United Nations says, more than 40 civilians, some of them children. Have you committed a war crime?[25]

This question is addressed not to the Israeli soldiers on the ground that day, but to *New York Times* readers. Will readers take the time and perhaps the courage to think carefully about the no-win situation the Israeli soldier faced?

Hoyt thinks not. He asserts that readers are not willing to consider shattering the paradigm of stereotypes:

> Supporters of Israel want coverage that stresses the terror caused by Hamas rockets fired ever deeper into Israeli territory, and are offended at so many pictures of Palestinian casualties. Supporters of the Palestinians want the coverage to focus on the suffering caused by Israel's bombs and missiles, and on the economic sanctions and border closings that isolated Gaza before the latest fighting began.[26]

Hoyt is using the apologia strategy of explanation to assert that the agency of the complaints against the *Times* lies not in what the *Times* is reporting but in the minds of the readers. Readers who have become passionate about one side or the other in "this intractable struggle" will not, he thinks, be satisfied with even the best, most evenhanded reporting. In effect, he is blaming the readers for their accusations of bias. The reporters and editors at the *Times* are, he implies, more evolved and more sophisticated because they can appreciate that both sides are simultaneously victims and perpetrators.

However, Hoyt explains that the *Times* has investigated charges of bias. For example, one reader said he suspected that a front-page picture . . . of a dead Palestinian girl being carried on a stretcher in a Gaza City hospital was a faked "propaganda photo" because, "A doctor does not examine a person face down." Hoyt talked to Patrick Witty, the photo editor who recommended the picture. Witty showed Hoyt "how he blew [the photo] up on a large computer screen and scanned it carefully for any signs of 'digital doctoring,'" and he also showed Hoyt examples of propaganda photos taken by both sides that Witty would not publish – "posed pictures of Palestinians looking at bodies or Israel's prime minister visiting a smiling soldier in a hospital."[27]

Moreover, Hoyt explains, the *Times* does admit errors. He cites one example. On December 29 Ethan Bronner, the Jerusalem *Times* bureau chief, wrote a front-page news analysis. Hoyt calls the analysis "deep and insightful" but admitted it contained one "slip." Bonner said that Israel would need "another peace treaty" with Hamas when Israel has had no peace treaties with that group. Bonner later told Hoyt that he meant cease fire, but one reader "saw [the slip] as a sign of bias or "at best sloppy reporting." Hoyt's explanation makes the argument that an error here or there (or sloppy reporting here or there) does not destroy the impartiality of the *Times'* coverage. Not all readers would agree.

Some of the *Times'* explanations sound more like justification, apologia strategy number five than they do like explanation, strategy number three. Hoyt describes Witty and others at the *Times* as "frustrated because Israel has barred [foreign] journalists from entering Gaza, and although the *Times* has two photographers in the region ready to go, it must rely on pictures taken by Palestinian photographers."[28] Witty said, "When I can't have my own person there, I have to question every picture that comes in – to an obsessive degree."[29]

To justify why the *Times'* body count of deaths in the conflict might occasionally be wrong, Hoyt gives this illustration:

> When Israeli bombs killed dozens at a United Nations school . . ., it was too dangerous for the newspaper's Palestinian [reporter], Taghreed El-Khodary . . . to go to the scene. She went instead to a hospital, where an official told her that 40 were killed, including 10 children and 5 women. The head surgeon and an ambulance driver said 45 were dead. United Nations officials, who were not on the scene, said 30 were killed. The *Times* emphasized the hospital's count of 40.[30]

So, he is saying, complications inherent in the dangerous situation make it almost impossible to determine an accurate body count – a justification of the error.

Downey, however, writes that dividing apologia into categories such as explanation and justification limits documentation of evolution in the genre or consideration of the context. She suggests considering the function of the apologia rather than the category of the remarks. In classical times, apologias were generally evoked by court cases. When someone was accused of an offense, the apologist presented a speech in the presence of the accuser, as part of a defense that might also involve witnesses, and the jury or assembly would deliver a verdict. If the apologist were judged guilty, the verdict would be immediately followed by a sentence. As Downey points out, the function of apologia in ancient times was survival through exoneration or vindication, for a guilty verdict meant "expulsion, imprisonment, exile, or death."[31]

Downey, in her article, "The Evolution of the Rhetorical Genre of Apologia," tracks changes in the rhetorical form since classical days. For example, in medieval times, the guilt of the accused was often decided in advance, and the only option open to an apologist was to plead for absolution, rather than exoneration or vindication, as in classical times. In contemporary times prior to 1960, she suggests, apologia often had dual motives. The motivation for Richard Nixon's "Checker's" speech was most obviously to refute slurs on his character that he had improperly kept money from a fund for reimbursing campaign expenses. In the speech he does not specifically identify his accusers, another difference from ancient and medieval times in which the identity of the accuser was clear. He says that he will keep one gift, a little dog named Checkers. Because of the timing of Nixon's speech when he was a vice presidential candidate, "the opportunity arose to exploit the situation for more than exoneration." [32] Nixon's apologia was a resounding success perhaps because the public was charmed by the pet, and it resulted in a bump in the polls for Nixon and the presidential candidate, Dwight Eisenhower. The function of Nixon's apologia was to reinstate credibility, which he famously did.

Since 1960, apologias, according to Downey, have suffered as a rhetorical form from the public distrust of politicians and bureaucrats and, indeed, leadership in general. Certainly, due to scandals at newspapers, including the Jayson Blair and Zachery Kouwe plagiarism scandals at the *New York Times*, as well as allegations of liberal bias, the *Times* has been subject to distrust as well. In addition, the proliferation of the media and its ability to mold public perception in modern times have contributed to changes in the apologia genre, for even frivolous accusations, when reported widely in the media, have the ability to damage reputations. Apologias since 1960 have been mostly staged events such as President Bill Clinton's speech in which he admitted his sexual relationship with Monica Lewinsky or the senate hearing in which Akio Toyoda, president of Toyota apologized for the company's problems with car accelerators. Such apologias, evaluated in the public perception rather than in a court of law, often do not result in closure, for either the apologist or the accuser, through an innocent or guilty verdict, as would an apologia in ancient times.[33]

Downey is highly critical of contemporary apologias which, she says, "reflect contradictory, self-serving motives . . . exploit audience ignorance and emotions . . . undermines facts and accuracy, and shuns confrontation of issues."[34] In her opinion, contemporary apologias, in the absence of any rules for the content or conduct of apologias, have become a "decisive rhetoric of manipulation."[35] Yet, she points out, "That this subversive form persisted implies the existence of some pragmatic function" which she thinks may be its use as a delaying tactic. Or, apologists may believe that "time heals, distorts, and forgets." Most alarmingly, she suggests that contemporary apologias function as "self-deception."[36]

Downey was not, of course, referring specifically to Hoyt's apologia column in the *Times*, and there are important differences from her examples. Hoyt's apologia is a newspaper column, not a speech, and it was written in response to criticisms of a newspaper, not an individual. The accusation is that of bias, not sexual impropriety or hiding a dangerous product flaw from the public. However, it may be useful to consider whether some of Downey's criticisms of the rhetorical form may be applicable to Hoyt's apologia. Hoyt acknowledges that the *Times* was caught in "a familiar crossfire" because recent criticisms of the *Times'* coverage on the part of pro-Israeli and pro-Palestinian readers has happened before. By implication, he is saying that this type of criticism will continue whenever the *Times* is covering a story involving the Israeli-Palestinian conflict. If Hoyt has accepted that prospect, why bother to write an apologia? He gives no indication that the *Times* plans to change anything in terms of its coverage. Nor does he evidence any belief that his apologia will convince disillusioned readers of the *Times'* dedication to balanced coverage. Is the apologia, as Downey suggests, a delaying tactic? Is he hoping that, if the *Times* continues its current policies toward assignment and selection of stories, that "time heals, distorts, and forgets." Is he engaging in self-deception? Perhaps not.

Perhaps Hoyt is focusing on the priority of serving the *Times'* core readership, irrespective of the fact that regional newspapers with different demographics may also run the *Times'* articles. Hoyt concludes his column, "Standing Between Enemies," by saying rather proudly, perhaps to his readers who, like him, do not identify themselves as pro-Israeli or pro-Palestinian, "Though the most vociferous supporters of Israel and the Palestinians do not agree, I think the *Times*, largely barred from the battlefield and reporting amid the chaos of war, has tried its best to do a fair, balanced and complete job." In other words, Hoyt's apologia justifies the *New York Times* coverage of the Gaza War by saying that, for an admittedly liberal newspaper, handicapped by having only one reporter on the ground, they have presented nuanced coverage. He is saying that the *Times'* coverage, while alienating "vociferous" supporters on both sides, does a good job of serving the *Times* core readership of urban Northeastern, culturally seen-it-all, and liberal New Yorkers who are able to appreciate the moral complexity that "both sides are both victims and perpetuators at the same time." So, is the *New York Times* coverage of the Gaza War biased? That depends on the definition of bias and the definition of the newspaper's audience.

Notes

1. T. El-Khodary and E. Bonner, "Israelis Say Strikes Against Hamas Will Continue," *New York Times*, 28 December 2008: www.nytimes.com/2008/12/28/world/middle east/28mideast.html (accessed 10 June 2010).
2. M. Mazzetti, "Striking Deep Into Israel, Hamas Employs an Upgraded Arsenal," *New York Times*, 31 December 2008: www.nytimes.com/2009/01/01/world/middleeast/01rockets.html (accessed 10 June 2010).
3. T. El-Khodary and I. Kershner, "Warning Not Enough for Gaza Families," *New York Times*, 5 January 2009: www.nytimes.com/2009/01/06/world/middleeast/06scene.html (accessed 10 June 2010).
4. After the Oslo Accords, troops did remain in and around Israeli settlements in the Gaza Strip until they were disbanded in August 2005.
5. P. Bantimaroudis and H. Ban, "Covering the Crisis in Somalia: Framing the Choices by the *New York Times* and the *Manchester Guardian*," in S.D. Reese, O.H. Gandy, Jr. and A.E. Grant (Eds.), *Framing Public Life: Perspectives on Media and Our Understanding of the Social World*, Mahwah, New Jersey: Lawrence Erlbaum Assoc., 2003, p. 176.
6. J. Abramson, "Talk to the Newsroom: Jill Abramson, Managing Editor," *New York Times*, 2 January 2009: www.nytimes.com/2009/01/02/business/media/05askthe times.html?hp=&pagewanted=a ll (accessed 10 June 2010).
7. C. Hoyt, "Standing Between Enemies," *New York Times*, 11 January 2009: www.nytimes.com/2009/01/11/opinion/11pubed.html?scp=1&sq=%22Standing%20 Between%20Enemies%22&st=cse (accessed 10 June 2010).
8. Quoted in Hoyt, "Standing Between Enemies."
9. J. Abramson, "Talk to the Newsroom: Jill Abramson, Managing Editor."
10. "C. Hoyt" (n.d.): http://topics.nytimes.com/top/opinion/thepubliceditor/index.html?scp=1-spot&sq=Clark%20Hoyt&st=cse (accessed 10 June 2010).
11. Hoyt, "Standing Between Enemies."
12. Ibid.
13. E. Koch, "The *New York Times*' Anti-Israel Bias," Realclearpolitics.com, 1 June 2006: www.realclearpolitics.com/articles/2006/06/the_new_york_times_antiisrael.html (accessed 10 June 2010).
14. P.R.R. White, "Media Objectivity and the Rhetoric of News Story Structure," in E. Ventola (Ed.), *Discourse and Community: Doing Functional Linguistics*, Tübingen, Germany: Narr, 2000, pp. 379–397.
15. D. Orient, "THE PUBLIC EDITOR; Is *The New York Times* a Liberal Newspaper?" *New York Times*, 25 July 2004: www.nytimes.com/2004/07/25/opinion/the-public-editor-is-the-new-york-times-a-liberal-newspaper.html?scp=1&sq=%22Is%20the%20 New%20York%20Times%20a%20Liberal%20Newspaper%22&st=cse (accessed 10 June 2010).
16. B. Nyhan and J. Reifler, "When Corrections Fail: The Persistence of Political Misperceptions," *Political Behavior* 32.2, 2010, p. 303.
17. B.L. Ware and W.A. Linkugel, "They Spoke in Defense of Themselves: On the Generic Criticism of Apologia," *Quarterly Journal of Speech* 59, 1973, pp. 273–274.
18. S.D. Downey, "The Evolution of the Rhetorical Genre of Apologia," *Western Journal of Communication* 57, 1993, pp. 42–64.
19. Ware and Linkugel, "They Spoke in Defense of Themselves: On the Generic Criticism of Apologia," pp. 282–283.
20. Hoyt, "Standing Between Enemies."
21. Ibid.
22. Quoted in Hoyt, "Standing Between Enemies."
23. Ibid.
24. S. Erlanger, "A Gaza War Full of Traps and Trickery," *New York Times*, 11 January 2009: www.nytimes.com/2009/01/11/world/middleeast/11hamas.html?scp=1&sq=

%22A%20Gaza%20War%20Full%20of%20Traps%20and%20Trickery%22&st=cse (accessed 10 June 2010).

25. S. Erlanger, "Weighing Crimes and Ethics in the Fog of Urban Warfare," *New York Times*, 17 January 2009: www.nytimes.com/2009/01/17/world/middleeast/17israel. html?scp=1&sq=%22Weighing%20Crimes%20and%20Ethics%22&st=cse (accessed 10 June 2010).
26. Hoyt, "Standing Between Enemies."
27. Ibid.
28. Hoyt, "Standing Between Enemies."
29. Quoted in Hoyt, "Standing Between Enemies."
30. Hoyt, "Standing Between Enemies."
31. Downey, "The Evolution of the Rhetorical Genre of Apologia," p. 47.
32. Ibid., p. 54.
33. Downey, "The Evolution of the Rhetorical Genre of Apologia," pp. 42–43, 55–56.
34. Ibid., p. 58.
35. Ibid., p. 58.
36. Ibid., p. 58.

18 Media ethics in times of war*

Yuval Cherlow

A.

When a democratic society experiences a state of war, it must deal with the conflict that necessarily exists between the idea of a free media on one hand and the war goals and the ability to achieve a victory on the other. A free media may prevent the possibility of achieving a victory: it exposes military secrets; it raises and airs discussion about the war's justification, and may damage the self confidence of the troops; it decreases the national morale; and it may move the public to extreme positions opposing the war. Additionally, at times the media may cause severe injury to individual privacy, for example by publishing reports and photographs of casualties even before the person's family is notified.

Then again, a free media is not only unavoidable due to the internet, the availability of cameras and videos and other technological devices which make it practically impossible to stem the flow of information, making the need for a free media much more important. Free media is the primary means that enables public discussion about the war's objectives, the ways to control the war, and to search for other solutions to the conflict that are better than military action.

The situation of the media in wartime has undergone a significant change in recent years that warrants a new discussion concerning basic assumptions about the goals and objectives of the media in wartime. In the past, the media was an addendum to the war. Most of the public's attention was given to the battlefield, so the discussion about the role of media was influenced by its ancillary role. The main ethical issue was how to balance between the effort to achieve victory in the battlefield and the importance of open discussion in order to supervise the goals of the war. Open media was often considered dangerous, mainly because of the enemy's ability to uncover military-related information through the media, potentially causing damage in the battlefield.

Today, the media is no longer an addendum, but an integral part of the battle.[1] The new technologies that bring the battlefield to every place in the world in real time, the world's transformation to a global village, and the negative public attitude to the violence used by states, have transformed the question of what will be presented from the battlefield in the world's media into a component that determines defeat or victory. The awareness of the limitations of force means that the struggle cannot be determined by military action alone. There are many components that, despite the fact that they are very far from the battlefield, have a huge influence on the outcome of the war: international public opinion, the UN and other international organizations and so on. The sources of information used by these organizations are mainly the open media, increasing its effect tremendously. Therefore, as mentioned, the role played by the media is increasing and there is a dramatic change in its status.

This new status raises new ethical dilemmas. In order to demonstrate them I'll focus on the public debate that occurred during the military operation against the Palestinian terrorists, which took place in the Gaza strip during December of 2009.[2] During that conflict, the media was criticized from two different, contradictory, directions. On one hand, there were a lot of complaints that the media supplied assistance to the terrorists. There were also complaints that the media exposed secret information by describing the troops' locations; the media distributed information about every injured soldier and weakened the public morale. As mentioned, these are traditional complaints towards the media.

In recent years, two new main issues have arisen. The first is a result of the awareness of the media's limitations. The media has actually adopted a policy of telling a story, instead of trying to describe and analyze the big picture. If there is a good story that looks interesting on the screen – it will be broadcast, regardless of the weight or the real relative importance of this event. As mentioned, the widespread technology means that many individual stories can find their way to the screen. Consequently, this causes a distortion of reality. Injured civilians, destroyed houses and crying children are much more impressive on screen than analyzing the impossible situation of a state being constantly attacked and targeted by missiles; therefore they are broadcast frequently. Hence, the information is distorted and the role played by the media is seen as negative.

The second issue is also a result of the new situation, in which victory depends not only on the achievements in the battlefield, but also on the ethical judgment of public opinion. During a war mistakes naturally occur, and there are always civilians that are injured. When terrorists hide in civilians' houses, this is unavoidable. Broadcasting such civilian casualties means giving the terrorists a very powerful weapon, weakening the military's ability to defeat them. When there is negative public opinion towards the legitimacy of the war itself, together with a misunderstanding of the difficulties of a battle against terrorists – these pictures result in a campaign to stop the war. That is exactly what the terrorists want to happen.

On the other hand, in the 2008–2009 Gaza war the media in Israel was criticized for not bringing the real picture to every living room. The claims from this side are that there is an essential need that the public be informed on what is being done in the Gaza strip. This is the only way to arouse public discussion about the operation's goals, to force the military commanders to understand that the military aspects are only part of the entire picture, and to "defend" the nation's young men and women who serve in the military from over-enthusiastic politicians. The importance of being moral and avoiding war crimes is not only an external necessity – it is an essential human and Jewish value, and the only way to achieve such morality is by exposing the situation to the public. For the media to hide any information, even such information that might weaken the troops, is a basic betrayal of ethics, putting that media in line with some of the worst dictators in history.

B.

Does Jewish tradition provide guidelines regarding these dilemmas? Unfortunately, there are no precise sources which might provide an answer this question. The reason for this situation is very clear. The last time that there was an independent Jewish state was more than 2,000 years ago. Therefore, discussions regarding state dilemmas are very rare in Jewish literature. Jewish communities worldwide did not often face situations in which they had power in their hands, and both war crimes and open media were unthinkable. Jewish tradition is affected by Jewish history, and this is a history of a minority living under the patronage of other powers. For a minority in exile, the most important thing was to survive. This was the basis for the Jewish response to any situation. Collaborating with any external power against fellow-Jews, and in particular supplying incriminating information, was one of the worst sins imaginable. There are special religious rulings regarding a *"moser"* (a person who delivers incriminating information to the gentile government), and every member of the community is authorized to do everything possible to stop such a *"moser,"* including killing him.[3] It is very important to emphasize that there are communities in Israel today that claim this should lead our current policy against anyone who delivers restricted information to the media – not going as far as killing the reporter, but that policy should to be guided by the rule of *"moser,"* especially during wartime. There are even a few people who claim that even an Israeli government can be identified as *"moser,"* if it is planning to withdraw from the parts of the Holy Land and to dismantle Jewish settlements. I think this opinion is not acceptable: there is a unique difference between a sovereign state and a minority tribe, and ignoring that may lead to tragic situations. From a more practical view, many horrible mistakes may be made without the important role played by the open media.

One source that should have been very productive in this regard is the Bible.[4] Most of the events described in the Bible are described as happening at a time in which there was an independent Israelite state. The Bible describes various military actions, and so it would seem to be the best source for rules of conduct during wartime. But actually there is very little that we can learn directly from the Bible: we are facing a new reality, which is very different than that known to the Bible. The role of the media is completely new. In the centuries that have passed since the biblical period, humanity in general has made a lot of progress regarding international law and values, and leaping directly from the Bible to our day is irresponsible. We can't transfer the way that war was conducted in the biblical period and apply it to our own times. We can't ignore and devaluate the progress that the world has made.

However, there are a few principles in Jewish law that can serve as leads in this contentious issue. In order to continue, we must first identify the main relevant topics, in order to appreciate the possible contribution of Jewish law in defining the role of the media during wartime.

C.

There are two basic differences between the principles of modern media in Western liberal societies and those of Jewish tradition. Both of these differences are not at all marginal, but very central to the issue.

The first major difference between Jewish tradition and the principles of free media is the dogma of the public's "right to know." This is one of the basic principles of modern media. The pre-assumption is that the public has the right to know everything, and information must be published unless there is a special, rare and unusual reason to prevent publication. Burden of proof is on whoever wants to prevent publication, and if he fails to do so the information is allowed to be published. Journalistic ethics claims even more – that there is an ethical obligation to publish any information that is possible unless there is a real obstacle to doing that, and a journalist who withholds information without good reason abuses his position and commits an ethical offense. In contrast, according to Jewish law, the public doesn't have any rights regarding information that may injure or even just cause embarrassment to the person in question.[5] Jewish law prohibits writing negative things publicly even if they are pure truth, unless there is a real need to do so.[6] If we try to define the main role of the media in Jewish law, we could say that instead of being about the right to know, Jewish law is based on the obligation or necessity to know. When there are important events that the public has a need to know in order to protect itself from criminals or harmful events, there is an obligation to advertise the information. But one should not publicize negative information without a real need.

The second point is the context. Jewish tradition sees everything in context. There is no uninhibited art without asking if it is moral; there can be no democratic decisions that contradict the religious codes; therefore, there can be no free media without investigating its influence on the entire issue that we are dealing with. Reporters are part of the nation; therefore they must consider the nation's needs when there are debating whether to publish information that may cause damage to the nation.

There is a big dispute between halakhic authorities on whether Jewish law has a place for what we call "the media" at all.[7] Some authorities consider the whole idea of free information to be opposed to religious principles, because the media does not and cannot take religious codes into consideration. Therefore, they claim, free information causes much more injustice than benefits, and we should try to limit it only to information that is really important and very necessary. My opinion is that a free media has a tremendously important function in our society. There can be no freedom of choice without freedom of expression. The ability to say things that are negative or even insulting when it's necessary should be expanded to cover everything that is important in a modern state. A society is obligated not only to protect people from being hurt by information about them.

Society must also advance ethically and morally, and that can be done only if its members are brave enough to face their failures and try to fix them. The Torah also directs us to eradicate sin from our society, and it is impossible to do that without having all of the relevant information. Nevertheless, the two principles of "need to know" and of protection from too much information are still very importannt, particularly at times when the nation is under attack or at war.

D.

What are the halakhic principles according to which we are to consider the media a very important component in public life?[28] The answer to this question is based on the understanding that the obligation to avoid advertising negative information about people may be offset by additional considerations that would actually oblige us to distribute that same information. The Torah commands that a person should be responsible for his fellow and when that fellow is facing risk, it is forbidden to remain silent and avoid involvement.[9] Indeed, one must do everything he can in order to protect or rescue the other person. This is also an obligation on society in general. The general commitment to eradicate evil is binding on the congregation or the state and must depend on having an open public flow of information. The leaders of the community are obligated to tackle crime and inappropriate behavior and are not permitted to close their eyes to evil. Another important role of such open information is to intimidate potential criminals. People who realize that their actions will be made public knowledge may think twice before their wrongdoing.

These principles are part of Jewish law. The basic book of religious commandments that defines those issues is *Shmirat Halashon* ("Guarding the Tongue").[10] The author, Rabbi Yisrael Meir Kagan (Poupko),[11] one of the greatest Torah scholars of the early twentieth century, was well-known for being very strict about publicizing negative or confusing information about people. Even so, a whole chapter of this book deals with the right, and even the statutory duty, to do so when necessary.[12] In fact, Rabbi Kagan formulated details defining the rules and limitations concerning speech about other people. Analyzing these rules demonstrates the sensitive way in which *halakhah* attempts to balance the necessity to confront evil and the wish to avoid violating the rules of "*Lashon Hara*" ("the evil tongue" – the general definition of all the rules about speech meant to prevent insulting and confusing others). The rules, as they are set out in the tenth chapter of *Shmirat Halashon*, are as follows: purity of motivation, so that the information will only be used for the relevant purpose; distinguishing between fact and commentary, and speaking or writing only about topics where the evidence is clear and proven; doing it in a way that will not cause any unnecessary damage; advertizing the information only if there is no other choice, and there is no alternative way to avoid the harm done by the person that the information is about.[13]

However, in order to use these principles to formulate a Jewish approach regarding the operation of the media during war, one cannot simply "copy and paste" them as they are. As mentioned above, the role of the media during war is much more complicated, and limits that we can force on individuals are irrelevant for states – and even more so for the international media. It would take a significant effort to "translate" halakhic principles that were formulated for individuals into the public field. However, I think that we are able to draw a kind of "road map" that may be thought of as the halakhic guidelines for reporters, editors, the IDF spokesman and politicians, when considering whether certain information is best kept hidden or published.

It should be emphasized that the aspect with which we are dealing here is the halakhic/legal one. However the purpose of this survey is not to suggest that this should become the state law, and not to recommend that reporters or editors should be sued or punished according to these rules. My opinion, as a member of the presidential press council, is that the state should limit its involvement in all fields of professional ethics, and in particular should leave media ethical dilemmas to the conscience and internal codes of the media organizations. The purpose of this survey is to search for essential principles that could serve as guidelines for Jewish media during war, and perhaps to contribute to the international debate about this sensitive issue as well.

E.

Consequently, what are the ethical rules of conduct for the media during wartime according to principles of Jewish law?

1. The media is not an external player, and therefore everyone who works for the media is part of the national war effort. Individuals who are distributing information privately should function as part of the national effort to achieve victory. The idea of looking at the media as an exceptional group that are exempt from the national effort is in contradiction to the prevalent attitude in Jewish law. Reporters and editors, publishers and private people, are part of the nation, and the fact that they are dealing with information doesn't exempt them from supporting the nation in its confrontation against its enemies. Indeed, this rule does not relate only to citizens or groups for whom the war is part of their personal interests; every human being should see himself as someone who is responsible for the promotion of justice in the world, and should support the righteous side of any conflict. There can be a major disagreement as to who the righteous side is, but there is no argument that once you decide who is right – you should be part of the effort to assist that side. If you are part of the nation, you should support your nation, unless the evil committed by your nation is so great that (in your opinion) it is better that your nation be defeated than be victorious.

2. The role of the media is more significant than that of an individual: as shown above, the way that the war is brought to every television and computer screen is definitely one of the components that influence the outcome of the war. Therefore, the media is part of the military effort, even if some would prefer

to deny this and to behave as if the media were only transferring objective information. This is true world-wide, but within the Jewish approach to the image of the war – it has an additional aspect. Jewish heritage sees the Jewish nation as a representative of the Divine. When the Jewish army acts in a way that is moral it is also glorifying the name of God. Therefore, it is vital that the image that is disseminated emphasize the army's moral behavior – of course only if that is the truth.

3.   Helping and supporting the nation does not mean covering up or hiding the various types of failures. Failures are an integral part of waging war, and they can appear in many aspects: the goals of the war might be completely wrong; many of the tactics used may be controversial, and there may be better alternatives to those that were selected; during the war, both individual soldiers and their commanders may perform acts that can be considered to be war-crimes. It is necessary that all these issues be discussed critically for two reasons: to avoid mistakes that may result in a lot of damage to the troops or even to the nation itself, and to avoid war crimes and other extreme activities that can happen during war. This is not only the media's prerogative; this is its main responsibility.

4.   The way to fulfill this mission is to use the halakhic guidelines. In spite of the fact that there are no direct rules in regarding the functions of media during wartime, we can use the rules that were originally formulated for individuals and translate them, with proper adaptation, to rules that can guide everyone involved in publicizing information from the battlefield. This is one of the ways that halakhic authorities formulate rules that are relevant to the modern Jewish state, compensating for the past 2,000 years during which such a state did not exist.

5.   The first rule is an internal one: each person should ask himself what is the real source that motivates him. Indeed, *halakhah* constantly emphasizes that acting in according to personal motives is only human and certainly not wrong. However, given the special way according to which *halakhah* rejects publicizing embarrassing information – even true information – such action is limited to necessity only, demanding that any information published be absolutely necessary.

6.   The second demand is the authenticity of the information. Obviously, this is part of the professional principles of journalism; a reporter who reports news that is not true is violating his mission. But this is also an ethical demand, because doing so means using the power that he has in order to harm those about whom he writes as well as all of the people who are being exposed to the information. Causing damage and hurting people is a moral sin, and in order to avoid this, the journalist must be precise and very careful.

7.   Distinguishing between facts and commentary is part of the wider meaning of "truth." *Halakhah* uses the term *"Avak Lashon Hara"* (The dust of the evil tongue) in order to forbid not only explicit lies but also using "tricks" in order to look like a righteous person while behaving like an evil one.[14] One of the techniques is to use all kinds of hints, craftiness and other ways of expression,

that enable saying negative things without seeming to do so. The obligation is to be completely honest when distributing information.

8. The big question is whether it is right to avoid publicizing true information that will cause a lot of damage to the nation, or to the just side of the conflict. As we have seen, the fact that the information is true is not enough. There should be a real need that the information be distributed, and it is prohibited to do so when there is no reason to do so, and definitely when doing so may cause real damage. The problem is that it's very difficult to define specific guidelines, because often public criticism and pointing out failures as they happen may actually contribute to eventually achieving the goals of the war. A second problem is the inability of the individual reporter to judge what is helpful and what can cause a disaster. All we can say is that this should be one of the factors that influences the decision whether or not to publish the information in question.

F.

Indeed, the principles that I have suggested above are based on religious foundations. This is the reason that we can speak about intentions, motivations and principles, not just consequences. Religious language also can demand an involvement in the issues, trying to resolve them by ways other than airing them in public. But when dealing with the question of media in time of war, the question is: can we transmute this religious discourse into legal principles, which may then guide the members of the media precisely how to act in time of war?

There are three possible answers to this question. The first is to dispute the very premise that the only way to influence the desired standards is through legal formulations.[15] Ethical principles can be incorporated in many ways other than through legislation. They can become part of the profession through education. One of the most difficult problems that we face is the fact that there is no need for any authorization or certification in order to practice journalism (a government-issued journalist's license is just a technical permit, not a sign of ethics or professionalism). But if there were a sort of continuing education program where ethical issues were discussed, it might have a much larger effect than legislation.

The second answer is that there is a variety of ways in which to formulate ethical principles: they can be part of an internal ethical code, that, though it not be precise, may be able to establish guidelines; the Israel Press Council could establish a voluntary institution for the investigation of complaints about ethics violations in war time, which would again serve as a guide for reporters, editors and others.

The third option is to try to do as much as possible to draft principles and to create a law. However, we should resist the government's involvement in shaping the free press as much as possible. In order to enable the media to play the role as criticizing government abuses of the legal system, it must be free of any restraints that the government would seek to impose on it. Therefore, there is almost no place for legislation, and we should encourage the media to limit its power with its own systems. However, in times of war, it might be justified to consider

Prokaryote, ganz nach rechts

legislation that would enforce the ethical principles that should guide journalists. In this framework, it is possible to translate topics such as motivation or goals into legal terms and to discuss such concepts as fairness and integrity. It is impossible to force the media to see itself as part of the war effort and to impose patriotism or cooperation with goals of the war by law, but it is possible to demand that the media not actually damage the war effort itself.

These three options are also relevant to today's media. Indeed, the ability to impose ethical principles supposedly does not exist anymore, because everyone who owns a mobile device is automatically a potential reporter and any owner of a video camera could become a broadcaster. Private information sources supposedly prevent any possibility of influencing the media. But it would be wrong to throw out all of the ethical principles, because most of the significant power still remains in the hands of the established media. The public refers to the established media more seriously and sees it as a source of information that is relatively objective. Therefore, there is great importance in its preserving the ethical rules, delicately maneuvering between its journalists' duty as citizens to participate in the war effort and the media's traditional role as an objective observer.

Throughout this paper, our assumption has been that the responsibility for the existence of the state is an ethical principle of the first degree. The citizens are responsible not only for their personal rights, but also for the survival and security of the state, and sometimes they are even called upon to sacrifice their lives for their country. This principle also requires them to take responsibility for the protection the state, and consequently there are ethical limits on freedom of speech and freedom of information in wartime.

Like any other ethical issue, the commitment to apply these principles is based on their inherent truth, even if legislation fails to impose them. Jewish tradition and law offers one of the ways to balance between theses different goals, in light of the fundamental principles of the general perception of "*Lashon Harah*" ("guarding the tongue").

Notes

* This article is an expanded version of a paper delivered at the conference on War and Peace in Jewish Tradition held by the Ariel University Center and Beit Morasha of Jerusalem in July 2009. I wish to thank Dr. Amnon Shapira, Dr. Yigal Levin and Mr. Jackie Goldstein for their help in preparing this version.
1. See M. Kalb and C. Saivetz, *The Israeli-Hezbollah War of 2006: The Media as a Weapon in Asymmetrical Conflict*, Cambridge, Mass: Harvard University, John F. Kennedy School of Government, 2007 (etext).
2. The questions raised by open media during wartime and the attempt to write a code of ethics were intensified during the Second Lebanon War of July 2006. The Israel Press Council established a special committee that discussed these issues and published a report, which can be accessed (in Hebrew) on the council's website: www.moaza.co.il/BRPortal/br/P102.jsp?arc=26997. See also D. Dor, S. Iram and O. Voldavsky, *"War Till the Last Moment": The Israeli Media in the Second Lebanon War*, Jerusalem: Keshev, The Center for the Protection of Democracy in Israel, 2007 (Hebrew).

3. See M. Maimonides, *Mishneh Torah – The Book of Torts*, Wounding and Damaging VIII (trans. H. Klein), New Haven and London: Yale University Press, 1954, pp. 188–192; M. Wolf, "Halakhic Connections between the Law of 'Moser' and the Law of 'Rodef'," in M. Addad and Y. Wolf (Eds.), *Crime and Social Deviance: Theory and Practice*, Ramat-Gan: Bar-Ilan University Press, 2002, pp. 215–249 (Hebrew with English abstract).

4. See Y. Ariel, "War Ethics in the Torah," in E. Bloom *et al.* (Eds.), *Values in the Trial of War: Ethics and War in the View of Judaism*, Jerusalem: The Mizrahi Family and Moreshet Publishers, 1985, pp. 80–90 (Hebrew).

5. See: T. Rashi, "'The Public's Right to Know' in the Code of Media Ethics Versus 'The Public's Obligation to Know' in Jewish Law," in T. Rashi and M. Zapt (Eds.), *Media and Judaism – A Collection of Essays*, Petah Tikvah: Keter Hazahav, 2008, pp. 47–62 (Hebrew). See also A. Hacohen, "On Freedom of Expression, Tolerance and Pluralism in Jewish Law," ibid. pp. 9–46 (Hebrew).

6. See Maimonides, *Mishneh Torah – The Book of Knowledge*, Ethics VII, 2 (trans. S. Glaezr), New York: Maimonides Publishing Company, 1927, pp. 224–225; N. Rakover, *Protection of Privacy in Jewish Law*, Jerusalem: The Jewish Legal Heritage Society, 2006, pp. 29–32 (Hebrew).

7. See T. Rashi, "Between Isolation and Knowledgeable Use: The Reaction of the Jewish Orthodox Leadership to the Mass Media in the Twentieth Century," *Mayyim MiDalyav* 19–20, 2008–9, pp. 399–424 (Hebrew); A.Y. Shvat, "Media and News – Positive Commandment or Negative," *Talelei Orot* 6, 1995, pp. 164–188 (Hebrew).

8. For more on this theme see A. Ariel, "*Lashon Hara* in a Democratic Public System," *Tsohar* 5, 2001, pp. 37–61; *Tsohar* 6, 2002, pp. 41–59 (Hebrew).

9. M. Maimonides, *Mishneh Torah – The Book of Torts*, Murder and the Preservation of Life I, 14 (trans. H. Klein), New Haven and London: Yale University Press, 1954, p. 198. Much has been written on this subject, for which see Y. Eldan, "'Do Not Stand by the Blood of Your Neighbor' and the Concept of Responsibility," *Akdamot: A Journal of Jewish Thought* 11, 2001, pp. 7–37 (Hebrew with English abstract).

10. Y.M. Kagan, *Sefer Shmirat Halashon*, Vilna: Metz, 1876 (Hebrew and in dozens of later editions).

11. Rabbi Yisrael Meir Ha-Kohen (Kagan) Poupko of Radun (1838–1933), was one of the leaders of European and worldwide Orthodox Jewry in the generation before the Holocaust. He was the head of the Radun Yeshiva and published dozens of works, the most influential of which were *Hafetz Hayim*, Vilna: Hillel Dvarzetz, 1873 (Hebrew and in dozens of later editions), and his halakhic commentary *Mishnah Berurah*, published over the years 1884–1907. Within the Jewish world Rabbi Yisrael Meir is often simply known by the name of his first book, "The Hafetz Hayim."

12. See Y. Cherlow, "'And You Shall Cast out the Evil From Israel': On the Policy Towards Publishing Embarrassing Items," in Rashi and Zapt (Eds.), *Media and Judaism*, pp. 79–96 (Hebrew).

13. For a different interpretation of the Jewish tradition on this matter see C.H. Cohen, "On Freedom of Opinion and of Speech in Jewish Tradition," in G. Frishtik (Ed.), *Human Rights in Judaism: Obligations and Privileges in Jewish Law*, Jerusalem: The Sanhedrin Institute, 1992, pp. 179–202 (Hebrew).

14. Maimonides, *Mishneh Torah – The Book of Knowledge*, Ethics VII, 4 (trans. S. Glazer), New York: Maimonides Publishing Company, 1927, pp. 226–227.

15. For an extensive discussion of this issue see A. Geva, "Ethics in Business," in A. Kasher (Ed.), *Introductions to Ethics* I, Jerusalem: The Hebrew University Magnes Press, 2009, pp. 99–143 (Hebrew).

Epilogue

War and peace in Jewish tradition – seven anomalies

Amnon Shapira and Yigal Levin

An examination of the eighteen individual papers that were included in this volume will easily reveal that the majority of them deal with matters of personal and collective morality in warfare. It should come as no surprise that such questions of morality have concerned the People of Israel from the time of the Bible through the rabbis of the Talmud and all the way to the modern State of Israel. However it is precisely this fact that raises the question of just how such a people managed to survive though such a long and often violent history.

The phenomenon of the Jews' survival is indeed a wonder: a small persecuted minority in a world that is generally intolerant of minorities, not only surviving but even managing to create some of the world's great cultural assets, in literature, philosophy and religion, but also in the fields of community life and social autonomy.

But this is not the only wonder. The people of Israel were exiled from the land of Canaan to Egypt and returned under Joshua, exiled by Nebuchadnezzar and returned under Cyrus, then exiled again by Titus the Roman, with a small number of Jews always remaining in the land. The Jews then returned to the land in waves, Nahmanides in the thirteenth century, the "Hasidim" in the eighteenth century, the more substantial Zionist immigrations of the late nineteenth century and the twentieth, especially after the wars of 1948 and 1967. And through all of this, the Jews were forced to fight for their very survival in their own land. One result of this is that the idea of "War and Peace" is a central theme of Jewish thought and historiography, not a marginal ideal. What is more, is that according to the theme that runs through this book, these constant struggles resulted in turning the people of Israel into an Athens, not a Sparta. Israel did not lose its values over all those years of conflict; on the contrary, those values were heightened and refined. In the years 2000–5 Israel was assaulted with a wave of Palestinian terrorist activity, known as "the second intifada" or "the El-Aqsa Intifada" that included massive suicide bombings of busses, discotheques and cafés. It is doubtful that any other civilian society in modern times has been attacked so violently by people living among and alongside it. Yet despite this, Professor Asa Kasher of Tel Aviv University, one of Israel's premier ethical philosophers and the author of the IDF code of ethics, wrote in an article published in the daily *Maariv* on October 1, 2010, that "the second intifada did not harm Israel's morality, rather,

Israel's sense of morality has become stronger." He reiterated and re-emphasized this theme in a lecture given before the senior faculty of social sciences at the Ariel University Center of Samaria on February 1, 2011. He deduced this "strengthening of Israel's morals" from a series of parameters that he examined in the military, the security service, the legal establishment and the civil service. And we wonder: how did this seemingly surprising trend come to be?

In what follows we will briefly trace seven distinctive phenomena, all connected to the moral aspects of war in Jewish tradition; phenomena that distinguish Jewish tradition from the norm in the ancient world. These phenomena have their origins in the Hebrew Bible, but they most certainly influenced the way in which Jewish tradition developed through the ages, all the way to the present day. We will address each of these phenomena in turn.

1. Neither "pacifism" nor "militarism"

In general, the Hebrew Bible does not preach "pacifism" (which in the Christian tradition traces its origins to the Sermon on the Mount in Matthew 5:38–44). On the other hand, the Bible also does not preach continuous "holy war," such as the Islamic *Jihad*. The Talmud stated this most succinctly – "if one comes to kill you – rise to kill him first" (BT *Sanhedrin* 73b). As shown in several of the papers in this volume, the idea of self-defense as a justification for war runs through Jewish tradition of all ages.

2. The purpose of war is to inherit the land, not imperialist expansion

The Bible forbids Israel to engage in war for the purpose of conquering the neighboring lands, which God had given to their own nations. Specifically listed are the lands of Edom (Deuteronomy 2:2–6), Moab (ibid. 9) and Ammon (ibid. 17–19). Such legislation, that forbids a nation from expanding beyond its own borders, is unparalleled in the world of the Ancient Near East. And while the biblical narrative does tell of David's wars and conquest of these and other nations (justified by the claim that "they attacked first"), the moral ideal was set, and the rabbis of the Talmud in fact condemn David for these acts.

3. "The call for peace" before war: talk first, shoot later

The book of Deuteronomy demands that before going to war, Israel first call on the opposing side to make peace: "When you draw near to a town to fight against it, offer it terms of peace" (Deuteronomy 20:10) – in practice, to negotiate a peaceful surrender. This rule came into practice in Moses' war against Sihon, when, after God commanded, "See, I have handed over to you King Sihon the Amorite of Heshbon and his land. Begin to take possession by engaging him in battle" (ibid. 2:24), Moses himself first negotiated: "So I sent messengers from the wilderness of Kedemoth to King Sihon of Heshbon with the following terms of peace" (ibid. 26). Although the incident itself ended in war because of Sihon's refusal to allow the Israelites passage, rabbinic exegesis understood Moses' Call for Peace as contravening God's specific commandment, establishing his own autonomous moral position which overrides even a divine commandment.[1]

4. A tradition of disobeying a corrupt or immoral political leadership

The 1945–46 Nuremburg Trials accentuated the existence of two opposing philosophies: one which demands absolute obedience to the laws and ordinances of a legally elected government, and the other according to which the rules of morality take precedent over those of the government. A similar dispute existed in the world of the Ancient Near East. In all of the cultures known to us, from Egypt to Assyria and Babylonia, the command of the king was imbued with divine authority which could not be disobeyed, and the laws of the state, harsh and cruel as they may have been, were absolute. The one exception to this rule was Israel. According to the laws of the Torah and the stories of the prophets, the king of Israel was but human, and his behavior, if contravening divine law, was constantly given to criticism. Thus the Hebrew midwives disobeyed the king's command to murder the Hebrew male children (Exodus 1:17) and Moses also disobeyed the king's command (ibid. 2:11–14). An additional example is that of Saul's servants who refused to kill the priests of Nob (1 Samuel 22:17). This was even true for divine commands, as in Abraham's refusal to accept God's collective punishment of Sodom (Genesis 18:23–33) and Moses' similar debate with God (Exodus 32:32).

The conclusion from these and many additional examples is that the Bible encourages defiance that stems from opposition to injustice, even if that injustice is supported by authority. Such opposition usually does not originate in written law but rather in ethical and moral values. As formulated by Benjamin Uffenheimer, "Instead of addressing kings and princes, fomenting overt uprising against regimes and governments, the prophets appeal to the masses, seeking to inspire a revolution in human hearts."[2]

5. The existence of limitations in times of war

There is a series of laws in the Bible that relate to the by-products of war: the humane treatment of a beautiful woman taken captive (Deuteronomy 21:10–14); the especially positive treatment of Israelites taken captive during war (2 Chronicles 28:10–15); the obligation to bury a person who had been killed in battle (Deuteronomy 21:22–23; this rule, which originally referred to Israelite casualties, was expanded to include foreigners, even bitter enemies, who are still to be respected as human beings – see Joshua 8:29; 10:26–27); the rule forbidding to cut down fruit trees in time of siege (Deuteronomy 20:19); the general demand for "purity of the camp" (Deuteronomy 20:10–15). The very existence of such laws may have served as a moderating factor in Israelite soldiers' behavior on the battlefield, but even if not, they do set standards of behavior that later Judaism considered to be binding.

6. The "ethical code" of war

There are several examples of a sort of "Code of Ethics" that takes effect in time of war. Two such examples follow:

a. The attempt to avoid harm to non-combatants, especially weaker members of society: "Remember what Amalek did to you on your journey out of Egypt, how he attacked you on the way, when you were faint and weary, and struck down all who lagged behind you; he did not fear God" (Deuteronomy 25:17–18). From the sins of Amalek we can infer the following codes of conduct: unlike Amalek, one must only attack after giving notice, and one must only fight against an army that is prepared for war and not against the weak, the tired, women and children. As we have stated, most of the biblical rules of war are unparalleled in Ancient Near Eastern sources, but this rule, demanding advance notice, actually was known in the ancient world, and transgressors could expect divine retribution.[3] Surprisingly, there are also signs of similar rules in the cultures of the Far East. Walzer quotes an ancient Hindi text according to which the following are not to be involved in warfare: "Those who look on without taking part, those afflicted with grief . . . those who are asleep, thirsty, or fatigued or are walking along the road, or have a task on hand unfinished, or who are proficient in fine art."[4] The mention of "those who are asleep, thirsty, or fatigued or are walking along the road" is reminiscent of the crime of which Amalek is accused in Deuteronomy 25:18, while "have a task on hand unfinished" reminds us of the list of those whom Deuteronomy 20:5–7 releases from going to war: those who have built a house and not yet lived in it, planted a vineyard and not yet enjoyed its fruit, and those who have become engaged to a woman but not yet married her.

b. Avoiding the devaluation of human life in wartime. The following story reflects the way in which human life seems to lose its value during wartime, and the way in which the Bible opposes unnecessary endangerment of the lives of Israelite soldiers:

> David said longingly, "O that someone would give me water to drink from the well of Bethlehem that is by the gate!" Then the three warriors broke through the camp of the Philistines, drew water from the well of Bethlehem that was by the gate, and brought it to David. But he would not drink of it; he poured it out to the Lord, for he said, "The Lord forbid that I should do this. Can I drink the blood of the men who went at the risk of their lives?" Therefore he would not drink it.
>
> (2 Samuel 23:15–17; 1 Chronicles 11:17–19)

After the three soldiers risked their lives to fulfill David's whim, David expressed sorrow, understanding that he should not have caused them to do so needlessly. This is not the only case in the Bible in which a military action is weighed against its internal-human cost. Walzer writes of Napoleon bragging to Metternich "that he could afford to lose 30,000 men a month."[5] From this statement we can see that even in modern times, a French patriot could become insensitive even to the lives of his own countrymen. This example makes the biblical consideration of human life even more important.

7. Reality versus utopia: the total elimination of war in the future world

Isaiah's vision of the future is one of the world's best-known expressions of hope:

> The word that Isaiah son of Amoz saw concerning Judah and Jerusalem. In the end of days the mountain of the Lord's house shall be established as the highest of the mountains, and shall be raised above the hills; all the nations shall stream to it. Many peoples shall come and say, 'Come, let us go up to the mountain of the Lord, to the house of the God of Jacob; that he may teach us his ways and that we may walk in his paths." For out of Zion shall go forth instruction and the word of the Lord from Jerusalem. He shall judge between the nations, and shall arbitrate for many peoples; they shall beat their swords into plowshares, and their spears into pruning hooks; nation shall not lift up sword against nation, neither shall they learn war any more.
>
> (Isaiah 2:1–4; see also Micah 4)

The meaning of the term "*aharit hayyamim*," often rendered "end of days," underwent a transformation within the Bible and later. In the Septuagint, this term is translated "*eschatos*," meaning "last" or "final." It is possible, that the original prophecies of Isaiah and Micah actually referred to a historical time of peace that would occur in the natural future, and it was later generations, faced with the fact that the prophecy had not yet come to be, who projected its fulfillment into an eschatological future, a utopia that would come to be at the end of history.

Indeed, biblical literature does cope with literary utopian models. However it should be emphasized that literary utopias are not created *ex nihilo*. The purpose of a literary utopia is to criticize an existing social reality. The writer of a utopia expresses his opinion on those elements that society must avoid at all cost, and those that society must seek to achieve at all costs.[6] By another definition, "Utopian writers criticize present conditions and outline vast revolutionary schemes without, however, describing the concrete steps necessary to realize them."[7] In this case, since the vision of "the end of days" envisages a future reality without war, it serves to criticize the extant reality of the world today, in which Israel and the nations exist in a constant state of warfare.

In conclusion, it is difficult to find a parallel, in the annals of the Ancient Near East, to the biblical ideal of a universal spiritual peace, of the conversion of weapons of destruction into tools of peace. It is equally difficult to find significant parallels to most of the ideas set forth in this epilogue; these are some of the unique concepts expressed in the Bible and incorporated into Jewish thought through the ages. It is our assertion that these principles had, and indeed have still, a vital part in the formation of the moral and ethical ideals expressed by Judaism throughout its history, a history of struggle and war, and also of a hope for that ultimate time of peace.

Notes

1. See also Numbers 21:21–26; H. Freedman and M. Simon (Eds.), *Midrash Numbers Rabbah* (trans. J.J. Slotki), London: Soncino, 1961, vol. II, Huqat XIX, ch. 33, p. 782.
2. B. Uffenheimer, *Early Prophecy in Israel*, Jerusalem: Magnes, 1999, p. 557.
3. See A. Altman, *The Historical Prologues of the Hittite Vassal Treaties*, Ramat-Gan: Bar-Ilan University Press, 2004, pp. 408–410.
4. Michael Walzer, *Just and Unjust Wars: A Moral Argument With Historical Illustrations*, London: Fakenham and Reading, 1978, p. 42 (n.*). See S.V. Viswanathan, *International Law in Ancient India*, Bombay 1925, p. 156. See also: *The Chinese Classics* (trans. and Ed. James Legge), vol. V; *The Ch'un Ts'ew with the Tso Chuen*, Oxford: Clarendon, 1893, p. 183.
5. Walzer, *Just and Unjust Wars*, p. 29.
6. Y. Amit, "Biblical Utopism," in M. Hovav (Ed.), *Reflections on the Bible – Selected Studies of the Bible Circle in Memory of Yishai Ron*, vol. V, Tel Aviv: Am Oved, 1988, pp. 52–57 and especially p. 54 (Hebrew).
7. A. Briggs (Ed.), *The Longman Encyclopedia*, Essex: Longman, 1990, p. 1103.

Bibliography

Abelman, R. and Hoover, S. *Religious Television: Controversies & Conclusions*, Norwood: Ablex, 1990.

Abrabanel, D.I. *Torah Commentary, Genesis*, Jerusalem: Bene Arbeel Publishing, 1964 (Hebrew).

Abramovitch, H. "Onvayzungen un bamerkungen," *Yidishe shprakh* 12, 1952, pp. 122–123.

Abramovitch, H. *Farshvundene geshtaltn: zikhroynes un siluetn*, Buenos Aires: Tsentral farband fun poylishe yidn in argentine, 1958.

Abramski, S. "The Revival of the Damascene Kingdom in the time of Solomon and its Mark on Historiography," in J. Blau and Y. Avishur (Eds.), *Studies in Bible and the Ancient Near East presented to Samuel E. Loewenstamm*, Jerusalem: Rubinstein, 1978, pp. 15–24 (Hebrew).

Abramson, J. "Talk to the Newsroom: Jill Abramson, Managing Editor," *The New York Times*, 2 January 2009.

Ackroyd, P.R. "יד *yad*," in G.J. Botterweck and H. Ringgren (Eds.), *Theological Dictionary of the Old Testament*, Grand Rapids: Eerdmans, 1986, vol. 5, pp. 410–411.

Adam, K.-P. "Law and Narrative: The Narratives of Saul and David Understood Within the Framework of a Legal Discussion on Homicide Law (Ex. 21:12–14)," *Zeitschrift für Altorientalische und Biblische Rechtsgeschichte* 14, 2008, pp. 311–335.

Adams, J.B. "A Qualitative Analyisis of Domestic and Foreign Networks on the AP-TAWire," *Gazette* 10, 1964, pp. 285–295.

Adams, W. (Ed.) *Television Coverage of the Middle East*, New Jersey: Ablex, 1981.

Adcock, F.E. *Roman Political Ideas and Practices*, Ann Arbor: University of Michigan Press, 1964.

Ahituv, Y. "The Wars of Israel and the Sanctity of Life," in Y. Gafni and A. Revitsky (Eds.), *Sanctity of Life and Martyrdom: Studies in Memory of Amir Yekutiel*, Jerusalem: Shazar Center, 1993, pp. 255–276 (Hebrew).

Albertz, R. "Monotheism and Violence: How to Handle a Dangerous Biblical Tradition," in J. van Ruiten and J. Cornelius de Vos (Eds.), *The Land of Israel in Bible, History and Theology – Studies in Honour of Ed Noort* (VT Sup. 124), Leiden – Boston: Brill, 2009, pp. 373–387.

Alroey, G. *The Quiet Revolution: Jewish Emigration from the Russian Empire, 1875–1924*, Jerusalem: Merkaz Zalman Shazar, 2008 (Hebrew).

Alter, R. *The Art of Biblical Narrative*, New York: Basic Books, 1981.

Altman, A. "Hittite Imperialism in Perspective: The Hittite and the Roman Treatment of Subordinate States Compared," in G. Wilhelm (Ed.), *Hattuša – Bogazköy: Das Hethiterreich im Spannungsfeld des Alten Orients*, 6 (Internationales Colloquium der Deutschen Orient-Gesellschaft, Würzburg 22.–24. März 2006), Wiesbaden: Harrassowitz Verlag, 2008, pp. 377–393.

Altman, A. "Tracing the Earliest Recorded Concepts of International Law (4): The Near East in the Late Bronze Age (1600–1200 BCE)," *Journal of the History of International Law* 11, 2009, pp. 125–187.

Altman, A. *The Historical Prologues of the Hittite Vassal Treaties*, Ramat-Gan: Bar-Ilan University Press, 2004.

Amiel, M.A. "Exile and Redemption," *Ha-mizrahi* 49, 1920, p. 6 (Hebrew).

Amiel, M.A. "More on the Ideological Foundations of Mizrahi," *Ha-tor* 16, 1935, p. 7 (Hebrew).

Amiel, M.A. "On the Disturbances and on Restraint," *Ha-zofeh*, 28 Tammuz 5698 [summer 1938], p. 3 (Hebrew).

Amiel, M.A. "On the Ideological Foundations of Mizrahi," *Ha-Tor* 3, 1935, p. 23 (Hebrew).

Amiel, M.A. "The Jewish Idea of Redemption," *Ha-boqer* 19, 1939, p. 2 (Hebrew).

Amiel, M.A. "The Prohibition of Murder with Respect to Arabs," *Tehumin* 10, 1989, p. 148 (1 page; Hebrew).

Amiel, M.A. *Darkhei Mosheh* vol. 2, *Darkhei Ha-qinyanim*, Warsaw: Neta Krohberg Printers, 1931 (Hebrew).

Amiel, M.A. *Discourses to my People*, Warsaw: Hacefira Publication, 1943 (Hebrew).

Amiel, M.A. *Principles of Halakhic Study*, Jerusalem: Mosad Harav Kook, 1939 (Hebrew).

Amiel, M.A. *Social Justice and our Legal and Moral Justice*, Tel Aviv: Torah Va-Avoda Movement, 1936 (Hebrew).

Amiel, M.A. *The Sabbath Queen: Essays and Speeches on the Sabbath*, Tel Aviv: Mizrachi Publication, 1937 (Hebrew).

Amiel, M.A. *To the Perplexed of the Age – Essays on the Essence of Judaism*, Jerusalem: Mosad Ha-Rav Kook, 1943 (Hebrew).

Amiel, M.A. *Zionism's Spiritual Problems*, Tel Aviv: The Mizrachi Organization, 1937 (Hebrew).

Amit, Y. "Biblical Utopism," in M. Hovav (Ed.), *Reflections on the Bible – Selected Studies of the Bible Circle in Memory of Yishai Ron*, vol. V, Tel Aviv: Am Oved, 1988, pp. 52–57 (Hebrew).

Amit, Y. *Judges with Introduction and Commentary*, Jerusalem: Magnes Press, 1999 (Hebrew).

Amit, Y. *The Book of Judges: The Art of Editing* (The Biblical Encyclopedia Library), Jerusalem and Tel Aviv: Bialik, 1992 (Hebrew).

Amit, Y. *The Book of Judges: The Art of Editing*, Leiden – Boston – Koln: Brill, 1998.

Amital, Y. "The Wars of Israel According to Maimonides," *Tehumin* 8, 1987, pp. 454–461 (Hebrew).

Anbar, M. *Joshua and the Covenant at Shechem (Jos. 24:1–28)*, Jerusalem: Bialik Institute, 1999 (Hebrew).

Andersen, F.I. "Genesis 14: An Enigma," in D.P. Wright, D.N. Freedman and A. Hurvitz (Eds.), *Pomegranates and Golden Bells: Studies in Biblical, Jewish, and Near Eastern Ritual, Law and Literature in honor of Jacob Milgrom*, Winona Lake: Eisenbrauns, 1995, pp. 497–508.

Anderson, A. *2 Samuel* (WBC), Waco: Word, 1984.

An-ski, S. (Shloyme Zaynvl Rapoport), "Khurbm galitsye," in *Gezamlte shriftn* vol. 4, Warsaw: Farlag An-ski, 1925, pp. 10–14.

Antin, M. *The Promised Land*, 1912, new ed., New York: Penguin, 1997

Ariel, A. "*Lashon Hara* in a Democratic Public System," *Tsohar* 5, 2001, pp. 37–61; *Tsohar* 6, 2002, pp. 41–59 (Hebrew).

Ariel, Y. "War Ethics in the Torah," in E. Bloom *et al.* (Eds.), *Values in the Trial of War: Ethics and War in the View of Judaism*, Jerusalem: The Mizrahi Family and Moreshet Publishers, 1985, pp. 80–90 (Hebrew).

Ariel, Y. *Mikdash Melekh: Studies in the Book of Kings*, Hispin: Midreshet Hagolan, 1994, (Hebrew).

Assaf, D. (Ed.), *Journey To a Nineteenth-Century Shtetl: The Memoirs of Yekhezkel Kotik*, Detroit: Wayne State University Press, 2002.

Assis, E. "Divine Versus Human Leadership: An Examination of Joshua's Succession," in M. Poorthuis and J. Schwartz (Eds.), *Saints and Role Models in Judaism and Christianity*, Leiden: Brill, 2004, pp. 25–42.

Assis, E. *From Moses to Joshua and from the Miraculous to the Ordinary: A Literary Analysis of the Conquest Narrative in the Book of Joshua*, Jerusalem: The Hebrew University Magnes Press, 2005 (Hebrew).

Av, N. *The Battle for Tiberias*, Tel Aviv: Ministry of Defense, 1991 (Hebrew).

Avineri, S. *The Zionist Idea*, Tel Aviv: Am Oved, 1980 (Hebrew).

Avraham, N. "On the Social Status of Elisha and the Disciples of the Prophets," in M. Heltzer and M. Malul (Eds.), *Teshurot leAvishur: Studies in the Bible and the Ancient Near East, in Hebrew and Semitic Languages*, Tel Aviv: Archeological Center Publications, 2004, pp. 41–54 (Hebrew).

Avraham, N. *2 Chronicles* (Olam Ha-Tanakh), Tel Aviv: Sifrei Hemed, 1995 (Hebrew).

Axskjöld, C.-J. *Aram as the Enemy Friend: the Ideological Role of Aram in the Composition of Genesis – 2 Kings*, Stockholm: Almqvist & Wiksell International, 1998.

Ayer, N.W. and Sons, *American Newspaper Annual and Directory*, Philadelphia: N.W. Ayer and Sons, 1914.

Bae, C.-H. "Comparative Studies of King Darius's Bisitun Inscription," Ph.D. dissertation, Harvard University, 2001.

Bahrani, Z. *Rituals of War: The Body and Violence in Mesopotamia*, New York: Zone Books, 2008.

Bailey, R.C. *David in Love and War*, Sheffield: Sheffield Academic Press, 1990.

Bainton, R. *Christian Attitudes towards War and Peace*, Nashville: Abingdon Press, 1960.

Ball, H. *Flight Out of Time: A Dada Diary (Documents of Twentieth-Century Art)*, Ed. John Elderfield, trans. Ann Raimes, Berkeley – Los Angeles – London: University of California Press, 1996.

Bantimaroudis, P. and Ban, H. "Covering the Crisis in Somalia: Framing the Choices by the *New York Times* and the *Manchester Guardian*," in S.D. Reese, O.H. Gandy, Jr. and A.E. Grant (Eds.), *Framing Public Life: Perspectives on Media and Our Understanding of the Social World*, Mahwah: Lawrence Erlbaum Associates, 2003, pp. 175–184.

Bar Ilan, M. *Biblical Numerology*, Rehovot: Association for Jewish Astrology and Numerology, 2005 (Hebrew).

Bar Ilan, M. *Genesis' Numerology*, Rehovot: Association for Jewish Astrology and Numerology, 2003 (Hebrew).

Bar-Efrat, S. *First Samuel With Introduction and Commentary*, Jerusalem: Magnes Press, 1996 (Hebrew).

Bar-On, M. "Status Quo Before or After? Israel's Security Policy 1949–1957," in M. Bar-On, *Smoking Borders: Studies in the Early History of the State of Israel, 1948–1967*, Jerusalem: Yad Ben Zvi, 2001, pp. 131–165 (Hebrew).

Baron, S.W. *Ancient and Medieval Jewish History*, New Brunswick: Rutgers University Press, 1972.

Baron, S.W. *History and Jewish Historians*, Philadelphia: The Jewish Publication Society of America, 1964.

Bartal, I. "The Image of Germany and German Jewry in East European Jewish Society During the 19th Century," in Isadore Twersky (Ed.), *Danzig, Between East and West: Aspects of Modern Jewish History*, Cambridge: Harvard University Press, 1985, pp. 3–17.

Bartal, I. "The Porets and the Arendar: The Depiction of Poles in Jewish Literature," *The Polish Review* 32, 1987, pp. 357–359.

Bartal, I. "Non-Jews and Gentile Society in East-European Hebrew and Yiddish literature, 1856–1914," Ph.D. Dissertation, Jerusalem: Hebrew University, 1980 (Hebrew).

Bartana, O. *End of Century and Beginning of Century*, Tel Aviv: Eked, 2001 (Hebrew).

Bartana, O. *Fantasy in Israeli Literature*, Tel Aviv: Hakibbutz Hameuchad, 1987 (Hebrew).

Bartov, O. "Defining Enemies, Making Victims: Germans, Jews, and the Holocaust," in A. Weiner (Ed.), *Landscaping the Human Garden: Twentieth-Century Population*, Stanford: Stanford University Press, 2003, pp. 155–156.

Bartov, O. *Mirrors of Destruction: War, Genocide and Modern Identity*, New York: Oxford University Press, 2000.

Baum, B.D. *The Rise and Fall of the Caucasian Race: A Political History of Racial Identity*, New York: New York University Press, 2006.

Beal, R.H. "The Ten Year Annals of Great King Muršili II of Hatti, year 1," in W.W. Hallo (Ed.), *The Context of Scripture: Canonical Compositions from the Biblical World* II, Leiden: Brill, 2000, p. 84.

Beckman, G. *Hittite Diplomatic Texts* (2nd ed.), Atlanta: Scholars Press, 1999.

Bell, C. *Ritual Theory, Ritual Practice*, New York: Oxford University Press, 1992.

Ben Attar, C. *Or Hachayim: Commentary on the Torah*; translated and annotated by Eliyahu Munk, Jerusalem: Lambda, 1999.

Ben Gurion, D. "The Book of Evil," *Ha'aretz*, 18 May 1939 (Hebrew).

Ben Gurion, D. "Towards the Future," *HaToren*, 25 June 1915 (Hebrew).

Ben-Dov, J. "Writing as Oracle and as Law: New Contexts for the Book-Find of King Josiah," in *Journal of Biblical Literature* 127, 2008, pp. 223–239.

Beneqvit, I.A. *Durkhgelebt un durkhgetrakht*, New York: Kultur federatsye, 1934.

Ben-Shalom, I. *The School of Shammai and the Zealots' Struggle against Rome*, Jerusalem: Yad Ben Zvi, 1993 (Hebrew).

Ben-Zvi, S. "Rabbi Kook's Self-Image: A New Reading in Light of Publication of *Eight Files*," MA Thesis, Jerusalem: Hebrew University, 2003 (Hebrew with English abstract).

Berlin, N.Z.Y. *Ha'amek Davar: A Commentary on the Torah*, commented and edited by M. Kupperman, Jerusalem: Luhot Frank, 2005 (Hebrew).

Bernshteyn, I. *Yudishe shprikhverter un rednsarten*, 1908, reprinted Wiesbaden: Fourier, 1988.

Binnun, Y. "'Comes to Ayyat. . .' – A New Solution for the Identification of Ai," in Z.H. Erlich and Y. Eshel (Eds.), *Judea and Samaria Research Studies – Proceedings of the 2nd Annual Meeting – 1992*, Kedumim – Ariel: The College of Judea and Samaria, 1993, pp. 43–64 (Hebrew).

Binnun, Y. "The Book of Joshua – *Peshat* and the Sages' Interpretation," in Z. Rimon (Ed.), *Morality, War and Conquest*, Alon Shevut: Tenuvot, 1994, pp. 31–40 (Hebrew).

Blackman, P. *Mishnayoth* III (pointed Hebrew text, English trans., introductions, notes, suppl., appendix; 2nd ed.), New York: Judaica Press, 1963.

Blake, W. "Auguries of Innocence," in J. Bronowski (Ed.), *A Selection of Poems and Letters*, London: Penguin Books, 1958, p. 67.

Blanco-Wissman, F. *"Er tat das Rechte": Beurteilungskriterien und Deuteronomismus in 1Kön 12–2Kön 25* (Abhandlungen zur Theologie des Alten und Neuen Testaments 93), Zurich: Theologischer Verlag Zurich, 2008.

Blank, S.H. "The Death of Zechariah in Rabbinic Literature," *Hebrew Union College Annual* 12–13, 1937–38, pp. 327–346.

Bleich, D. "Preemptive War in Jewish Law," *Tradition* 21, 1983, pp. 3–41.

Bleich, J.D. "Preemptive War in Jewish Law," *Contemporary Halakhic Problems* vol. 3, New York: Ktav, 1989, pp. 251–292.

Blidstein, G.J. "Holy War in Maimonidean Law," in J. Kraemer (Ed.), *Perspectives on Maimonides: Philosophical and Historical Studies*, Oxford: Littman Library of Jewish Civilization, 1991, pp. 209–220.

Blidstein, G.J. *Political Concepts in Maimonidean Halakha*, Ramat Gan: Bar-Ilan University Press, 1983 (Hebrew).

Blidstein, G.J. *Political Concepts in Maimonidean Halakha* (2nd ed.), Ramat Gan: Bar-Ilan University Press, 2001 (Hebrew).

Blidstein, Y. "Holy War in Maimonidean Law," in J. Kraemer (Ed.), *Perspectives on Maimonides*, Oxford: Oxford University Press, 1991, pp. 209–221.

Blidstein, Y. "The Treatment of Hostile Civilian Populations: The Contemporary Halachic Discussion in Israel," *Israel Studies* 1, 1996, pp. 27–44.

Bloom, E. *et al.* (Eds.) *Values in the Trial of War: Ethics and War in the View of Judaism*, Jerusalem: The Mizrahi Family and Moreshet Publishers, 1985 (Hebrew).

Bodner, K. "Crime Scene Investigation: A Text Critical Mystery and the Strange Death of Ishbosheth," *Journal of Hebrew Scriptures* 7, 2007, article 13 (www.arts.ualberta.ca/ JHS/Articles/article_74.pdf).

Boling, R.G. *Judges* (Anchor Bible), Garden City: Doubleday, 1975.

Borgenicht, L. *The Happiest Man: The Life of Louis Borgenicht as Told to Harold Friedman*, New York: Putnam's Sons, 1942.

Borokhov, B. "Di oyfgaben fun der yidisher filologye," in Sh. Niger (Ed.), *Der pinkes*, Vilna: B.A. Kletskin, 1912–13, p. 11.

Boudin, L.B. *Socialism and War*, New York: New Review Publishing, 1916.

Bourdieu, P. *La Distinction: Critique sociale de jugement*, Paris: Les Editions de Minuit, 1979.

Breish, M.Y. *Chelkat Yaakov*, vol. II, Orach Chaim, 96, Tel Aviv: Published by family of author, 1992 (Hebrew).

Brinker, M. *Jean-P. Sartre*, Tel Aviv: Ministry of Defense, 1992 (Hebrew).

Brodsky, H. "Did Abram Wage a Just War?," *Jewish Bible Quarterly* 31, 2003, pp. 167–173.

Brown, F., Driver, S.R. and Briggs, C.A. *The Brown-Driver-Briggs Hebrew and English Lexicon*, Peabody: Hendrickson, 1999.

Broyde, M. "Only the Good Die Young?," *Meorot: A Forum of Modern Orthodox Discourse* 6, 2006, pp. 1–2.

Broyde, M. *The Bounds of Wartime Military Conduct in Jewish Law: An Expansive Conception*, Herbert Berman Memorial Lecture 2004, Flushing: Center for Jewish Studies, Queens College, CUNY, 2006.

Brug, M. "From the Top of Masada to the Heart of the Ghetto: Myth as History," in D. Ohana and R.S. Westreich (Eds.), *Myth and Memory: Transfiguration of Israeli Consciousness*, Jerusalem: Van-Leer Institute and Hakibutz Hameuhad, 1998, pp. 203–227 (Hebrew).

Buddenbaum, J. "Network News Coverage of Religion," in J. Ferret (Ed.), *Channels of Belief: Religion & American Commercial Television*, Ames: Iowa State University Press, 1990, pp. 57–78.

Bundi, D. *How?* Jerusalem: Shalem Center, 2008.

Burkert, W. *The Orientalizing Revolution: Near Eastern Influence on Greek Culture in Early Archaic Age* (trans. Margaret E. Pinder and W. Burkert), Cambridge – London: Harvard University Press, 1992.

Cahan, I.L. *Der yid: vegn zikh un vegn andere in zayne shprikhverter un rednsortn*, New York: YIVO, 1933.

Cahnman, W.J. *Jews & Gentiles: A Historical Sociology of their Relations*, New Brunswick: Transaction, 2004.

Callaway, J.A. "Ai (et-Tell): Problem Site for Biblical Archaeologists," in L.G. Perdue (Ed.), *Archaeology and Biblical Interpretation; Essays in Memory of D. Glenn Rose*, Atlanta: John Knox Press, 1987, pp. 87–99.

Caplan, K. "The Holocaust in Contemporary Israeli Haredi Popular Religion," *Modern Judaism* 22, 2, 2002, pp. 142–168.

Caputo, J. *The Prayers and Tears of Jacques Derrida: Religion Without Religion*, Bloomington: Indiana University Press, 1997.

Carmignac, J. "Precisions apportees au vocabulaire de l'Hebreu biblique par la guerre des fils de lumiere contre les fils de tenebre," *Vetus Testamentum* 5, 1955, pp. 357–359.

Carmy, S. "The Origin of Nations and the Shadow of Violence: Theological Perspectives on Canaan and Amalek," in L. Schiffman and T.B. Wulowelsky (Eds.), *War and Peace in Jewish Tradition*, New York: Yeshiva University Press, 2007, pp. 163–199.

Caro, J. *Code of Hebrew Law Shulhan Aruk*, Orach Chaim (trans. C.N. Denburg), Montreal: Jurisprudence Press, 1954–55.

Cavenaugh, W.T. "A Fire Strong Enough to Consume the House: The Wars of Religion and the Rise of the Nation State," in J. Milbank and S. Oliver (Eds.), *The Radical Orthodox Reader*, London – New York: Routledge, 2009, pp. 314–337.

Cazeaux, J. "Le livre de Josué: De la conquête au dernier des Justes," in S. Trigano (Ed.), *Guerre et paix dans le jidaïsme*, Paris: In Press, 2004, pp. 43–62.

Chapman, C.R. *The Gendered Language of Warfare in the Israelite-Assyrian Encounter* (Harvard Semitic Monographs 62), Winona Lake: Eisenbrauns, 2004.

Charlesworth, J.H. (Ed.) *The Dead Sea Scrolls: Hebrew, Aramaic, and Greek Texts with English Translations*, vol. 2, Tübingen: J.C.B. Mohr, 1995.

Chavel, C.D. *The Book of Commandments of Maimonides with the Glosses of Nahmanides*, Jerusalem: Mosad Harav Kook, 1981 (Hebrew).

Cherlow, S. "The Tzaddiq is the Foundation of the World: Rav Kook's Esoteric Mission and Mystical Experience," Ph.D. Dissertation, Ramat-Gan: Bar-Ilan University, 2003 (Hebrew with English abstract).

Cherlow, Y. "'And You Shall Cast out the Evil From Israel': On the Policy Towards Publishing Embarrassing Items," in T. Rashi and M. Zapt (Eds.), *Media and Judaism – A Collection of Essays*, Petah Tikvah: Keter Hazahav, 2008, pp. 79–96 (Hebrew).

Cifola, B. *Analysis of Variants in the Assyrian Royal Titulary from the Origins to Tiglath-Pileser III*, Napoli: Istituto Universitario Orientale, 1995

Coady, C.A.J. *Morality and Political Violence*, New York: Cambridge University Press, 2008.

Cohen, C.H. "On Freedom of Opinion and of Speech in Jewish Tradition," in G. Frishtik (Ed.), *Human Rights in Judaism: Obligations and Privileges in Jewish Law*, Jerusalem: The Sanhedrin Institute, 1992, pp. 179–202 (Hebrew).

Cohen, G.L. "The Book of Joshua as Reflected in Midrashic Exegesis," in M.L. Frankel and H. Deitcher (Eds.), *Understanding the Bible in Our Times: Implications for Education* (Studies in Jewish Education IX), Jerusalem: The Hebrew University Magnes Press, 2003, pp. 47–59 (Hebrew with English abstract).

Cohen, J. *Living Letters of Law: Ideas of the Jew in Medieval Christianity*, Berkeley: University of California Press, 1999, pp. 23–66.

Cohen, M. (Ed.) *Kings I & II, Mikra'ot Gedolot 'Haketer': A Revised and Augmented Scientific Edition of 'Mikra'ot Gedolot' Based on the Aleppo Codex and Early Medieval Mss,* Jerusalem: Keter, 1995 (Hebrew).

Cohen, M.R. *A Dreamer's Journey,* Glenco: Free Press, 1949.

Cohen, N. "On the Origin of the Name 'Fonye'," *Yeda-'Am* 10, 1964, p. 19 (1 page; Hebrew with English abstract).

Cohen, S.A. "The Quest for a Corpus of Jewish Military Ethics in Modern Israel," *Journal of Israeli History* 26, 2007, pp. 35–66.

Cohen, S.Y. "The Birth of the Booklet *Regarding the Commandment of the Land,*" in Z.Y. Kook, *In the Paths of Israel (LNtivot Yisrael),* Bet El: Me'Avnei Hamakom, 3rd printing, 2007, vol. 2, pp. 607–608 (Hebrew).

Cohen, Y. "Focus on Israel: Twenty-Five Years of Foreign Media Reporting," *Encyclopaedia Judaica,* decennial edition 1983–92, Jerusalem: Keter, 1994, pp. 46–56.

Cohen, Y. "Foreign Press Corps as an Indicator of International News Interest," *Gazette* 56, 1995, pp. 89–99.

Conklin, B. *Oath Formulas in Biblical Hebrew,* Winona Lake: Eisenbrauns, 2011.

Cook, M. "The New Testament: Confronting its Impact on Jewish-Christian Relations," in S. Scholz (Ed.), *Biblical Studies Alternatively – An Introductory Reader,* New Jersey: Prentice Hall, 2003, pp. 291–307.

Cook, P.J. and Ludwig, J. *Guns in America: National Survey on Private Ownership and Use of Firearms,* National Institute of Justice, May 1997. Available at: www.ncjrs.gov/pdffiles/165476.pdf.

Cooper, A.D. *David,* London: J. Cape, 1943.

Craigie, P.C. *The Problem of War in the Old Testament,* Grand Rapids: Eerdmans, 1978.

Day, J. "Gibeon and the Gibeonites in the Old Testament," in R. Rezetko, T.H. Lim and W.B. Aucker (Eds.), *Reflection and Refraction: Studies in Biblical Historiography in Honour of A. Graeme Auld,* Leiden – Boston: Brill, 2007, pp. 117–120.

Day, P.L. "Abishai the Sātān in 2 Samuel 19:17–24," *Catholic Biblical Quarterly* 49, 1987, pp. 546–547.

de Hoop, R. "Saul the Sodomite: Genesis 18–19 as the Opening Panel of a Polemic Triptych on King Saul," in E. Noort and E. Tigchelaar (Eds.), *Sodom's Sin: Genesis 18–19 and Its Interpretations,* Leiden: Brill, 2004, pp. 17–26.

Delbrück, H. *Numbers in History,* London: University of London Press, 1913.

Demsky, A. "The Genealogy of Asher (1 Chron. 7:30–40)," *Eretz-Israel* 24, 1993, pp. 68–73 (Hebrew).

Deploige, J. and Deneckere, G. (Eds.) *Mystifying the Monarch: Studies on Discourse, Power and History,* Amsterdam: Amsterdam University Press, 2006.

Derrida, J. "Violence and Metaphysics: An Essay on the Thought of Emannuel Levinas," in *Writing and Difference* (trans. A. Bass), Chicago: University of Chicago Press, 1978, pp. 97–192.

Dietler, M. and Hayden, B. *Feasts: Archaeological and Ethnographic Perspectives,* Washington DC: Smithsonian Books, 2001.

Dietrich, W. "David, Amnon und Abschalom (2 Samuel 13): Literarische, textliche und historische Erwägungen zu den ambivalenten Beziehungen eines Vaters zu seinen Söhnen," *Textus* 23, 2007, pp. 115–143.

Donner, H. and Röllig, W. *Kanaanäische und aramäische Inschriften* (2nd ed.), Wiesbaden: Harrassowitz, 1966–69.

Dor, D., Iram, S. and Velodevsky, O. *"War Until the Last Minute": The Israeli Media in the Second Lebanon War,* Jerusalem: Keshev, The Center for the Protection of Democracy in Israel, 2007 (Hebrew).

Dossin, G. *Correspondance de Šamsi-Addu* (Archives royals de Mari I), Paris: Imprimerie nationale, 1950.

Downey, S.D. "The Evolution of the Rhetorical Genre of Apologia," *Western Journal of Communication* 57, 1993, pp. 42–64.

Driver, S.R. *A Treatise on the Use of the Tenses in Hebrew and Some Other Syntactical Questions* (2nd ed.), Grand Rapids: Eerdmans, 1998.

Drori, A. "Mokraja-Kaligurka," *He-avar* 19, 1972, pp. 231–232 (Hebrew with English abstract).

Edelman, D. "Solomon's Adversaries Hadad, Rezon and Jeroboam: A Trio of Bad Guy Characters Illustrating the Theology of Immediate Retribution," in S.W. Holloway and L.K. Handy (Eds.), *The Pitcher is Broken: Memorial Essays for Gosta W. Ahlström*, Sheffield: Sheffield Academic Press, 1995, pp. 166–191.

Edrei, A. "Holocaust Memorial: A Paradigm of Competing Memories in the Religious and Secular Societies in Israel," in D. Mendels (Ed.), *On Memory*, Bern: Peter Lang, 2007, pp. 37–100.

Edrei, A. "Law, Interpretation and Ideology: The Renewal of the Jewish Laws of War in the State of Israel," *Cardozo Law Review* 28, 2006, pp. 187–227.

Efrati, N. "Captives, Ransoming of," in F. Skolnic (Ed.), *Encyclopedia Judaica* (2nd ed.), vol. 4, New York: Keter Publishing House, 2007, pp. 456–457.

Ehrenberg, Y.M. "The Prohibition of Transferring the Territories of the Land of Israel to non-Jews," *Tehumin* 10, 1899, pp. 26–33 (Hebrew).

Ehrlich, A.B. *Mikrâ Ki-pheschutô*, Berlin: M. Poppelauer's Buchhandlung, 1890 (print-offset New York: Ktav Publishing House 1969) (Hebrew).

Ehrlich, C.S. "Joshua, Judaism, and Genocide," in J. Targarona Borrás and A. Sáenz-Badillos (Eds.), *Jewish Studies at the Turn of the Twentieth Century I: Proceedings of the 6th EAJS Congress, Toledo, July 1998*, vol. I–II, Leiden: Brill, 1999, pp. 117–124.

Elberg, S. "A Holocaust Remembrance," *Hapardes* 66, 9, 1992, preliminary page (Hebrew).

Elberg, S. "The Warsaw Ghetto Uprising," *Hapardes* 63, 6, 1989, pp. 2–3 (Hebrew).

Eldan, Y. "'Do Not Stand by the Blood of Your Neighbor' and the Concept of Responsibility," *Akdamot: A Journal of Jewish Thought* 11, 2001, pp. 7–37 (Hebrew with English abstract).

Elgavish, D. "Objective of Baasha's War against Asa," in G. Galil and M. Weinfeld (Eds.), *Studies in Historical Geography and Biblical Historiography Presented to Zecharia Kallai*, Leiden – Boston – Köln: Brill, 2000, pp. 141–149.

Elgavish, D. "Restraint in the Wars between Israel and Judah," in Z.H. Erlich and Y. Eshel (Eds.), *Judea and Samaria Research Studies: Proceedings of the 4th Annual Meeting – 1994*, Kedumim – Ariel: The College of Judea and Samaria, 1995, pp. 59–68 (Hebrew with English abstract).

Elgavish, D. "The Divisions of the Spoils of War in the Bible and in the Ancient Near East," *Zeitschrift für Altorientalische und Biblische Rechtsgeschichte* 8, 2002, pp. 242–273.

Elgavish, D. "The Encounter of Abram and Melchizedek: Covenant Establishment," in A. Wénin (Ed.), *Studies in the Book of Genesis: Literature, Redaction and History (Bibliotheca Ephemeridum Theologicarum Lovaniensium CLV)*, Leuven: University Press, 2001, pp. 495–508.

Elgavish, D. "War and Peace in the Relationships between Israel and Judah," M.A. Thesis, Ramat-Gan: Bar-Ilan University, 1978 (Hebrew).

El-Khodary, T. and Bonner, E. "Israelis Say Strikes Against Hamas Will Continue," *The New York Times*, 28 December 2008.

El-Khodary, T. and Kershner, I. "Warning Not Enough for Gaza Families," *The New York Times*, 5 January 2009.

Elksteins, M. *Rites of Spring: The Great War and the Birth of the Modern Age*, New York: Anchor Books, 1989.

Emerton, J. "The Riddle of Genesis XIV," *Vetus Testamentum* 21, 1971, pp. 403–439.

Engelman, M. *Four Years of Relief and War Work by the Jews of America, 1914–1918*, New York: Shoen, 1918.

Epstein, Y.M. *Aruch Hashulchan*, Orach Chaim vol. III 301:52, Pietrikow: Yosef Tzvi Lew, 1905 (Hebrew).

Erickson, E. and Hamilton, J.M. "Foreign Reporting Enhanced by Parachute Journalism," *Newspaper Research Journal* 27, 2006, pp. 33–47.

Erlanger, S. "A Gaza War Full of Traps and Trickery," *The New York Times*, 11 January 2009.

Erlanger, S. "Weighing Crimes and Ethics in the Fog of Urban Warfare," *The New York Times*, 17 January 2009.

Eshkoli (Wagman), H. "Religious Zionist Responses in Mandatory Palestine to the Warsaw Ghetto Uprising," *Holocaust and Genocide Studies* 11, 2, 1997, pp. 213–238.

Etzioni, A. *Security First: For a Muscular, Moral Foreign Policy*, New Haven: Yale University Press, 2007.

Etzioni, A. and Marsh, J.H. "What We're Fighting For: A Letter from America," in A. Etzioni and J.H. Marsh (Eds.), *Rights vs. Public Safety After 9/11: America in the Age of Terrorism*, Lanham: Rowman & Littlefield, 2003, pp. 101–125.

Falk, Z.W. "Gestures Expressing Affirmation," *Journal of Semitic Studies* 4, 1959, pp. 268–269.

Feinstein, M. *Igrot Moshe*, vol. VIII 18 (on Shulcan Aruch Orach Chaim 301:7), Ed. Shabtai Avraham Hacohen Rappoport, Jerusalem: Published by family of author, 1996 (Hebrew).

Ferre, J. (Ed.) *Channels of Belief: Religion & American Commercial Television*, Ames: Iowa State University Press, 1990.

Finkelstein, L. (Ed.) *Sifre on Deuteronomy*, New York: The Jewish Theological Seminary, 1993.

Finley, M.I. "The Fifth Century Athenian Empire: A Balance Sheet," in P. Low (Ed.), *The Athenian Empire*, Edinburgh: Edinburgh University Press, 2008, pp. 14–40.

Fischer, J.A. "War and Peace: A Methodological Consideration," in A.J. Tambasco (Ed.), *Blessed Are the Peacemakers; Biblical Perspectives on Peace and Its Social Foundations*, New York: Paulist Press, 1989, pp. 17–39.

Fishman, Y.L.H. "A Giant of Thought in *Halakhah* and *Aggadah*," in Y.L.H. Fishman (Ed.), *Festschrift Presented to Rabbi Moses Avigdor Amiel*, Jerusalem: Mosad Harav Kook, 1943, pp. 1–12.

Fleming, D.E. "The Seven-Day Siege of Jericho in Holy War," in R. Chazan, W.W. Hallo and L.H. Schiffman (Eds.), *Ki Baruch Hu: Ancient Near Eastern, Biblical, and Judaic Studies in Honor of Baruch A. Levine*, Winona Lake: Eisenbrauns, 1999, pp. 211–228.

Fletcher, G.P. and Ohlin, J.D. "The Collective Dimension of War," in G.P. Fletcher and J.D. Ohlin (Eds.), *Defending Humanity: When Force is Justified and Why*, New York: Oxford University Press, 2008, pp. 180–181.

Fokkelman, J. *Narrative Art and Poetry in the Books of Samuel, Volume One: King David*, Assen: Van Gorcum, 1990.

Fokkelman, J.P. *Narrative Art in Genesis: Specimens of Stylistic and Structural Analysis*, Amsterdam: Van Gorcum, 1975.

Fossum, J.E. *The Name of God and the Angel of the Lord. Samaritan and Jewish Concepts of Intermediation and the Origin of Gnosticism* (Wissenschaftliche Untersuchungen zum Neuen Testament 36), Tübingen: J.C.B. Mohr [Paul Siebeck], 1985.

Fowler, M.D. "The Meaning of 'Lipne YHWH' in the Old Testament," *Zeitschrift für die Alttestamentliche Wissenschaft* 99, 1987, p. 390.

Franke, S. *Konigsinschriften und Konigsideologie*, Munster: Lit, 1995.

Frankel, J. *Prophecy and Politics: Socialism, Nationalism, and the Russian Jews 1862–1917*, New York: Cambridge University Press, 1981.

Freedman, H. and Simon, M. (Eds.) *Midrash Numbers Rabbah* (trans. J.J. Slotki), London: Soncino, 1961.

Fretheim, T.E. *First and Second Kings*, Louisville: Westminster John Knox Press, 1994.

Frick, F.S. *A Journey through the Hebrew Scriptures* (2nd ed.), Belmont: Wadsworth/Thomson, 2003.

Friedman, M. "The Haredim and the Holocaust," *The Jerusalem Quarterly* 53, 1980, pp. 86–114.

Friedman, Sh. "How Much Anthropomorphism? Allowing the *Aggada* to Speak for Itself," *Sidra* 22, 2007, pp. 89–152 (Hebrew).

Frisch, A. "Shemaiah the Prophet versus King Rehoboam: Two Opposed Interpretations of the Schism (1 Kings XII 21–24)," *Vetus Testamentum* 38, 1988, pp. 466–468.

Frisch, A. "The Solomon Stories in the Book of Kings," Ph.D. dissertation, Ramat-Gan: Bar-Ilan University, 1986 (Hebrew).

Funkenstein, A. "The Dialectics of Assimilation," *Jewish Social Studies* 1, 1995, pp. 1–13.

Galil, G. *The Chronology of the Kings of Israel and Judah*, Leiden: Brill, 1996.

Galtung, J. and Ruge, M. "The Structure of Foreign News," *International Journal of Peace Research* 1, 1965, pp. 65–91.

Garsiel, M. *2 Samuel* (Olam Ha-Tanakh), Tel Aviv: Sifrei Hemed, 2007 (Hebrew).

Garsiel, M. *Biblical Names: A Literary Study of Midrashic Derivations and Puns* (trans. P. Hackett), Ramat-Gan: Bar-Ilan University Press, 1991.

Garsiel, M. *The Beginning of the Kingdom in Israel: Studies in the Book of Samuel*, vol. 1, Tel Aviv: The Open University, 2008, p. 154 (Hebrew).

Gesenius, W., Kautzch, E. and Cowley, A.E. *Hebrew Grammar*, Oxford: Clarendon Press, 1910.

Geva, A. "Ethics in Business," in A. Kasher (Ed.), *Introductions to Ethics I*, Jerusalem: The Hebrew University Magnes Press, 2009, pp. 99–143 (Hebrew).

Gevaryahu, H.M.Y. "From the Bible Study Group at David Ben-Gurion's House: On the Prophet Elisha," *Beit Mikra* 33, 1988, pp. 189–208 (Hebrew).

Ghorpade, S. "Sources and Access: How Foreign Correspondents Rate Washington DC," *Journal of Communication* 34, 1984, pp. 32–40.

Gibson, J.J. "The Theory of Affordances," in R. Shaw and J. Bransford (Eds.), *Perceiving, Acting and Knowing*, Hillsdale: Lawrence Erlbaum Associates, 1977, pp. 67–82.

Gibson, J.J. *The Ecological Approach to Visual Perception*, Boston: Houghton Mifflin, 1979.

Gichon, M. "The Veracity of Biblical Battles," in Y. Eshel (Ed.), *Judea and Samaria Research Studies – Proceedings of the 6th Annual Meeting – 1996*, Kedumim – Ariel: The College of Judea and Samaria, 1997, pp. 17–33 (Hebrew with English abstract).

Gilbert, P. *Terrorism, Security and Nationality: An Introductory Study in Applied Political Philosophy*, London – New York: Routledge, 1994.

Gilboa, E. "Public Diplomacy: The Missing Component in Israel's Foreign Policy," *Israel Affairs* 12/4, 2006, pp. 715–747.

Gisborne, M. "A Curia of Kings: Sulla and Royal Imagery," in O. Hekster and R. Fowler (Eds.), *Imaginary Kings: Royal Images in the Ancient Near East, Greece and Rome* (Oriens et Occidens 11), Munich: Franz Steiner, 2005, pp. 105–124.

Goerg, M. "Der 'Satan': der 'Vollstrecker' Gottes?," *Biblische Notizen* 82, 1996, pp. 9–12.

Goetze, A. (Ed.), *Keilschrifturkunden aus Boghazköi, 23. Historische Texte*, Berlin: Akademie-Verlag, 1928.

Goldstein, E.L. *The Price of Whiteness: Jews, Race, and American Identity*, Princeton: Princeton University Press, 2006.

Goldstein, Y. "The Reply of a Lazy Historian," *Kivunim Hadashim* 13, 2006, pp. 157–169 (Hebrew).

Goldstein, Y. "Why was Ben Gurion Interested in Rewriting History?" *Ha'aretz*, 14 May, 2006 (Hebrew).

Goodblatt, D. *The Monarchic Principle: Studies in Jewish Self-Government in Antiquity* (Texte und Studien zum Antiken Judentum 38), Tübingen: Mohr, 1994.

Goodman, N. "Pacifism and Nonviolence: Another Jewish View," in J.P. Burns (Ed.), *War and Its Discontents: Pacifism and Quietism in the Abrahamic Traditions*, Washington DC: Georgetown University Press, 1996, pp. 67–73.

Goodnick Westenholz, J. *Legends of the Kings of Akkade*, Winona Lake: Eisenbrauns, 1997.

Gordon, C.H. "War and Peace: The Theoretical Structure of Israelite Society," in V.D. Sanua (Ed.), *Fields of Offerings; Studies in Honor of Raphael Patai*, Rutherford: Fairleigh Dickinson University Press, 1983, pp. 299–303.

Goren, D., Cohen, A.A. and Caspi, D. "Reporting of the Yom-Kippur War from Israel," *Journalism Quarterly* 52, 1975, pp. 199–206.

Goren, S. "A Question and a Response on the Matter of the Heroes of Masada," *Or Hamizrach* 7, 3–4, 1960, pp. 22–27 (Hebrew).

Görg, M. "Mythos und Geschichte in Jos 10, 12–14," *Aegyptiaca – Biblica; Notizen und Beiträge zu den Beziehungen zwischen Ägypten und Israel*, Wiesbaden: Otto Harrassowitz, 1991, pp. 347–360.

Gotesfeld, K. *Vos ikh gedenk fun mayn lebn*, New York: Fareynikte galitsyaner yidn in amerike, 1960.

Gottwald, N.K. "Theological Education as a Theory-Praxis Loop: Situating the Book of Joshua in a Cultural, Social, Ethical and Theological Matrix," in J.M. Rogerson, M. Davies and M. Daniel Carrol R. (Eds.), *The Bible in Ethics* (JSOT Sup. 207), Sheffield: Sheffield Academic Press, 1995, pp. 107–118.

Grayson, A.K. *Assyrian Rulers of the Third and Second Millennia BC (to 1115 BC)* (RIMA I), Toronto: University of Toronto Press, 1987.

Grayson, A.K. *Babylonian Historical-Literary Texts* (Toronto Semitic Studies 3), Toronto: University of Toronto Press, 1975.

Greenberg, G. "Myth and Catastrophe in Simha Elberg's Religious Thought," *Tradition* 26, 1, 1991, pp. 35–64.

Greenberg, M. "Rabbinic Reflections on Defying Illegal Orders: Amasa, Abner and Joab," *Judaism* 19, 1970, pp. 30–37.

Greenstein, E.L. "Interpreting the Bible by Way of Its Ancient Cultural Milieu," in M.L. Frankel and H. Deitcher (Eds.), *Understanding the Bible in Our Times: Implications for Education* (Studies in Jewish Education IX), Jerusalem: The Hebrew University Magnes Press, 2003, pp. 61–73 (Hebrew with English abstract).

Grossman, Y. "Dual Meaning in the Biblical Narrative and its Contribution to Molding the Story," Ph.D. dissertation, Ramat-Gan: Bar-Ilan University, 2006 (Hebrew).

Grottanelli, C. *Kings and Prophets: Monarchic Power, Inspired Leadership and Sacred Text in Biblical Narrative*, New York: Oxford University Press, 1999.

Gutel, N. "Combat in Areas Saturated With Civilian Population," *Tehumin* 23, 2003, pp. 18–42 (Hebrew).

Gutman, I. "Jews – Poles – Antisemitism," in I. Bartal and I. Gutman (Eds.), *The Broken Chain: Polish Jewry through the Ages. II. Society, Culture, Nationalism*, Jerusalem: Merkaz Zalman Shazar, 2001, pp. 612–617 (Hebrew).

Hacohen, A. "On Freedom of Expression, Tolerance and Pluralism in Jewish Law," in T. Rashi and M. Zapt (Eds.), *Media and Judaism – A Collection of Essays*, Petah Tikvah: Keter Hazahav, 2008, pp. 9–46 (Hebrew).

Hager-Lau, J. *The Redemption and the Magnificence*: *Guarantor's Expressions in Redemption of Captives from Ancient Times until our Days*, Jerusalem: The Religious Institute in Or-Ezion, 2009 (Hebrew).

Hakohen-Levin, P.Y. "A Dangerous Illusion because of a Forgotten Principle," *Beit Ya'akov* 32, 1962, p. 2 (1 page; Hebrew).

Halberstam, Y.Y. *Shut Divei Yatziv*, Orach Chaim, 148:3, Netanya: Machon Shefa Chaim, 1996 (Hebrew).

Hall, S. "The Rediscovery of Ideology: Return of the Repressed in Media Studies," in M. Gurevitch, T. Bennett, J. Curran and J. Woollacott (Eds.), *Culture, Society & the Media*, London: Methuen, 1982, pp. 56–90.

Halpern-Amaru, B. "The Killing of the Prophets," *Hebrew Union College Annual* 54, 1983, pp. 153–180.

Hamilton, J.M. and Jenner, E. "Redefining Foreign Correspondence," *Journalism* 5, 2004, pp. 301–321.

Hamilton, M. "The Past as Destiny: Historical Visions in Sam'al and Judah under Assyrian Hegemony," *Harvard Theological Review* 91, 1998, pp. 215–250.

Hamilton, V.P. *The Book of Genesis* (NICOT), Grand Rapids: Eerdmans, 1990.

Hanson, P.D. "War, Peace and Justice in Early Israel," *Bible Review* 3, 3, 1987, pp. 32–45.

Hardin, R.F. *Civil Idolatry: Desacralizing and Monarchy in Spenser, Shakespeare, and Milton*, Cranbury: Associated University Press, 1992.

Harris, W.V. *War and Imperialism in Republican Rome*, Oxford 1979.

Hartland, E.S. *Primitive Law*, Port Washington: Kennikat Press, 1924, reissued 1970.

Hasanovitz, E. *One of Them: Chapters from a Passionate Autobiography*, New York: Houghton Mifflin, 1918.

Heffelfinger, K.M. "'My Father is King': Chiefly Politics and the Rise and Fall of Abimelech," *Journal for the Study of the Old Testament* 33, 2009, pp. 277–292.

Hegel, G.W. *Outlines of the Philosophy of Right* (trans. T.M. Knox), Oxford – New York: Oxford University Press, 2008.

Heidegger, M. *Being and Time* (trans. J. Macquarrie and E. Robinson), New York: Harper and Row, 1962.

Held, A. *Oral History Collection of the Labor Movement* (YIVO), box #2, pp. 14–15.

Heller, J. *From Brit Shalom to Ichud: Judah Leib Magnes and the Struggle for a Binational State in Palestine*, Jerusalem: Magnes, 2003 (Hebrew).

Hellinger, M. "War and Peace in Jewish Tradition: Between Idealism and Realism," in S. Avineri (Ed.), *War and Peace*, Jerusalem: Zalman Shazar Center, 2010, pp. 73–98 (Hebrew).

Herman, G. "The Exilarchate in the Sasanian Era," Ph.D. dissertation, the Hebrew University, Jerusalem, 2005.

Herman, G. *Morality and Behavior in Democratic Athens*, Cambridge: Cambridge University Press, 2006.

Herman, J.L. *Trauma and Recovery*, Tel Aviv: Am Oved, 1994 (Hebrew).

Herman, T. "Ihud- A Peace Movement in a Test of Fire," in *State, Government and International Relations* 33, 1980, pp. 31–72 (Hebrew).

Hertzberg, H.W. *I and II Samuel* (Old Testament Library), London: SCM Press.

Herwig, H.H. "Germany," in R.F. Hamilton and H.H. Herwig (Eds.), *The Origins of World War I*, Cambridge: Cambridge University Press, 2003, pp. 163–164.

Herzog, I. "On the Establishment of the State and Its Wars," *Tehumin* 4, 1983, pp. 13–24 (Hebrew).

Herzog, I. *Responsa Heichal Yitzhak Orach Haim*, Jerusalem: Committee for the Publication of the Works of Rabbi Herzog, 1972 (Hebrew).

Heschel, A.J. *The Sabbath: Its Meaning for Modern Man*, New York: Farrar, Straus and Giroux, 1951.

Hess, R.S. "Joshua 10 and the Sun that Stood Still," *Buried History* 35, 1999, pp. 26–33.

Hess, S. *International News & Foreign Correspondents*, Washington DC: The Brookings Institution, 1996.

Hess, S. *Through Their Eyes: Foreign Correspondents in the United States*, Washington DC: The Brookings Institution, 2005.

Hester, A. "An Analysis of News Flow from Developed and Developing Nations," *Gazette* 7, 1971, pp. 29–43.

Higham, J. *Strangers in the Land: Patterns of American Nativism 1860–1925* (2nd ed.), New York: Atheneum, 1978.

Hindess, B. *Discourses of Power: From Hobbes to Foucault*, Oxford: Blackwell, 1996.

Hobbs, T.R. *2 Kings*, Waco: Word Books, 1985.

Hobbs, T.R. *A Time for War: A Study of Warfare in the Old Testament*, Wilmington: Michael Glazier, 1989.

Hoffman, E. *Shtetl: The Life and Death of a Small Town and the World of Polish Jews*, New York: Houghton Mifflin, 1997.

Hoffmeier, J.K. "The Structure of Joshua 1–11 and the Annals of Thutmose III," in A.R. Millard, J.K. Hoffmeier and D.W. Baker (Eds.), *Faith, Tradition and History: Old Testament Historiography in Its Near Eastern Context*, Winona Lake: Eisenbrauns, 1994, pp. 165–179.

Hoffner, H.A. Jr. "Deeds of Šuppiluliuma," fragments 11, 13, in W.W. Hallo (Ed.), *The Context of Scripture: Canonical Compositions from the Biblical World* II, Leiden: Brill, 2000, p. 186.

Holladay, J.S. Jr. "The Day(s) the Moon Stood Still [Jos. 10:12–13]," *Journal of Biblical Literature* 87, 1968, pp. 166–178.

Holmes, R. *On War and Morality*, Princeton: Princeton University Press, 1989.

Holzer, E. *Military Activism in Religious Zionist Thought*, Jerusalem: Shalom Hartman Institute, 2009 (Hebrew).

Hoover, S. *Religion in the News*, Thousand Oaks: Sage, 1998.

Horovitz, H.S. (Ed.) *Siphre D'be Rab*, Jerusalem: Wahrmann, 1966 (Hebrew with German introduction).

Horowitz, E. *Reckless Rites: Purim and the Legacy of Jewish Violence*, Princeton: Princeton University Press, 2006.

Hoyt, C. "Standing Between Enemies," *The New York Times*, 11 January 2009.

Humbert, P. "Etendre la main," *Vetus Testamentum* 12, 1962, pp. 383–395.

Hundert, G. "The Implications of Jewish Economic Activities for Christian-Jewish Relations in the Polish Commonwealth," in C. Abramsky, M. Jachimczyk and A. Polonsky (Eds.), *The Jews in Poland*, Oxford: Basil Blackwell, 1986, pp. 55–63.

Hundert, G.D. *Jews in Poland-Lithuania in the Eighteenth Century: A Genealogy of Modernity*, Berkeley: University of California Press, 2004.

Ihde, D. *Postphenomenology: Essays in the Postmodern Context*, Evanston: Illinois Northwestern University Press, 1993.

Ilam, I. "The Declaration of Independence, the Drama, the Myth and the Historical Truth," *Kivunim Hadashim* 12, 2005, pp. 92–119 (Hebrew).

Isaacs, A. "A Socio-Cultural Inquiry into the Link between Jewish and General Culture in Light of the Teachings of Rabbi Moses Avigdor Amiel," in Y. Amir (Ed.), *The Way of the Spirit: Festschrift in Honor of Eliezer Schweid* vol. 1, Jerusalem: Van Leer Institute and the Hebrew University, 2005, pp. 409–438 (Hebrew).

Isaacs, A. "Zionism as an Apolitical Spiritual Revolution in the Teachings of Rabbi Moses Avigdor Amiel," in A. Sagi and D. Schwartz (Eds.), *A Century of Religious Zionism* vol. 1, Ramat-Gan: Bar-Ilan University Press, 2003, pp. 287–306 (Hebrew).

Ish-Shalom, M. (Ed.) *Seder Eliyahu Rabbah ve-Seder Eliyahu Zuta*, Vienna: Bamberger, 1902; Jerusalem: Wohrman, 1969, p. 39 (Hebrew).

Ismail, B.K. and Cavigneaux, A. "Dādušas Siegestele IM 95200 aus Ešnunna. Die Inschrift," *Baghdader Mitteilungen* 34, 2003, pp. 129–156.

Jacobs, J. (Ed.) *American Jewish Year Book* 5676, Philadelphia: The Jewish Publication Society, 1915–16.

James, W. "The Moral Equivalent of War," in J.J. McDermott (Ed.), *The Writings of William James: A Comprehensive Edition*, New York: Random House, 1968, pp. 660–671.

Japhet, S. *I & II Chronicles – A Commentary* (OTL), Louisville: Westminster John Knox, 1993.

Japhet, S. *The Ideology of the Book of Chronicles and its Place in Biblical Thought* (trans. Anna Barber), Frankfurt am Main: Lang, 1997.

Jeffery, R. *Hugo Grotius in International Thought*, New York – London: Palgrave Macmillan, 2006.

Johnson, J.T. *Military and Contemporary Warfare*, New Haven: Yale University Press, 1994.

Johnson, J.T. *The Just War Tradition and the Restraint of War*, Princeton: Princeton University Press, 1981.

Johnstone, W. "The Deuteronomistic Cycles of 'signs' and 'wonders' in Exodus 1–13," in A.G. Auld (Ed.), *Understanding Poets and Prophets: Essays in Honour of George Wishart Anderson* (SJOT Sup. 152), Sheffield: Sheffield Academic Press, 1993, pp. 166–185.

Jones, G.H. *1 and 2 Kings. Volume II, 1 Kings 17:1–2 Kings 25:30*, London: Marshall Morgan & Scott, 1984.

Judah Halevi, *The Kuzari: An Argument for the Faith of Israel* (trans. H. Hirschfeld), New York: Schocken Books, 1964.

Jünger, E. *In Stahlgewitter* (46th ed.), Stuttgart: Klett-Cotta Verlag, 2007.

Kaddari, M.Z. קוף, *Dictionary of Biblical Hebrew*, Ramat Gan: Bar-Ilan University Press, 2006, pp. 940–941 (Hebrew).

Kagan, Y.M. *Hafetz Hayim*, Vilna: Hillel Dvarzetz, 1873 (Hebrew and in dozens of later editions).

Kagan, Y.M. *Sefer Shmirat Halashon*, Vilna: Metz, 1876 (Hebrew and in dozens of later editions).

Kahana, I.Z. *Research on Responsa Literature*, Jerusalem: Mosad Harav Kook, 1973 (Hebrew).

Kahana, M. "Prolegomena to a New Edition of the Sifre on Numbers," Ph.D. Dissertation, The Hebrew University, Jerusalem, 1982.

Kahana, M. *Sifre Zuta on Deuteronomy: Citations from a New Tannaitic Midrash*, Jerusalem: Magnes, 2002.

Kalb, M. and Saivetz, C. *The Israeli-Hezbollah War of 2006: The Media as a Weapon in Asymmetrical Conflict*, Cambridge: Harvard University, John F. Kennedy School of Government, 2007 (etext).

Kalimi, I. "Murder in the Jerusalem Temple – The Chronicler's story of Zechariah: Literary and Theological Features, Historical Credibility and Impact," *Revue Biblique* 117, 2010, pp. 200–209.

Kalimi, I. "The Murders of the Messengers: Stephen versus Zechariah and the Ethical Values of 'New' versus 'Old' Testament," *Australian Biblical Review* 56, 2008, pp. 69–73.

Kamalipur, Y. (Ed.) *The US Media and the Middle East: Image & Perception*, Westport: Praeger, 1995.

Kant, I. "Perpetual Peace: A Philosophical Sketch," in H. Reiss (Ed.), *Kant's Political Writings* (2nd ed.; trans. H.B. Nisbet), Cambridge: Cambridge University Press, 1991, pp. 93–130.

Kapiszewski, A. "Polish-Jewish Conflicts in the United States at the Beginning of World War I," *Polish American Studies* 48, 1991, pp. 63–78.

Kapiszewski, A. *Conflicts Across the Atlantic: Essays on Polish-Jewish Relation in the United States During World War I and in the Interwar Period*, Krakow: Ksiegarnia Akademicka, 2004.

Kaplan, Z.J. "Rabbi Joel Teitelbaum, Zionism, and Hungarian Ultra-Orthodoxy," *Modern Judaism* 24, 2, 2004, pp. 165–178.

Kassow, S. "Shtetl," in G. Hundert (Ed.), *The YIVO Encyclopedia of Jews in Eastern Europe* vol. 2, YIVO and Yale University Press, 2008, pp. 1732–1736.

Katz, J. *The "Shabbes Goy": A Study in Halachic Flexibility* (trans. Y. Lerner), Philadelphia: Jewish Publication Society, 1989.

Kaufman, T. *Know Him in All Your Ways: The Concept of the Divine and Worship through Corporeality in Early Hasidism*, Ramat-Gan: Bar-Ilan University, 2009 (Hebrew).

Kaufman, Y. *The Army According to Halacha: Laws of War and of the Army*, Jerusalem: Kol Mevaser, 1994 (Hebrew).

Kaufman, Y. "A Time for War vs. A Time for Peace according to the Natziv," *Merhavim* 6, 1997, pp. 285–297 (Hebrew).

Kearney, R. *The God Who May Be: A Hermeneutics of Religion*, Bloomington: Indiana University Press, 2001.

Keefe, A.A. "Rapes of Women/Wars of Men," *Semeia* 61, 1993, pp. 79–97.

Keel, O. *Wirkmächtige Siegeszeichen im Alten Testament*, Göttingen: Vandenhoeck & Ruprecht, 1974.

Kelle, B.E. and Ames, F.R. (Eds.) *Writing and Reading War: Rhetoric, Gender, and Ethics in Biblical and Modern Contexts* (SBL Symposium Series 42), Atlanta: Society of Biblical Literature, 2008.

Khaykin, Y. *Yidishe Bleter in Amerike*, New York: Published by the author, 1946.

Kimelman, R. "Non-Violence in the Talmud," *Judaism* 17, 1968, pp. 316–334.

Kimelman, R. "The Laws and Restrictions of War," in I.M. Gafni and A. Ravitzky (Eds.), *Sanctity of Life and Martyrdom*, Jerusalem: Zalman Shazar Center, 1992, pp. 233–254 (Hebrew).

Klapper, A. "Warfare, Ethics and Jewish Law," *Meorot: A Forum of Modern Orthodox Discourse* 6, 2006, pp. 2–9.

Klaus, N. *Pivot Patterns in the Former Prophets*, Sheffield: Sheffield Academic Press, 1999.

Klein, J. *Job* (Olam Hatanakh), Tel Aviv: Davidson Azati, 1996 (Hebrew).

Klein, R.W. "Abijah's Campaign Against the North (2 Chr 13) – What were the Chronicler's Sources?," *Zeitschrift für die Alttestamentliche Wissenschaft* 95, 1983, pp. 210–217.

Kliesch, R. "News Media Presence and Southeast Asia," *Journalism Quarterly* 57, 1980, pp. 255–261.

Klingender, F.D. *Marxism and Modern Art*, London: Lawrence and Wishart, 1975.

Knight, A. "Re-inventing the Wheel: Australian Foreign Correspondents in Southeast Asia," *Media Asia* 22, 1995, pp. 9–17.

Knoppers, G.N. "'Battling against Yahweh': Israel's War against Judah in 2 Chr 13:2–20," *Revue Biblique* 100, 1993, pp. 511–532.

Knoppers, G.N. *1 Chronicles 10–29: A New Translation with Introduction and Commentary* (Anchor Bible), New York: Doubleday, 2004.

Koch, E. "The *New York Times*' Anti-Israel Bias," *The New York Times*, 1 June 2006.

Koehler, L. and Baumgartner, W. *Hebräisches und Aramäisches Lexikon zum Alten Testament*, Leiden: Brill, 1974.

Koenigsberg, R. *Nations Have the Right to Kill*, New York: The Library of Social Science, 2009.

Kook, A.I.H. "Israel's Destiny and Nationhood," in M.Y. Zuriel (Ed.), *Otzrot Ha-Reayah [An Anthology of Writings by Rabbi Kook]* vol. 1, Sha`albim: M.Y. Zuriel, 1988, pp. 693–708 (Hebrew).

Kook, A.I.H. *Ain Ayeh, Berakhot 1*, Jerusalem: Mosad Harav Kook, 1987 (Hebrew).

Kook, A.I.H. *Arpelei Tohar*, Jerusalem: Rabbi Z.Y. Kook Publications, 1983 (Hebrew).

Kook, A.I.H. *Eder Ha-Yaqar*, Jerusalem: Mosad Harav Kook, 1967 (Hebrew).

Kook, A.I.H. *Eight Papers*, Hebron – Kiryat-Arba – Jerusalem: Pozner Publication, 1999 (Hebrew).

Kook, A.I.H. *Mishpat Kohen*, Jerusalem: Mosad Harav Kook, 1985 (Hebrew).

Kook, A.I.H. *Mizvot Re'ayah*, Jerusalem: Mosad Harav Kook, 1985 (Hebrew).

Kook, A.I.H. *Olat Re'ayah*, Jerusalem: Mosad Harav Kook, 1989 (Hebrew).

Kook, A.I.H. *Orot*, Jerusalem: Mosad Harav Kook, 1982 (Hebrew).

Kook, A.I.H. *Orot Ha-Emunah*, Jerusalem: NP, 1985 (Hebrew).

Kook, A.I.H. *Orot Ha-Qodesh*, Jerusalem: Mosad Harav Kook, 1983 (Hebrew).

Kook, A.I.H. *The Sabbath of the Land*, Jerusalem: Mosad Harav Kook, 1979 (Hebrew).

Kook, Z.Y. "The 19th Psalm of the State of Israel," in Z.Y. Kook, *In the Paths of Israel (LNtivot Yisrael)*, Bet El: Me'Avnei Hamakom, 3rd printing, 2007, vol. 2, pp. 355–367 (Hebrew).

Kook, Z.Y. *Regarding the Commandment of the Land*, n.p., Jerusalem, Iyar 5708 [May, 1948], reprinted in *In the Paths of Israel (L'Ntivot Yisrael)*, vol. 1, pp. 168–183 (Hebrew).

Koole, J.L. *Isaiah III. Vol. 1: Isaiah 40–48* (Historical Commentary on the Old Testament) (trans. A.P. Runia), Kampen: Kok Pharos, 1997.

Kopelov, Y. *Amol in amerike*, Warsaw: Brzoza, 1928.

Koren, Y. "Morality in *Halakha*: Genocide, Divine Command and Halakhic Reasoning," *Akdamot* 18, 2007, pp. 41–54 (Hebrew).

Kot, J. *The Human Memory*, Tel Aviv: Matar, 2007 (Hebrew).

Kotik, Y. *Mayne zikhroynes*, Warsaw: A. Gitlin, 1913.

Kruger, H.A.J. "Sun and Moon Marking Time: A Cursory Survey of Exegetical Possibilities in Joshua 10:9–14," *Journal of Northwest Semitic Languages* 26, 2000, pp. 137–152.

Kruglak, T. *The Foreign Correspondents: A Study of the Men & Women Reporting for the American Information Media in Western Europe*, Geneva: Librairie E. Droz, 1955.

Kuhn, K.G. "Beiträge zum Verständnis der Kriegsrolle von Qumran," *Theologische Literaturzeitung* 81, 1956, pp. 25–30.

Kushner, M. *Lebn un kamf fun a kloakmakher*, New York: Published by a committee from local 9, International Ladies' Garment Workers Union, 1960.

L'Orange, H.P. *Studies on the Iconography of Cosmic Kingship in the Ancient World*, New Rochelle: Caratzas Brothers, 1982.

LaBarbera, R. "The Man of War and the Man of God: Social Satire in 2 Kings 6:8–7:20," *Catholic Biblical Quarterly* 46, 1984, pp. 637–651.

Lamm, N. "Amalek and the Seven Nations: A Case of Law vs. Morality," in L. Schiffman and J.B. Wolowelsky (Eds.), *War and Peace in Jewish Tradition*, New York: Yeshiva University Press, 2007, pp. 201–238.

Laniado, S. *Keli Yaqar on the Former Prophets. 2 Kings*, Jerusalem: Makhon Ha-ketav, 1994 (Hebrew).

Latvus, K. "From Army Campsite to Partners in Peace: The Changing Role of the Gibeonites in the Redaction Process of Josh. x 1–8; xi 19," in K.-D. Schunck and M. Augustin (Eds.), *"Lasset uns Brücken bauen . . ."; Collected Communications to the XVth Congress of the International Organization for the Study of the Old Testament, Cambridge, 1995*, Frankfurt: P. Lang, 1998, pp. 111–115.

Leach, E. "Anthropological Approaches to the Study of the Bible During the Twentieth Century," in E. Leach and D.A. Aycock (Eds.), *Structuralist Interpretations of Biblical Myth*, Cambridge: Cambridge University Press, 1983, pp. 7–32.

Lederman, J. *Battle Lines*, New York: Henry Holt, 1992.

Legge, J. (Ed. and trans.) *The Chinese Classics* vol. V; *The Ch'un Ts'ew with the Tso Chuen*, Oxford: Clarendon, 1893.

Leibowitz, Y. "After Kibiyeh," in E. Goldman (Ed.), *Judaism, Human Values, and the Jewish State*, Cambridge, MA: Harvard University Press, 1995, pp. 185–190.

Lemaire, A. "The Tel Dan Stele as a Piece of Royal Historiography," *Journal for the Study of the Old Testament* 23, 1988, pp. 3–14.

Letters of Rabbi A.I H. Kook, Jerusalem: Mosad Harav Kook, 1981 (Hebrew).

Levey, G.B. "Judaism and the Obligation to Die for the State," in M. Walzer (Ed.), *Law, Politics, and Morality in Judaism*, Princeton: Princeton University Press, 2006, pp. 182–208.

Levin, S. *Memories of my Life* vol. 3, (trans. Z. Vislevsky), Tel Aviv: Dvir, 1935 (Hebrew).

Levinson, B. "The First Constitution: Rethinking the Origins of Rule of Law and Separation of Powers in Light of Deuteronomy," *Cardozo Law Review* 27, 2006, pp. 1853–1888.

Levinson, B. "The Reconceptualization of Kingship in Deuteronomy and the Deuteronomistic History's Transformation of Torah," *Vetus Testamentum* 51, 2001, pp. 511–534.

Lewis, B. *Semites and Anti-Semites*, London: Weidenfeld & Nicolson, 1986, pp. 100–109.

Lewis, B. *The Sargon Legend: A Study of the Akkadian Text and the Tale of the Hero Who Was Exposed at Birth* (American Schools of Oriental Research Dissertation Series 4), Cambridge: ASOR, 1980.

Licht, J. "War," in B. Mazar *et al.* (Eds.) *Encyclopaedia Biblica* vol. 4, Jerusalem: Bialik, 1962, p. 1061 (Hebrew).

Lichtenstein, A. "Morality and War," *Techumin* 4, 1983, pp. 180–194 (Hebrew);

Lichtheim, M. *Ancient Egyptian Literature: The Late Period* vol. III (3rd ed.), Berkeley: University of California Press, 2006.

Lichtheim, M. *Ancient Egyptian Literature: The New Kingdom* vol. II (3rd ed.), Berkeley: University of California Press, 2006.

Lifshutz, E. "Repercussions of the Beiles Trial in the United States," *Zion* 28, 1963, pp. 206–222 (Hebrew).

Liulevicius, V.G. *War Land on the Eastern Front: Culture, National Identity, and the German Occupation in World War I*, Cambridge: Cambridge University Press, 2000.

Lohr, E. *Nationalizing the Russian Empire: The Campaign against Enemy Aliens During World War I*, Cambridge, MA: Harvard University Press, 2003.

Lopez, R.S. *The Birth of Europe*, New York: M. Evans, 1962.

Lorberbaum, M. *Politics and the Limits of Law: Secularizing the Political in Medieval Jewish Thought*, Stanford: Stanford University Press, 2001.

Luebke, F.C. *Bonds of Loyalty: German-Americans and World War I*, Dekalb: Northern Illinois University Press, 1974.

Luz, E. (Ed.) *Pacifism and Torah: Works by A.S Tamares*, Jerusalem: Dinur Center, 1992 (Hebrew).

Luz, E. "*Halakhah* and *Aggadah* in Rabbi Kook's Teachings," *AJS Review: Journal of the Association for Jewish Studies* 11, 1986, Hebrew section, pp. 1–23.

MacMahan, J. "Realism, Morality and War," in T. Nardin (Ed.), *The Ethics of War and Peace: Religious and Secular Perspectives*, Princeton: Princeton University Press, 1996, pp. 78–92.

Magidov, Y. *Der shpigl fun der ist sayd*, New York: Published by the author, 1923.

Maharal, *Gevurot ha-shem*, Benei-Berak: Yahadut Publication, 1980 (Hebrew).

Maimon, S. *An Autobiography* (trans. from the German by J.C. Murray 1888), reprinted Urbana: University of Illinois Press, 2001.

Maimonides, M. "Letter to Obadiah the Proselyte," in I. Twersky (Ed.), *A Maimonides Reader*, Springfield: Behrman House, 1972, pp. 475–476.

Maimonides, M. *Mishneh Torah – The Book of Adoration*, Ed. according to the Bodleian (Oxford) Codex with an English Translation by M. Hyamson, Talmudic References and Hebrew Footnotes by C.M. Brecher, Jerusalem: Feldheim Publishers, 1981.

Maimonides, M. *Mishneh Torah – The Book of Judges* (Ed. Sh. Frankel), Jerusalem: Congregation Bnei Yosef, 1999 (Hebrew).

Maimonides, M. *Mishneh Torah – The Book of Knowledge* (trans. S. Glaezr), New York: Maimonides Publishing Company, 1927.

Maimonides, M. *Mishneh Torah – The Book of Torts* (trans. H. Klein), New Haven – London: Yale University Press, 1954.

Maimonides, M. *The Code of Maimonides, Book 3: The Book of Seasons* (trans. S. Gandz and H. Klein), New Haven: Yale University Press, 1961.

Maimonides, M. *The Code of Maimonides, Book 5: The Book of Holiness* (trans. L.I. Rabinowitz and P. Grossman), New Haven – London: Yale University Press, 1965.

Maimonides, M. *The Code of Maimonides, Book 10: The Book of Cleanliness* (trans. H. Danby), New Haven: Yale University Press, 1954.

Maimonides, M. *The Code of Maimonides, Book 13: The Book of Civil Laws* (trans. J.J. Rabinowitz), New Haven – London: Yale University Press, 1949.

Maimonides, M. *The Code of Maimonides, Book 14: The Book of Judges* (trans. A. Hershman), New Haven: Yale University Press, 1949.

Maimonides, M. *The Commandments: Sefer Ha-Mitzvoth of Maimonides: Volume One: The Positive Commandments* (trans. C.B. Chavel), London – New York: Soncino, 1967.

Maimonides, M. *The Guide of the Perplexed* (trans. S. Pines), Chicago: University of Chicago, 1963.

Malachi, E.R. (Ed.) *Igrot Sofrim*, New York: By Dr. Simon Miller, 1931 (Hebrew).

Malamat, A. "Campaigns to the Mediterranean by Iahdunlim and Other Early Mesopotamian Rulers," in T. Jacobsen (Ed.), *Studies in Honor of B. Landsberger*, Chicago: University of Chicago Press, 1965, pp. 365–373.

Mapel, D. "Realism and the Ethics of War and Peace," in T. Nardin (Ed.), *The Ethics of War and Peace: Religious and Secular Perspectives*, Princeton: Princeton University Press, 1996, pp. 180–200.

Mapu, A. *Ayit Tsavua* ("The Hypocrite," 1858–1864), in *The Complete Works of Abraham Mapu*, Tel Aviv: Dvir, 1959, pp. 373–376 (Hebrew).

Margalit, B. "The Day the Sun did not Stand Still: A New Look at Joshua X 8–15," *Vetus Testamentum* 42, 1992, pp. 466–491.

Mark, Y. "A zamlung volksfarglaykhen," *Yidishe sprakh* 5, 1945, pp. 99–140.

Marrus, R.M. "Jewish Resistance to the Holocaust," *Journal of Contemporary History* 30, 1, 1995, pp. 83–110.

Marx, S. *Shakespeare and the Bible*, Oxford: Oxford University Press, 2000.

Mayes, A.D.H. "Deuteronomy 29, Joshua 9, and the Place of the Gibeonites in Israel," in N. Lohfink (Ed.), *Das Deuteronomium; Entstehung, Gestalt und Botschaft*, Leuven: Peeters, 1985, pp. 321–325.

Mazar, A. *Archaeology of the Land of the Bible, 10,000–586 B.C.E.* (ABRL), New York: Doubleday, 1990.

Mazor, L. "The Rise and Fall of the Book of Joshua in the *Mamlakhti* School System in View of Ideological Shifts in Israeli Society," in M.L. Frankel and H. Deitcher (Eds.), *Understanding the Bible in Our Times: Implications for Education* (Studies in Jewish Education IX), Jerusalem: The Hebrew University Magnes Press, 2003, pp. 21–46 (Hebrew with English abstract).

Mazzetti, M. "Striking Deep Into Israel, Hamas Employs an Upgraded Arsenal," *The New York Times*, 31 December 2008.

McCune, M. *"The Whole Wide World Without Limits": International Relief, Gender Politics, and American Jewish Women, 1890–1913*, Detroit: Wayne State University Press, 2005.

Mechilta D'Rabbi Ishmael, Ed. H.S. Horovitz and I.A. Rabin, Frankfurt am Main: J. Kauffmann Press, 1931 (Hebrew).

Medan, Y. "The Question of the Conquest of the Land Following Moral Values – A Look at the Book of Joshua," in Z. Rimon (Ed.), *Morality, War and Conquest*, Alon Shevut: Tenuvot, 1994, pp. 19–30 (Hebrew).

Meidan, B. *Birkat Meir: Veyada'ata Vehashevotah*, Netivot: B. Meidan, 2003 (Hebrew).

Melamed, A. *Philosopher-King in Medieval and Renaissance Jewish Political Thought*, Albany: SUNY Press, 2003.

Menahem Mendel of Chernobyl, *Me'or Einayim*, Jerusalem: Me'or Einayim Yeshivah, 1975.

Mendelsohn, E. *The Jews of East Central Europe Between the World Wars*, Bloomington: Indiana University Press, 1983.

Michman, D. "The Meaning of Jewish Resistance during the Holocaust: Some Theoretical Observations," *Dappim Leheker Tekufat Hashoa* 12, 1995, pp. 7–41 (Hebrew).

Midrash Devarim Rabbah, edited from the Oxford Manuscript 147 with an Introduction and Notes by S. Lieberman, Jerusalem: Wahrmann, 1964 (Hebrew).

Midrash HaGadol on the Pentateuch: Deuteronomy (Ed. Sh. Fisch), Jerusalem: Mosad Harav Kook, 1972 (Hebrew).

Midrash HaGadol on the Pentateuch: Numbers (Ed. Z.M. Rabinowitz), Jerusalem: Mosad Harav Kook, 1967 (Hebrew).

Midrash Rabbah, Leviticus (trans. H. Freedman and M. Simon), London: Soncino Press, 1939.

Midrash Tanhuma (based on S. Buber edition), Exodus and Leviticus (trans. with introduction, indices, and brief notes by J.T. Townsend), Hoboken: Ktav, 1989.

Midrash Tankhuma, Numbers, Beha'alotcha (trans. J.T. Townsend), Jersey City: Ktav Publishing House, 2003.

Midrash Tanna'im on Deuteronomy (Ed. D. Hoffman), Berlin: Poppelauer 1909.

Midrash Vayyikra Rabbah, A Critical Edition by M. Margulies, London: Ararat, 1954, p. 386 (Hebrew).

Miller, P.D. "The Story of the First Commandment: The Book of Joshua," in A.D.H. Mayes and R.B. Salters (Eds.), *Covenant as Context; Essays in Honour of E.W. Nicholson*, Oxford: Oxford University Press, 2003, pp. 310–324.

Miller, P.D. *The Divine Warrior in Early Israel*, Cambridge: Harvard University Press, 1973, pp. 155–165.

Miller, P.D. and Flint, P.W. (Eds.) *The Book of Psalms. Composition and Reception* (Vetus Testamentum Sup. 99), Leiden – Boston: Brill, 2005.

Mintz, M. (Ed.) *The Letters of Ber Borokhov*, Tel Aviv: Am Oved, 1989 (Hebrew).

Mintz, M. *New Times – New Tunes: Ber Borokhov 1914–1917*, Tel Aviv: Am Oved, 1988 (Hebrew).

Mittleman, A. *Hope in a Democratic Age*, New York: Oxford University Press, 2009.

Molin, G. "What is a *Kidon*?," *Journal of Semitic Studies* 1, 1956, pp. 334–337.

Moran, W.L. *The Amarna Letters*, Baltimore: Johns Hopkins University Press, 1992.

Morris, B. "Yosef Nahmani and the Arab Question in 1948," in *1948 and After* (rev. ed.), Oxford: Oxford University Press, 2004, pp. 171–180.

Morris, B. *Israel's Border Wars 1949–1956*, Oxford: Clarendon Press, 1999.

Morrison, D. and Tumber, H. "The Foreign Correspondent: Dateline London," *Media, Culture & Society* 7, 1985, pp. 445–470.

Mosse, G.L. *Fallen Soldiers: Reshaping the Memory of the World Wars*, New York: Oxford, 1990.

Mosse, G.L. *Image of Man: The Creation of Modern Masculinity*, New York: Oxford, 1996.

Mothersill, M. *Beauty Restored*, New York: Adams Bannister Cox, 1991.

Mowlana, H. "Who Covers America?," *The Journal of Communication* 25, 1975, pp. 86–91.

Na'aman, N. "The 'Conquest of Canaan' in the Book of Joshua and in History," in I. Finkelstein and N. Na'aman (Eds.), *From Nomadism to Monarchy: Archaeological Aspects of Early Israel*, Jerusalem: Yad Yitzhak Ben-Zvi and the Israel Exploration Society, 1994, pp. 218–281.

Na'aman, N. "The Law of the Altar in Deuteronomy and the Cultic Site Near Shechem," in S.L. McKenzie and T. Römer (Eds.), *Rethinking the Foundations: Historiography in the Ancient World and in the Bible, Essays in Honour of John Van Seters*, Berlin: Walter de Gruyter, 2000, pp. 141–161.

Nachshon, A. "The Lord's Demands of Gentiles in the Historical and Prophetic Books of the Bible," Ph.D. dissertation, Ramat-Gan: Bar-Ilan University, 2003, pp. 41–43 (Hebrew).

Nachshon, A. and I. "Moral-Psychological Manipulation in a Prophetic Story: An Interdisciplinary Analysis," *Moreshet-Israel* 7, 2010, pp. 31–45 (Hebrew with English abstract).

Nadell, P. "The Journey to America by Steam: The Jews of Eastern Europe in Transition," *American Jewish History* 71, 1981, pp. 269–284.

Nadler, A.L. "Piety and Politics: The Case of the Satmar Rebbe," *Judaism* 31, 2, 1982, pp. 135–152.

Nahmanides, M. (Ramban – Mosheh Ben Nahman), *Commentary on the Torah*, (trans. from the Hebrew and annotated with index by C.B. Chavel), New York: Shilo, 1976.

Nahmanides, M. (Ramban – Mosheh Ben Nahman), *Hasagot HaRamban to the Book of Commandments* (Ed. C.B. Chavel), Jerusalem: Mosad Harav Kook, 1981 (Hebrew).

Nair, M. "The Foreign Media Correspondent: Dateline Washington DC," *Gazette* 48, 1991, pp. 59–64.

Naor, M. *The Eighth Column*, Tel Aviv: Hakibutz Hameuchad, 2006 (Hebrew).

Narveson, J. "Pacifism: A Philosophical Analysis," in R. Wasserstrom (Ed.), *Morality and War*, Belmont: Wadsworth, 1970, pp. 63–77.

Narveson, J. "Violence and War," in T. Regan (Ed.), *Matters of Life and Death*, Philadelphia: Temple University Press, 1980, pp. 109–147.

Nathans, B. *Beyond the Pale: The Jewish Encounter with Late Imperial Russia*, Berkeley: University of California Press, 2002.

Neher, A. *The Teachings of Maharal*, Jerusalem: Reuben Mass, 2003 (Hebrew).

Neryah, M.Z. "The People of Masada's Suicide in Halakha," *Alei Mishmeret* 14, 1961, pp. 3–14 (Hebrew).

Neuman, K. "To Blotto or to Blot Out," *Jerusalem Report*, 10 July 2006.

Niditch, S. *War in the Hebrew Bible: A Study in the Ethics of Violence*, Oxford: Oxford University Press, 1993.

Noort, E. "Josua und Amalek: Exodus 17:8–16," in R. Roukema (Ed.), *The Interpretation of Exodus: Studies in Honour of Cornelis Houtman*, Leuven: Peeters, 2006, pp. 155–170.

Noort, E. "The Traditions of Ebal and Gerizim: Theological Positions in the Book of Joshua," in M. Vervenne and J. Lust, *Deuteronomy and Deuteronomic Literature, Festschrift C.H.W. Brekelmans*, Leuven: Peeters, 1997, pp. 161–180.

Norman, D.A. "Affordances, Conventions, and Design," *Interactions* 6, 1999, pp. 38–41.

Norman, D.A. *Emotional Design: Why We Love (Or Hate) Everyday Things*, New York: Basic Books, 2004.

Norman, D.A. *The Psychology of Everyday Things*, New York: Basic Books, 1988.

Noth, M. *Das Buch Josua* (2nd ed.), Tübingen: Mohr, 1953.

Noy, S. *Traumatic Stress Situation*, Tel Aviv: Shoken, 2000 (Hebrew).

Oakeshott, R.E. *The Archaeology of Weapons: Arms and Armour from Prehistory to Age of Chivalry*, London: Lutterworth Press, 1960.

Ober, J. "Classical Greek Times," in M. Howard, G. Andreopoulos and M.R. Schulman (Eds.), *The Laws of War: Constraints on Warfare in the Western World*, New Haven: Yale University Press, 1994, pp. 12–26, 227–230.

Oded, B. "Ahaz's Appeal to Tiglath-Pileser III in the Context of the Assyrian Policy of Expansion," in M. Heltzer, A. Segal and D. Kaufman (Eds.), *Studies in the Archaeology and History of Ancient Israel in Honour of Moshe Dothan*, Haifa: Haifa University Press, 1993, pp. 63–71.

Ophir, A. "H-Hour," in A. Ophir (Ed.), *Fifty to Forty-Eight: Critical Moments in the History of the State of Israel*, Tel Aviv – Jerusalem: Hakibutz Hameuchad, 1999, pp. 15–33 (Hebrew).

Orend, B. "War," E.N. Zalta (Ed.), *The Stanford Encyclopedia of Philosophy* (Fall 2008 Edition), (http://plato.stanford.edu/archives/fall2008/entries/war/).

Orend, B. *The Morality of War*, Toronto: Broadview Press, 2006.

Orient, D. "THE PUBLIC EDITOR; Is *The New York Times* a Liberal Newspaper?" *The New York Times*, 25 July 2004.

Orpaz, Y. *The Pilgrim*, Tel Aviv: Hakibbutz Hameuchad, 1982 (Hebrew).

Orpaz, Y. *The Voyage of Daniel*, Tel Aviv: Am Oved, 1986 (Hebrew).

Paperna, A.Y. *Kol ha-ktavim* (Ed. I. Zmora), Tel Aviv: Machbarot le-Sifrut, 1952 (Hebrew).

Parkinson, R.B. *The Tale of Sinuhe and Other Ancient Egyptian Poems, 1940–1640 BC*, Oxford: Oxford University Press, 1997.

Passmore, J.A. "The Dreariness of Aesthetics," in W. Elton (Ed.), *Aesthetics and Language*, Oxford: Blackwell, 1954, pp. 36–55.

Paul, S. *Isaiah 40–66 with Introduction and Commentary*, Jerusalem: Magnes Press, 2008, pp. 257–258 (Hebrew).

Payne, J.B. "The Validity of the Numbers in Chronicles," *Bibliotheca Sacra* 136, 1979, pp. 109–128, 206–220.

Pedelty, M. *War Stories: The Culture of Foreign Correspondents*, New York – London: Routledge, 1995.

Perl, J. "Postmodern Disarmament," in S. Zabala (Ed.), *Weakening Philosophy*, Montreal: McGill-Queen's University Press, 2006, pp. 326–347.

Pienaar, D.N. "Some Observations on Conquest Reports in the Book of Joshua," *Journal of Northwest Semitic Languages* 30, 2004, pp. 151–164.

Pinsky, R. *The Life of David*, New York: Schocken.

Pitkänen, P. "Memory, Witnesses and Genocide in the Book of Joshua," in J.G. McConville and K. Möller (Eds.), *Reading the Law: Studies in Honour of Gordon J. Wenham*, New York – London: T&T Clark, 2007, pp. 267–282.

Polish, D. *Give Us a King: Legal-Religious Sources of Jewish Sovereignty*, Hoboken: Ktav, 1989.

Polonsky, A. "Introduction – The Shtetl: Myth and Reality," *Polin* 17, 2004, pp. 5–10.

Pongratz-Leisten, B. "Toponyme als Ausdruck assyrischen Herrschaftsanspruchs," in B. Pongratz-Leisten, H. Kühne and P. Xella (Eds.), *Beiträge zu altorientalischen und mittelmeerischen Kulturen. FS W. Röllig* (Alter Orient Altes Testament 247), Neukirchen-Vluyn, 1997, pp. 325–344.

Porath, H. "Each Eye will See God's Return to Zion," *Petahim* 2, 32, 1975, pp. 3–12 (Hebrew).

Prager, M. *Sparks of Glory* (trans. M. Schreiber), New York: Shengold, 1974.

Propp, W.H.C. *Exodus 1–18* (Anchor Bible), New York: Doubleday, 1999.

Rabinovitch, N. "The Opinion of Nahmanides Regarding Conquest of the Land," *Tehumin* 4, 1986, pp. 302–306 (Hebrew).

Radner, K. *Die Macht des Namens: Altorientalische Strategien zur Selbsterhaltung* (Santag 8), Wiesbaden: Harrassowitz, 2005.

Rakover, N. *Protection of Privacy in Jewish Law*, Jerusalem: The Jewish Legal Heritage Society, 2006 (Hebrew).

Rakower, N. *The Laws of Independence Day and Jerusalem Day*, Jerusalem: Ministry of Religions, 1973 (Hebrew).

Rappaport, J. "The American Yiddish Press and the European Conflict," *Jewish Social Studies* 19, 1957, pp. 113–128.

Rappaport, J. *Hands Across the Sea: Jewish Immigrants and World War I*, Lanham: Hamilton Books, 2005.

Rashi, T. "Between Isolation and Knowledgeable Use: The Reaction of the Jewish Orthodox Leadership to the Mass Media in the Twentieth Century," *Mayyim MiDalyav* 19–20, 2008–9, pp. 399–424 (Hebrew).

Rashi, T. "'The Public's Right to Know' in the Code of Media Ethics Versus 'The Public's Obligation to Know' in Jewish Law," in T. Rashi and M. Zapt (Eds.), *Media and Judaism – A Collection of Essays*, Petah Tikvah: Keter Hazahav, 2008, pp. 47–62 (Hebrew).

Ravitzky, A. "Kings and Laws in Medieval Jewish Thought (Nissim of Gerona vs. Isaac Abravanel)," in L. Landman (Ed.), *Scholars and Scholarship: The Interaction between Judaism and Other Cultures*, New York: Yeshiva University Press, 1990, pp. 67–90.

Ravitzky, A. "Prohibited War in Jewish Tradition," in T. Nadrin (Ed.), *The Ethics of War and Peace: Religious and Secular Perspectives*, Princeton: Princeton University Press, 1996, pp. 115–127.

Ravitzky, A. "Prohibited Wars" in Walzer (Ed.), *Law, Politics and Morality in Judaism*, Princeton: Princeton University Press, 2006, pp. 173–174.

Ravitzky, A. *Freedom Inscribed – Diverse Voices of the Jewish Religious Thought*, Tel Aviv: Am Oved, 1999 (Hebrew).

Reisman, W. and Antoniou, C. (Eds.) *The Laws of War*, New York: Vintage, 1994.

Reyzin, A. *Epizodn fun mayn lebn*, Vilna: Kletskin, 1929.

Reyzin, Z. *Leksikon fun der yidisher literatur, prese un filologye*, Vilna: Kletskin, 1927.

Rich, D.A. "Russia," in R.F. Hamilton and H.H. Herwig (Eds.), *The Origins of World War I*, Cambridge: Cambridge University Press, 2003, pp. 204–205.

Rich, J. "Fear, Greed and Glory: The Causes of Roman War-Making in the Middle Republic," J. Rich and G. Shipley (Eds.), *War and Society in the Roman World*, London: Routledge, 1993, pp. 38–68.

Richter, S. *The Deuteronomistic History and the Name Theology: lešakkēn šemô šām in the Bible and the Ancient Near East*, Berlin: De Gruyter, 2002.

Ricks, S.D. and Sroka, J.J. "King, Coronation, and Temple: Enthronement Ceremonies in History," in D.W. Parry (Ed.), *Temples of the Ancient World: Ritual and Symbolism*, Salt Lake City: Deseret, 1994, pp. 236–271.

Riggsby, A. *Caesar in Gaul and Rome: War in Words*, Austin: University of Texas Press, 2006.

Riklin, Sh. "A New Proposal for the Identification of the City Hai near Ma'aleh Michmash," in Y. Eshel (Ed.), *Judea and Samaria Research Studies – Proceedings of the 5th Annual Meeting – 1995*, Kedumim – Ariel: The College of Judea and Samaria, 1996, pp. 27–32 (Hebrew).

Robinson, J. *The Second Book of Kings*, Cambridge: Cambridge University Press, 1976.

Robinson, R.B. "The Coherence of the Jericho Narrative: A Literary Reading of Joshua 6," in B. von Rüdiger, T. Krüger and H. Utzschneider (Eds.), *Konsequente Traditionsgeschichte: Festschrift für Klaus Baltzer*, Freiburg – Göttingen: Universitätsverlag – Vandenhoeck & Ruprecht, 1993, pp. 311–335.

Rodin, D. *War and Self Defense*, Oxford: Oxford University Press, 2004.

Rofé, A. "Joshua son of Nun in the History of Biblical Tradition," *Tarbiz* 73, 2003–4, pp. 333–364 (Hebrew with English abstract).

Rofé, A. *Introduction to the Literature of the Hebrew Bible*, Jerusalem: Simor, 2009.

Rofé, A. *The Prophetical Stories: The Narratives About the Prophets in the Hebrew Bible, Their Literary Types and History*, Jerusalem: Magnes Press, 1988.

Rolnik, Y. *Zikhroynes*, New York: With the help of the David Ignatoff Fund, 1954.

Rom-Shiloni, D. *God in an Age of Destruction and Exile: Biblical Theology*, Jerusalem: Magnes Press, 2009, pp. 185–192 (Hebrew).

Roness, Y.A. "Halakha, Ideology and Interpretation – Rabbi Shaul Yisraeli on The Status of Defensive War," *Jewish Law Association Studies* 20, 2010, pp. 184–195.

Rorty, R. *Philosophy and the Mirror of Nature*, Princeton: Princeton University Press, 1979.

Rosenak, A. "General and Jewish Culture in the Thought of Rabbi M.A. Amiel: A Socio-Cultural Model," in Y. Amir (Ed.), *The Path of the Spirit: The Eliezer Schweid Jubilee*, vol. I, (*Jerusalem Studies in Jewish Thought*, XVIII), Jerusalem: The Hebrew University of Jerusalem, pp. 409–438 (Hebrew).

Rosenak, A. "*Halakhah*, Thought, and the Idea of Holiness in the Writings of Rabbi Haim David Halevi," in R. Elior and P. Schafer (Eds.), *Creation and Re-Creation in Jewish Thought: Festschrift in Honor of Joseph Dan*, Tübingen: Mohr Siebeck, 2005, pp. 309–338.

Rosenak, A. "Unity of Opposites in the teachings of Maharal: A Study of his Writings and their Implications for Jewish Thought in the Twentieth and Twenty-first Centuries" (Hebrew; in preparation).

Rosenak, A. *Prophetic Halakhah: The Philosophy of Halakhah in the Teachings of Rabbi Kook*, Jerusalem: Magnes Press, 2007 (Hebrew).

Rosenak, A. *Rabbi Kook*, Jerusalem: Zalman Shazar Center, 2006 (Hebrew).

Rosenberg, S. "War and Peace – Joshua and Isaiah," in Z. Rimon (Ed.), *Morality, War and Conquest*, Alon Shevut: Tenuvot, 1994, pp. 41–52 (Hebrew).

Rosengren, K. "International News: Methods, Data, Theory," *International Journal of Peace Research* 11, 1974, pp. 74–80.

Rosman, M.J. "Jewish Perceptions of Insecurity and Powerlessness in 16th–18th Century Poland," *Polin* 1, 1986, pp. 19–27.

Rosman, M.J. *The Lords' Jews: Magnate-Jewish Relations in the Polish-Lithuanian Commonwealth During the Eighteenth Century*, Cambridge: Harvard University Press, 1990.

Roth, M. *Kol Mevaser*, Jerusalem: Mosad Harav Kook, 1955 (Hebrew).

Rowlett, L.L. *Joshua and the Rhetoric of Violence: A New Historical Analysis* (JSOT Sup. 226), Sheffield: Sheffield Academic Press, 1996.

Rozenson, I. "The Story of the Failure at Ai and the Literary Structure of Joshua 1–11," *Beit Mikra* 42, 1997, pp. 137–143 (Hebrew).

Sa`adyah Ga'on, *With Perfect Faith: The Foundation of Jewish Belief [Sefer ha-emunot ve-ha-de`ot]*, J.D. Bleich (Ed.), New York: Ktav Publishing House, 1983.

Sadan, D. *A Bowl of Raisins, or, A Thousand and One Jokes*, Tel Aviv: Mordecai Newman, 1950 (Hebrew).

Sagi, A. "Religious Command vrs. Legal System – a Chapter in the Thought of Rabbi Shim'on Shkop," *Da`at* 35, 1995, pp. 99–114 (Hebrew with English abstract).

Sagi, A. "The Punishment of Amalek in Jewish Tradition: Coping with the Moral Problem," *Harvard Theological Review* 87, 1994, pp. 323–346.

Said, E. *Covering Islam*, New York: Pantheon, 1981.

Salmon, Y. "The Emergence of a Jewish Nationalist Consciousness in Europe During the 1860s and 1870s," *AJS Review* 16, 1–2, 1991, pp. 107–132.

Salmon, Y. "Tradition and Modernity in Early religious-Zionist Thought," *Tradition* 18, 1, 1979, pp. 79–98.

Samet, E. *The Elisha Chapters*, Ma'ale Adumim: Ma'aliyot, 2003, pp. 462–463 (Hebrew).

Sanders, P. "So May God Do to Me!," *Biblica* 85, 2004, pp. 91–98.

Sarid, M. "The Declaration of the State – The Historical Truth about the Fateful Vote," *Kivunim Hadashim* 13, 2006, pp. 155–157 (Hebrew).

Sartre, J.-P. *La nausée* (trans. H. Lazar), Tel Aviv: Siman Kriya, 1978 (Hebrew).

Sasson, J. *The Military Establishment at Mari* (Studia Pohl 3), Rome: Pontifical Biblical Institute, 1969.

Satlow, M.L. "'And On the Earth You Shall Sleep': Talmud Torah and Rabbinic Asceticism," *The Journal of Religion* 83:2, 2003, pp. 204–222.

Schaack, T. *Die Ungeduld des Papiers* (BZAW 262), Berlin: De Gruyter, 1998.

Scheler, M. and Schiller, M. *Der Genius des Krieges und der Deutsche Krieg (1915)*, Whitefish: Kessinger, 2010.

Schmidt, C. *Die Apokalypse des Subjekts*, Bielefeld: Aisthesis Verlag, 2003.

Schonfeld, M. *The Holocaust Victims Accuse*, New York: Neturei Karta of U.S.A., 1977.

Schwartz, D. "The Revolutionary Consciousness of the Religious Zionist Movement Since 1902," *Annual of Rabbinic Judaism* 3, 2000, pp. 175–184.

Schwartz, D. *Faith at the Crossroads*, Tel Aviv: Am Oved, 1996 (Hebrew).

Schwartz, D. *The Land of Israel in Religion Zionist Thought*, Tel Aviv: Am Oved, 1997 (Hebrew).

Schwarzbaum, H. "Jews and Gentiles in Folklore," *Yeda-'Am* 15, 1971, pp. 55–61 (Hebrew with English abstract).

Segal, J.B. "Numerals in the Old Testament," *Journal of Semitic Studies* 10, 1965, pp. 2–20.

Seidman, H. *The Warsaw Ghetto Diaries*, Southfield: Targum Press, 1997.

Shalom-Guy, H. "Three-Way Intertextuality: Some Reflections of Abimelech's Death in Thebez in Biblical Narrative," *Journal for the Study of the Old Testament* 34, 2010, pp. 419–432.

Shanor, D. *News from Abroad*, New York: Columbia University Press, 2003.

Shapira, A. *Democratic Values in the Hebrew Bible*, Tel Aviv: Hakibbutz Hameuchad, 2009 (Hebrew).

Shapira, A. *The First Democracy in the Bible: Ancient Foundations of Democratic Values*, Tel Aviv: Hillel Ben-Hayyim, 2009 (Hebrew).

Sharf, Z. *Three Days, 12–14 May 1948*, Tel Aviv: Am Oved, 1965 (Hebrew).

Shaviv, Y. "The Torah's War against War," in *Batzir Avi'ezer: Studies Related to Society and Forbidden Work on the Sabbath*, Alon Shvut: Tzomet, 1989, pp. 111–126 (Hebrew).

Sheehan, J.J. *Where Have All the Soldiers Gone? The Transformation of Modern Europe*, Boston: Houghton Mifflin, 2008.

Shemesh, Y. "The Elisha Stories as Saints' Legends," *Journal of Hebrew Scriptures* 8, 2008, pp. 2–14.

Shemesh, Y. "The Elisha Stories: A Literary Analysis," Ph.D. dissertation, Ramat-Gan: Bar-Ilan University, 1997 (Hebrew).

Sheshar, M. "Yom Hakadish Hakelali," *Turei Yeshurun* 8, 1967, pp. 3–4 (Hebrew).

Shochetman, E. *And He Established it for Jacob as a Law*, Jerusalem: Kol Mevaser, 1995 (Hebrew).

Shub, D. *Fun di amolike yorn*, New York: Cyco, 1970.

Shulman, V. "In di yorn fun der ershter velt-milkhome," in A. Menes (Ed.), *Di yidn in poyln*, New York: By a committee, 1946, pp. 751–758.

Shvat, A.Y. "Media and News – Positive Commandment or Negative," *Talelei Orot* 6, 1995, pp. 164–188 (Hebrew).

Sibley, F. "Aesthetics and Nonaesthetics," *Philosophical Review* 74, 1965, p. 137.

Siddall, L.R. "Tiglath-Pileser III's Aid to Ahaz: A New Look at the Problems of the Biblical Accounts in Light of the Assyrian Sources," *Ancient Near Eastern Studies* 46, 2009, pp. 93–106.

Simon, A.E. "Are we still Jews?," in A.E. Simon (Ed.), *Are We Still Jews?: Essays*, Tel Aviv: Sifriyat Ha-Poalim, Hebrew University School of Education and the Jewish Theological Seminary of America, 1983, pp. 9–46 (Hebrew).

Singer, I.J. *Fun a velt vos iz nishtu mer*, New York: Matones, 1946.

Slaatta, T. "Transnational Politics and News Production. Norwegian Correspondents on the Brussels Beat," in S. Hjarvard (Ed.), *News in a Globalised Society*, Goteborg: Nordicum, 2001, pp. 129–148.

Smith, H.P. *Critical and Exegetical Commentary on the Books of Samuel* (ICC), Edinburgh: T&T Clark, 1969.

Soloveitchik, J.B. *Faith and Destiny: From Holocaust to the State of Israel* (trans. L. Kaplan), Hoboken: Ktav, 2000.

Soloveitchik, J.B. *Kol Dodi Dofek: Listen – My Beloved Knocks* (translated and annotated by D.Z. Gordon), Hoboken: Ktav, 2006.

Soyer, D. *Jewish Immigrant Associations and American Identity in New York 1880–1939*, Detroit: Wayne State University Press, 1997 (reprinted 2001).

Speiser, E.A. *Genesis* (Anchor Bible), Garden City: Doubleday, 1964.

Spiegel, N. *War and Peace in Ancient Greek Literature*, Jerusalem: Magnes, 1986 (Hebrew).

Statman, D. "Humiliation, Dignity and Self-Respect," *Philosophical Psychology* 13, 4, 2000, pp. 523–540.

Statman, D. "On the Success Condition for Legitimate Self-Defence," *Ethics* 118, 2008, pp. 659–686.

Stauber, R. "The Jewish Response during the Holocaust: The Educational Debate in Israel in the 1950s," *Shofar* 22, 4, 2005, pp. 57–66.

Stein, D. "The Limits of Religious Optimism: The 'Hazon Ish' and the Alter of Novardok on 'Bittahon'," *Tradition* 43, 2, 2010, pp. 31–48.

Steinberger, Y.A. "The Tenth of Tevet as a Memorial Day for the Holocaust," *Shana Beshana*, 1991, pp. 311–320 (Hebrew).

Steinberger, Y.A. "The Tenth of Tevet: The Holocaust Memorial Day which became the General Day of Reciting the Kaddish," *Shana Beshana*, 1990, pp. 378–385 (Hebrew).

Sternberg, M. *The Poetics of Biblical Narrative*, Bloomington: Indiana University Press, 1987.

Stone, S.L. "On the Interplay of Rules, 'Cases' and Concepts in Rabbinic Legal Literature: Another Look at the Aggadot of Ḥoni the Circle Drawer," *Dinei Israel* 24, 2007, pp. 125–155.

Strange, J. "The Book of Joshua – Origin and Dating," *Scandinavian Journal of the Old Testament* 16, 2002, pp. 44–51.

Stuart, D. *Hosea-Jonah* (WBC 31), Waco: Word Books, 1987.

Stutchkov, N. *Der oytser fun der yidisher shprakh*, New York: YIVO, 1950.

Szajkowski, Z. "Sufferings of Jewish Emigrants to America in Transit to America through Germany," *Jewish Social Studies* 39, 1977, pp. 105–116.

Szajkowski, Z. *Jews, Wars, and Communism: The Attitude of American Jews in World War I, the Russian Revolutions of 1917, and Communism (1914–1945)*, New York: Ktav, 1972.

Tadmor, H. "Chronology," in B. Mazar *et al.* (Eds.), *Encyclopaedia Biblica* vol. 4, Jerusalem: Bialik, 1962, pp. 261–262 (Hebrew).

Tadmor, H. "Mesopotamia," in B. Mazar (Ed.), *Encyclopaedia Biblica* vol. 5, Jerusalem: Bialik, 1958, pp. 88–89 (Hebrew).

Tadmor-Shimoni, T. "From Cosmopolitan Socialism to Jewish Cultural Nationalism – The Case of Louis Miller," *Yahadut Zémanenu – Contemporary Jewry* 8, 1993, pp. 23–38 (Hebrew with English abstract).

Teichman, J. *Pacifism and the Just War*, Oxford: Basil Blackwell, 1986.

Teitelbaum, J. *'Al HaGeulah V'al HaTemurah*, New York: Sender Deutsch, 1967 (Hebrew).

Teitelbaum, J. *Vayoel Moshe*, New York: Yerushalayim, 1960 (Hebrew).

Tekhorsh, K.P. *Rabbi M.A. Amiel's Teachings on Halakhah and Aggadah*, Jerusalem: Religious Publication Society and Mosad Harav Kook, 1943 (Hebrew).

Tevet, S. *Kin'at David: The Life of David Ben-Gurion*, vols. 1–4, Jerusalem – Tel Aviv: Shoken, 1976–2004 (Hebrew).

Teveth, S. "Who changed the General Command Order," *Haaretz*, 9 September 1994, pp. b5–b6 (Hebrew).

The Mishnah (Everyman's Mishnah Series, trans. E. Levin, Ed. Bernard Susser), Jerusalem: Eliner Library, Department for Torah Education and Culture in the Diaspora of the World Zionist Organization, 1990.

Thucydides, *The Peloponnesian War* (trans. M. Hammond, with an Introduction and Notes by P.J. Rhodes), Oxford: Oxford University Press, 2009.

Tiffen, R. *The News from Southeast Asia: The Sociology of Newsmaking*, Singapore: Institute of Southeast Asian Studies, 1978.

Tishby, I. *The Wisdom of the Zohar*, Jerusalem: Mosad Bialik, 1961 (Hebrew).

Trigano, S. "Les guerres de Josué: origine et violence," in S. Trigano (Ed.), *Guerre et paix dans le jidaïsme*, Paris: In Press, 2004, pp. 13–22.

Trundle, M. *Greek Mercenaries: From the Late Archaic Period to Alexander*, London – New York: Routledge, 2004.

Tsukerman, B. *Zikhroynes*, New York: Yidisher kemfer, 1962.

Twersky, I. *Raabad of Posquieres: A Twelfth-Century Talmudist*, Philadelphia: Jewish Publication Society of America, 1980.

Tyan, E. "Djihad," in H.A.R. Gibb *et al.* (Eds.), *The Encyclopaedia of Islam* vol. 2, Leiden: E.J. Brill, 1983, pp. 538–540.

Tydor-Baumel, J. "Reactions to the Uprising among the Ultra-Orthodox," *Dappim Leheker Tekufat Hashoa* 12, 1995, pp. 289–308 (Hebrew).

Uffenheimer, B. *Early Prophecy in Israel*, Jerusalem: Magnes, 1999.

Unger, A.P. *Mayn heymshtetl strykov*, New York: Arbeter Ring, 1957.

van der Toorn, K. *Family Religion in Babylonia, Syria and Israel* (Studies in the History and Culture of the Ancient Near East 7), Leiden: E.J. Brill, 1996.

Van Seters, J. "Joshua's Campaign of Canaan and Near Eastern Historiography," *Scandinavian Journal of the Old Testament* 2, 1990, pp. 1–12.

Van Seters, J. *Abraham in History and Tradition*, New Haven: Yale University Press, 1975.

Van Seters, J. *The Biblical Saga of King David*, Winona Lake: Eisenbrauns, 2009.

Vaynshteyn, B. *Fertsik yor in der yidisher arbeter bavegung*, New York: Veker, 1924.

Viswanathan, S.V. *International Law in Ancient India*, Bombay: [N.P.], 1925.

Von Der Linden, H. "Just War Theory and U.S. Military Hegemony," in M.W. Brough, J.W. Lango and H. Von Der Linden (Eds.), *Rethinking the Just War Tradition*, New York: SUNY Press, 2007, pp. 56–57.

von Rad, G. *Holy War in Ancient Israel* (trans. and Ed. M.J. Dawn), Grand Rapids: Eerdmans, 1991.

Waltke, B.K. and O'Connor, M. *An Introduction to Biblical Hebrew Syntax*, Winona Lake: Eisenbrauns, 1990.

Walton, J.H. "Joshua 10:12–15 and Mesopotamian Celestial Omen Texts," in A.R. Millard, J.K. Hoffmeier and D.W. Baker (Eds.), *Faith, Tradition and History: Old Testament Historiography in Its Near Eastern Context*, Winona Lake: Eisenbrauns, 1994, pp. 181–190.

Walzer, M. "Commanded and Permitted Wars," in M. Walzer (Ed.), *Law, Politics and Morality in Judaism*, Princeton: Princeton University Press, 2006, pp. 149–168.

Walzer, M. "War and Peace in the Jewish Tradition," in T. Nadrin (Ed.), *The Ethics of War and Peace: Religious and Secular Perspectives*, Princeton: Princeton University Press, 1996, pp. 95–114.

Walzer, M. *Arguing About War*, New Haven: Yale University Press, 2004.

Walzer, M. *Just and Unjust Wars*, New York: Basic Books, 1977.

Walzer, M. *Just and Unjust Wars: A Moral Argument With Historical Illustrations*, London: Fakenham and Reading, 1978.

Ware, B.L. and Linkugel, W.A. "They Spoke in Defense of Themselves: On the Generic Criticism of Apologia," *Quarterly Journal of Speech* 59, 1973, pp. 273–274.

Weinberg, J.J. *Seridei Esh*, Jerusalem: Mosad Harav Kook, 1977 (Hebrew).

Weinfeld, M. "Judges 1.1–2.5: The Conquest Under the Leadership of the House of Judah," in A.G. Auld (Ed.), *Understanding Poets and Prophets: Essays in Honour of George Wishart Anderson* (SJOT Sup. 152), Sheffield: Sheffield Academic Press, 1993, pp. 388–400.

Weinreich, M. *History of the Yiddish Language* (trans. J.A. Fishman), Chicago: University of Chicago Press, 1980.

Weisgal, M. *So Far: An Autobiography*, New York: Random House, 1971.

Weissmandel, H.M.D. *Min Hameitzar*, New York: Emunah, 1944 (Hebrew).

Wells, R.H. *Shakespeare on Masculinity*, Cambridge: Cambridge University Press, 2000.

Wertheimer, J. *Unwelcome Strangers: East European Jews in Imperial Germany*, New York: Oxford University Press, 1987.

Westermann, C. "Peace (Shalom) in the Old Testament," in P.B. Yoder and W.M. Swartley (Eds.), *The Meaning of Peace: Biblical Studies*, Louisville: Westminster John Knox Press, 1992, pp. 16–48.

Whedbee, J.W. "On Divine and Human Bonds: The Tragedy of the House of David," in G. Tucker, D. Peterson and R. Wilson (Eds.), *Canon, Theology, and Old Testament Interpretation: Essays in Honor of Brevard S. Childs*, Philadelphia: Fortress Press, 1988, pp. 147–165.

White, H. "The Value of Narrativity in the Representation of Reality," *Critical Inquiry* 7, 1980, pp. 5–27.

White, P.R.R. "Media Objectivity and the Rhetoric of News Story Structure," in E. Ventola (Ed.), *Discourse and Community: Doing Functional Linguistics*, Tübingen, Germany: Narr, 2000, pp. 379–397.

Wiernik, P. "The Jew in Russia," in C.S. Bernheimer (Ed.), *The Russian Jew in the United States*, Philadelphia: John C. Winston, 1905, pp. 18–31.

Wilcke, C. "Der Tod im Leben der Babylonier," in J. Assmann and R. Trauzettel (Eds.), *Tod, Jenseits und Identität. Perspektiven einer kulturwissenschaftlichen Thanatologie*, Freiburg: Karl Alber Verlag, 2002.

Wilcke, C. "Göttliche und menschliche Weisheit im Alten Orient: Magie und Wissenschaft, Mythos und Geschichte," in A. Assmann (Ed.), *Weisheit. Archäologie der literarischen Kommunikation 3*, Munich: Fink, 1991, pp. 259–270.

Wilhelm, J.R. "The World Press Corps Dwindles: A Fifth World Survey of Foreign Correspondents," paper read at the Association for Education in Journalism Convention, Carbondale, Illinois, August 1972.

Wise, M., Abegg, M. and Cook, E. *The Dead Sea Scrolls: A New Translation*, San Francisco: Harper, 1996.

Wittgenstein, L. *Tractatus Logico-Philosophicus* (trans. D.F. Pears and B.F. McGuinness; with an introduction by Bertrand Russell), London: Routlege and Kegan Paul, 1961.

Wolf, M. "Halakhic Connections between the Law of 'Moser' and the Law of 'Rodef'," in M. Addad and Y. Wolf (Eds.), *Crime and Social Deviance: Theory and Practice*, Ramat-Gan: Bar-Ilan University Press, 2002, pp. 215–249 (Hebrew with English abstract).

Wood, J.A. *Perspectives on War in the Bible*, Macon: Mercer University Press, 1998.

Wright, J.L. "A Book-Oriented Approach to the Study of a Major War Theme," in B.E. Kelle and F.R. Ames (Eds.), *Writing and Reading War: Rhetoric, Gender, and Ethics in Biblical and Modern Contexts*, Atlanta: Society of Biblical Literature, 2008, pp. 33–56.

Wright, J.L. "Chariots: Evidence and Evolution," in A. Berlejung, G. Lehmann, J. Kamlah and M. Daviau (Eds.), *Encylopaedia of Material Culture in the Biblical World*, Tübingen: Mohr Siebeck, forthcoming 2011.

Wright, J.L. "Commensal Politics in Ancient Western Asia, Part II," *Zeitschrift für alttestamentliche Wissenschaft* 122, 2010, pp. 333–352.

Wright, J.L. "Making a Name for Oneself: Masculinity, Martial Valor and Procreation in Ancient Israel," *Journal for the Study of the Old Testament* 36, 2011, pp. 128–145.

Wright, J.L. "Seeking, Finding and Writing in Ezra-Nehemiah," in M. Boda and P. Reddit (Eds.), *The (Dis-)Unity of Ezra-Nehemiah*, Sheffield: Sheffield Phoenix Press, 2008, pp. 277–304.

Wu Yuhong *A Political History of Eshnunna, Mari and Assyria during the Early Old Babylonian Period: From the End of Ur III to the Death of Samsi-Adad*, Changchun: Institute of History of Ancient Civilizations, Northeast Normal University, 1994.

Wyatt, N. "Arms and the King," in M. Dietrich and I. Kottsieper (Eds.), *"Und Mose schrieb dieses Lied auf": Studien zum Alten Testament und zum Alten Orient*, Münster: Ugarit-Verlag, 1998, pp. 833–882.

Yadin, Y. *The Scroll of the War of the Sons of Light against the Sons of Darkness*, Oxford: Oxford University Press, 1962.

Yegar, M. *The Growth of the Israeli Foreign Information Policy Apparatus*, Herzliya: Lahav, 1986, (Hebrew).

Yisraeli, S. "Operation Jonathan in the Light of Halacha," in N. Gutel (Ed.), *Havat Binyamin* vol.1, Kfar Darom: The Institute for Torah and Land, 5752 [1992], pp. 126–133 (Hebrew).

Yisraeli, S. "The Siege of Beirut in Light of the Halacha," in N. Gutel (Ed.), *Havat Binyamin* vol.1, Kfar Darom: The Institute for Torah and Land, 5752 [1992], pp. 11–119 (Hebrew).

Yisraeli, S. *Amud Ha-Yimini*, Tel Aviv: Moreshet, 1966 (Hebrew).

Yoder, J.H. *The Politics of Jesus*, Grand Rapids: Eerdmans, 1972.

Yosef, O. *Book of Responsa Yabia Omer*, Orach Chaim, Jerusalem: Midrash Bnei Zion, 1995 (Hebrew).

Younger, K.L. Jr. "The 'Conquest' of the South (Jos 10,28–39)," *Biblische Zeitschrift* 9, 1995, pp. 255–264.

Zabala, S. (Ed.), *The Future of Religion*, New York: Columbia University Press, 2005.

Zaharopoulos, T. "Cultural Proximity in International News Coverage: 1988 US Presidential Election in the Greek Press," *Journalism Quarterly* 67, 1990, pp. 1990–1994.

Zakovitch, Y. "Teaching the Book of Joshua in Our Times," in M.L. Frankel and H. Deitcher (Eds.), *Understanding the Bible in Our Times: Implications for Education* (Studies in Jewish Education IX), Jerusalem: The Hebrew University Magnes Press, 2003, pp. 11–20 (Hebrew with English abstract).

Zakovitch, Y. "To Cause His *Name* to Dwell There – To Put his *Name* There," *Tarbiz*, 41, 1971–72, pp. 338–340 (Hebrew).

Zand, E. "Did Rashi Embrace the Idea of Autonomous Morality in His Commentary on the Account of the Battle Against Sihon?," *Iggud* 1, 2008, pp. 103–124 (Hebrew).

Zenner, W.P. "Middlemen Minority Theories and the Jews: Historical Survey and Assessment," *Working Papers in Yiddish and East European Jewish Studies* 31, 1978, pp. 1–30.

Zevin, S.Y. "On the Question of the Conscription of Yeshiva Students" in A. Shapira (Ed.), *Draft According to the Halacha*, Jerusalem: Torah and Labor Guardians, 1993, pp. 217–220 (Hebrew).

Zevin, S.Y. "War in the Light of the Halacha," in S.Y. Zevin, *In the Light of the Halacha* (new ed.), Jerusalem: Bet Hillel, 2004, pp. 84–90 (Hebrew).

Zevit, Z. "The Problem of Ai: New Theory Rejects the Battle as Described in the Bible but Explains How the Story Evolved," *Biblical Archaeology Review* 11, 2, 1985, pp. 58–69.

Zgoll, A. "'Einen Namen will ich mir Machen' – Die Sehnsucht nach Unsterblichkeit im Alten Orient," *Saeculum* 54, 2003, pp. 1–11.

Zhitlovsky, C. *Zikhroynes fun mayn lebn*, New York: Zhitlovsky's Jubilee Committee, 1935.

Zimran, Y. "And He Heard their Voice: On God's Changing His Mind in Response to Human Prayer," M.A. thesis, Ramat-Gan: Bar-Ilan University, 2009 (Hebrew).

Zohar, N. "Can a War Be Morally 'Optional'?," *Journal of Political Philosophy* 4, 1996, pp. 229–241.

Zohar, N. "Morality and War: A Critique of Bleich's Oracular Halakha," in D.H. Frank (Ed.), *Commandment and Community: New Essays in Jewish Legal and Political Philosophy*, Albany: SUNY Press, 1995, pp. 245–258.

Zohar, Z. "'On the Basis of Judaism in its Entirety': Rabbi Amiel's Polemic against the Enlightenment, Secularism, Nationalism, Mizrahi, and Agudah," in N. Ilan (Ed.), *A Good Eye: Dialogue and Polemic in Israeli Culture*, Tel Aviv: Ha-Kibutz Ha-Meuchad Publications, 1999, pp. 313–348 (Hebrew).

Zoriel, M.Y. (Ed.), *"Shemen ra`anan," Ozrot Hareayah*, Tel Aviv: Yeshivat Sha'alabim, 1988 (Hebrew).

General index

Index of references

An index of references to the Hebrew Bible, the Dead Sea Scrolls, the New Testament, the Talmud, the Midrash and later commentaries

Hebrew Bible

Genesis
3:3; 115
3:7; 33
3:22; 115
3:22–3; 59
4:8; 90
5:20–22; 63
6–7; 91
9:5–6; 134
9:6; 87
12; 76
13:10; 12
14; 9, 11
14:1–14; 11
14:21; 17
15:1; 123, 137
18:23–33; 272
18:2–8, 24:14; 24
19; 14
19; 91
26:28, 30–31; 29
27:41; 28
27:41–45; 90
27:46; 34
31:52; 135
32:30; 61
34; 91
34:26; 18
34:30; 22
37; 90
37:22; 99
49:23, 50:15; 34

Exodus
1:17; 272
3–4; 57
3–12; 25, 57
3–14; 57
3:20; 52, 54, 57
4:17; 54, 58
7:4–5; 54
7:19–20, 8:1–2,12–13, 9:22–3,
    10:12–13,21–2; 54
9:16, 15:3; 69
14:15,16,21,26,27; 54
14:24; 27
15; 51
15:3,6,11,12; 51
15:12; 54
17:9–13; 54
17:10–13; 40
17:16; 54
19:16; 56
21:12–14; 99
31:1; 124
32; 84
32:27; 90
32:32; 272

Leviticus
7:11; 125
23:22; 163

Numbers
14:44–45; 39
21:1–3; 25
21:5; 34